John David Kratzer

GOOD WRITERS

An Anthology of Excellent English

Edited by
R. Samuel Thorpe, Ph.D.

First Edition • June 1994

ISBN: 0-9631249-7-8
Library of Congress Catalog Card Number: 94-90230

Printed in the USA by

*M*ORRIS
PUBLISHING

3212 E. Hwy 30
Kearney, NE 68847
800-650-7888

Contact Morris Publishing for a FREE
guide to publishing your own book.

ACKNOWLEDGMENTS

To my parents, Kitty and Bud Hewitt, who have encouraged and supported me in this publishing effort and so many other efforts in my life, I give my gratitude and love.

To my sweet wife, Chrissy, and my wonderful children, James, John, Ben, and Anna, all of whom have always been supportive, encouraging and patient with Daddy's struggles and endeavors, I give my most profound and tenderest love and appreciation.

God bless all of you in the richest ways.

INTRODUCTION

How can a person become a better writer? There are many courses and books which attempt to train people to write better. Some of the techniques utilized by these works include writing exercises, grammatical studies, and topics studies on subjects like the use of dependent clauses, words that should not be used, etymology, and ways to put "life" into writing through action verbs. Many students experience frustration with such methodology; the task of becoming a better writer seems relentlessly time-consuming and tedious.

Students also reflect culture in their use of language. Slang and improper English usage find entrance into printed and vocal news media, magazines, television, and commerce. Over time these intrusions become common and accepted by most people who assume that such verbiage "must be all right" if it appears publicly.

These two problems, the apparent difficulty of formal writing education and cultural acquiescence to popular linguistic misuse, provoke an enigmatic reputation for the knowledge of good writing. How can we overcome the problem? In this case, the answer is relatively simple yet requires intentional effort from students.

Read--Read--Read! More importantly, read good writers! The answer to our problem is read; good writing comes from good reading. So much of modern American writing is an average to poor quality style that uses little vocabulary and unimaginative forms. If students read writers who use excellent formal style and imaginative constructions with diverse vocabularies, they will improve their writing abilities. Good writing is better caught than taught. Certainly, some specific habits of misuse can be recognized and improved by a teacher, but if the student resolves to notice the vocabularies and structures used by the good writers, the specific habits can be self-corrected.

To this end has this book been constructed. Some of the best classical English and American writers have been selected to expose students to excellent style in poetry and prose. "Hope springs eternal" that students will recognize the improvement in their written work after they have read this book and be inspired to continue a life-long program of reading good writers. Perhaps in a few years, more good writers will appear on our modern literary scene.

R. Samuel Thorpe
1993

TABLE OF CONTENTS

Page

Introduction

How to Read This Book 1

Washington Irving (1783-1859) 2
  Knickerbocker's History of New York: Book III

Charles Dickens (1812-1870) 8
  A Christmas Carol

Charlotte Brontë (1816-1855) 46
  Jane Eyre: Chapter 27

Mary Ann Evans or George Eliot (1819-1880) 69
  Silas Marner: Chapter 1

Frederick Douglass (1817-1895) 85
  Narrative of the Life of Frederick Douglass,
  An American Slave: Chapter 10

Sir Arthur Conan Doyle (1859-1930) 110
  The Case of the Dying Detective

Francis Thompson (1859-1907) 124
  The Hound of Heaven

G. K. Chesterton (1874-1936) 129
  "A Piece of Chalk"
  "On Lying in Bed"
  "The Wind and the Trees"

Mary Webb (1881-1927) 138
  Precious Bane

Appendices 340

HOW TO READ THIS BOOK

As you read Good Writers, note certain things besides the ideas and plots. Notice the feelings you have, the effects that the scenes or statements create in you, and the beauty of the settings. Place yourself in them. Feel free to express emotion; cry, laugh, shout if necessary! Experience the literary work.

After you recognize your experience, note how the author uses the language to produce this experience. What verbs are used to suggest or describe certain actions? How does the author make the emotions of the characters or narrator come alive to you? How diverse is the vocabulary? Please keep a good, complete dictionary handy, mark enigmatic words in the text, and after the personal experience of the book, find the precise meanings of these words.

Subsequent to your reading experience, immediately try your own hand by writing an essay, a critique of the work, or a poem that expresses the emotions of the experience. This practice helps inculcate certain stylistic skills of the good writer just read into your own style. Another interesting and helpful exercise is a rewrite. Read a newspaper or magazine article, then intentionally rewrite the story in formal style or rewrite creatively; take whatever creative approach that appeals to you at the time. Such an example is:

Magazine: "Two Virginians, George Mason and James Madison, played major roles in the drama that created the Constitution and the Bill of Rights. Both favored a national government that would unify the country, and both firmly believed in personal rights."

Rewrite: "Could these sovereign states ever be unified? Both George Mason and James Madison believed they could, through national government. But, since many people in these states feared tyranny, indeed some had recently fought England to free themselves from such, care had to be given to ensure personal right; not just in Virginia, the home of these two great leaders, but in all states. Fortunately, both men invested much of their thought in the creation of our Constitution, which includes a Bill of Rights.

Finally, reread this book. You will be amazed how much you missed on the first run. Second readings allow you to look specifically for certain scenes or thoughts and help generate deeper thoughts on the ideas produced by the writings.

Above all, read to enjoy, to exercise your thinking, and to enrich your life.

WASHINGTON IRVING
(1783-1859)

Wit extraordinaire! An apt description of Washington Irving's work. Irving's youth was spent in New York, where he explored the Hudson River, Sleepy Hollow, and other picturesque places in the area. As he lived and learned among the transplanted Scots, Dutch, and English villagers, Irving heard with rapt interest the superstitions and folklore that inspired many of his favorite tales.

Though Irving studied law, he never really adopted the profession. At the young age of 26, he published Diedrich Knickerbocker's History of New York, which made him famous. This History, ostensibly from the point of view of a patriotic Dutch American, is filled with insightful satire, wit, and wisdom. Irving's description of major government leaders of Dutch New Amsterdam will make readers laugh out loud, as well as recognize the mature and practical political perspectives he provides.

For most of his adult life, Irving was America's best known and respected author. He was a congenial, happy man, loved by his countrymen, and sought by international lovers of fine English literature. Irving never married and lived peaceably on his estate, Sunnyside, in the Sleepy Hollow area near the Hudson River until his death in 1859.

Knickerbocker's History of New York, one of Irving's best works, combines historical facts with local Dutch legend and humor to create a whimsical way to consider history. The effect is great fun. Perhaps if history, and all other fields of academic endeavor, could continually be viewed with such a "grain of salt," conflicts and disagreements between people might be reduced.

Judge = looked at in satire,
but liked by the narrator
because no govt. is good govt.

2

A HISTORY OF NEW YORK

Book Three
In Which Is Recorded the Golden Reign of
Wouter Van Twiller

Chapter One

Of the renowned Walter Van Twiller—his unparalleled virtues—and likewise his unutterable wisdom in the law-case of Wancle Schoonhoven and Barent Bleecker—and the great admiration of the public thereat

Grievous and very much to be commiserated is the task of the feeling historian who writes the history of his native land. If it fall to his lot to be the sad recorder of calamity or crime, the mournful page is watered with his tears; nor can he recall the most prosperous and blissful era without a melancholy sigh at the reflection that it has passed away forever! I know not whether it be owing to an immoderate love for the simplicity of former times, or to that certain tenderness of heart incident to all sentimental historians, but I candidly confess that I cannot look back on the happier days of our city, which I now describe, without a sad dejection of the spirits. With a faltering hand do I withdraw the curtain of oblivion that veils the modest merit of our venerable ancestors, and as their figures rise to my mental vision, humble myself before the mighty shades.

Such are my feelings when I revisit the family mansion of the Knickerbockers, and spend a lonely hour in the chamber where hang the portraits of my forefathers, shrouded in dust, like the forms they represent. With pious reverence do I gaze on the countenances of those renowned burghers, who have preceded me in the steady march of existence--whose sober and temperate blood now meanders through my veins, flowing slower and slower in its feeble conduits, until its current shall soon be stopped forever!

These, say I to myself, are but frail memorials of the mighty men who flourished in the days of the patriarchs; but who, alas! have long since mouldered in that tomb toward which my steps are insensibly and irresistibly hastening! As I pace the darkened chamber, and lose myself in melancholy musings, the shadowy images around me almost seem to steal once more into existence--their countenances to assume the animation of life--their eyes to pursue me in every movement! Carried away by the delusions of fancy, I almost imagine myself surrounded by the shades of the departed, and holding sweet converse with the worthies of antiquity! Ah, hapless Diedrich! born in a degenerate age, abandoned to the buffetings of fortune--a stranger and a weary pilgrim in thy native land--blest with no weeping wife, nor family of help-less children; but doomed to wander neglected through those crowded streets, and elbowed by foreign upstarts from those fair abodes where once thine ancestors held sovereign empire!

Let me not, however, lose the historian in the man, nor suffer the doting recollections of age to overcome me, while dwelling with fond garrulity on the virtuous days of the patriarchs--on those sweet days of simplicity and ease which never more will dawn on the lovely island of Manna-hata!

The renowned Wouter (or Walter) Van Twiller was des-cended from a long line of Dutch burgomasters, who had successively dozed away their lives and grown fat upon the bench of magistracy in Rotterdam; and who had comported themselves with such singular wisdom and propriety that they were never either heard or talked of--which, next to being universally applauded, should be the object of ambition of all sage magistrates and rulers.

The surname of Twiller is said to be a corruption of the original *Twijfler*, which in English means *doubter*; a name admirably descriptive of his deliberative habits. For, though he was a man shut up within himself like an oyster, and of such a profoundly reflective turn that he scarcely ever spoke except in monosyllables, yet did he never make up his mind on any doubtful point. This was clearly accounted for by his adherents, who affirmed that he always conceived every object on so comprehensive a scale that he had not room in his head to turn it over and examine both sides of it, so that he always remained in doubt, merely in consequence of the astonishing magnitude of his ideas!

There are two opposite ways by which some men get into notice--one by talking a vast deal and thinking a little, and the other by holding their tongues and not thinking at all. By the first, many a vaporing, superficial pretender acquires the reputation of a man of quick parts; by the other, many a vacant dunderpate, like the owl, the stupidest of birds, comes to be complimented by a discerning world with all the attri-butes of wisdom. This, by the way, is a mere casual remark, which I would not for the universe have it thought I apply to Governor Van Twiller. On the contrary, he was a very wise Dutchman, for he never said a foolish thing--and of such invincible gravity that he was never known to laugh, or even to smile, through the course of a long and prosperous life. Certain, however, it is, there never was a matter proposed, however simple, and on which your common narrow-minded mortals would rashly determine at the first glance, but what the renowned Wouter put on a mighty, mysterious, vacant kind of look, shook his capacious head, and, having smoked for five minutes with redoubled earnestness, sagely observed that "he had his doubts about the matter"--which in process of

4

time gained him the character of a man slow in belief, and not easily imposed on.

The person of this illustrious old gentleman was as regularly formed, and nobly proportioned, as though it had been molded by the hands of some cunning Dutch statuary, as a model of majesty and lordly grandeur. He was exactly five feet six inches in height and six feet five inches in circumference. His head was a perfect sphere, and of such stupendous dimensions that Dame Nature, with all her sex's ingenuity, would have been puzzled to construct a neck capable of supporting it; wherefore she wisely declined the attempt, and settled it firmly on the top of his backbone, just between the shoulders. His body was of an oblong form, particularly capacious at bottom; which was wisely ordered by Providence, seeing that he was a man of sedentary habits, and very averse to the idle labor of walking. His legs, though exceeding short, were sturdy in proportion to the weight they had to sustain; so that when erect he had not a little the appearance of a robustious beer-barrel, standing on skids. His face, that infallible index of the mind, presented a vast expanse, perfectly unfurrowed or deformed by any of those lines and angles which disfigure the human countenance with what is termed expression. Two small gray eyes twinkled feebly in the midst, like two stars of lesser magnitude in the hazy firmament; and his full-fed cheeks, which seemed to have taken toll of everything that went into his mouth, were curiously mottled and streaked with dusty red, like a Spitzenberg apple.

His habits were as regular as his person. He daily took his four stated meals, appropriating exactly an hour to each; he smoked and doubted eight hours, and he slept the remaining twelve of the four-and-twenty. Such was the renowned Wouter Van Twiller--a true philosopher, for his mind was either elevated above, or tranquilly settled below, the cares and perplexities of this world. He had lived in it for years without feeling the least curiosity to know whether the sun revolved round it, or it round the sun; and he had watched, for at least half a century, the smoke curling from his pipe to the ceiling, without once troubling his head with any of those numerous theories, by which a philosopher would have perplexed his brain, in accounting for its rising above the surrounding atmosphere.

In his council he presided with great state and solemnity. He sat in a huge chair of solid oak, hewn in the celebrated forest of the Hague, fabricated by an experienced timmerman of Amsterdam, and curiously carved about the arms and feet into exact imitations of gigantic eagle's claws. Instead of a scepter, he swayed a long Turkish pipe, wrought with jasmine and amber, which had been presented to a Stadtholder of Holland at the conclusion of a treaty with one of the petty

Barbary powers. In this stately chair would he sit, and this magnificent pipe would he smoke, shaking his right knee with a constant motion, and fixing his eye for hours together upon a little print of Amsterdam which hung in a black frame against the opposite wall of the council chamber. Nay, it has even been said that when any deliberation of extraordinary length and intricacy was on the carpet, the renowned Wouter would absolutely shut his eyes for full two hours at a time, that he might not be disturbed by external objects--and at such times the internal commotion of his mind was evinced by certain regular guttural sounds, which his admirers declared were merely the noise of conflict made by his contending doubts and opinions.

It is with infinite difficulty I have been enabled to collect these biographical anecdotes of the great man under consideration. The facts respecting him were so scattered and vague, and divers of them so questionable in point of authenticity, that I have had to give up the search after many, and decline the admission of still more, which would have tended to heighten the coloring of his portrait.

I have been the more anxious to delineate fully the person and habits of the renowned Van Twiller, from the consideration that he was not only the first but also the best governor that ever presided over this ancient and respectable province; and so tranquil and benevolent was his reign that I do not find throughout the whole of it a single instance of any offender being brought to punishment--a most indubitable sign of a merciful governor, and a case unparalleled, excepting in the reign of the illustrious King Log, from whom, it is hinted, the renowned Van Twiller was a lineal descendant.

The very outset of the career of this excellent magistrate was distinguished by an example of legal acumen that gave flattering presage of a wise and equitable administration. The morning after he had been solemnly installed in office, and at the moment that he was making his breakfast, from a prodigious earthen dish, filled with milk and Indian pudding, he was suddenly interrupted by the appearance of one Wandle Schoonhoven, a very important old burgher of New Amsterdam, who complained bitterly of one Barent Bleecker, inasmuch as he fraudulently refused to come to a settlement of accounts, seeing that there was a heavy balance in favor of the said Wandle. Governor Van Twiller, as I have already observed, was a man of few words; he was likewise a mortal enemy to multiplying writings--or being disturbed at his breakfast. Having listened attentively to the statement of Wandle Schoonhoven, giving an occasional grunt, as he shoveled a spoonful of Indian pudding into his mouth--either as a sign that he relished the dish or comprehended the story--he called unto him his constable, and pulling out of his breeches pocket a huge jack-knife, dispatched it after the

6

defendant as a summons, accompanied by his tobacco-box as a warrant.

This summary process was as effectual in those simple days as was the seal-ring of the great Haroun Alraschid among the true believers. The two parties being confronted before him, each produced a book of accounts written in a language and character that would have puzzled any but a High Dutch commentator, or a learned decipherer of Egyptian obelisks, to understand. The sage Wouter took them one after the other, and having poised them in his hands, and attentively counted over the number of leaves, fell straightway into a very great doubt, and smoked for half an hour without saying a word; at length, laying his finger beside his nose, and shutting his eyes for a moment, with the air of a man who has just caught a subtle idea by the tail, he slowly took his pipe from his mouth, puffed forth a column of tobacco-smoke, and with marvelous gravity and solemnity prounounced--that having carefully counted over the leaves and weighed the books, it was found that one was just as thick and as heavy as the other--therefore it was the final opinion of the court that the accounts were equally balanced--therefore Wandle should give Barent a receipt, and Barent should give Wandle a receipt--and the constable should pay the costs.

This decision being straightway made known diffused general joy throughout New Amsterdam, for the people immediately perceived that they had a very wise and equitable magistrate to rule over them. But its happiest effect was that not another lawsuit took place throughout the whole of his administration--and the office of constable fell into such decay that there was not one of those local scouts known in the province for many years. I am the more particular in dwelling on this transaction, not only because I deem it one of the most sage and righteous judgements on record, and well worthy the attention of modern magistrates, but because it was a miraculous event in the history of the renowned Wouter--being the only time he was ever known to come to a decision in the whole course of his life.

Commiserate = to show sympathy

Garrulity = talkativeness

Propriety = character, true nature

Comported = behaved

Capacious = large

Evinced = proved

Acumen = keenness

Prestige = foreshadowing

Prodigious = Extraordinary

7

CHARLES DICKENS
(1812-1870)

The master of the use of English vocabulary is undoubtedly Charles Dickens. His works flood with a diversity of words yet each perfectly fit for its use. Dickens is also the master of characterization. Without redundancy, he created hundreds of unique individuals for his works, often as many as 20, 30, or more for one book, and made them come alive to the reader. Probably, Dickens possessed an acute ability of observation and recollection as well as imagination, wherewith his powers of expression enlivened these personalities. His many experiences with various social and economic classes of people in England, America, and other countries no doubt added to his repertoire of characters.

Dickens also has an enormous power to emotionally move readers. From terrible sorrow and pity, his stories carry our hopes and expectations to heightened joy and love. None of his tales are wholly encompassed by one feeling or mood, hence to read him is truly an experience beyond simple, cognitive recognition.

Though Dickens was a precocious child, destined, it seemed, to great education, his father experienced severe financial failure and poverty, which forced Dickens and his numerous siblings into the child labor force in England. Such a state was heart-rending as well as back-breaking. The family's poverty was devastating. Through his sorrow, Dickens was prepared by his feelings and his suffering to become the master writer of his future.

Oddly, Dickens, humor drew the first attention of publishers. His reports for newspapers and the attorneys for which he worked attracted publishers, who requested that he write more lighthearted tales and sketches. From this opportunity emerged Pickwick Papers (1836-37), one of Dickens' most famous and successful works. These sketches made his career; henceforth he was the toast of Europe and America for the remainder of his life.

Though his works tend to be rather lengthy, any effort by students to work through them produces great rewards both in experience and improved writing skills. Dickens' historic and famous short novel, A Christmas Carol, has been beloved by readers since its first publication. In this work, Dickens displays humor in the midst of pathetic conditions of heart and body, but finishes the story with a warm appreciation for the humane and loving capabilities of humankind. The reality of true conversion of life from sourness, anger, and bitterness to the joy of personal generosity is clearly the theme of the book, which uses Christmas, renowned for warmth and generosity in remembrance of God's "good will toward men," as the setting for Ebenezer Scrooge's dramatic change.

A CHRISTMAS CAROL

Stave One
Marley's Ghost

Marley was dead, to begin with. There is no doubt what-ever about that. The register of his burial was signed by the clergyman, the clerk, the undertaker, and the chief mourner. Scrooge signed it. And Scrooge's name was good upon 'Change for anything he chose to put his hand to.

Scrooge knew he was dead? Of course he did. How could it be otherwise? Scrooge and he were partners for I don't know how many years. Scrooge was his sole executor, his sole administrator, his sole assign, his sole residuary legatee, his sole friend, and sole mourner.

Scrooge never painted out Old Marley's name. There it stood, years afterward, above the warehouse door: *Scrooge and Marley*. Sometimes people new to the business called Scrooge Scrooge, and sometimes Marley, but he answered to both names. It was all the same to him.

Once upon a time--of all the good days in the year, on Christmas Eve--old Scrooge sat busy in his countinghouse. It was cold, bleak, biting weather: foggy withal: and he could hear the people in the court outside, go wheezing up and down, beating their hands upon their breasts, and stamping their feet upon the pavement stones to warm them. The city clocks had only just gone three, but it was quite dark already. The fog came pouring in at every chink and keyhole, and was so dense without, that although the court was of the nar-rowest, the houses opposite were mere phantoms.

The door of Scrooge's countinghouse was open, that he might keep his eye upon his clerk, who, in a dismal little cell beyond, a sort of tank, was copying letters. Scrooge had a very small fire, but the clerk's fire was so very much smaller that it looked like one coal. But he couldn't replenish it, for Scrooge kept the coalbox in his own room; and so surely as the clerk came in with the shovel the master predicted that it would be necessary for them to part. Wherefore the clerk put on his white comforter and tried to warm himself at the candle, in which effort, not being a man of imagination, he failed.

"A merry Christmas, Uncle! God save you!" cried a cheerful voice. It was the voice of Scrooge's nephew, who came upon him so quickly that this was the first intimation he had of his approach.

"Bah!" said Scrooge. "Humbug!"

He had so heated himself with rapid walking in the fog and frost, this nephew of Scrooge's, that he was all in glow; his face was ruddy and handsome; his eyes sparkled, and his breath smoked again.

"Christmas a humbug, Uncle!" said Scrooge's nephew. "You don't mean that, I am sure."

"I do," said Scrooge. "Merry Christmas! What right have you to be merry? What reason have you to be merry? You're poor enough."

"Come, then," returned his nephew gaily. "What right have you to be dismal? What reason have you to be morose? You're rich enough."

"Out upon merry Christmas!" returned the uncle. "What's Christmas time to you but a time for paying bills without money, a time for finding yourself a year older and not an hour richer, a time for balancing your books and having every item in 'em through a round dozen of months presented dead against you? If I could work my will," said Scrooge indignantly, "every idiot who goes about with 'Merry Christmas' on his lips should be boiled with his own pudding, and buried with a stake of holly through his heart. He should!"

"Uncle!" pleaded the nephew.

"Nephew!" returned the uncle sternly. "Keep Christmas in your own way, and let me keep it in mine."

"There are many things from which I might have derived good, by which I have not profited, I dare say," returned the nephew. "Christmas among the rest. But I am sure I have always thought of Christmas time, when it has come round-- apart from the veneration due to its sacred name and origin, if anything belonging to it can be apart from that--as a good time; a kind, forgiving, charitable, pleasant time; the only time I know of the long calendar of the year, when men and women seem by one consent to open their shut-up hearts freely, and to think of people below them as if they really were fellow passengers to the grave, and not another race of creatures bound on other journeys. And therefore, Uncle, though it has never put a scrap of gold or silver in my pocket, I believe that it has done me good and will do me good; and I say God bless it!"

"You're quite a powerful speaker, sir," said Scrooge. "I wonder you don't go into Parliament."

"Don't be angry, Uncle. Come! Dine with us tomorrow."

Scrooge said that he would see him--yes, indeed he did. He went the whole length of the expression, and said that he would see him in that extremity first.

"But why?" cried Scrooge's nephew. "Why?"

"Why did you get married?" said Scrooge.

"Because I fell in love."

"Because you fell in love!" growled Scrooge, as if that were the only one thing in the world more ridiculous than a merry Christmas.

"I want nothing from you; I ask nothing of you; why cannot we be friends?"

"Good afternoon," said Scrooge.

"I am sorry, with all my heart, to find you so resolute. We have never had any quarrel to which I have been a party. But I have made the trial in homage to Christmas, and I'll keep my Christmas humor to the last. So, a Merry Christmas, Uncle!"

"Good afternoon!" said Scrooge.

"And a Happy New Year!"

"Good afternoon!" said Scrooge.

His nephew left the room without an angry word, notwithstanding. He stopped at the outer door to bestow the greetings of the season on the clerk, who, cold as he was, was warmer than Scrooge; for he returned them cordially.

"There's another fellow," muttered Scrooge, who overheard him. "My clerk, with fifteen shillings a week and a wife and family, talking about a merry Christmas. I'll retire to Bedlam."

This lunatic, in letting Scrooge's nephew out, had let two other people in. They were portly gentlemen, pleasant to behold, and now stood, with their hats off, in Scrooge's office. They had books and papers in their hands, and bowed to him.

"Scrooge and Marley's, I believe," said one of the gentlemen, referring to his list. "Have I the pleasure of addressing Mr. Scrooge or Mr. Marley?"

"Mr. Marley has been dead these seven years," Scrooge replied. "He died seven years ago, this very night."

"We have no doubt his liberality is well represented by his surviving partner," said the gentleman, presenting his credentials.

"At this festive season of the year, Mr. Scrooge," said the gentleman, taking up a pen, "it is more than usually desirable that we should make some slight provision for the poor and destitute, who suffer greatly at the present time. Many thousands are in want of common necessaries, hundreds of thousands are in want of common comforts, sir."

"Are there no prisons?" asked Scrooge.

"Plenty of prisons," said the gentleman, laying down the pen again.

"And the Union workhouses?" demanded Scrooge. "Are they still in operation?"

"They are. Still," returned the gentleman, "I wish I could say they were not."

"The Treadmill and the Poor Law are in full vigor, then?" said Scrooge.

"Both very busy, sir."

"Oh! I was afraid, from what you said at first, that something had occurred to stop them in their useful course," said Scrooge. "I am very glad to hear it."

"Under the impression that they scarcely furnish Christian cheer of mind or body to the multitude," returned the gentleman, "a few of us are endeavoring to raise a fund to buy the Poor some meat and drink and means of warmth. We choose this time, because it is a time of all others, when Want is keenly felt, and Abundance rejoices. What shall I put you down for?"

"Nothing!" Scrooge replied.

"You wish to be anonymous?"

"I wish to be left alone," said Scrooge. "Since you ask me what I wish, gentlemen, that is my answer. I don't make merry myself at Christmas, and I can't afford to make idle people merry. I help to support the establishments I have mentioned--they cost enough, and those who are badly off must go there."

"Many can't go there; many would rather die."

"If they would rather die," said Scrooge, "they had better do it, and decrease the surplus population. Besides--excuse me--I don't know that."

"But you might know it," observed the gentleman.

"It's not my business." Scrooge returned. "It's enough for a man to understand his own business, and not to interfere with other people's. Mine occupies me constantly. Good afternoon, gentlemen!"

Seeing clearly that it would be useless to pursue their point, the gentlemen withdrew. Scrooge resumed his labor with an improved opinion of himself, and in a more facetious temper than was usual with him.

At length the hour of shutting up the countinghouse arrived. With an ill will Scrooge dismounted from his stool and tacitly admitted the fact to the expectant clerk in the tank, who instantly snuffed his candle out and put on his hat.

"You'll want all day tomorrow, I suppose?" said Scrooge.

"If quite convenient, sir."

"It's not convenient," said Scrooge. "and it's not fair. If I was to stop half-a-crown for it, you'd think yourself ill-used, I'll be bound?"

The clerk smiled faintly.

"And yet," said Scrooge, "you don't think *me* ill-used, when I pay a day's wages for no work."

The clerk observed that it was only once a year.

"A poor excuse for picking a man's pocket every twenty-fifth of December!" said Scrooge, buttoning his greatcoat to the chin. "But I suppose you must have the whole day. Be here all the earlier the next morning."

The clerk promised that he would; and Scrooge walked out with a growl. The office was closed in a twinkling, and the clerk, with the long ends of his white comfortor dangling below his waist (for he boasted no greatcoat), went down a slide on Cornhill, at the end of a lane of boys, twenty times, in honor of its being Christmas Eve, and then ran home to Camden Town as hard as he could pelt, to play at blindman's buff.

Scrooge took his melancholy dinner in his usual melancholy tavern; and having read all the newspapers, and beguiled the rest of the evening with his banker's book, went home to bed. He lived in chambers which had once belonged to his deceased partner. They were a gloomy suite of rooms, in a lowering pile of building up a yard, where it had so little business to be, that one could scarcely help fancying it must have run there when it was a young house, playing at hide-and-seek with other houses, and have forgotten the way out again. It was old enough now, and dreary enough; for nobody lived in it but Scrooge, the other rooms being all let out as offices. The yard was so dark that even Scrooge, who knew its every stone, was fain to grope with his hands. The fog and frost so hung about the black old gateway of the house that it seemed as if the Genius of the Weather sat in mournful meditation on the threshold.

Now it is a fact that there was nothing at all particular about the knocker on the door, except that it was very large. It is also a fact that Scrooge had seen it, night and morning, during his whole residence in that place; now Scrooge had as little of what is called fancy about him as any man in the City of London, even including--which is a bold word--the corporation, aldermen, and livery. Let it also be borne in mind that Scrooge had not bestowed one thought on Marley since his last mention of his seven-years dead partner that afternoon. And then let any man explain to me, if he can, how it happened that Scrooge, having his key in the lock of the door, saw in the knocker, without its undergoing any intermediate process of change--not a knocker, but Marley's face.

Marley's face. It was not in impenetrable shadow, as the other objects in the yard were, but had a dismal light about it, like a bad lobster in a dark cellar. It was not angry or ferocious, but looked at Scrooge as Marley used to look, with ghostly spectacles turned up on its ghostly forehead. The hair was curiously stirred, as if by breath of hot air; and, though the eyes were wide open, they were perfectly motionless. That, and its livid color, made it horrible; but its horror seemed to be in spite of the face, and beyond its control, rather than a part of its own expression.

As Scrooge looked fixidly at this phenomenon, it was a knocker again.

To say that he was not startled, or that his blood was not conscious of a terrible sensation to which it had been a stranger from infancy, would be untrue. But he put his hand upon the key he had relinquished, turned it sturdily, walked in, and lighted his candle.

He *did* pause, with a moment's irresolution, before he shut the door; and he *did* look cautiously behind it first, as if he half expected to be terrified with the sight of Marley's pigtail sticking out into the hall. But there was nothing on the back of the door except the screws and nuts that held the knocker on, so he said, "Pooh, pooh!" and closed it with a bang.

Up Scrooge went. Darkness is cheap, and Scrooge liked it. But before he shut his heavy door he walked through his rooms to see that all was right. He had just enough recollection of the face to desire to do that.

Sitting-room, bedroom, lumber room. All as they should be. Nobody under the table, nobody under the sofa; a small fire in the grate; spoon and basin ready; and the little saucepan of gruel (Scrooge had a cold in his head) upon the hob.

"Humbug!" said Scrooge, and walked across the room.

After several turns, he sat down again. As he threw his head back in the chair, his glance happened to rest upon a bell, a disused bell that hung in the room and communicated for some purpose now forgotten with a chamber in the highest story of the building. It was with great astonishment, and with a strange, inexplicable dread, that as he looked, he saw this bell begin to swing. It swung so softly in the outset that it scarcely made a sound; but soon it rang out loudly, and so did every bell in the house.

This might have lasted half a minute, or a minute, but it seemed an hour. The bells ceased as they had begun, together. They were succeeded by a clanking noise, deep down below, as if some persons were dragging a heavy chain over the casks in the wine merchant's cellar.

The cellar door flew open with a booming sound, and then he heard the noise much louder, on the floors below; then coming up the stairs; then coming straight toward his door.

"It's humbug still!" said Scrooge. "I won't believe it."

His color changed, though, when, without a pause, it came on through the heavy door and passed into the room before his eyes. Upon its coming in, the dying flame leaped up, as though it cried, "I know him! Marley's ghost!" and then fell again.

The same face; the very same. Marley in his pigtail, usual waistcoat, tights, and boots; and tassels on the latter bristling like his pigtail, and his coat skirts, and the hair upon his head. The chain he drew was clasped about his middle. It was long and wound about him like a tail; and it was made (for Scrooge observed it closely) of cashboxes, keys, padlocks, ledgers, deeds, and heavy purses wrought in steel. His body was transparent, so that Scrooge, observing him and looking through his waistcoat, could see the two buttons on his coat behind.

"How now!" said Scrooge, caustic and cold as ever. "What do you want with me?"

"Much!" Marley's voice, no doubt about it.

"Who are you?"

"Ask me who I *was*."

14

"Who *were* you, then?" said Scrooge, raising his voice. "You're particular, for a shade." He was going to say "to a shade," but substituted this, as more appropriate.

"In life I was your partner, Jacob Marley."

"Can you--can you sit down?" asked Scrooge, looking at him.

"I can."

Scrooge asked the question because he didn't know whether a ghost so transparent might find himself in a condition to take a chair; and felt that in the event of its being impossible, it might involve the necessity of an embarrassing explanation. But the ghost sat down on the opposite side of the fireplace, as if he were quite used to it.

"You don't believe in me," observed the Ghost.

"I don't," said Scrooge. "You may be an undigested bit of beef, a blot of mustard, a crumb of cheese, a fragment of an underdone potato. There's more of gravy than of grave about you, whatever you are!"

Scrooge was not much in the habit of cracking jokes, nor did he feel in his heart by any means waggish then. The truth is that he tried to be smart, as a means of distracting his own attention, and keeping down his terror, for the specter's voice disturbed the very marrow of his bones.

To sit staring at those fixed glazed eyes, in silence for a moment, would play, Scrooge felt, the very deuce with him. There was something very awful, too, in the specter's being provided with an infernal atmosphere of his own. Scrooge could not feel it himself, but this was clearly the case; for though the Ghost sat perfectly motionless, its hair and skirts and tassels were still agitated as by the hot vapor from an oven.

"You see this toothpick?" said Scrooge, returning quickly to the charge for the reason just assigned, and wishing, though it were only for a second, to divert the vision's stony gaze from himself.

"I do," replied the Ghost.

"You are not looking at it," said Scrooge.

"But I see it," said the Ghost, "notwithstanding."

"Well!" returned Scrooge. "I have but to swallow this, and be for the rest of my days persecuted by a legion of goblins, all of my own creation. Humbug, I tell you; humbug!"

At this the spirit raised a frightful cry, and shook its chain with such a dismal and appalling noise that Scrooge held on tight to his chair to save himself from falling in a swoon. But how much greater was his horror when, the phantom taking off the bandage round its head, as if it were too warm to wear indoors, its lower jaw dropped down upon its breast!

Scrooge fell upon his knees, and clasped his hands before his face.

"Mercy!" he said. "Dreadful apparition, why do you trouble me?"

"It is required of every man," the Ghost returned, "that the spirit within him should walk abroad among his fellow men, and travel far and wide; and if that spirit goes not forth in life, it is condemned to do so after death. It is doomed to wander through the world--oh, woe is me!--and witness what it cannot share, but might have shared on earth, and turned to happiness!"

Again the specter raised a cry, and shook its chain and wrung its shadowy hands.

"You are fettered," said Scrooge, trembling. "Tell me why?"

"I wear the chain I forged in life," replied the Ghost. "I made it link by link, and yard by yard; I girded it on of my own free will, and of my own free will I wore it. Is its pattern strange to you?"

Scrooge trembled more and more.

"Or would you know," pursued the Ghost, "the weight and length of the strong coil you bear yourself? It was full as heavy and as long as this seven Christmas Eves ago. You have labored on it since. It is a ponderous chain!"

Scrooge glanced about him on the floor, in the expectation of finding himself surrounded by some fifty or sixty fathoms of iron cable; but he could see nothing.

"Jacob," he said imploringly. "Old Jacob Marley, tell me more. Speak comfort to me, Jacob!"

"I have none to give," the Ghost replied. "It comes from other regions, Ebenezer Scrooge, and is conveyed by other ministers, to other kinds of men. Nor can I tell you what I would. A very little more is all that is permitted to me. I cannot rest, I cannot stay, I cannot linger anywhere. My spirit never walked beyond our countinghouse--mark me!--in life my spirit never roved beyond the narrow limits of our money-changing hole; and weary journeys lie before me!"

It was a habit with Scrooge, whenever he became thoughtful, to put his hands in his breeches' pockets. Pondering on what the Ghost had said, he did so now, but without lifting up his eyes, or getting off his knees.

"You must have been very slow about it, Jacob," Scrooge observed in a businesslike manner, though with humility and deference.

"Slow!" the Ghost repeated.

"Seven years dead," mused Scrooge. "And traveling all the time?"

"The whole time," said the Ghost. "No rest, no peace. Incessant torture of remorse."

"You might have got over a great quantity of ground in seven years," said Scrooge.

The Ghost, on hearing this, set up another cry and clanked its chain so hideously in the dead silence of the night, that the Ward would have been justified in indicting it for a nuisance.

"Oh! Captive, bound and double-ironed," cried the phantom, "not to know that ages of incessant labor, by immortal creatures, for this earth must pass into eternity before the good of which it is susceptible is all developed. Not to know that any Christian spirit working kindly in its little sphere, whatever it may be, will find its mortal life too short for its vast means of usefulness. Not to know that no space of regret can make amends for one life's opportunities misused! Yet such was I! Oh! such was I!"

"But you were always a good man of business, Jacob," faltered Scrooge, who now began to apply this to himself.

"Business!" cried the Ghost, wringing its hands again. "Mankind was my business. The common welfare was my business; charity, mercy, forbearance, and benevolence were all my business. The dealings of my trade were but a drop of water in the comprehensive ocean of my busines!"

It held up its chain at arm's length, as if that were the cause of all its unavailing grief, and flung it heavily upon the ground again.

"At this time of the rolling year," the specter said, "I suffer most. Why did I walk through crowds of fellow beings with my eyes turned down, and never raise them to that blessed Star which led the Wise Men to a poor abode? Were there no poor homes to which its light would have conducted me?"

Scrooge was very much dismayed to hear the specter going on at this rate, and began to quake exceedingly.

"Hear me!" cried the Ghost. "My time is nearly gone."

"I will," said Scrooge. "But don't be hard upon me! Don't be flowery, Jacob! Pray!"

"How it is that I appear before you in a shape that you can see, I may not tell. I have sat invisible beside you many and many a day."

It was not an agreeable idea. Scrooge shivered and wiped the perspiration from his brow.

"That is no light part of my penance," pursued the Ghost. "I am here tonight to warn you that you have yet a chance and hope of escaping my fate. A chance and hope of my procuring, Ebenezer."

"You were always a good friend to me," said Scrooge. "Thank 'ee!"

"You will be haunted," resumed the Ghost, "by Three Spirits."

Scrooge's countenance fell almost as low as the Ghost's had done.

"Is that the chance and hope you mentioned, Jacob?" he demanded in a faltering voice?

"It is."

"I--I think I'd rather not," said Scrooge.

"Without their visits," said the Ghost, "you cannot hope to shun the path I tread. Expect the first tomorrow, when the bell tolls one."

"Couldn't I take 'em all at once, and have it over?" hinted Scrooge.

"Expect the second on the next night at the same hour. The third, upon the next night when the last stroke of twelve has ceased to vibrate. Look to see me no more; and look that, for your own sake, you remember what has passed between us!"

When it had said these words, the specter took its wrapper from the table and bound it round its head, as before. Scrooge knew this by the smart sound its teeth made, when the jaws were brought together by the bandage. He ventured to raise his eyes again, and found his supernatural visitor confronting him in an erect attitude, with its chain wound over and about its arm.

The apparition walked backward from him; and at every step it took, the window raised itself a little, so that when the specter reached it, it was wide open. It beckoned Scrooge to approach, which he did. When they were within two paces of each other, Marley's Ghost held up its hand, warning him to come no nearer. Scrooge stopped. The specter floated out upon the bleak, dark night. Scrooge followed to the window, desperate in his curiosity. He looked out.

The air was filled with phantoms, wandering hither and thither in restless haste, and moaning as they went. Every one of them wore chains like Marley's Ghost; some few (they might be guilty governments) were linked together; none were free. Many had been personally known to Scrooge in their lives. The misery with them all was, clearly, that they sought to interfere, for good, in human matters, and had lost the power forever.

Whether these creatures faded into mist, or mist enshrouded them, he could not tell. But they and their spirit voices faded together; and the night became as it had been when he walked home.

Scrooge closed the window and examined the door by which the Ghost had entered. It was double-locked, as he had locked it with his own hands, and the bolts were undisturbed. He tried to say, "Humbug!" but stopped at the first syllable. And being, from the emotion he had undergone, or the fatigues of the day, or his glimpse of the Invisible World, or the dull conversation of the Ghost, or the lateness of the hour, much in need of repose, went straight to bed without undressing, and fell asleep upon the instant.

When Scrooge awoke, it was so dark that, looking out of bed, he could scarcely distinguish the transparent window from the opaque walls of his chamber. He was endeavoring to pierce the darkness with his ferret eyes, when the chimes of a neighboring church struck the four quarters. So he listened for the hour.

To his great astonishment, the heavy bell went on from six to seven, and from seven to eight, and regularly up to twelve; then stopped. Twelve! It was past two when he went to bed. The clock was wrong. An icicle must have got into the works. Twelve!

"Why, it isn't possible," said Scrooge, "that I can have slept through a whole day and far into another night. It isn't possible that anything has happened to the sun, and this is twelve at noon!"

Marley's ghost bothered him exceedingly. Every time he resolved within himself, after mature inquiry, that it was all a dream, his mind flew back again, like a strong spring released, to its first position, and presented the same problem to be worked all though: Was it a dream or not?

Scrooge lay in this state until the chime had gone three quarters more, when he remembered, on a sudden, that the Ghost had warned him of a visitation when the bell tolled one.

He resolved to lie awake until the hour was passed; and, considering that he could no more go to sleep than go to heaven, this was perhaps the wisest resolution in his power.

The quarter was so long, that he was more than once convinced that he must have sunk into a doze unconsciously and missed the clock. At length it broke upon his listening ear.

"The hour itself," said Scrooge triumphantly, "and nothing else!"

He spoke before the hour bell sounded, which it now did with a deep, dull, hollow, melancholy one. Light flashed up in the room upon the instant, and the curtains of his bed were drawn.

The curtains of his bed were drawn aside, I tell you, by a hand. Not the curtains at his feet, nor the curtains at his back, but those to which his face was addressed. The curtains of his bed were drawn aside; and Scrooge, starting up into a half-recumbent attitude, found himself face to face with the unearthly visitor who drew them; as close to it as I am now to you, and I am standing in the spirit at your elbow.

It was a strange figure--like a child; yet not so like a child as like an old man, viewed through some supernatural medium, which gave him the appearance of having receded from the view, and being diminished to a child's proportions.

Its hair, which hung about its neck and down its back, was white as if with age; and yet the face had not a wrinkle in it, and the tenderest bloom was on the skin. It held a branch of fresh green holly in its hand; and, in singular contradiction of that wintry emblem, had its dress trimmed with summer flowers.

But the strangest thing about it was that from the crown of its head there sprung a bright clear jet of light, by which all this was visible; and which was doubtless the occasion of its using, in its duller moments, a great extinguisher for a cap, which it now held under its arm.

Even this, though, when Scrooge looked at it with increasing steadiness, was *not* its strangest quality. For as its belt sparkled and glittered, now in one part and now in another, and what was light one instant, at another time was dark, so the figure itself fluctuated in its distinctness, being now a thing with one arm, now with one leg, now with twenty legs, now a pair of legs without a head, now a head without a body; of which dissolving parts, no outline would be visible in the dense gloom wherein they melted away. And in the very wonder of this, it would be itself again; distinct and clear as ever.

"Are you the Spirit, sir, whose coming was foretold to me?" asked Scrooge.

"I am!"

The voice was soft and gentle. Singularly low, as if instead of being so close beside him, it were at a distance.

"Who and what are you?" Scrooge demanded.

"I am the Ghost of Christmas Past."

"Long Past?" inquired Scrooge, observant of its dwarfish stature.

"No. Your past."

Scrooge then made bold to inquire what business brought him there.

"Your welfare!" said the Ghost.

Scrooge expressed himself much obliged, but could not help thinking that a night of unbroken rest would have been more conducive to that end.

The Spirit must have heard him thinking, for it said, "Your reclamation, then. Take heed!"

It put out its strong hand as it spoke, and clasped him gently by the arm.

"Rise! And walk with me!"

"I am a mortal," Scrooge remonstrated, "and liable to fall."

"Bear but a touch of my hand there," said the Spirit, laying it upon his heart, "and you shall be upheld in more than this!"

As the words were spoken, they passed through the wall and stood upon an open country road, with fields on either hand. The city had entirely vanished. Not a vestige of it was to be seen. The darkness and the mist had vanished with it, for it was a clear, cold, winter day, with snow upon the ground.

"Good Heaven!" said Scrooge, clasping his hands together, as he looked about him. "I was bred in this place. I was a boy here!"

The Spirit gazed upon him mildly. Its gentle touch, though it had been light and instantaneous, appeared still present to the old man's sense of feeling. He was conscious of a thousand odors floating in the air, each one connected with a thousand thoughts and hopes and joys and cares, long, long forgotten.

"You recollect the way?" inquired the Spirit.

"Remember it!" cries Scrooge with fervor. "I could walk it blindfold."

"Strange to have forgotten it for so many years!" observed the Ghost. "Let us go on."

They walked along the road, Scrooge recognizing every gate and post and tree, until a little market town appeared in the distance, with its bridge, its church, and winding river. Some shaggy ponies were now seen trotting toward them with boys upon their backs, who called to other boys in country gigs and carts, driven by farmers. "These are but shadows, of the things that have been," said the Ghost. "They have no consciousness of us."

Scrooge knew and named them every one. Why was he rejoiced beyond all bounds to see them? Why did his cold eye glisten, and his heart leap up as they went past. Why was he filled with gladness when he heard them give each other Merry Christmas, as they parted at crossroads and byways, for their several homes? What was Merry Christmas to Scrooge? Out upon merry Christmas! What good had it ever done to him?

"The school is not quite deserted," said the Ghost. "A solitary child, neglected by his friends, is left there still."

They went, the Ghost and Scrooge, across the hall to a door at the back of the house. It opened before them and disclosed a long, bare, meloncholy room, made barer still by lines of plain deal forms and desks. At one of these a lonely boy was reading near a feeble fire; and Scrooge sat down upon a form, and wept to see his poor forgotten self as he had used to be.

Not a latent echo in the house, not a squeak and scuffle from the mice behind the paneling, not a drip from the half-thawed water-spout in the dull yard behind, not a sigh among the leafless boughs of one despondent poplar, not the idle swinging on an empty storehouse door, no, not a clicking in the fire, but fell upon the heart of Scrooge with softening influence, and gave a freer passage to his tears.

"I wish," Scrooge muttered, putting his hand in his pocket and looking about him, after drying his hands with his cuff, "but it's too late now."

"What is the matter?" asked the Spirit.

"Nothing," said Scrooge. "Nothing. There was a boy singing a Christmas carol at my door last night. I should have like to have given him something; that's all."

The Ghost smiled thoughtfully and waved its hands, saying as it did so, "Let us see another Christmas!"

Scrooge's former self grew large at the words, and the room became a little darker and more dirty. The panels shrunk, the windows cracked; fragments of plasters fell out of the ceiling, and the naked laths were shown instead; but how all this was brought about, Scrooge knew no more than you do.

He was not reading now, but walking up and down despairingly. Scrooge looked at the Ghost and, with a mournful shaking of his head, glanced anxiously toward the door.

It opened; and a little girl, much younger than the boy, came darting in, and putting her arms about his neck, and often kissing him, addressed him as her "Dear, dear brother."

"I have come to bring you home, dear brother!" said the child, clapping her tiny hands, and bending down to laugh. "To bring you home, home, home!"

"Home, little Fan?" returned the boy.

"Yes!" said the child, brimful of giggles. "Home, for good and all. Home, forever and ever. Father is so much kinder than he used to be, that home's like Heaven. He spoke so gently to me one dear night when I was going to bed, that I was not afraid to ask him once more if you might come home; and he said Yes you should; and sent me in a coach to bring you. And you're to be a man," said the child, opening her eyes; "and are never to come back here; but first we're to be together all the Christmas long, and have the merriest time in all the world."

"Always a delicate creature, whom a breath might have withered," said the Ghost. "But she had a large heart!"

"So she had," cried Scrooge. "You're right. I will not gainsay it, Spirit. God forbid!"

"She died a woman," said the Ghost, "and had, as I think, children."

"One child," Scrooge returned.

"True," said the Ghost. "Your nephew!"

Scrooge seemed uneasy in his mind, and answered briefly, "Yes."

Although they had but that moment left the school behind them, they were now in the busy thoroughfares of a city, where shadowy passengers passed and repassed, where shadowy carts and coaches battled for the way, and all the strife and tumult of a real city were. It was made plain

22

enough, by the dressing of the shops, that here too it was Christmas time again; but it was evening, and the streets were lighted up.

The Ghost stopped at a certain warehouse door, and asked Scrooge if he knew it.

"Know it?" said Scrooge. "Was I apprenticed here?"

They went in. At sight of an old gentleman in a Welsh wig, sitting behind such a high desk, that if he had been two inches taller he must have knocked his head against the ceiling, Scrooge cried in great excitement, "Why it's old Fezziwig! Bless his heart; it's Fezziwig alive again!"

Old Fezziwig laid down his pen and looked up at the clock, which pointed to the hour of seven. He rubbed his hands, adjusted his capacious waistcoat, laughed all over himself, from his shoes to his organ of benevolence, and called out in a comfortable, oily, rich, fat, jovial voice, "Yo ho, there! Ebenezer! Dick!"

Scrooge's former self, now grown a young man, came briskly in, accompanied by his fellow 'prentice.

"Dick Wilkins, to be sure!" said Scrooge to the Ghost. "Bless me, yes. There he is."

"Yo ho, my boys!" said Fezziwig. "No more work tonight. Christmas Eve, Dick. Christmas, Ebenezer! Let's have the shutters up," cried old Fezziwig, with a sharp clap of his hands, "before a man can say Jack Robinson!"

You wouldn't believe how those two fellows went at it! They charged into the street with the shutters--one, two, three--had 'em up in their places--four, five, six--barred 'em and pinned 'em--seven, eight, nine--and came back before you could have got to twelve, panting like race horses.

"Hilli-ho!" cried old Fezziwig, skipping down from the high desk with wonderful agility. "Clear away, my lads, and let's have lots of room here! Hilli-ho, Dick! Chirrup, Ebenezer!"

Every movable was packed off, as if it were dismissed from public life for evermore; the floor was swept and watered, the lamps were trimmed, fuel was heaped upon the fire; and the warehouse was as snug and warm and dry and bright a ballroom as you would desire to see upon a winter's night.

In came a fiddler with a music book and went up to the lofty desk and made an orchestra of it, and tuned like fifty stomach-aches. In came Mrs. Fezziwig, one vast, substantial smile. In came the three Miss Fezziwigs, beaming and lovable. In came the six young followers whose hearts they broke. In came all the young men and women employed in the business. In came the housemaid with her cousin, the baker. In came the cook with her brother's particular friend, the milkman. In came the boy from over the way, who was suspected of not having board enough from his master; trying to hide himself behind the girl from next door but one, who was proved to have had her ears pulled by her mistress. In they all came, one after another, some shyly, some boldly, some gracefully, some awkwardly, some pushing, some pulling; in they all came, anyhow and everyhow. Away they all went, twenty couples at once; hands half round and back again the other way; down the middle and up again; round and round in various stages of affectionate grouping; old top couple always turning up in the wrong place; new top couple starting off again, as soon as they got there; all top couples at last, and not a bottom one to help them!

There were more dances, and there were forfeits, and more dances, and there was cake, and there was negus, and there was a great piece of Cold Roast, and there was a great piece of Cold Boiled, and there were mince pies and plenty of beer.

When the clock struck eleven, this domestic ball broke up. Mr. and Mrs. Fezziwig took their stations, one on either side of the door, and, shaking hands with every person individually as he or she went out, wished him or her a Merry Christmas. When everybody had retired but the two 'prentices, they did the same to them; and thus the cheerful voices dies away, and the lads were left to their beds, which were under a counter in the back shop.

During the whole of this time Scrooge had acted like a man out of his wits. His heart and soul were in the scene, and with his former self. He corroborated everything, remembered everything, enjoyed everything, and underwent the strangest agitation. It was not until now, when the bright faces of his former self and Dick were turned from them, that he remembered the Ghost, and became conscious that it was looking full upon him, while the light upon its head burned very clear.

"A small matter," said the Ghost, "to make these silly folks so full of gratitude."

"Small!" echoed Scrooge.

The Spirit signed to him to listen to the two apprentices, who were pouring out their hearts in praise of Fezziwig; and when he had done so, said, "Why! Is it not? He has spent but a few pounds of your mortal money, three or four perhaps. Is that so much that he deserves this praise?"

"It isn't that," said Scrooge, heated by the remark and speaking unconsciously like his former, not his latter self. "It isn't that, Spirit. He has the power to render us happy or unhappy; to make our service light or burdensome; a pleasure or a toil. The happiness he gives is quite as great as if it cost a fortune."

He felt the Spirit's glance, and stopped.

"What is the matter?" asked the Ghost.

"Nothing particular," said Scrooge.

"Something, I think?" the Ghost insisted.

"No," said Scrooge. "No. I should like to be able to say a word or two to my clerk just now. That's all."

"My time grows short," observed the Spirit. "Quick!"

This was not addressed to Scrooge, or to any one whom he could see, but it produced an immediate effect. For again Scrooge saw himself. He was older now, a man in the prime of life. His face had not the harsh and rigid lines of later years, but it had begun to wear the signs of care and avarice. There was an eager, greedy, restless motion in the eye, which showed the passion that had taken root, and where the shadow of the growing tree would fall.

He was not alone, but sat by the side of a fair young girl in whose eyes there were tears, which sparkled in the light that shone out of the Ghost of Christmas Past.

"It matters little," she said softly. "Another idol has displaced me."

"What idol has displaced you?" he rejoined.

"A golden one."

"This is the evenhanded dealing of the world!" he said. "There is nothing on which it is so hard as poverty; and there is nothing it professes to condemn with such severity as the pursuit of wealth!"

"You fear the world too much," she answered, gently. "All your other hopes have merged into the hope of being beyond the chance of its morbid reproach. I have seen your noble aspirations fall off one by one, until the master passion, Gain, engrosses you. Have I not?"

"What then?" he retorted. "Even if I have grown so much wiser, what then? I am not changed toward you."

She shook her head.

"Our contract is an old one. It was made when we were both poor and content to be so, until, in good season, we could improve our worldly fortune by our patient industry. You are changed. When it was made you were another man."

"I was a boy," he said impatiently.

"Your own feeling tells you that you were not what you are," she returned. "I am."

"Have I ever sought release?"

"In words, no, never."

"In what, then?"

"In a changed nature, in an altered spirit, in another atmosphere of life, another Hope as its great end. In everything that made my love of any worth or value in your sight."

He was about to speak; but, with her head turned from him, she resumed.

"The memory of what is past half makes me hope you will--have pain in this. A very, very brief time, and you will dismiss the recollection of it, gladly, as an unprofitable dream, from which it happened well that you awoke. May you be happy in the life you have chosen!"

She left him and they parted.

"Spirit!" said Scrooge. "Show me no more!"

"One shadow more!" exclaimed the Ghost.

"No more!" cried Scrooge.

But the relentless Ghost pinioned him in both his arms, and forced him to observe what happened next.

They were in another scene and place, a room, not very large or handsome, but full of comfort. Near the winter fire sat a beautiful young girl, so like that last that Scrooge believed it was the same, until he saw her, now a comely matron, sitting opposite her daughter. The noise in this room was perfectly tumultuous, for there were more children there than Scrooge in his agitated state of mind could count. The consequences were uproarious beyond belief, but no one seemed to care; on the contrary, the mother and daughter laughed heartily and enjoyed it very much, and the latter, soon beginning to mingle in the sports.

But now a knocking at the door was heard, and such a rush immediately ensued that she with laughing face and plundered dress was borne toward it in the center of a flushed and boisterous group, just in time to greet the father, who came attended by a man laden with Christmas toys and presents. Then the shouting and the struggling, and the onslaught that was made on the defenseless porter! It is enough that, by degrees, the children and their emotions got out of the parlor, and by one stair at a time, up to the top of the house, where they went to bed.

And now Scrooge looked on more attentively than ever, when the master of the house, having his daughter leaning fondly on him, sat down with her and her mother at his own fireside; and when he thought that such another creature, quite as graceful and as full of promise, might have called him Father, and been a springtime in the haggard winter of his life, his sight grew very dim indeed.

"Spirit!" said Scrooge. "Remove me from this place."

"I told you these were shadows of the things that have been," said the Ghost. "That they are what they are, do not blame me!"

"Leave me! Take me back. Haunt me no longer!"

In the struggle--if that can be called a struggle in which the Ghost, with no visible resistance on its own part was undisturbed by an effort of its adversary--Scrooge observed that its light was burning high and bright; and dimly connecting that with its influence over him, he seized the extinguisher-cap, and by a sudden action pressed it down upon its head.

The Spirit dropped beneath it, so that the extinguisher covered its whole form; but though Scrooge pressed it down with all his force, he could not hide the light, which streamed from under it.

He was conscious of being exhausted and overcome by an irresistible drowsiness, and, further, of being in his own bedroom. He gave the cap a parting squeeze, in which his hand relaxed, and had barely time to reel to bed before he sank into a heavy sleep.

Stave Three
The Second of the Three Spirits

Awakening in the middle of a prodigiously tough snore, and sitting up in bed to get his thoughts together, Scrooge had no occasion to be told that the bell was again upon the stroke of one. He felt that he was restored to consciousness in the right nick of time, for the especial purpose of holding a conference with the second messenger despatched to him through Jacob Marley's intervention.

Now, being prepared for almost anything, he was not by any means prepared for nothing; and consequently, when the bell struck one and no shape appeared, he was taken with a violent fit of trembling. This idea taking full possession of his mind, he got up softly and shuffled in his slippers to the door.

The moment Scrooge's hand was on the lock, a strange voice called him by his name and bade him enter. He obeyed.

It was his own room. There was no doubt about that. But it had undergone a surprising transformation. The walls and ceiling were so hung with living green, that it looked a perfect grove, from every part of which bright gleaming berries glistened.

"Come in!" exclaimed the Ghost. "Come in and know me better, man!"

Scrooge entered timidly, and hung his head before this Spirit. He was not the dogged Scrooge he had been; and though the Spirit's eyes were clear and kind, he did not like to meet them.

"I am the Ghost of Christmas Present," said the Spirit. "Look upon me!"

Scrooge reverently did so. It was clothed in one simple deep green robe, or mantle, bordered with white fur. This garment hung so loosely on the figure that its capacious breast was bare, as if disclaiming to be warded or concealed by any artiface. Its feet, observable beneath the ample folds of the garment, were also bare, and on its head it wore no other covering than a holly wreath, set here and there with shining icicles. Its dark brown curls were long and free. Girded round its middle was an antique scabbard, but no sword was in it.

"Touch my robe!"

Scrooge did as he was told, and held it fast.

They stood in the city streets on Christmas morning, where (for the weather was severe) the people made a rough but brisk and not unpleasant kind of music, in scraping the snow from the pavement in front of their dwellings. The sky was gloomy, and the shortest streets were choked up with a dingy mist, half thawed, half frozen, whose heavier particles descended in a shower of sooty atoms, as if all the chimneys in Great Britain had, by one consent, caught fire and were blazing away to their dear heart's content. There was nothing very cheerful in the climate or the town, and yet was there an air of cheerfulness abroad that the clearest summer air and brightest summer sun might have endeavored to diffuse in vain.

It was a remarkable quality of the Ghost that, notwithstanding his gigantic size, he could accommodate himself to any place with ease; and that he stood beneath a low roof quite as gracefully and like a supernatural creature as it was possible he could have done in any lofty hall.

And perhaps it was the pleasure the good Spirit had in showing off this power of his, or else it was his own kind, generous, hearty nature, and his sympathy with all poor men, that led him straight to Scrooge's clerk's; for there he went, and took Scrooge with him, holding to his robe; and on the threshold of the door the Spirit smiled, and stopped to bless Bob Cratchit's dwelling with the sprinklings of his torch. Think of that! Bob had but fifteen bob a week himself; he pocketed on Saturdays but fifteen copies of his Christian name; and yet the Ghost of Christmas Present blessed his four-roomed house!

Then up rose Mrs. Cratchit, Cratchit's wife, dressed out but poorly, but brave in ribbons. She laid the cloth, assisted by Belinda Cratchit, second of her daughters, also brave in ribbons; while Master Peter Cratchit plunged a fork into the saucepan of potatoes. And now two smaller Cratchits, boy and girl, came treading in, screaming that outside the baker's they had smelled the goose and known it for their own; and basking in luxurious thoughts of sage and onion, these young Cratchits danced about the table.

"What has ever got your precious father, then?" said Mrs. Cratchit. "And your brother, Tiny Tim! And Martha wasn't as late last Christmas Day by half an hour!"

"Here's Martha, Mother," said a girl appearing as she spoke.

"Here's Martha, Mother!" cried the two young Cratchits. "Hurrah! There's such a goose, Martha!"

"Why, bless your heart alive, my dear, how late you are!" said Mrs. Cratchit, kissing her a dozen times, and taking off her shawl and bonnet for her with officious zeal.

"No, no! There's Father coming," cried the two young Cratchits, who were everywhere at once. "Hide, Martha, hide!"

So Martha hid herself, and in came little Bob, the father, with at least three foot of comforter exclusive of the fringe hanging down before him, and his threadbare clothes darned up and brushed, to look seasonable, and Tiny Tim upon his shoulder. Alas for Tiny Tim, he bore a little crutch, and had his limbs supported by an iron frame!

"Why, where's our Martha?" cried Bob Cratchit, looking round.

"Not coming," said Mrs. Cratchit.

"Not coming!" said Bob, with a sudden declension in his high spirits; for he had been Tim's blood horse all the way from church, and had come home rampant. "Not coming upon Christmas Day!"

Martha didn't like to see him disappointed, if it were only in joke, so she came out prematurely from behind the closet door and ran into his arms, while the two young Cratchits hustled Tiny Tim and bore him off into the washhouse, that he might hear the pudding singing in the copper.

"And how did little Tim behave?" asked Mrs. Cratchit, when she had rallied Bob on his credulity, and Bob had hugged his daughter to his heart's content.

"As good as gold," said Bob, "and better. Somehow he gets thoughtful, sitting by himself so much, and thinks the strangest things you ever heard. He told me, coming home, that he hoped the people saw him in the church, because he was a cripple, and it might be pleasant to them to remember upon Christmas Day who made lame beggars walk, and blind men see."

There never was such a goose. Bob said he didn't believe there ever was such a goose cooked. Its tenderness and flavor, size and cheapness, were the themes of universal admiration. Eked out by apple sauce and mashed potatoes, it was a sufficient dinner for the whole family; indeed, as Mrs. Cratchit said with great delight (surveying one small atom of a bone upon the dish), they hadn't eaten it all at last! Yet every one had had enough, and the youngest Cratchits, in particular, were steeped in sage and onion to the eyebrows! But now the plates being changed by Miss Belinda, Mrs. Cratchit left the room--too nervous to bear witness--to take the pudding up and bring it in.

Suppose it should not be done enough! Suppose it should break in turning out! Suppose somebody should have got over the wall of the back yard, and stolen it. All sorts of horrors were supposed.

Hallo! A great deal of steam! The pudding was out of the copper. In half a minute Mrs. Cratchit entered--flushed but smiling proudly--with the pudding, like a speckled cannon ball, so hard and firm, blazing in half-a-quartern of ignited brandy, and bedight with Christmas holly stuck into the top.

Oh, a wonderful pudding! Everybody had something to say about it, but nobody said or thought it was at all a small pudding for a large family. It would have been flat heresy to do so.

At last the dinner was all done, the cloth was cleared, the hearth swept, and the fire made up. The compound in the jug being tasted, and considered perfect, apples and oranges were put upon the table, and a shovel full of chestnuts on the fire. Then all the Cratchit family drew around the hearth, in what Bob Cratchit called a circle, meaning a half one; and at Bob Cratchit's elbow stood the family display of glass. Two tumblers and a custard cup without a handle.

These held the hot stuff from the jug, however, as well as golden goblets would have done; and Bob served it out with beaming looks, while the chestnuts on the fire sputtered and cracked noisily. Then Bob proposed, "A Merry Christmas to us all, my dears. God bless us!"

Which all the family re-echoed.

"God bless us every one!" said Tiny Tim, the last of all.

He sat very close to his father's side, upon his little stool. Bob held his withered little hand in his, as if he loved the child and wished to keep him by his side and dreaded that he might be taken from him.

"Spirit," said Scrooge, with an interest he had never felt before, "tell me if Tiny Tim will live."

"I see a vacant seat," replied the Ghost, "in the poor chimney corner, and a crutch without an owner, carefully preserved. If these shadows remain unaltered by the Future, the child will die."

"No, no," said Scrooge. "Oh, no, kind Spirit! Say he will be spared."

"If these shadows remain unaltered by the Future, none other of my race," returned the Ghost, "will find him here. What then? If he be like to die, he had better do it, and decrease the surplus population."

Scrooge hung his head to hear his own words quoted by the Spirit, and cast his eyes upon the ground. But he raised them on hearing his own name.

"Mr. Scrooge!" said Bob; "I'll give you Mr. Scrooge, the Founder of the Feast!"

"The Founder of the Feast, indeed!" cried Mrs. Cratchit, reddening. "I wish I had him here. I'd give him a piece of my mind to feast upon, and I hope he'd have a good appetite for it."

"My dear," said Bob; "the children! Christmas Day."

"It should be Christmas Day, I am sure," said she, "on which one drinks the health of such an odious, stingy, hard, unfeeling man as Mr. Scrooge. You know he is Robert! Nobody knows it better than you do, poor fellow!"

"My dear," was Bob's mild answer. "Christmas Day."

"I'll drink his health for your sake and the Day's," said Mrs. Cratchit, "not for his. Long life to him! A merry Christmas and a happy New Year! He'll be very merry and very happy, I have no doubt!"

The children drank the toast after her. It was the first of their proceedings which had no heartiness in it. Tiny Tim drank it last of all, but he didn't care twopence for it. Scrooge was the Ogre of the family. The mention of his name cast a dark shadow on the party, which was not dispelled for full five minutes.

They were not a handsome family; they were not well dressed; their shoes were far from being waterproof; their clothes were scanty; and Peter might have known, and very likely did, the inside of a pawnbroker's. But they were happy, grateful, pleased with one another, and contented with the time; and when they faded, and looked happier yet in the bright sprinklings of the Spirit's torch at parting, Scrooge had his eye upon them, and especially on Tiny Tim, until the last.

By this time it was getting dark and snowing pretty heavily; and, as Scrooge and the Spirit went along the streets, the brightness of the roaring fires in kitchens, parlors, and all sorts of rooms, was wonderful. Here, the flickering of the blaze showed preparations for a cozy dinner, with hot plates baking through and through before the fire, and deep red curtains, ready to be drawn to shut out cold and darkness. There, all the children of the house were running out into the snow to meet their married sisters, brothers, cousins, aunts, and to be the first to greet them.

But if you had judged from the numbers of people on their way to friendly gatherings, you might have thought that no one was at home to give them welcome when they got there, instead of every house expecting company, and piling up its fires half-chimney high. Blessings on it, how the Ghost exulted!

And now, without a word of warning from the Ghost, they stood upon a bleak and desert moor, where monstrous masses of rude stone were cast about as though it were the burial of giants; and water spread itself wheresoever it listed; or would have done so, but for the frost that held it prisoner; and nothing grew but moss and furze and coarse, rank grass. Down in the west the setting sun had left a streak of firey red, which glared upon the desolation for an instant like a sullen eye, and frowning lower, lower, lower yet, was lost in the thick gloom of darkest night.

"What place is this?" asked Scrooge.

"A place where miners live, who labor in the bowels of the earth," returned the Spirit. "But they know me. See!"

31

A light shone from the window of the hut, and swiftly they advanced toward it. Passing through the wall of mud and stone, they found a cheerful company assembled round a glowing fire. An old, old man and woman, with their children and their children's children, and another generation beyond that, all decked out gaily in their holiday attire. The old man, in a voice that seldom rose above the howling of the wind upon the barren waste, was singing them a Christmas song; it had been a very old song when he was a boy; and from time to time they all joined in the chorus. So surely as they raised their voices, the old man got quite blithe and loud; and so surely as they stopped, his vigor sank again.

Again the Ghost sped on, through the lonely darkness over an unknown abyss. It was a great surprise to Scrooge, while thus engaged, to hear a hearty laugh.

It was a much greater surprise to find himself in a bright, dry, gleaming room, with the Spirit standing smiling by his side, and looking at his nephew with approving affability!

"Ha! Ha!" laughed Scrooge's nephew. "Ha, ha, ha! He said that Christmas was a humbug, as I live! He believed it, too!"

"More shame for him, Fred!" said Scrooge's niece, indignantly. Bless these women! They never do anything by halves. They are always in earnest.

She was very pretty, exceedingly pretty. With a dimpled, surprised-looking, capital face, a ripe little mouth that seemed made to be kissed--as no doubt it was. Altogether she was what you would have called provoking, you know, but satisfactory, too. Oh, perfectly satisfactory.

"He's a comical fellow," said Scrooge's nephew, "that's the truth; and not so pleasant as he might be. However, his offenses carry their own punishment, and I have nothing to say against him."

"I'm sure he is very rich, Fred," hinted Scrooge's niece. "At least you always tell *me* so."

"What of that, my dear!" said Scrooge's nephew. "His wealth is of no use to him. He don't do any good with it. He don't make himself comfortable with it."

"I have no patience with him," observed Scrooge's niece.

"Oh, I have!" said Scrooge's nephew. "I am sorry for him; I couldn't be angry with him if I tried. Who suffers by his ill whims! Himself, always. Here he takes it into his head to dislike us, and he won't come and dine with us. What's the consequence? He don't lose much of a dinner."

"Indeed, I think he loses a very good dinner," interrupted Scrooge's niece. Everybody else said the same, and they must be allowed to have been competent judges, because they had just had dinner.

"Well, I am very glad to hear it," said Scrooge's nephew.

"I was only going to say," said Scrooge's nephew, "that the consequence of his taking a dislike to us, and not making merry with us, is, I think, that he loses some pleasant moments which could do him no harm. I am sure he loses pleasanter companions than he can find in his own thoughts, either in his moldy old office or his dusty chambers. I mean to give him the same chance every year, whether he likes it or not, for I pity him."

After a while they played at forfeits, for it is good to be children sometimes, and never better than at Christmas. There was then a game at blindman's buff. There might have been twenty people there, young and old, but they all played, and so did Scrooge.

The Ghost was greatly pleased to find him in this mood, and looked upon him with such favor that he begged like a boy to be allowed to stay until the guests departed. But this the Spirit said could not be done.

"Here is a new game," said Scrooge. "One half-hour, Spirit, only one!"

It was a game called "Yes and No," where Scrooge's nephew had to think of something, and the rest must find out what; he only answering to their questions yes or no, as the case was. The brisk fire of questioning to which he was exposed, elicited from him that he was thinking of an animal, a live animal, a rather disagreeable animal, a savage animal, an animal that growled and grunted sometimes, and talked sometimes, and lived in London, and walked about the streets, and wasn't made a show of, and wasn't led by anybody, and didn't live in a menagerie, and was never killed in a market, and was not a horse, or an ass, or a cow, or a bull, or a tiger, or a dog, or a pig, or a cat, or a bear. At every fresh question that was put to him, this nephew burst into a fresh roar of laughter and was so inexpressibly tickled, that he was obliged to get up off the sofa and stamp.

At last the plump sister, falling into a similar state, cried out, "I have found it out! I know what it is, Fred! I know what it is!"

"What is it?" cried Fred.

"It's your Uncle Scro-o-o-o-oge!"

Which it certainly was.

"He has given us plenty of merriment, I am sure," said Fred, "and it would be ungrateful not to drink his health. Here is a glass of mulled wine ready to our hand at the moment; and I say, 'Uncle Scrooge!'"

"Well! Uncle Scrooge!" they cried.

"A Merry Christmas and a Happy New Year to the old man, wherever he is!" said Scrooge's nephew. "He wouldn't take it from me, but may he have it, nevertheless. Uncle Scrooge!"

The whole scene passed off in the breath of the last word spoken by his nephew; and he and the Spirit were again upon their travels.

Much they saw, and far they went, and many homes they visited, but always with a happy end. The Spirit stood beside sick beds, and they were cheerful; on foreign lands, and they were close at home; by struggling men, and they were patient in their greater hope; by poverty, and it was rich.

It was a long night, if it were only a night; but Scrooge had his doubts of this, because the Christmas holidays appeared to be condensed into the space of time they passed together. It was strange, too, that while Scrooge remained unaltered in his outward form, the Ghost grew older, clearly older. Scrooge had observed this change, but never spoke of it, until they left a children's Twelfth Night party, when, looking at the Spirit as they stood together in an open place, he noticed that his hair was gray.

"Are spirits' lives so short?" asked Scrooge.

"My life upon this globe is very brief," replied the Ghost. "It ends tonight."

"Tonight!" cried Scrooge.

"Tonight at midnight. Hark! The time is drawing near."

"Forgive me if I am not justified in what I ask," said Scrooge, looking intently at the Spirit's robe, "but I see something strange, and not belonging to yourself, protruding from your skirts. Is it a foot or a claw?"

"It might be a claw, for the flesh there is upon it," was the Spirit's sorrowful reply. "Look here."

From the foldings of its robe it brought two children; wretched, abject, frightful, hideous, miserable. They knelt down at its feet and clung upon the outside of its garment.

"Oh, Man! Look here. Look, look, down here!" exclaimed the Ghost.

They were a boy and girl. Yellow, meager, ragged, scowling, wolfish; but prostate, too, in their humility.

"Spirit! Are they yours?" Scrooge could say no more.

"They are Man's," said the Spirit, looking down upon them. "And they cling to me, appealing from their fathers. This boy is Ignorance. This girl is Want. Beware of them both, and all of their degree, but most of all beware this boy, for on his brow I see that written which is Doom, unless the writing be erased. Deny it!" cried the Spirit, stretching out its hand toward the city.

"Have they no refuge or resource?" cried Scrooge.

"Are there no prisons!" said the Spirit, turning on him for the last time with his own words. "Are there no workhouses?"

The bell struck twelve.

Scrooge looked about him for the Ghost, and saw it not. As the last stroke ceased to vibrate, he remembered the prediction of old Jacob Marley and, lifting up his eyes, beheld a solemn Phantom, draped and hooded, coming like a mist along the ground toward him.

Stave Four
The Last of the Spirits

It was shrouded in a deep black garment, which concealed its head, its face, its form, and left nothing of it visible save one outstretched hand. But for this it would have been difficult to detach its figure from the night, and separate it from the darkness by which it was surrounded.

"I am in the presence of the Ghost of Christmas Yet To Come?" said Scrooge.

The Spirit answered not, but pointed onward with its hand.

"You are about to show me shadows of the things that have not happened, but will happen in the time before us," Scrooge pursued. "Is that so, Spirit?"

The upper portion of the garment was contracted for an instant in its folds, as if the Spirit had inclined its head. That was the only answer he received.

"Lead on!" said Scrooge. "Lead on! The night is waning fast, and it is precious time to me, I know. Lead on Spirit!"

The phantom moved away as it had come toward him. Scrooge followed in the shadow of its dress, which bore him up, he thought, and carried him along.

The Spirit stopped beside one little knot of business men. Observing that the hand was pointed to them, Scrooge advanced to listen to their talk.

"No," said a great fat man with a monstrous chin, "I don't know much about it either way. I only know he's dead."

"When did he die?" inquired another.

"Last night, I believe."

"Why, what was the matter with him?" asked a third, taking a vast quantity of snuff out of a very large snuffbox. "I thought he'd never die."

"God knows," said the first, with a yawn.

"What has he done with his money?" asked a red-faced gentleman with a pendulous excrescence on the end of his nose, that shook like the gills of a turkey cock.

"I haven't heard," said the man with the large chin, yawning again. "Left it to his company, perhaps. He hasn't left it to me. That's all I know."

This pleasantry was received with a general laugh.

"Well, I am the most disinterested among you, after all," said the first speaker, "for I never wear black gloves, and I never eat lunch. But I'll offer to go, if anybody else will. When I come to think of it, I'm not at all sure that I wasn't his most particular friend; for we used to stop and speak whenever we met. By, by!"

Speakers and listeners strolled away and mixed with other groups. Scrooge knew the men, and looked toward the Spirit for an explanation.

The Phantom glided on into a street. Its finger pointed to two persons meeting. Scrooge listened again, thinking that the explanation might lie there.

He knew these men, also, perfectly. They were men of business, very wealthy, and of great importance.

He had made a point always of standing well in their esteem in a business point of view.

"How are you?" said one.

"How are you?" returned the other.

"Well!" said the first. "Old Scratch has got his own at last, hey?"

"So I am told," returned the second. "Cold, isn't it!"

"Seasonable for Christmas time. You are not a skater, I suppose?"

"No. No. Something else to think of. Good morning!"

Not another word. That was their meeting, their conversation, and their parting.

Scrooge was at first inclined to be surprised that the Spirit should attach importance to conversations apparently so trivial, but feeling assured that they must have some hidden purpose. He resolved to treasure up every word he heard, and everything he saw and especially to observe the shadow of himself when it appeared. For he had an expectation that the conduct of his future self would give him the clue he missed, and would render the solution of these riddles easy.

He looked about in that very place for his own image, but another man stood in his accustomed corner, and though the clock pointed to his usual time of day for being there, he saw no likeness of himself among the multitudes that poured in through the porch.

They left the busy scene and went into an obscure part of the town, where Scrooge had never penetrated before, although he recognized its situation and its bad repute. The ways were foul and narrow, the shops and houses wretched, the people half-naked, drunken, slipshod, ugly. Alleys and archways, like so many cesspools, disgorged their offenses of smell and dirt and life upon the straggling streets.

Far in this den of infamous resort, there was a low-browed, beetling shop, below a penthouse roof, where iron, old rags, bottles, bones, and greasy offal were brought. Secrets that few would like to scrutinize were bred and hidden in mountains of unseemly rags, masses of corrupted fat, and sepulchers of bones. Sitting in among the wares he dealt in, by a charcoal stove made of bricks, was a gray-haired rascal, nearly seventy-five years of age.

Scrooge and the Phantom came into the presence of this man, just as a woman with a heavy bundle slunk into the shop. But she had scarcely entered, when another woman, similarly laden, came in too; and she was closely followed by a man in faded black, who was no less startled by the sight of them, than they had been upon the recognition of each other. After a short period of blank astonishment, in which the old man with the pipe had joined them, they all three burst into a laugh.

"Let the charwoman alone to be the first!" cried she who had entered first. "Let the laundress alone to be the second; and let the undertaker's man alone to be the third. Look here, old Joe, here's a chance! If we haven't all three met here without meaning it!"

"We're all suitable to our calling, we're well matched. Come into the parlor."

"What odds then! What odds, Mrs. Dilber?" said the woman. "Every person has a right to take care of themselves. He always did!"

"That's true indeed!" said the laundress. "No man more so."

"Why, then, don't stand staring as if you was afraid, woman. Who's the wiser? We're not going to pick holes in each other's coats, I suppose?"

"Very well, then!" cried the woman. "That's enough. Who's the worse for the loss of a few things like these? Not a dead man, I suppose."

"No, indeed," said Mrs. Dilber, laughing.

"If he wanted to keep 'em after he was dead, a wicked old screw," pursued the woman, "why wasn't he natural in his lifetime? If he had been, he'd have had somebody to look after him when he was struck with Death, instead of lying gasping out his last there, alone by himself."

"It's the truest word that ever was spoke," said Mrs. Dilber. "It's a hard judgment on him."

"I wish it was a little heavier judgment," replied the woman; "and it should have been, you may depend upon it, if I could have laid my hands on anything else. Open that bundle, old Joe, and let me know the value of it. Speak out plain. I'm not afraid to be the first, nor afraid for them to see it. We know pretty well that we were helping ourselves, before we met here, I believe. It's no sin. Open the bundle, Joe."

But the gallantry of her friends would not allow of this; and the man in faded black, mounting the breach first, produced his plunder. It was not extensive. A seal or two, a pencil case, a pair of sleeve buttons, and a brooch of no great value, were all. They were severally examined and appraised by old Joe.

"That's your account," said Joe, "and I wouldn't give another sixpence, if I was to be boiled for not doing it. Who's next?"

Mrs. Dilber was next. Sheets and towels, a little wearing apparel, two old-fashioned silver teaspoons, a pair of sugar tongs, and a few boots.

"I always give too much to ladies. It's a weakness of mine, and that's the way I ruin myself," said old Joe. "That's your account."

"And now undo my bundle, Joe," said the first woman.

Joe went down on his knees for the greater convenience of opening it, and having unfastened a great many knots, dragged out a large heavy roll of some dark stuff.

"What do you call this?" said Joe. "Bed curtains!"

"Ah!" returned the woman, laughing and leaning forward on her crossed arms. "Bed curtains!"

"You don't mean to say you took 'em down, rings and all, with him lying there?" said Joe.

"Yes, I do," replied the woman. "Why not?"

"You were born to make your fortune," said Joe, "and you'll certainly do it."

"I certainly shan't hold my hand, when I can get anything in it by reaching out, for the sake of such a man as he was, I promise you, Joe," returned the woman, coolly. "Don't drop that oil upon the blankets, now."

"His blankets?" asked Joe.

"Whose else's do you think?" replied the woman. "He isn't likely to take cold without 'em, I dare say."

"I hope he didn't die of anything catching? Eh?" said old Joe, stopping in his work and looking up.

"Don't you be afraid of that," returned the woman. "I ain't so fond of his company that I'd loiter abut him for such things, if he did."

Scrooge listened to this dialogue in horror. As they sat grouped about their spoil, in the scanty light afforded by the old man's lamp, he viewed them with a detestation and disgust which could hardly have been greater, though they had been obscene demons, marketing the corpse itself.

"Spirit!" said Scrooge, shuddering from head to foot. "I see, I see. My life tends that way, now. Merciful Heaven what is this!"

He recoiled in terror, for the scene had changed, and now he almost touched a bed, a bare, uncurtained bed, on which, beneath a ragged sheet, there lay something covered up which, though it was dumb, announced itself in awful language.

"Spirit!" he said. "This is a fearful place. In leaving it I shall not leave its lesson, trust me. Let us go!"

Still the Ghost pointed with unmoved finger to the head.

"If there is any person in the town who feels emotion caused by this man's death," said Scrooge, quite agonized, "show that person to me, Spirit, I beseech you!"

The Phantom spread its dark robe before him for a moment, like a wing, and withdrawing it, revealed a room by daylight, where a mother and her children were.

She was expecting someone, and with anxious eagerness, for she walked up and down the room, started at every sound, looked out from the window, glanced at the clock, tried, but in vain, to work with her needle, and could hardly bear the voices of her children in their play.

At length the long-expected knock was heard. She hurried to the door and met her husband, a man whose face was careworn and depressed, though he was young. There was a remarkable expression in it now, a kind of serious delight of which he felt ashamed, and which he struggled to repress.

"It is good," she said, "or bad?"--to help him.

"Bad," he answered.

"We are quite ruined?"

"No. There is hope yet, Caroline."

"If he relents," she said, amazed, "there is! Nothing is past hope, if such a miracle has happened."

"He is past relenting," said her husband. "He is dead."

She was a mild and patient creature, if her face spoke truth, but she was thankful in her soul to hear it, and she said so, with clasped hands. She prayed for forgiveness the next moment, and was sorry; but the first was the emotion of her heart.

"Let me see some tenderness connected with a death," said Scrooge; "or that dark chamber, Spirit, which we left just now, will be forever present to me."

The Ghost conducted him through several streets familiar to his feet; and as they went along, Scrooge looked here and there to find himself, but nowhere was he to be seen. They entered poor Bob Cratchit's house.

Quiet. Very quiet. The noisy little Cratchits were as still as statues in one corner, and sat looking up at Peter, who had a book before him. The mother and her daughters were engaged in sewing. But surely they were very quiet!

" 'And He took a child, and set him in the midst of them.' "

Where had Scrooge heard these words? He had not dreamed them. The boy must have read them out as he and the Spirit crossed the threshold. Why did he not go on?

The mother laid her work upon the table, and put her hand up to her face.

"The color hurts my eyes," she said.

The color? Ah, poor Tiny Tim!

"They're better now again," said Cratchit's wife. "It makes them weak by candlelight; and I wouldn't show weak eyes to your father when he comes home, for the world. It must be near his time."

"Past it rather," Peter answered, shutting up his book. "But I think he has walked a little slower than he used, these few last evenings, Mother."

They were very quiet again. At last she said, in a steady, cheerful voice that only faltered once, "I have known him walk with--I have known him walk with Tiny Tim upon his shoulder, very fast, indeed."

"And so have I," cried Peter. "Often."

"And so have I," exclaimed another. So had all.

"But he was very light to carry," she resumed, intent upon her work, "and his father loved him so, that it was no trouble; no trouble. And there is your father at the door!"

His tea was ready for him on the hob, and they all tried who should help him to it most. Then the two young Cratchits got upon his knees and laid, each child, a little cheek against his face, as if they said, "Don't mind it, Father. Don't be grieved!"

Bob was very cheerful with them, and spoke pleasantly to all the family. He looked at the work upon the table, and praised the industry and speed of Mrs. Cratchit and the girls. They would be done long before Sunday, he said.

"Sunday! You went today, then, Robert?" said his wife.

"Yes, my dear," returned Bob. "I wish you could have gone. It would have done you good to see how green a place it is. But you'll see it often. I promised him that I would walk there on a Sunday. My little, little child!" cried Bob. "My little child!"

He broke down all at once. He couldn't help it. If he could have helped it, he and his child would have been farther apart perhaps than they were.

He left the room and went upstairs into the room above, which was lighted cheerfully, and hung with Christmas. There was a chair set close beside the child and there were signs of someone having been there lately. Poor Bob sat down in it, and when he had thought a little and composed himself, he kissed the little face. He was reconciled to what had happened, and went down again quite happy.

They drew about the fire, and talked, the girls and mother working still. Bob told them of the extraordinary kindness of Mr. Scrooge's nephew, whom he had scarcely seen but once, and who, meeting him in the street that day, and seeing that he looked a little--"just a little down, you know," said Bob, inquired what had happened to distress him. "On which," said Bob, "for he is the pleasantest-spoken gentleman you ever heard, I told him. 'I am heartily sorry for it, Mr. Cratchit,' he said, 'and heartily sorry for your good wife.'"

Mrs. Cratchit kissed him, his daughters kissed him, the two young Cratchits kissed him, and Peter and himself shook hands. Spirit of Tiny Tim, thy childish essence was from God!

"Specter," said Scrooge, "something informs me that our parting moment is at hand. I know it, but I know not how. Tell me what man that was whom we saw lying dead?"

The Ghost of Christmas Yet To Come conveyed him, as before--though at a different time, he thought, indeed, there seemed no order in these latter visions, save that they were in the Future--into the resorts of businessmen, but showed him not himself. Indeed, the Spirit did not stay for anything, but went straight on, as to the end just now desired, until besought by Scrooge to tarry for a moment.

"This Court," said Scrooge, "through which we hurry now, is where my place of occupation is, and has been for a length of time."

The Spirit stopped; the hand was pointed elsewhere.

A churchyard. Here, then, the wretched man whose name he had now to learn, lay underneath the ground.

"Before I draw nearer to that stone to which you point," said Scrooge, "answer me one question. Are these the shadows of the things that Will be, or are they shadows of the things that May be, only?"

Still the Ghost pointed downward to the grave by which it stood.

Scrooge crept toward it, trembling as he went, and following the finger, read upon the stone of the neglected grave his own name. *Ebenezer Scrooge.*

"No, Spirit! Oh, no, no!" he cried, tight clutching at its robe. "Hear me! I am not the man I was. I will not be the man I must have been but for this intercourse. Why show me this, if I am past all hope!"

The kind hand trembled.

"I will honor Christmas in my heart, and try to keep it all the year. I will live in the Past, the Present, and the Future. The Spirits of all three shall strive within me. I will not shut out the lessons that they teach. Oh, tell me I may sponge away the writing on this stone!"

In his agony he caught the spectral hand. It sought to free itself, but he was strong in his entreaty, and detained it. The Spirit, stronger yet, repulsed him.

Holding up his hands in a last prayer to have his fate reversed, he saw an alteration in the Phantom's hood and dress. It shrunk, collapsed, and dwindled down into a bedpost.

Stave Five
The End of It

Yes! And the bedpost was his own. The bed was his own, the room was his own. Best and happiest of all, the Time before him was his own, to make amends in!

41

"I will live in the Past, the Present, and the Future!" Scrooge repeated, as he scrambled out of bed. "The Spirits of all three shall strive within me. Oh, Jacob Marley! Heaven, and the Christmas time be praised for this! I say it on my knees, old Jacob, on my knees!"

"They are not torn down," cried Scrooge, folding one of his bed curtains in his arms; "they are not torn down, rings and all. They are here--I am here--the shadows of the things that would have been may be dispelled. They will be. I know they will!"

His hands were busy with his garments all this time, turning them inside out, putting them on upside down, tearing them, mislaying them, making them parties to every kind of extravagance.

He was checked in his transports by the churches ringing out the lustiest peals he had ever heard.

Running to the window, he opened it and put out his head. No fog, no mist; clear, bright, jovial, stirring, cold; cold, piping for the blood to dance to; golden sunlight; heavenly sky; sweet fresh air; merry bells. Oh, glorious. Glorious!

"What's today?" cried Scrooge, calling downward to a boy in Sunday clothes, who perhaps had loitered in to look about him.

"Today!" replied the boy. "Why, Christmas Day."

"Eh?" returned the boy, with all his might of wonder.

"What's today, my fine fellow?" said Scrooge.

"It's Christmas Day!" said Scrooge to himself. "I haven't missed it. The Spirits have done it all in one night.

"Do you know the poulterer's in the next street but one, at the corner?" Scrooge inquired.

"I should hope I did," replied the lad.

"An intelligent boy!" said Scrooge. "A remarkable boy! Do you know whether they've sold the prize turkey that was hanging up there?"

"What, the one as big as me?" returned the boy.

"Yes, my buck!"

"It's hanging there now," replied the boy.

"Is it?" said Scrooge. "Go and buy it and tell 'em to bring it here, that I may give them the direction where to take it. Come back with the man, and I'll give you a shilling. Come back with him in less than five minutes, and I'll give you half a crown!"

The boy was off like a shot.

"I'll send it to Bob Cratchit's," whispered Scrooge, rubbing his hands and splitting with a laugh. "He shan't know who sends it. It's twice the size of Tiny Tim.

"Why here's the turkey. Hallo! Whoop! How are you! Merry Christmas!"

It was a turkey! He never could have stood upon his legs, that bird. He would have snapped 'em short off in a minute, like sticks of sealing wax.

"Why, it's impossible to carry that to Camden Town," said Scrooge. "You must have a cab."

The chuckle with which he paid for the cab, and the chuckle with which he recompensed the boy, were only to be exceeded by the chuckle with which he sat down, breathless, and chuckled till he cried.

He dressed himself "all in his best," and at last got out into the streets. The people were by this time pouring forth, and walking with hands behind him, Scrooge regarded every one with a delighted smile.

He had not gone far, when coming on toward him he beheld the portly gentleman who had walked into his countinghouse the day before and said, "Scrooge and Marley's, I believe?" It sent a pang across his heart to think how this old gentleman would look upon him when they met, but he knew what path lay straight before him, and he took it.

"My dear sir," said Scrooge, quickening his pace, and taking the old gentleman by both hands. "How do you do?"

"Mr. Scrooge?"

"Yes," said Scrooge. "Allow me to ask your pardon. And will you have the goodness--" Here Scrooge whispered in his ear.

"My dear Mr. Scrooge, are you serious?"

"If you please," said Scrooge. "Not a farthing less. A great many back payments are included in it, I assure you. Will you do me that favor?"

"My dear sir," said the other, shaking hands with him. "I don't know what to say."

"Don't say anything, please," retorted Scrooge. "Come and see me."

"I will!" cried the old gentleman. And it was clear he meant to do it.

"Thank'ee," said Scrooge. "I am much obliged to you. I thank you fifty times. Bless you!"

He went to church, and walked about the streets, and watched the people hurrying to and fro, and patted the children on the head, and found that everything could yield him pleasure. In the afternoon he turned his steps toward his nephew's house.

He passed the door a dozen times before he had the courage to go up and knock.

"Is your master at home, my dear?" said Scrooge to the girl. Nice girl! Very.

"Yes, sir."

"Where is he, my love?" said Scrooge.

"He's in the dining-room, sir, along with mistress. I'll show you upstairs, if you please."

"Thank'ee. He knows me," said Scrooge, with his hand already on the dining-room lock. "I'll go in here, my dear."

He turned it gently, and sidled his face in round the door. They were looking at the table (which was spread out in great array); for these young housekeepers are always nervous on such points, and like to see that everything is right.

"Fred!" said Scrooge.

Dear heart alive, how his niece by marriage started.

"Why, bless my soul!" cried Fred. "Who's that?"

"It's I. Your uncle Scrooge. I have come to dinner. Will you let me in, Fred?"

Let him in! It is a mercy he didn't shake his arm off. He was at home in five minutes. Nothing could be heartier. Wonderful party, wonderful games, wonderful unanimity, wonderful happiness!

But he was early at the office next morning. If he could only be there first and catch Bob Cratchit coming late! That was the thing he had set his heart upon.

And he did it; yes, he did! Bob was full eighteen minutes and a half behind his time. Scrooge sat with his door wide open, that he might see him come into the tank.

His hat was off before he opened the door, his comforter too. He was on his stool in a jiffy, driving away with his pen, as if he were trying to overtake nine o'clock.

"Hallo!" growled Scrooge, in his accustomed voice as near as he could feign it. "What do you mean by coming here at this time of day?"

"I am very sorry, sir," said Bob. "I am behind my time."

"You are!" repeated Scrooge. "Yes, I think you are. Step this way, sir, if you please."

"It's only once a year, sir," pleaded Bob, appearing from the tank.

"Now, I'll tell you what, my friend," said Scrooge. "I am not going to stand this sort of thing any longer. And therefore," he continued, "I am about to raise your salary!"

Bob trembled, and got a little nearer to the ruler. He had a momentary idea of knocking Scrooge down with it, holding him, and calling to the people in the court for help and a straight-waistcoat.

"A Merry Christmas, Bob!" said Scrooge, with an earnestness that could not be mistaken, as he clapped him on the back. "A merrier Christmas, Bob, my good fellow, than I have given you for many a year! I'll raise your salary and endeavor to assist your struggling family, and we will discuss your affairs this very afternoon."

Scrooge was better than his word. He did it all, and infinitely more; and to Tiny Tim, who did not die, he was a second father. He became as good a friend, as good a master, and as good a man, as the good old city knew, or any other good old city, town, or borough, in the good old world. Some people laughed to see the alteration in him, but he let them laugh, and little heeded them. His own heart laughed; and that was quite enough for him.

He had no further intercourse with Spirits, but lived upon the Total Abstinence Principle, ever afterward; and it was always said of him, that he knew how to keep Christmas well, if any man alive possessed the knowledge. May that be truly said of us, and all of us! And so, as Tiny Tim observed, God Bless Us, Every One!

Theology = must love ourselves to love others

Characterization = many different, memorable characters

CHARLOTTE BRONTË
(1816-1855)

Born in Yorkshire, England, in 1816, Charlotte, one of five sisters, learned to write primarily at home. Her books reflect the magic and mystery of the moors of Yorkshire, desolate, perhaps dangerous, marshlands renowned in English folklore and literature. The haunting beauty of the moor inspired Charlotte's gothic romances, such as Jane Eyre, but the power of Christian righteousness also pervades her stories.

The Brontë sisters, daughters of an Anglican minister, bore their difficult lives with dignity and faith. The deaths of their mother and two sisters put great responsibility on their shoulders. They each worked as governesses and Charlotte also became a teacher of French. Charlotte married after her two sisters died, but she, too, expired soon after.

Readers might assume that such tragedy might breed bitterness or pity in the Brontë's writings. Their stories, however, reveal a strong faith in the goodness of God, the triumph of righteousness, and the reward of good moral character. The settings of their books are replete with the suspense and darkness of life, but the strength of morality in the heroes and heroines lighten the landscape with the assurance of ultimate well-being for those who follow God's ways.

SSSSSSSSSSSSSSSSSSSSSSSS

JANE EYRE

Chapter 27

Some time in the afternoon I raised my head, and looking round and seeing the western sun gilding the sign of its decline on the wall, I asked, "What am I to do?"

But the answer my mind gave--"Leave Thornfield at once"--was so prompt, so dread, that I stopped my ears. I said I could not bear such words now. "That I am not Edward Rochester's bride is the least part of my woe," I alleged: "that I have wakened out of most glorious dreams, and found them all void and vain, is a horror I could bear and master; but that I must leave him decidedly, instantly, entirely, is intolerable. I cannot do it."

But, then, a voice within me averred that I could do it and foretold that I should do it. I wrestled with my own resolution: I wanted to be weak that I might avoid the awful passage of further suffering I saw laid out for me; and Conscience, turned tyrant, held Passion by the throat, told her tauntingly, he had yet dipped her dainty foot in the slough, and swore that with that arm of iron he would thrust her down to unsounded depths of agony.

"Let me be torn away, then!" I cried. "Let another help me!"

"No; you shall tear yourself away, none shall help you: you shall yourself pluck out your right eye; yourself cut off your right hand: your heart shall be the victim, and you the priest to transfix it."

I rose up suddenly, terror-struck at the solitude which so ruthless a judge haunted,--at the silence which so awful a voice filled. My head swam as I stood erect. I perceived that I was sickening from excitement and inanition; neither meat nor drink had passed my lips that day, for I had taken no breakfast. And, with a strange pang, I now reflected that, long as I had been shut up here, no message had been sent to ask how I was, or to invite me to come down: not even little Adèle had tapped at the door; not even Mrs. Fairfax had sought me. "Friends always forget those whom fortune forsakes," I murmured, as I undrew the bolt and passed out. I stumbled over an obstacle: my head was still dizzy, my sight was dim, and my limbs were feeble. I could not soon recover myself. I fell, but not on to the ground; an outstretched arm caught me. I looked up--I was supported by Mr. Rochester, who sat in a chair across my chamber threshold.

"You come out at last," he said. "Well, I have been waiting for you long, and listening; yet not one movement have I heard, no one sob: five minutes more of that death-like hush, and I should have forced the lock like a burglar. So you shun me?--you shut yourself up and grieve me with vehemence. You are passionate: I expected a scene of some kind. I was prepared for the hot rain of tears; only I wanted them to be shed on my breast: now a senseless floor has received them, or your drenched handkerchief. But I err: you have not wept at all! I see a white cheek and a faded eye, but no trace of tears. I suppose, then, your heart has been weeping blood?

"Well, Jane! not a word of reproach? Nothing bitter-- nothing poignant? Nothing to cut a feeling or sting a passion? You sit quietly where I have placed you, and regard me with a weary, passive look.

"Jane, I never meant to wound you thus. If the man who had but one little ewe lamb that was dear to him as a daughter, that ate of his bread and drank of his cup, and lay in his bosom, had by some mistake slaughtered it at the shambles, he would not have rued his bloody blunder more than I now rue mine. Will you ever forgive me?"

Reader, I forgave him at the moment on the spot. There was such deep remorse in his eye, such true pity in his tone, such manly energy in his manner; and besides, there was such unchanged love in his whole look and mien--I forgave him all: yet not in words, not outwardly; only at my heart's core.

"You know I am a scoundrel, Jane?" ere long he inquired wistfully--wondering, I suppose, at my continued silence and tameness, the result rather of weakness than of will.

"Yes, sir."

"Then tell me so roundly and sharply--don't spare me."

"I cannot: I am tired and sick. I want some water." He heaved a sort of shuddering sigh, and taking me in his arms, carried me downstairs. At first I did not know to what room he had borne me; all was cloudy to my glazed sight: presently I felt the reviving warmth of a fire; for, summer as it was, I had become icy cold in my chamber. He put wine to my lips; I tasted it and revived; then I ate something he offered me, and was soon myself. I was in the library--sitting in his chair--he was quite near. "If I could go out of life now, without too sharp a pang, it would be well for me," I thought; "then I should not have to make the effort of cracking my heartstrings in rending them from among Mr. Rochester's. I must leave him, it appears. I do not want to leave him--I cannot leave him."

"How are you now, Jane?"

"Much better, sir; I shall be well soon."

"Taste the wine again, Jane."

I obeyed him; then he put the glass on the table, stood before me, and looked at me attentively. Suddenly he turned away, with an inarticulate exclamation, full of passionate emotion of some kind; he walked fast through the room and came back; he stooped towards me as if to kiss me; but I remembered caresses were now forbidden. I turned my face away and put his aside.

"What!--How is this?" he exclaimed hastily. "Oh, I know! you won't kiss the husband of Bertha Mason? You consider my arms filled and my embraces appropriated?"

"At any rate, there is neither room nor claim for me, sir."

"Why, Jane? I will spare you the trouble of much talking; I will answer for you--Because I have a wife already, you would reply.--I guess rightly?"

"Yes."

"If you think so, you must have a strange opinion of me; you must regard me as a plotting profligate--a base and low rake who has been simulating disinterested love in order to draw you into a snare deliberately laid, and strip you of honour and rob you of self-respect. What do you say to that? I see you can say nothing: in the first place, you are faint still, and have enough to do to draw your breath; in the second place, you cannot yet accustom yourself to accuse and revile me, and besides, the flood-gates of tears are opened, and they would rush out if you spoke much; and you have no desire to espostulate, to upbraid, to make a scene: you are thinking how *to act—talking* you consider is of no use. I know you--I am on my guard."

"Sir, I do not wish to act against you," I said; and my unsteady voice warned me to curtail my sentence.

"Not in *your* sense of the word, but in *mine* you are scheming to destroy me. You have as good as said that I am a married man--as a married man you will shun me, keep out of my way: just now you have refused to kiss me. You intend to make yourself a complete stranger to me: to live under this roof only as Adèle's governess; if ever I say a friendly word to you, if ever a friendly feeling inclines you again to me, you will say,--'That man had nearly made me his mistress: I must be ice and rock to him'; and ice and rock you will accordingly become."

I cleared and steadied my voice to reply: "All is changed about me, sir; I must change too--there is no doubt of that; and to avoid fluctuations of feeling, and continual combats with recollections and associations, there is only one way-- Adèle must have a new governess, sir."

"Oh, Adèle will go to school--I have settled that already; nor do I mean to torment you with the hideous associations and recollections of Thornfield Hall--this accursed place--this tent of Achan--this insolent vault, offering the ghastliness of living death to the light of the open sky--this narrow stone hell, with its one real fiend, worse than a legion of such as we imagine. Jane, you shall not stay here, nor will I. I was wrong ever to bring you to Thornfield Hall, knowing as I did how it was haunted. I charged them to conceal from you, before I ever saw you, all knowledge of the curse of the place; merely because I feared Adèle never would have a governess to stay if she knew with what inmate she was housed, and my plans would not permit me to remove the maniac elsewhere--though I possess an old house, Ferndean Manor, even more retired and hidden than this, where I could have lodged her safely enough, had not a scruple about the unhealthiness of the situation, in the heart of a wood, made my conscience recoil from the arrangement. Probably those damp walls would soon have eased me of her charge: but to each villain his own vice; and mine is not a tendency to indirect assassination, even of what I most hate.

"Concealing the mad-woman's neighbourhood from you, however, was something like covering a child with a cloak and laying it down near a upastree: that demon's vicinage is poisoned, and always was. But I'll shut up Thornfield Hall: I'll nail up the front door and board the lower windows: I'll give Mrs. Poole two hundred a year to live here and *my wife*, as you term that fearful hag: Grace will do much for money, and she shall have her son, the keeper at Grimsby Retreat, to bear her company and be at hand to give her aid in the paroxysms, when *my wife* is prompted by her familiar to burn people in their beds at night, to stab them, to bite their flesh from their bones, and so on--"

49

"Sir," I interrupted him, "you are inexorable for that unfortunate lady: you speak of her with hate--with vindictive antipathy. It is cruel--she cannot help being mad."

"Jane, my little darling (so I will call you, for so you are), you don't know what you are talking about; you misjudge me again: it is not because she is mad I hate her. If you were mad, do you think I should hate you?"

"I do indeed, sir."

"Then you are mistaken, and you know nothing about me, and nothing about the sort of love of which I am capable. Every atom of your flesh is as dear to me as your own: in pain and sickness it would still be dear. Your mind is my treasure, and if it were broken, it would be my treasure still: if you raved, my arms should confine you, and not a strait waist-coat--your grasp, even in fury, would have a charm for me: if you flew at me as wildly as that woman did this morning, I should receive you in an embrace, at least as fond as it would be restrictive. I should not shrink from you with disgust as I did from her: in your quiet moments you should have no watcher and no nurse but me; and I could hang over you with untiring tenderness, though you gave me no smile in return; and never weary of gazing into your eyes, though they had no longer a ray of recognition for me.--But why do I follow that train of ideas? I was talking of removing you from Thornfield. All, you know, is prepared for prompt departure: to-morrow you shall go. I only ask you to endure one more night under this roof, Jane; and then, farewell to its miseries and terrors for ever! I have a place to repair to, which will be a secure sanctuary from hateful reminiscences, from unwelcome intrusion--even from falsehood and slander."

"And take Adèle with you, sir," I interrupted; "she will be a companion for you."

"What do you mean, Jane? I told you I would send Adèle to school; and what do I want with a child for a companion, and not my own child,--a French dancer's bastard? Why do you importune me about her! I say, why do you assign Adèle to me for a companion?"

"You spoke of a retirement, sir; and retirement and solitude are dull: too dull for you."

"Solitude! solitude!" he reiterated with irritation. "I see I must come to an explanation. I don't know what sphynx-like expression is forming in your countenance. *You* are to share my solitude. Do you understand?"

I shook my head: it required a degree of courage, excited as he was becoming, even to risk that mute sign of dissent. He had been walking fast about the room, and he stopped, as if suddenly rooted to one spot. He looked at me long and hard: I turned my eyes from him, fixed them on the fire, and tried to assume and maintain a quiet, collected aspect.

"Now for the hitch in Jane's character," he said at last, speaking more calmly than from his look I had expected him to speak. "The reel of silk has run smoothly enough so far; but I always knew there would come a knot and a puzzle: here it is. Now for vexation, and exasperation, and endless trouble! By God! I long to exert a fraction of Samson's strength, and break the entanglement like tow!"

He recommenced his walk, but soon again stopped, and this time just before me.

"Jane! will you hear reason?" (he stooped and approached his lips to my ear); "because, if you won't, I'll try violence." His voice was hoarse; his look that of a man who is just about to burst an insufferable bond and plunge headlong into wild license. I saw that in another moment, and with one impetus of frenzy more, I should be able to do nothing with him. The present--the passing second of time--was all I had in which to control and restrain him: a movement of repulsion, flight, fear would have sealed my doom,--and his. But I was not afraid: not in the least. I felt an inward power; a sense of influence, which supported me. The crisis was perilous; but not without its charm: such as the Indian, perhaps, feels when he slips over the rapid in his canoe. I took hold of his clenched hand, loosened the contorted fingers, and said to him, soothingly--

"Sit down; I'll talk to you as long as you like, and hear all you have to say, whether reasonable or unreasonable."

He sat down: but he did not get leave to speak directly. I had been struggling with tears for some time: I had taken great pains to repress them, because I knew he would not like to see me weep. Now, however, I considered it well to let them flow as freely and as long as they liked. If the flood annoyed him, so much the better. So I gave way and cried heartily.

Soon I heard him earnestly entreating me to be composed. I said I could not while he was in such a passion.

"But I am not angry, Jane: I only love you too well; and you had steeled your little pale face with such a resolute, frozen look, I could not endure it. Hush, now, and wipe your eyes."

His softened voice announced that he was subdued; so I, in my turn, became calm. Now he made an effort to rest his head on my shoulder, but I would not permit it. Then he would draw me to him: no.

"Jane! Jane!" he said, in such an accent of bitter sadness it thrilled along every nerve I had; "you don't love me, then? It was only my station, and the rank of my wife, that you valued? Now that you think me disqualified to become your husband, you recoil from my touch as if I were some toad or ape."

These words cut me; yet what could I do or say? I ought probably to have done or said nothing; but I was so tortured by a sense of remorse at thus hurting his feelings, I could not control the wish to drop balm where I had wounded.

"I *do* love you," I said, "more than ever: but I must not show or indulge the feeling: and this is the last time I must express it."

"The last time, Jane! What! do you think you can live with me, and see me daily, and yet, if you still love me, be always cold and distant?"

"No, sir; that I am certain I could not; and therefore I see there is but one way: but you will be furious if I mention it."

"Oh, mention it! If I storm, you have the art of weeping."

"Mr. Rochester, I must leave you."

"For how long, Jane? For a few minutes, while you smooth your hair--which is somewhat dishevelled; and bathe your face--which looks feverish?"

"I must leave Adèle and Thornfield. I must part with you for my whole life: I must begin a new existence among strange faces and strange scenes."

"Of course: I told you you should. I pass over the madness about parting from me. You mean you must become a part of me. As to the new existence, it is all right: you shall yet be my wife: I am not married. You shall be Mrs. Rochester-- both virtually and nominally. I shall keep only to you so long as you and I live. You shall go to a place I have in the south of France: a whitewashed villa on the shores of the Mediterranean. There you shall live a happy, and guarded, and most innocent life. Never fear that I wish to lure you into error--to make you my mistress. Why did you shake your head? Jane, you must be reasonable, or in truth I shall again become frantic."

His voice and hand quivered: his large nostrils dilated; his eye blazed: still I dared to speak.

"Sir, your wife is living: that is a fact acknowledged this morning by yourself. If I lived with you as you desire, I should then be your mistress: to say otherwise is sophistical--is false."

"Jane, I am not a gentle-tempered man--you forget that: I am not long-enduring; I am not cool and dispassionate. Out of pity to me and yourself, put your finger on my pulse, feel how it throbs, and--beware!"

He bared his wrist, and offered it to me: the blood was forsaking his cheek and lips, they were growing livid; I was distressed on all hands. To agitate him thus deeply, by a resistance he so abhorred, was cruel: to yield was out of the question. I did what human beings do instinctively when they are driven to utter extremity--looked for aid to one higher than man: the words "God help me!" burst involuntarily from my lips.

"I am a fool!" cried Mr. Rochester suddenly. "I keep telling her I am not married, and do not explain to her why. I forget she knows nothing of the character of that woman, or of the circumstances attending my infernal union with her. Oh, I am certain Jane will agree with me in opinion, when she knows all that I know! Just put your hand in mine, Janet--that I may have the evidence of touch as well as sight, to prove you are near me--and I will in a few words show you the real state of the case. Can you listen to me?"

"Yes, sir; for hours if you will."

"I ask only minutes. Jane, did you ever hear or know that I was not the eldest son of my house: that I had once a brother older than I?"

"I remember Mrs. Fairfax told me so once."

"And did you ever hear that my father was an avaricious, grasping man?"

"I have understood something to that effect."

"Well, Jane, being so, it was his resolution to keep the property together; he could not bear the idea of dividing his estate and leaving me a fair portion: all, he resolved, should go to my brother, Rowland. Yet as little could he endure that a son of his should be a poor man. I must be provided for by a wealthy marriage. He sought me a partner betimes. Mr. Mason, a West India planter and merchant, was his old acquaintance. He was certain his possessions were real and vast: he made inquiries. Mr. Mason, he found, had a son and daughter; and he learned from him that he could and would give the latter a fortune of thirty thousand pounds: that sufficed. When I left college, I was sent out to Jamaica, to espouse a bride already courted for me. My father said nothing about her money; but he told me Miss Mason was the boast of Spanish Town for her beauty: and this was no lie. I found her a fine woman, in the style of Blanche Ingram: tall, dark, and majestic. Her family wished to secure me because I was of a good race; and so did she. They showed her to me in parties, splendidly dressed. I seldom saw her alone, and had very little private conversation with her. She flattered me, and lavishly displayed for my pleasure her charms and accomplishments. All the men in her circle seemed to admire her and envy me. I was dazzled, stimulated: my senses were excited; and being ignorant, raw, and inexperienced, I thought I loved her. There is no folly so besotted that the idiotic rivalries of society, the prurience, the rashness, the blindness of youth, will not hurry a man to its commission. Her relatives encouraged me; competitors piqued me; she allured me: a marriage was achieved almost before I knew where I was. Oh, I have no respect for myself when I think of that act!--an agony of inward contempt masters me. I never loved, I never esteemed, I did not even know her. I was not sure of the existence of one virtue in her nature: I had

53

marked neither modesty, nor benevolence, nor candour, nor refinement in her mind or manners--and, I married her:-- gross, grovelling, mole-eyed blockhead that I was! With less sin I might have--But let me remember to whom I am speaking.

"My bride's mother I had never seen: I understood she was dead. The honeymoon over, I learned my mistake; she was only mad, and shut up in a lunatic asylum. There was a younger brother, too--a complete dumb idiot. The elder one, whom you have seen (and whom I cannot hate, whilst I abhor all his kindred, because he has some grains of affection in his feeble mind, shown in the continued interest he takes in his wretched sister, and also in a dog-like attachment he once bore me), will probably be in the same state one day. My father and my brother Rowland knew all this; but they thought only of the thirty thousand pounds, and joined in the plot against me.

"These were vile discoveries; but except for the treachery of concealment, I should have made them no subject of reproach to my wife, even when I found her nature wholly alien to mine, her tastes obnoxious to me, her cast of mind common, low, narrow, and singularly incapable of being led to anything higher, expanded to anything larger--when I found that I could not pass a single evening, not even a single hour of the day with her in comfort; that kindly conversation could not be sustained between us, because whatever topic I started, immediately received from her a turn at once coarse and trite, perverse and imbecile--when I perceived that I should never have a quiet or settled household, because no servant would bear the continued outbreaks of her violent and unreasonable temper, or the vexations of her absurd, contradictory, exacting orders--even then I restrained myself: I eschewed upbraiding, I curtailed remonstrance; I tried to devour my repentance and disgust in secret; I repressed the deep antipathy I felt.

"Jane, I will not trouble you with abominable details: some strong words shall express what I have to say. I lived with that woman upstairs four years, and before that time she had tried me indeed: her character ripened and developed with frightful rapidity; her vices sprang up fast and rank: they were so strong, only cruelty could check them, and I would not use cruelty. What a pigmy intellect she had, and what giant propensities! How fearful were the curses those propensities entailed on me! Bertha Mason, the true daughter of an infamous mother, dragged me through all the hideous and degrading agonies which must attend a man bound to a wife at once intemperate and unchaste.

"My brother in the interval was dead, and at the end of the four years my father died too. I was rich enough now-- yet poor to hideous indigence: a nature the most gross,

54

impure, depraved I ever saw, was associated with mine, and called by the law and by society a part of me. And I could not rid myself of it by any legal proceedings: for the doctors now discovered that *my wife* was mad--her excesses had prematurely developed the germs of insanity. Jane, you don't like my narrative; you look almost sick--shall I defer the rest to another day?"

"No, sir, finish it now; I pity you--I do earnestly pity you."

"Pity, Jane, from some people is a noxious and insulting sort of tribute, which one is justified in hurling back in the teeth of those who offer it; but that is the sort of pity native to callous, selfish hearts; it is a hybrid, egotistical pain at hearing of woes, crossed with ignorant contempt for those who have endured them. But that is not your pity, Jane; it is not the feeling of which your whole face is full at this moment--with which your eyes are now almost overflowing-- with which your heart is heaving--with which your hand is trembling in mine. Your pity, my darling, is the suffering mother of love: its anguish is the very natal pang of the divine passion. I accept it, Jane; let the daughter have free advent--my arms wait to receive her."

"Now, sir, proceed; what did you do when you found she was mad?"

"Jane, I approached the verge of despair; a remnant of self-respect was all that intervened between me and the gulf. In the eyes of the world, I was doubtless covered with grimy dishonour; but I resolved to be clean in my own sight-- and to the last I repudiated the contamination of her crimes, and wrenched myself from connection with her mental defects. Still, society associated my name and person with hers; I yet saw her and heard her daily: something of her breath (faugh!) mixed with the air I breathed; and besides, I remembered I had once been her husband--that recollection was then, and is now, inexpressibly odious to me; moreover, I knew that while she lived I could never be the husband of another and better wife; and, though five years my senior (her family and her father had lied to me even in the particular of her age), she was likely to live as long as I, being as robust in frame as she was infirm in mind. Thus, at the age of twenty-six, I was hopeless.

"One night I had been awakened by her yells--(since the medical men had pronounced her mad, she had, of course, been shut up)--it was a fiery West Indian night; one of the description that frequently precede the hurricanes of those climates. Being unable to sleep in bed, I got up and opened the window. The air was like sulpher-streams--I could find no refreshment anywhere. Mosquitoes came buzzing in and hummed sullenly round the room; the sea, which I could hear from thence, rumbled dull like an earthquake--black clouds were casting up over it; the moon was setting in the waves, broad and red, like a hot cannon-ball--she threw her last bloody glance over a world quivering with the ferment of tempest. I was physically influenced by the atmosphere and scene, and my ears were filled with the curses the maniac still shrieked out; wherein she momentarily mingled my name with such a tone of demon-hate, with such language!--no professed harlot ever had a fouler vocabulary than she: though two rooms off, I heard every word--the thin partitions of the West India house opposing but slight obstruction to her wolfish cries.

" 'This life,' said I at last, 'is hell: this is the air--those are the sounds of the bottomless pit! I have a right to deliver myself from it if I can. The sufferings of this mortal state will leave me with the heavy flesh that now cumbers my soul. Of the fanatic's burning eternity I have no fear: there is not a future state worse than this present one--let me break away, and go home to God!' "

"I said this whilst I knelt down at, and unlocked a trunk which contained a brace of loaded pistols: I meant to shoot myself. I only entertained the intention for a moment; for, not being insane, the crisis of exquisite and unalloyed despair, which had originated the wish and design of self-destruction, was past in a second.

"A wind fresh from Europe blew over the ocean and rushed through the open casement: the storm broke, streamed, thundered, blazed, and the air grew pure. I then framed and fixed a resolution. While I walked under the dripping orange-trees of my wet garden, and amongst its drenched pomegranates and pineapples, and while the refulgent dawn of the tropics kindled round me--I reasoned thus, Jane--and now listen; for it was true Wisdom that consoled me in that hour, and showed me the right path to follow.

"The sweet wind from Europe was still whispering in the refreshed leaves, and the Atlantic was thundering in glorious liberty; my heart, dried up and scorched for a long time, swelled to the tone, and filled with living blood--my being longed for renewal--my soul thirsted for a pure draught. I saw hope revive--and felt regeneration possible. From a flowery arch at the bottom of my garden I gazed over the sea--bluer than the sky: the old world was beyond; clear prospects opened thus:--

" 'Go,' said Hope, 'and live again in Europe: there it is not known what a sullied name you bear, nor what a filthy burden is bound to you. You may take the maniac with you to England; confine her with due attendance and precautions at Thornfield: then travel yourself to what clime you will, and form what new tie you like. That woman, who has so abused your long-suffering, so sullied your name, so outraged your honour, so blighted your youth, is not your wife, nor are you her husband. See that she is cared for as her condition demands, and you have done all that God and humanity require of you. Let her identity, her connection with yourself, be buried in oblivion: you are bound to impart them to no living being. Place her in safety and comfort: shelter her degradation with secrecy, and leave her.'

"I acted precisely on this suggestion. My father and brother had not made my marriage known to their acquaintance; because, in the very first letter I wrote to apprise them of the union--having already begun to experience extreme disgust of its consequences, and, from the family character and constitution, seeing a hideous future opening to me--I added an urgent charge to keep it secret: and very soon the infamous conduct of the wife my father had selected for me was such as to make him blush to own her as his daughter-in-law. Far from desiring to publish the connection, he became as anxious to conceal it as myself.

"To England, then, I conveyed her; a fearful voyage I had with such a monster in the vessel. Glad was I when I at last got her to Thornfield, and saw her safely lodged in that third-storey room, of whose secret inner cabinet she has now for ten years made a wild beast's den--a goblin's cell. I had some trouble in finding an attendant for her, as it was necessary to select one on whose fidelity dependence could be placed; for her ravings would inevitably betray my secret: besides, she had lucid intervals of days--sometimes weeks--which she filled up with abuse of me. At last I hired Grace Poole from the Grimsby Retreat. She and the surgeon, Carter (who dressed Mason's wounds that night he was stabbed and worried) are the only two I have ever admitted to my confidence. Mrs. Fairfax may indeed have suspected something, but she could have gained no precise knowledge as to facts. Grace has, on the whole, proved a good keeper; though, owing partly to a fault of her own, of which it appears nothing can cure her, and which is incident to her harassing profession, her vigilance has been more than once lulled and baffled. The lunatic is both cunning and malignant; she has never failed to take advantage of her guardian's temporary lapses; once to secrete the knife with which she stabbed her brother, and twice to possess herself of the key of her cell, and issue therefrom in the night-time. On the first of these occasions, she perpetrated the attempt to burn me in my bed; on the second, she paid that ghastly visit to you. I thank Providence, who watched over you, that she then spent her fury on your wedding apparel, which perhaps brought back vague reminiscences of her own bridal days: but on what might have happened, I cannot endure to reflect. When I think of the thing which flew at my throat this morning, hanging its black and scarlet visage over the nest of my dove, my blood curdles--"

"And what, sir," I asked, while he paused, "did you do when you had settled her here? Where did you go?"

"What did I do, Jane? I transformed myself into a will-o-the-wisp. Where did I go? I pursued wanderings as wild as those of the March-spirit. I sought the Continent, and went devious through all its lands. My fixed desire was to seek and find a good and intelligent woman, whom I could love: a contrast to the fury I left at Thornfield--"

"But you could not marry, sir."

"I had determined and was convinced that I could and ought. It was not my original intention to deceive, as I have deceived you. I meant to tell my tale plainly, and make my proposals openly: and it appeared to me so absolutely rational that I should be considered free to love and be loved, I never doubted some woman might be found willing and able to understand my case and accept me, in spite of the curse with which I was burdened."

"Well, sir?"

"When you are inquisitive, Jane, you always make me smile. You open your eyes like an eager bird, and make every now and then a restless movement, as if answers in speech did not flow fast enough for you, and you wanted to read the tablet of one's heart. But before I go on, tell me what you mean by your 'Well, sir?' It is a small phrase very frequent with you; and which many a time has drawn me on and on through interminable talk: I don't very well know why."

"I mean,--What next? How did you proceed? What came of such an event?"

"Precisely! and what do you wish to know now?"

"Whether you found any one you liked: whether you asked her to marry you; and what she said."

"I can tell you whether I found any one I liked, and whether I asked her to marry me: but what she said is yet to be recorded in the book of Fate. For ten long years I roved about, living first in one capital, then another: sometimes in St. Petersburg; oftener in Paris; occasionally in Rome, Naples, and Florence. Provided with plenty of money and the passport of an old name, I could choose my own society: no circles were closed against me. I sought my ideal of a woman amongst English ladies, French countesses, Italian signoras, and German gräfinnen. I could not find her. Sometimes, for a fleeting moment, I thought I caught a glance, heard a tone, beheld a form, which announced the realization of my dream: but I was presently undeceived. You are not to suppose that I desired perfection, either of mind or person. I longed only for what suited me--for the antipodes of the Creole: and I longed vainly. Amongst them all I found not one whom, had I been ever so free, I--warned as I was of the risks, the horrors, the loathings of incongruous unions--would have asked to marry me. Disappointment made me reckless. I tried dissipation-- never debauchery: that I hated, and hate. That was my Indian Messalina's attribute: rooted disgust at it and her restrained me much, even in pleasure. Any enjoyment that bordered on riot seemed to approach me to her and her vices, and I eschewed it.

"Yet I could not live alone; so I tried the companionship of mistresses. The first I chose was Céline Varens--another of those steps which make a man spurn himself when he recalls them. You already know what she was, and how my liaison with her terminated. She had two successors: an Italian, Giacinta, and a German, Clara; both considered singularly handsome. What was their beauty to me in a few weeks? Giacinta was unprincipled and violent: I tired of her in three months. Clara was honest and quiet; but heavy, mindless, and unimpressible: not one whit to my taste. I was glad to give her a sufficient sum to set her up in a good line of business, and so get decently rid of her. But, Jane, I see by your face you are not forming a very favorable opinion of me just now. You think me an unfeeling, loose-principled rake: don't you?"

"I don't like you so well as I have done sometimes, indeed, sir. Did it not seem to you in the least wrong to live in that way, first with one mistress and then another? You talk of it as a mere matter of course."

"It was with me; and I did not like it. It was a grovelling fashion of existence: I should never like to return to it. Hiring a mistress is the next worse thing to buying a slave: both are often by nature, and always by position, inferior: and to live familiarly with inferiors is degrading. I now hate the recollection of the time I passed with Céline, Giacinta, and Clara."

I felt the truth of these words; and I drew from them the certain inference, that if I were so far to forget myself and all the teaching that had ever been instilled into me, as-- under any pretext--with any justification--through any temptation--to become the successor of these poor girls, he would one day regard me with the same feeling which now in his mind desecrated their memory. I did not give utterance to this conviction: it was enough to feel it. I impressed it on my heart, that it might remain there to serve me as aid in the time of trial.

"Now, Jane, why don't you say 'Well, sir?' I have not done. You are looking grave. You disapprove of me still, I see. But let me come to the point. Last January, rid of all mistresses--in a harsh, bitter frame of mind, the result of a useless, roving, lonely life--corroded with disappointment, sourly disposed against all men, and especially against all *woman* kind (for I began to regard the notion of an intellectual, faithful, loving woman as a mere dream) recalled by business, I came back to England.

"On a frosty winter afternoon, I rode in sight of Thornfield Hall. Abhorred spot! I expected no peace--no pleasure there. On a stile in Hay Lane I saw a quiet little figure sitting by itself. I passed it as negligently as I did the pollard willow opposite to it: I had no presentiment of what it would be to me; no inward warning that the arbitress of my life--my genius for good or evil--waited there in humble guise. I did not know it, even when, on the occasion of Mesrour's accident, it came up and gravely offered me help. Childish and slender creature! It seemed as if a linnet had hopped to my foot and proposed to bear me on its tiny wing. I was surly; but the thing would not go: it stood by me with strange perseverance, and looked and spoke with a sort of authority. I must be aided, and by that hand: and aided I was.

"When once I had pressed the frail shoulder, something new--a fresh sap and sense--stole into my frame. It was well I had learnt that this elf must return to me--that it belonged to my house down below--or I could not have felt it pass away from under my hand, and seen it vanish behind the dim hedge, without singular regret. I heard you come home that night, Jane, though probably you were not aware that I thought of you or watched for you. The next day I observed you--myself unseen--for half an hour, while you played with Adèle in the gallery. It was a snowy day, I recollect, and you could not go out of doors. I was in my room; the door was ajar: I could both listen and watch. Adèle claimed your outward attention for a while; yet I fancied your thoughts were elsewhere: but you were very patient with her, my little Jane; you talked to her and amused her a long time. When at last she left you, you lapsed at once into deep reverie: you betook yourself slowly to pace the gallery. Now and then, in passing a casement, you glanced out at the thick-falling snow; you listened to the sobbing wind, and again you paced gently on and dreamed. I think those day visions were not dark: there was a pleasurable illumination in your eye occasionally, a soft excitement in your aspect, which told of no bitter, bilious, hypochondriac brooding: your look revealed rather the sweet musings of youth when its spirit follows on willing wings the flight of Hope up and on to an ideal heaven. The voice of Mrs. Fairfax, speaking to a servant in the hall, wakened you: and how curiously you smiled to and at yourself, Janet! There was so much sense in your smile: it was very shrewd, and seemed to make light of your own abstraction. It seemed to say--'My fine visions are all very well, but I must not forget they are absolutely unreal. I have a rosy sky and a green flowery Eden in my brain; but without, I am perfectly aware, lies at my feet a rough tract to travel, and around me gather black tempests to encounter.' You ran downstairs and demanded of Mrs. Fairfax some occupation: the weekly house accounts to make up, or something of that sort, I think it was. I was vexed with you for getting out of my sight.

"Impatiently I waited for evening, when I might summon you to my presence. An unusual--to me--a perfectly new character I suspected was yours: I desired to search it deeper and know it better. You entered the room with a look and air at once shy and independent: you were quaintly dressed-- much as you are now. I made you talk: ere long I found you full of strange contrasts. Your garb and manner were restricted by rule; your air was often diffident, and altogether that of one refined by nature, but absolutely unused to society, and a good deal afraid of making herself disadvantageously conspicuous by some solecism or blunder; yet when addressed, you lifted a keen, a daring, and a glowing eye to your interlocutor's face: there was penetration and power in each glance you gave; when plied by close questions, you found ready and round answers. Very soon you seemed to get used to me: I believe you felt the existence of sympathy between you and your grim and cross master, Jane; for it was astonishing to see how quickly a certain pleasant ease tran- quillised your manner: snarl as I would, you showed no surprise, fear, annoyance, or displeasure at my moroseness; you watched me, and now and then smiled at me with a simple yet sagacious grace I cannot describe. I was at once content and stimulated with what I saw: I liked what I had seen, and wished to see more. Yet, for a long time, I treated you distantly, and sought your company rarely. I was an intellectual epicure, and wished to prolong the gratification of making this novel and piquant acquaintance: besides, I was for a while troubled with a haunting fear that if I handled the flower freely its bloom would fade--the sweet charm of freshness would leave it. I did not then know that it was no transitory blossom, but rather the radiant resemblance of one, cut in an indestructible gem. Moreover, I wished to see whether you would seek me if I shunned you--but you did not; you kept in the schoolroom as still as your own desk and easel; if by chance I met you, you passed me as soon, and with as little token of recognition, as was consistent with respect. Your habitual expression in those days, Jane, was a thoughtful look; not despondent, for you were not sickly; but not buoyant, for you had little hope, and no actual pleasure. I wondered what you thought of me, or if you ever thought of me, and resolved to find this out.

"I resumed my notice of you. There was something glad in your glance, and genial in your manner, when you conversed: I saw you had a social heart; it was the silent schoolroom--it was the tedium of your life--that made you mournful. I permitted myself the delight of being kind to you; kindness stirred emotion soon: your face became soft in expression, your tones gentle; I liked my name pronounced by your lips in a grateful happy accent. I used to enjoy a chance meeting with you, Jane, at this time: there was a curious hesitation in your manner: you glanced at me with a slight trouble--a hovering doubt: you did not know what my caprice might be--

whether I was going to play the master and be stern, or the friend and be benignant. I was now too fond of you often to simulate the first whim; and, when I stretched my hand out cordially, such bloom and light and bliss rose to your young, wistful features, I had much ado often to avoid straining you then and there to my heart."

"Don't talk any more of those days, sir," I interrupted, furtively dashing away some tears from my eyes; his language was torture to me; for I knew what I must do--and do soon--and all these reminiscences, and these revelations of his feelings, only made my work more difficult.

"No, Jane," he returned: "what necessity is there to dwell on the Past, when the Present is so much surer--the Future so much brighter?"

I shuddered to hear the infatuated assertion.

"You see now how the case stands--do you not?" he continued. "After a youth and manhood passed half in unutterable misery and half in dreary solitude, I have for the first time found what I can truly love--I have found *you*. You are my sympathy--my better self--my good angel. I am bound to you with a strong attachment. I think you good, gifted, lovely: a fervent, a solemn passion is conceived in my heart; it leans to you, draws you to my centre and spring of life, wraps my existence about you, and, kindling in pure, powerful flame, fuses you and me in one.

"It was because I felt and knew this, that I resolved to marry you. To tell me that I had already a wife is empty mockery: you know now that I had but a hideous demon. I was wrong to attempt to deceive you; but I feared a stubbornness that exists in your character. I feared early instilled prejudice: I wanted to have you safe before hazarding confidences. This was cowardly: I should have appealed to your nobleness and magnanimity at first, as I do now--opened to you plainly my life of agony--described to you my hunger and thirst after a higher and worthier existence--shown to you, not my *resolution* (that word is weak), but my resistless *bent* to love faithfully and well, where I am faithfully and well loved in return. Then I should have asked you to accept my pledge of fidelity and to give me yours. Jane--give it me now."

A pause.

"Why are you silent, Jane?"

I was experiencing an ordeal: a hand of fiery iron grasped my vitals. Terrible moment: full of struggle, blackness, burning! Not a human being that ever lived could wish to be loved better than I was loved; and him who thus loved me I absolutely worshipped: and I must denounce love and idol. One drear word comprised my intolerable duty--"Depart!"

"Jane, you understand what I want of you? Just this promise--'I will be yours, Mr. Rochester.' "

"Mr. Rochester, I will *not* be yours."

Another long silence.

"Jane!" recommenced he, with a gentleness that broke me down with grief, and turned me stone-cold with ominous terror--for this still voice was the pant of a lion rising--"Jane, do you mean to go one way in the world, and to let me go another?"

"I do."

"Jane" (bending towards and embracing me), "do you mean it now?"

"I do."

"And now?" softly kissing my forehead and cheek.

"I do," extricating myself from restraint rapidly and completely.

"Oh, Jane, this is bitter! This--this is wicked. It would not be wicked to love me."

"It would to obey you."

A wild look raised his brows--crossed his features: he rose; but he forbore yet. I laid my hand on the back of a chair for support: I shook, I feared--but I resolved.

"One instant, Jane. Give one glance to my horrible life when you are gone. All happiness will be torn away with you. What then is left? For a wife I have but the maniac upstairs: as well might you refer to some corpse in yonder churchyard. What shall I do, Jane? Where turn for a companion and for some hope?"

"Do as I do: trust in God and yourself. Believe in heaven. Hope to meet again there."

"Then you will not yield?"

"No."

"Then you condemn me to live wretched and to die accursed?" His voice rose.

"I advise you to live sinless, and I wish you to die tranquil."

"Then you snatch love and innocence from me? You fling me back on lust for a passion--vice for an occupation?"

"Mr. Rochester, I no more assign this fate to you than I grasp at it for myself. We were born to strive and endure--you as well as I: do so. You will forget me before I forget you."

"You make me a liar by such language: you sully my honour. I declared I could not change: you tell me to my face I shall change soon. And what a distortion in your judgment, what a perversity in your ideas, is proved by your conduct! Is it better to drive a fellow-creature to despair than to transgress a mere human law, no man being injured by the breach? For you have neither relatives nor acquaintances whom you need fear to offend by living with me?"

This was true: and while he spoke my very conscience and reason turned traitors against me, and charged me with crime in resisting him. They spoke almost as loud as Feeling: and that clamoured wildly. "Oh comply!" it said. "Think of his misery; think of his danger--look at his state when left alone; remember his headlong nature; consider the recklessness following on despair--soothe him; save him; love him; tell him you love him and will be his. Who in the world cares for *you*? or who will be injured by what you do?"

Still indomitable was the reply--"*I* care for myself. The more solitary, the more friendliness, the more unsustained I am, the more I will respect myself. I will keep the law given by God; sanctioned by man. I will hold to the principles received by me when I was sane, and not mad--as I am now. Laws and principles are not for the times when there is no temptation: they are for such moments as this, when body and soul rise in mutiny against their rigour; stringent are they; inviolate they shall be. If at my individual convenience I might break them, what would be their worth? They have a worth--so I have always believed; and if I cannot believe it now, it is because I am insane--quite insane: with my veins running fire, and my heart beating faster than I can count its throbs. Preconceived opinions, foregone determinations, are all I have at this hour to stand by: there I plant my foot."

I did. Mr. Rochester, reading my countenance, saw I had done so. His fury was wrought to the highest: he must yield to it for a moment, whatever followed; he crossed the floor and seized my arm and grasped my waist. He seemed to devour me with his flaming glance: physically, I felt, at the moment, powerless as stubble exposed to the draught and glow of a furnace: mentally, I still possessed my soul, and with it the certainty of ultimate safety. The soul, fortunately, has an interpreter--often an unconscious, but still a truthful interpreter--in the eye. My eye rose to his; and while I looked in his fierce face I gave an involuntary sigh; his grip was painful, and my overtaxed strength almost exhausted.

"Never," said he, as he ground his teeth, "never was anything at once so frail and so indomitable. A mere reed she feels in my hand!" (And he shook me with the force of his hold.) "I could bend her with my finger and thumb: and what good would it do if I bent, if I uptore, if I crushed her? Consider that eye: consider the resolute, wild, free thing looking out of it, defying me, with more than courage--with a stern triumph. Whatever I do with its cage, I cannot get at it--the savage, beautiful creature! If I tear, if I rend the slight prison, my outrage will only let the captive loose. Conqueror I might be of the house; but the inmate would escape to heaven before I could call myself possessor of its clay dwelling-place. And it is you, spirit--with will and energy, and virtue and purity--that I want: not alone your brittle frame. Of yourself you could come with soft flight and nestle against my heart, if you would: seized against your will, you will elude the grasp like an essence--you will vanish ere I inhale your fragrance. Oh! come, Jane, come!"

As he said this, he released me from his clutch, and only looked at me. The look was far worse to resist than the frantic strain: only an idiot, however, would have succumbed now. I had dared and baffled his fury; I must elude his sorrow: I retired to the door.

"You are going, Jane?"

"I am going, sir."

"You are leaving me?"

"Yes."

"You will not come? You will not be my comforter, my rescuer? My deep love, my wild woe, my frantic prayer, are all nothing to you?"

What unutterable pathos was in his voice! How hard it was to reiterate firmly, "I am going."

"Jane!"

"Mr. Rochester!"

"Withdraw, then,--I consent; but remember, you leave me here in anguish. Go up to your own room; think over all I have said, Jane, cast a glance on my sufferings--think of me."

He turned away; he threw himself on his face on the sofa. "Oh, Jane! my hope--my love--my life!" broke in anguish from his lips. Then came a deep, strong sob.

I had already gained the door; but, reader, I walked back-- walked back as determinedly as I had retreated. I knelt down by him; I turned his face from the cushion to me; I kissed his cheek; I smoothed his hair with my hand.

"God bless you, my dear master!" I said. "God keep you from harm and wrong--direct you, solace you--reward you well for your past kindness to me."

"Little Jane's love would have been my best reward," he answered; "without it, my heart is broken. But Jane will give me her love: yes--nobly, generously."

Up the blood rushed to his face; forth flashed the fire from his eyes; erect he sprang; he held his arms out; but I evaded the embrace, and at once quitted the room.

"Farewell!" was the cry of my heart as I left him. Despair added, "Farewell for ever!"

That night I never thought to sleep; but a slumber fell on me as soon as I lay down in bed. I was transported in thought to the scenes of childhood: I dreamt I lay in the red-room at Gateshead; that the night was dark, and my mind impressed with strange fears. The light that long ago had struck me into syncope, recalled in this vision, seemed glidingly to mount the wall, and tremblingly to pause in the centre of the obscured ceiling. I lifted up my head to look: the roof resolved to clouds, high and dim; the gloom was such as the moon imparts to vapours she is about to sever. I watched her come--watched with the strangest anticipation; as though some word of doom were to be written on her disk. She broke forth as never moon yet burst from cloud: a hand first penetrated the sable folds and waved them away; then, not a moon, but a white human form shone in the azure, inclining a glorious brow earthward. It gazed and gazed on me. It spoke to my spirit: immeasurably distant was the tone, yet so near, it whispered in my heart--

"My daughter, flee temptation."

"Mother, I will."

So I answered after I had waked from the trance-like dream. It was yet night, but July nights are short: soon after midnight, dawn comes. "It cannot be too early to commence the task I have to fulfil," thought I. I rose: I was dressed; for I had taken off nothing but my shoes. I knew where to find in my drawers some linen, a locket, a ring. In seeking these articles, I encountered the beads of a pearl necklace Mr. Rochester had forced me to accept a few days ago. I left that; it was not mine: it was the visionary bride's who had melted in air. The other articles I made up in a parcel; my purse, containing twenty shillings (it was all I had), I put in my pocket: I tied on my straw bonnet, pinned my shawl, took the parcel and my slippers, which I would not put on yet, and stole from my room.

"Farewell, kind Mrs. Fairfax!" I whispered, as I glided past her door. "Farewell, my darling Adèle!" I said, as I glanced towards the nursery. No thought could be admitted of entering to embrace her. I had to deceive a fine ear: for aught I knew it might now be listening.

I would have got past Mr. Rochester's chamber without a pause; but my heart momentarily stopping its beat at that threshold, my foot was forced to stop also. No sleep was there: the inmate was walking restlessly from wall to wall; and again and again he sighed while I listened. There was a heaven--a temporary heaven--in this room for me, if I chose: I had but to go in and to say--

"Mr. Rochester, I will love you and live with you through life till death," and a fount of rapture would spring to my lips. I thought of this.

That kind master, who could not sleep now, was waiting with impatience for day. He would send for me in the morning; I should be gone. He would have me sought for: vainly. He would feel himself forsaken; his love rejected: he would suffer; perhaps grow desperate. I thought of this too. My hand moved towards the lock: I caught it back, and glided on.

Drearily I wound my way downstairs: I knew what I had to do, and I did it mechanically. I sought the key of the side-door in the kitchen; I sought, too, a phial of oil and a feather; I oiled the key and the lock. I got some water, I got some bread: for perhaps I should have to walk far; and my strength, sorely shaken of late, must not break down. All this I did without one sound. I opened the door, passed out, shut it softly. Dim dawn glimmered in the yard. The great gates were closed and locked; but a wicket in one of them was only latched. Through that I departed: it, too, I shut; and now I was out of Thornfield.

A mile off, beyond the fields, lay a road which stretched in the contrary direction to Millcote; a road I had never travelled, but often noticed, and wondered where it led: thither I bent my steps. No reflection was to be allowed now: not one glance was to be cast back; not even one forward. Not one thought was to be given either to the past or to the future. The first was a page so heavenly sweet--so deadly sad--that to read one line of it would dissolve my courage and break down my energy. The last was an awful blank: something like the world when the deluge was gone by.

I skirted fields, and hedges, and lanes till after sunrise. I believe it was a lovely summer morning: I knew my shoes, which I had put on when I left the house, were soon wet with dew. But I looked neither to rising sun, nor smiling sky, nor wakening nature. He who is taken out to pass through a fair scene to the scaffold, thinks not of the flowers that smile on his road, but of the block and axe-edge; of the disseverment of bone and vein; of the grave gaping at the end: and I thought of drear flight and homeless wandering--and oh! with agony I thought of what I left. I could not help it. I thought of him now--in his room--watching the sunrise; hoping I should soon come to say I would stay with him and be his. I longed to be his; I panted to return: it was not too late; I could yet spare him the bitter pang of bereavement. As yet my flight, I was sure, was undiscovered. I could go back and be his comforter--his pride; his redeemer from misery, perhaps from ruin. Oh, that fear of his self-abandonment--far worse than my abandonment--how it goaded me! It was a barbed arrow-head in my breast; it tore me when I tried to extract it; it sickened me when remembrance thrust it farther in. Birds began singing in brake and copse: birds were faithful to their mates; birds were emblems of love. What was I? In the midst of my pain of heart and frantic effort of principle, I abhorred myself. I had no solace from self-approbation: none even from self-respect. I had injured--wounded--left my master. I was hateful in my own eyes. Still I could not turn, nor retrace one step. God must have led me on. As to my own will or conscience, impassioned grief had trampled one and stifled the other. I was weeping wildly as I walked along my solitary way; fast, fast I went like one delirious. A weakness, beginning inwardly, extending to the limbs, seized me, and I fell: I lay on the ground some minutes, pressing my face to the wet turf. I had some fear--

or hope--that here I should die: but I was soon up; crawling forwards on my hands and knees, and then again raised to my feet--as eager and as determined as ever to reach the road.

When I got there, I was forced to sit to rest under the hedge; and while I sat, I heard wheels, and saw a coach come on. I stood up and lifted my hand; it stopped. I asked where it was going: the driver named a place a long way off, and where I was sure Mr. Rochester had no connections. I asked for what sum he would take me there; he said thirty shillings; I answered I had but twenty; well, he would try to make it do. He further gave me leave to get into the inside, as the vehicle was empty: I entered, was shut in, and it rolled on its way.

Gentle reader, may you never feel what I then felt! May your eyes never shed such stormy, scalding, heart-wrung tears as poured from mine. May you never appeal to Heaven in prayers so hopeless and so agonised as in that hour left my lips; for never may you, like me, dread to be the instrument of evil to what you wholly love.

No adultry

Eyre = really did like Thornfield →
  stuck to principle

68

GEORGE ELIOT
(Mary Ann Evans)
(1819 - 1880)

Though she has been called an agnostic and "free-thinker," Mary Ann Evans reveals a truly deep spiritual understanding of God's character and love in her books. She has a mature perception, especially relevant for modern times, of women in ministry. The best example of this clarity comes through Dinah, a major character in Adam Bede. Evans' books are exceptionally pleasant as reading experiences, particularly the endings. Her stories all seem to end as they should, the way we would think God would have them.

Evans' stories center on the rural life of the Midlands of England, where she spent her youth. Her books exude the peace and contentment characteristic of life in the village culture, as well as warmth and intimacy in her characters. Silas Marner (1861) is Evans' best. The story has charm, adventure, mystery, and faith. Though difficulties arise in the lives of her heroes and heroines, she clearly connects the benevolent providence of God with the satisfactory, and pleasing, end to the story.

§§§§§§§§§§§§§§§§§§§§§§§§§

SILAS MARNER

The Weaver of Raveloe
Part I
Chapter I

In the days when the spinning-wheels hummed busily in the farmhouses--and even great ladies, clothed in silk and thread-lace, had their toy spinning-wheels of polished oak--there might be seen in districts far away among the lanes, or deep in the bosom of the hills, certain pallid undersized men, who, by the side of the brawny country-folk looked like the remnants of a disinherited race. The shepherd's dog barked fiercely when one of those alien-looking men appeared on the upland, dark against the early winter sunset; for what dog likes a figure bent under a heavy bag?--and these pale men rarely stirred abroad without that mysterious burden. The shepherd himself, though he had good reason to believe that the bag held nothing but flaxen thread, or else the long rolls of strong linen spun from that thread, was not quite sure that this trade of weaving, indispensable though it was, could be carried on entirely without the help of the Evil One. In that far-off time superstition clung easily round every person or thing that was at all unwonted, or even intermittent and occasional merely, like the visits of the pedler or the knife-grinder. No one knew where wandering men had their homes or their origin; and how was a man to be explained unless you at least knew somebody who knew his father or mother? To the peasants of old times, the world outside their own direct experience was a region of vagueness and mystery: to their untravelled thought a state of wandering was a conception as dim as the winter life of the swallows that came back with the spring; and even a settler, if he came from distant parts, hardly ever ceased to be viewed with a remnant of distrust, which would have prevented any surprise if a long course of inoffensive conduct on his part had ended in the commission of a crime; especially if he had any reputation for knowledge, or showed any skill in handicraft. All cleverness, whether in the rapid use of that difficult instrument the tongue, or in some other art unfamiliar to villagers, was in itself suspicious: honest folk, born and bred in a visible manner, were mostly not overwise or clever--at least, not beyond such a matter as knowing the signs of the weather; and the process by which rapidity and dexterity of any kind were acquired was so wholly hidden, that they partook of the nature of conjuring. In this way it came to pass that those scattered linen-weavers--emigrants from the town into the country-- were to be the last regarded as aliens by their rustic neighbors, and usually contracted the eccentric habits which belong to a state of loneliness.

In the early years of this century, such a linen-weaver, named Silas Marner, worked at his vocation in a stone cottage that stood among the nutty hedgerows near the village of Raveloe, and not far from the edge of a deserted stone-pit. The questionable sound of Silas's loom, so unlike the natural cheerful trotting of the winnowing-machine, or the simpler rhythm of the flail, had a half-fearful fascination for the Raveloe boys, who would often leave off their nutting or birds'-nesting to peep in at the window of the stone cottage, counter-balancing a certain awe at the mysterious action of the loom, by a pleasant sense of scornful superiority, drawn from the mockery of its alternating noises, along with the bent, treadmill attitude of the weaver. But sometimes it happened that Marner, pausing to adjust an irregularity in his thread, became aware of the small scoundrels, and, though chary of his time, he liked their intrusion so ill that he would descend from his loom, and opening the door, would fix on them a gaze that was always enough to make them take to their legs in terror. For how was it possible to believe that those large brown protuberant eyes in Silas Marner's pale face really saw nothing very distinctly that was not close to them, and not rather that their dreadful stare could dart cramp, or rickets, or a wry mouth at any boy who happened to be in the rear? They had, perhaps, heard their fathers and mothers hint that Silas Marner could cure folk's rheumatism if he had a mind, and add, still more darkly, that if you could only speak the devil fair enough, he might save you the cost of the doctor. Such strange lingering echoes of the old demon-worship might perhaps even now be caught by the diligent listener among the gray-haired peasantry; for the rude mind with difficulty associates the ideas of power and benignity. A shadowy conception of power that by much persuasion can be induced to refrain from inflicting harm, is the shape most easily taken by the sense of the Invisible in the minds of men who have always been pressed close by primitive wants, and to whom a life of hard toil has never been illuminated by any enthusiastic religious faith. To them pain and mishap present a far wider range of possibilities than gladness and enjoyment: their imagination is almost barren of the images that feed desire and hope, but is all overgrown by recollections that are a perpetual pasture to fear. "Is there anything you can fancy that you would like to eat?" I once said to an old laboring man, who was in his last illness, and who had refused all the food his wife had offered him. "No," he answered, "I've never been used to nothing but common victual, and I can't eat that." Experience had bred no fancies in him that could raise the phantasm of appetite.

And Raveloe was a village where many of the old echoes lingered, undrowned by new voices. Not that it was one of those barren parishes lying on the outskirts of civilization-- inhabited by meagre sheep and thinly scattered shepherds: on the contrary, it lay in the rich central plain of what we are pleased to call Merry England, and held farms which, speaking from a spiritual point of view, paid highly desirable tithes. But it was nestled in a snug well-wooded hollow, quite an hour's journey on horseback from any turnpike, where it was never reached by the vibrations of the coach-horn, or of public opinion. It was an important-looking village, with a fine old church and large churchyard in the heart of it, and two or three large brick-and-stone homesteads, with well-walled orchards and ornamental weathercocks, standing close upon the road, and lifting more imposing fronts than the rectory, which peeped from among the trees on the other side of the churchyard:--a village which showed at once the summits of its social life, and told the practised eye that there was no great park and manor-house in the vicinity, but that there were several chiefs in Raveloe who could farm badly quite at their ease, drawing enough money from their bad farming, in those war times, to live in a rollicking fashion, and keep a jolly Christmas, Whitsun and Easter tide.

It was fifteen years since Silas Marner had first come to Raveloe; he was then simply a pallid young man, with prominent short-sighted brown eyes, whose appearance would have had nothing strange for people of average culture and

71

experience; but for the villagers near whom he had come to settle it had mysterious peculiarities which corresponded with the exceptional nature of his occupation, and his advent from an unknown region called "North'ard." So had his way of life:--he invited no comer to step across his door-sill, and he never strolled into the village to drink a pint at the Rainbow, or to gossip at the wheelwright's: he sought no man or woman, save for the purposes of his calling, or in order to supply himself with necessaries; and it was soon clear to the Raveloe lasses that he would never urge one of them to accept him against her will--quite as if he had heard them declare that they would never marry a dead man come to life again. This view of Marner's personality was not without another ground than his pale face and unexampled eyes; for Jem Rodney, the mole-catcher, averred that one evening as he was returning homeward he saw Silas Marner leaning against a stile with a heavy bag on his back, instead of resting the bag on the stile as a man in his senses would have done; and that, on coming up to him, he saw that Marner's eyes were set like a dead man's, and he spoke to him, and shook him, and his limbs were stiff, and his hands clutched the bag as if they'd been made of iron; but just as he had made up his mind that the weaver was dead, he came all right again, like, as you might say, in the winking of an eye, and said "Good-night," and walked off. All this Jem swore he had seen, more by token that it was the very day he had been mole-catching on Squire Cass's land, down by the old saw-pit. Some said Marner must have been in a "fit," a word which seemed to explain things otherwise incredible; but the argumentative Mr. Macey, clerk of the parish, shook his head, and asked if anybody was ever known to go off in a fit and not fall down. A fit was a stroke, wasn't it? and it was in the nature of a stroke to partly take away the use of a man's limbs and throw him on the parish, if he'd got no children to look to. No, no; it was no stroke that would let a man stand on his legs, like a horse between the shafts, and then walk off as soon as you can say "Gee!" But there might be such a thing as a man's soul being loose from his body, and going out and in, like a bird out of its nest and back; and that was how folks got over-wise, for they went to school in this shell-less state to those who could teach them more than their neighbors could learn with their five senses and the parson. And where did Master Marner get his knowledge of herbs from--and charms too, if he liked to give them away? Jem Rodney's story was no more than what might have been expected by anybody who had seen how Marner had cured Sally Oates, and made her sleep like a baby, when her heart had been beating enough to bust her body, for two months and more, while she had been under the doctor's care. He might cure more folks if he would; but he was worth speaking fair, if it was only to keep him from doing you a mischief.

It was partly to this vague fear that Marner was indebted for protecting him from the persecution that his singularities might have drawn upon him, but still more to the fact that, the old linen-weaver in the neighboring parish of Tarley being dead, his handicraft made him a highly welcome settler to the richer housewives of the district, and even to the more provident cottagers, who had their little stock of yarn at the year's end. Their sense of his usefulness would have counteracted any repugnance or suspicion which was not confirmed by a deficiency in the quality or the tale of the cloth he wove for them. And the years rolled on without producing any change in the impressions of the neighbors concerning Marner, except the change from novelty to habit. At the end of fifteen years the Raveloe men said just the same things about Silas Marner as at the beginning: they did not say them quite so often, but they believed them much more strongly when they did say them. There was only one important addition which the years had brought: it was, that Master Marner had laid by a fine sight of money somewhere, and that he could buy up "bigger men" than himself.

But while opinion concerning him had remained nearly stationary, and his daily habits had presented scarcely any visible change, Marner's inward life had been a history and a metamorphosis, as of every fervid nature must be when it has fled or been condemned to solitude. His life, before he came to Raveloe, had been filled with the movement, the mental activity, and the close fellowship which, in that day as in this, marked the life of an artisan early incorporated in a narrow religious sect, where the poorest layman has the chance of distinguishing himself by gifts of speech, and has, at the very least, the weight of a silent voter in the government of his community. Marner was highly thought of in that little hidden world, known to itself as the church assembling in Lantern Yard; he was believed to be a young man of exemplary life and ardent faith; and a peculiar interest had been centred in him ever since he had fallen, at a prayer-meeting, into a mysterious rigidity and suspension of consciousness, which, lasting for an hour or more, had been mistaken for death. To have sought a medical explanation for this phenomenon would have been held by Silas himself, as well as by his minister and fellow-members, a wilful self-exclusion from the spiritual significance that might lie therein. Silas was evidently a brother selected for a peculiar discipline; and though the effort to interpret this discipline was discouraged by the absence, on his part, of any spiritual vision during his outward trance, yet it was believed by himself and others that its effect was seen in an accession of light and fervor. A less truthful man than he might have been tempted into the subsequent creation of a vision in the form of resurgent memory; a less sane man might have believed in such a creation; but Silas was both sane and honest, though, as with many honest and fervent men, culture had not defined any channels for his sense of mystery, and so it spread itself over the proper pathway of inquiry and knowledge. He had inherited from his mother some acquaintance with medicinal herbs and their preparation--a little store of wisdom which she had imparted to him as a solemn bequest--but of late years he had had doubts about the lawfulness of applying this knowledge, believing that herbs could have no efficacy without prayer, and that prayer might suffice without herbs; so that his inherited delight to wander through the fields in search of foxglove and dandelion and coltsfoot began to wear to him the character of a temptation.

Among the members of his church there was one young man, a little older than himself, with whom he had long lived in such close friendship that it was the custom of their Lantern Yard brethren to call them David and Jonathan. The real name of the friend was William Dane, and he, too, was regarded as a shining instance of youthful piety, though somewhat given to over-severity toward weaker brethren, and to be so dazzled by his own light as to hold himself wiser than his teachers. But whatever blemishes others might discern in William, to his friend's mind he was faultless; for Marner had one of those impressible self-doubting natures which, at an inexperienced age, admire imperativeness and lean on contradiction. The expression of trusting simplicity in Marner's face, heightened by that absence of special observation, that defenceless, deer-like gaze which belongs to large prominent eyes, was strongly contrasted by the self-complacent suppression of inward triumph that lurked in the narrow slanting eyes and compressed lips of William Dane. One of the most frequent topics of conversation between the two friends was Assurance of salvation: Silas confessed that he could never arrive at anything higher than hope mingled with fear, and listened with longing wonder when William declared that he had possessed unshaken assurance ever since, in the period of his conversion, he had dreamed that he saw the words "calling and election sure" standing by themselves on a white page in the open Bible. Such colloquies have occupied many a pair of pale-faced weavers, whose unnurtured souls have been like young winged things, fluttering forsaken in the twilight.

It had seemed to the unsuspecting Silas that the friendship had suffered no chill even from his formation of another attachment of a closer kind. For some months he had been engaged to a young servant-woman, waiting only for a little increase to their mutual savings in order to their marriage; and it was a great delight to him that Sarah did not object to William's occasional presence in their Sunday interviews. It was at this point in their history that Silas's cataleptic fit occurred during the prayer-meeting; and amidst the various queries and expressions of interest addressed to him by his fellow-members William's suggestion alone jarred with the general sympathy toward a brother thus singled out for special dealings. He observed that, to him, this trance looked more like a visitation of Satan than a proof of divine favor, and exhorted his friend to see that he hid no accursed thing within his soul. Silas, feeling bound to accept rebuke and admonition as a brotherly office, felt no resentment, but only pain, at his friend's doubts concerning him; and to this was soon added some anxiety at the perception that Sarah's manner toward him began to exhibit a strange fluctuation between an effort at an increased manifestation of regard and involuntary signs of shrinking and dislike. He asked her if she wished to break off their engagement; but she denied this: their engagement was known to the church, and had been recognized in the prayer-meeting; it could not be broken off without strict investigation, and Sarah could render no reason that would be sanctioned by the feeling of the community. At this time the senior deacon was taken dangerously ill, and, being a childless widower, he was tended night and day by some of the younger brethren or sisters. Silas frequently took his turn in the night-watching with William, the one relieving the other at two in the morning. The old man, contrary to expectation, seemed to be on the way to recovery, when one night Silas, sitting up by his bedside, observed that his usual audible breathing had ceased. The candle was burning low, and he had to lift it to see the patient's face distinctly. Examination convinced him that the deacon was dead—had been dead some time, for the limbs were rigid. Silas asked himself if he had been asleep, and looked at the clock: it was already four in the morning. How was it that William had not come? In much anxiety he went to seek for help, and soon there were several friends assembled in the house, the minister among them, while Silas went away to his work, wishing he could have met William to know the reason of his non-appearance. But at six o'clock, as he was thinking of going to seek his friend, William came, and with him the minister. They came to summon him to Lantern Yard, to meet the church members there; and to his inquiry concerning the cause of the summons the only reply was, "You will hear." Nothing further was said until Silas was seated in the vestry, in front of the minister, with the eyes of those who to him represented God's people fixed solemnly upon him. Then the minister, taking out a pocket-knife, showed it to Silas, and asked him if he knew where he had left that knife? Silas said he did not know that he had left it anywhere out of his own pocket—but he was trembling at this strange interrogation. He was then exhorted not to hide his sin, but to confess and repent. The knife had been found in the bureau by the departed Deacon's bedside--found in the place where the little bag of church money had lain, which the minister himself had seen the day before. Some hand had removed that bag; and whose hand could it be if not of the man to whom the knife belonged? For some time Silas was mute with astonishment: then he said, "God will clear me: I know nothing about the knife being there, or the money being gone. Search me and my dwelling; you will find nothing but three pound five of my own savings, which William Dane knows I have had these six months." At this William groaned, but the minister said, "The proof is heavy against you, brother Marner. The money was taken in the night last past, and no man was with our departed brother but you, for William Dane declares to us that he was hindered by sudden sickness from going to take his place as usual, and you yourself said that he had not come; and, moreover, you neglected the dead body."

"I must have slept," said Silas. Then, after a pause, he added, "Or I must have had another visitation like that which you have all seen me under, so that the thief must have come and gone while I was not in the body, but out of the body. But, I say again, search me and my dwelling, for I have been nowhere else."

The search was made, and it ended--in William Dane's finding the well-known bag, empty, tucked behind the chest of drawers in Silas's chamber! On this William exhorted his friend to confess, and not hide his sin any longer. Silas turned a look of keen reproach on him, and said, "William, for nine years that we have gone in and out together have you ever known me to tell a lie? But God will clear me."

"Brother," said William, "how do I know what you may have done in the secret chambers of your heart, to give Satan an advantage over you?"

Silas was still looking at his friend. Suddenly a deep flush came over his face, and he was about to speak impetuously, when he seemed checked again by some inward shock, that sent the flush back and made him tremble. But at last he spoke feebly, looking at William.

"I remember now--the knife wasn't in my pocket."

William said, "I know nothing of what you mean." The other persons present, however, began to inquire where Silas meant to say the knife was, but he would give no further explanation: he only said, "I am sore stricken; I can say nothing. God will clear me."

On their return to the vestry there was further deliberation. Any resort to legal measures for ascertaining the culprit was contrary to the principles of the church in Lantern Yard, according to which prosecution was forbidden to Christians, even had the case held less scandal to the community. But the members were bound to take measures

76

for finding out the truth, and they resolved on praying and drawing lots. This resolution can be a ground of surprise only to those who are unacquainted with that obscure religious life which has gone on in the alleys of our towns. Silas knelt with his brethren, relying on his own innocence being certified by immediate divine interference, but feeling that there was sorrow and mourning behind for him even then--that his trust in man had been cruelly bruised. *The lots declared that Silas Marner was guilty.* He was solemnly suspended from church-membership, and called upon to render up the stolen money; only on confession, as the sign of repentance, could he be received once more within the folds of the church. Marner listened in silence. At last, when every one rose to depart, he went toward William Dane and said, in a voice shaken by agitation,--

"The last time I remember using my knife was when I took it out to cut a strap for you. I don't remember putting it in my pocket again. *You* stole the money, and you have woven a plot to lay the sin at my door. But you may prosper, for all that: there is no just God that governs the earth righteously, but a God of lies, that bears witness against the innocent."

There was a general shudder at this blasphemy.

William said meekly, "I leave our brethren to judge whether this is the voice of Satan or not. I can do nothing but pray for you, Silas."

Poor Marner went out with that despair in his soul--that shaken trust in God and man, which is little short of madness to a loving nature. In the bitterness of his wounded spirit, he said to himself, "*She* will cast me off too." And he reflected that, if she did not believe the testimony against him, her whole faith must be upset as his was. To people accustomed to reason about the forms in which their religious feeling has incorporated itself, it is difficult to enter into that simple, untaught state of mind in which the form and the feeling have never been severed by an act of reflection. We are apt to think it inevitable that a man in Marner's position should have begun to question the validity of an appeal to the divine judgment by drawing lots; but to him this would have been an effort of independent thought such as he had never known; and he must have made the effort at a moment when all his energies were turned into the anguish of disappointed faith. If there is an angel who records the sorrows of men as well as their sins, he knows how many and deep are the sorrows that spring from false ideas for which no man is culpable.

Marner went home, and for a whole day sat alone, stunned by despair, without any impulse to go to Sarah and attempt to win her belief in his innocence. The second day he took refuge from benumbing unbelief by getting into his loom and working away as usual; and before many hours were past, the minister and one of the deacons came to him with the message from Sarah that she held her engagement to him at an end. Silas received the message mutely, and then turned away from the messengers to work at his loom again. In little more than a month from that time, Sarah was married to William Dane; and not long afterward it was known to the brethren in Lantern Yard that Silas Marner had departed from the town.

Chapter II

Even people whose lives have been made various by learning sometimes find it hard to keep a fast hold on their habitual views of life, on their faith in the Invisible, nay, on the sense that their past joys and sorrows are a real experience, when they are suddenly transported to a new land, where the beings around them know nothing of their history, and share none of their ideas--where their mother earth shows another lap, and human life has other forms than those on which their souls have been nourished. Minds that have been unhinged from their old faith and love, have perhaps sought this Lethean influence of exile, in which the past becomes dreamy because its symbols have all vanished, and the present too is dreamy because its symbols have all vanished, and the present too is dreamy because it is linked with no memories. But even *their* experience may hardly enable them thoroughly to imagine what was the effect on a simple weaver like Silas Marner, when he left his own country and people and came to settle in Raveloe. Nothing could be more unlike his native town, set within sight of the wide-spread hillsides, than this low, wooded region, where he felt hidden even from the heavens by the screening trees and hedgerows. There was nothing here, when he rose in the deep morning quiet and looked out on the dewy brambles and rank tufted grass, that seemed to have any relation with that life centring in Lantern Yard, which had once been to him the altar-place of high dispensations. The whitewashed walls; the little pews where well-known figures entered with a subdued rustling, and where first one well-known voice and then another, pitched in a peculiar key of petition, uttered phrases at once occult and familiar, like the amulet worn on the heart; the pulpit where the minister delivered unquestioned doctrine, and swayed to and fro, and handled the book in a long-accustomed manner; the very pauses between the couplets of the hymn, as it was given out, and the recurrent swell of voices in song: these things had been the channel of divine influences to Marner--they were the fostering of his religious emotions--they were Christianity and God's kingdom upon earth. A weaver who finds hard words in his hymn-book knows nothing of parental love, but only knows one face and one lap toward which it stretches its arms for refuge and nurture.

And what could be more unlike that Lantern Yard world than the world in Raveloe?--orchards looking lazy with neglected plenty; the large church in the wide churchyard, which men gazed at lounging at their own doors in service-time; the purple faced farmers jogging along the lanes or turning in at the Rainbow; homesteads, where men supped heavily and slept in the light of the evening hearth, and where women seemed to be laying up a stock of linen for the life to come.   There were no lips in Raveloe from which a word could fall that would stir Silas Marner's benumbed faith to a sense of pain. In the early ages of the world, we know, it was believed that each territory was inhabited and ruled by its own divinities, so that a man could cross the bordering heights and be out of the reach of his native gods, whose presence was confined to the streams and the groves and the hills among which he had lived from his birth. And poor Silas was vaguely conscious of something not unlike the feeling of primitive men, when they fled thus, in fear or in sullenness, from the face of an unpropitious deity. It seemed to him that the Power he had vainly trusted in among the streets and at the prayer-meetings was very far away from this land in which he had taken refuge, where men lived in careless abundance, knowing and needing nothing of that trust which, for him, had been turned to bitterness. The little light he possessed spread its beams so narrowly that frustrated belief was a curtain broad enough to create for him the blackness of night.

His first movement after the shock had been to work in his loom; and he went on with this unremittingly, never asking himself why, now he was come to Raveloe, he worked far on into the night to finish the tale of Mrs. Osgood's table-linen sooner than she expected--without contemplating beforehand the money she would put into his hand for the work. He seemed to weave, like the spider, from pure impulse, without reflection. Every man's work, pursued steadily, tends in this way to become an end in itself, and so to bridge over the loveless chasms of his life. Silas's hand satisfied itself with throwing the shuttle, and his eye with seeing the little squares in the cloth complete themselves under his effort. Then there were the calls of hunger; and Silas, in his solitude, had to provide his own breakfast, dinner, and supper, to fetch his own water from the well, and put his own kettle on the fire; and all these immediate promptings helped, along with the weaving, to reduce his life to the unquestioning activity of a spinning insect. He hated the thought of the past; there was nothing that called out his love and fellowship toward the strangers he had come amongst; and the future was all dark, for there was no Unseen Love that cared for him. Thought was arrested by utter bewilderment, now its old narrow pathway was closed, and affection seemed to have died under the bruise that had fallen on its keenest nerves.

But at last Mrs. Osgood's table-linen was finished, and Silas was paid in gold. His earnings in his native town, where he worked for a wholesale dealer, had been after a lower rate; he had been paid weekly, and of his weekly earnings a large proportion had gone to objects of piety and charity. Now, for the first time in his life, he had five bright guineas put into his hand; no man expected a share of them, and he loved no man that he should offer him a share. But what were the guineas to him who saw no vista beyond countless days of weaving? It was needless for him to ask that, for it was pleasant to him to feel them in his palm, and look at their bright faces, which were all his own: it was another element of life, like the weaving and the satisfaction of hunger, subsisting quite aloof from the life of belief and love from which he had been cut off. The weaver's hand had known the touch of hard-won money even before the palm had grown to its full breadth; for twenty years, mysterious money had stood to him as the symbol of earthly good, and the immediate object of toil. He had seemed to love it little in the years when every penny had its purpose for him; for he loved the *purpose* then. But now, when all purpose was gone, that habit of looking toward the money and grasping it with a sense of fulfilled effort made a loan that was deep enough for the seeds of desire; and as Silas walked homeward across the field in the twilight, he drew out the money and thought it was brighter in the gathering gloom.

About this time an incident happened which seemed to open a possibility of some fellowship with his neighbors. One day, taking a pair of shoes to be mended, he saw the cobbler's wife seated by the fire, suffering from the terrible symptoms of heart disease and dropsy, which he had witnessed as the precursors of his mother's death. He felt a rush of pity at the mingled sight and remembrance, and recalling the relief his mother had found from a simple preparation of foxglove, he promised Sally Oates to bring her something that would ease her, since the doctor did her no good. In this office of charity, Silas felt, for the first time since he had come to Raveloe, a sense of unity between his past and present life, which might have been the beginning of his rescue from the insect-like existence into which his nature had shrunk. But Sally Oates's disease had raised her into a personage of such interest and importance among the neighbors, and the fact of her having found relief from drinking Silas Marner's "stuff" became a matter of general discourse. When Doctor Kimble gave physic, it was natural that it should have an effect; but when a weaver, who came from nobody knew where, worked wonders with a bottle of brown waters, the occult character of the process was evident. Such a sort of thing had not been known since the Wise Woman at Tarley died; and she had charms as well as "stuff": everybody went to her when their children had fits. Silas Marner must be a person of the same sort, for how did he know what would bring back Sally Oates's breath, if he didn't know a fine sight more than that? The Wise Woman had words that she muttered to herself, so that you couldn't hear what they were, and if she tied a bit of red thread round the child's toe the while, it would keep off the water in the head. There were women in Raveloe, at that present time, who had worn one of the Wise Woman's little bags round their necks, and in consequence, had never had an idiot child, as Ann Coulter had. Silas Marner could very likely do as much, and more; and now it was all clear how he should have come from unknown parts, and be so "comical-looking." But Sally Oates must mind and not tell the doctor, for he would be sure to set his face against Marner: he was always angry about the Wise Woman, and used to threaten those who went to her that they should have none of his help any more.

Silas now found himself and his cottage suddenly beset by mothers who wanted him to charm away the whooping-cough or bring back the milk, and by men who wanted stuff against the rheumatics or the knots in the hands; and, to secure themselves against refusal, the applicants brought silver in their palms. Silas might have driven a profitable trade in charms as well as in his small list of drugs; but money on this condition was not temptation to him: he had never known an impulse toward falsity, and he drove one after another away with growing irritation, for the news of him as a wise man had spread even to Tarley, and it was long before people ceased to take long walks for the sake of asking his aid. But the hope in his wisdom was at length changed into dread, for no one believed him when he said he knew no charms and could work no cures, and every man and woman who had an accident or a new attack after applying to him, set the misfortune down to Master Marner's ill-will and irritated glances. Thus it came to pass that his movement of pity toward Sally Oates, which had given him a transient sense of brotherhood, heightened the repulsion between him and his neighbors, and made his isolation more complete.

Gradually the guineas, the crowns, and the half-crowns grew to a heap, and Marner drew less and less for his own wants, trying to solve the problem of keeping himself strong enough to work sixteen hours a day on as small an outlay as possible. Have not men, shut up in solitary imprisonment, found an interest in marking the moments by straight strokes of a certain length on the wall, until the growth of the sum of straight strokes, arranged in triangles, has become a mastering purpose? Do we not wile away moments of inanity or fatigued waiting by repeating some trivial movement or sound, until the repetition has bred a want, which is incipient habit? That will help us to understand how the love of accumulating money grows an absorbing passion in men whose imaginations, even in the very beginning of their hoard, showed them no purpose beyond it. Marner wanted the heaps of ten to grow into a square, and then into a larger square; and every added guinea, while it was itself a satisfaction, bred a new desire. In this strange world, made a hopeless riddle to him, he might, if he had had a less intense nature, have sat weaving, weaving--looking toward the end of his pattern, or toward the end of his web, till he forgot the riddle, and everything else but his immediate sensations; but the money had come to mark off his weaving into periods, and the money not only grew, but it remained with him. He began to think it was conscious of him, as his loom was, and he would on no account have exchanged those coins, which had become his familiars, for other coins with unknown faces. He handled them, he counted them, till their form and color were like the satisfaction of a thirst to him; but it was only in the night, when his work was done, that he drew them out to enjoy their companionship. He had taken up some bricks in his floor underneath his loom, and here he had made a hole in which he set the iron pot that contained his guineas and silver coins, covering the bricks with sand whenever he replaced them. Not that the idea of being robbed presented itself often or strongly to his mind: hoarding was common in country districts in those days; there were old laborers in the parish of Raveloe who were known to have their savings by them, probably inside their flock-beds; but their rustic neighbors, though not all of them as honest as their ancestors in the days of King Alfred, had not imaginations bold enough to lay a plan of burglary. How could they have spent the money in their own village without betraying themselves? They would be obliged to "run away"--a course as dark and dubious as a balloon journey.

So, year after year, Silas Marner had lived in this solitude, his guineas rising in the iron pot, and his life narrowing and hardening itself more and more into a mere pulsation of desire and satisfaction that had no relation to any other being. His life had reduced itself to the functions of weaving and hoarding, without any contemplation of an end toward which the functions tended. The same sort of process has perhaps been undergone by wiser men, when they have been cut off from faith and love--only, instead of a loom and a heap of guineas, they have had some erudite research, some ingenious project, or some well-knit theory. Strangely Marner's face and figure shrank and bent themselves into a constant mechanical relation to the objects of his life, so that he produced the same sort of impression as a handle or a crooked tube, which has no meaning standing apart. The prominent eyes that used to look trusting and dreamy now looked as if they had been made to see only one kind of thing that was very small, like tiny grain, for which they hunted everywhere, and he was so withered and yellow that, though he was not yet forty, the children always called him "Old Master Marner."

Yet even in this stage of withering a little incident happened which showed that the sap of affection was not all gone. It was one of his daily tasks to fetch his water from a well a couple of fields off, and for this purpose, ever since he came to Raveloe, he had had a brown earthenware pot, which he held as his most precious utensil among the very few conveniences he had granted himself. It had been his companion for twelve years, always standing on the same spot, always lending its handle to him in the early morning, so that its form had an expression for him of willing helpfulness, and the impress of its handle on his palm gave a satisfaction mingled with that of having the fresh clear water. One day as he was returning from the well, he stumbled against the step of the stile, and his brown pot, falling with force against the stones that overarched the ditch below him, was broken in three pieces. Silas picked up the pieces and carried them home with grief in his heart. The brown pot could never be of use to him any more, but he stuck the bits together and propped the ruin in its old place for a memorial.

This is the history of Silas Marner, until the fifteenth year after he came to Raveloe. The livelong day he sat in his loom, his ear filled with its monotony, his eyes bent close down on the slow growth of sameness in the brownish web, his muscles moving with such even repetition that their pause seemed almost as much a constraint as the holding of his breath. But at night came his revelry: at night he closed his shutters, and made fast his doors, and drew forth his gold. Long ago the heap of coins had become too large for the iron pot to hold them, and he had made for them two thick leather bags, which wasted no room in their resting-place, but lent themselves flexibly to every corner. How the guineas shone as they came pouring out of the dark leather mouths! The silver bore no large proportion in amount to the gold, because the long pieces of linen which formed his chief work were always partly paid for in gold, and out of the silver he supplied his own bodily wants, choosing always the shillings and sixpences to spend in this way. He loved the guineas best, but he would not change the silver--the crowns and halfcrowns that were his own earnings, begotten by his labor; he loved them all. He spread them out in heaps and bathed his hands in them; then he counted them and set them up in regular piles, and felt their rounded outline between his thumb and fingers, and thought fondly of the guineas that were only half earned by the work in his loom, as if they had been unborn children--thought of the guineas that were coming slowly through the coming years, through all his life, which spread far away before him, the end quite hidden by countless days of weaving. No wonder his thoughts were still with his loom and his money when he made his journeys through the fields and the lanes to fetch and carry home his work, so that his steps never wandered to the hedge-banks and the laneside in search of the once familiar herbs: these too belonged to the past, from which his life had shrunk away, like a rivulet that has sunk far down from the grassy fringe of its old breadth into a little shivering thread, that cuts a groove for itself in the barren sand.

But about the Christmas of that fifteenth year a second great change came over Marner's life, and his history became blent in a singular manner with the life of his neighbors.

FREDERICK DOUGLASS
(1817-1895)

Frederick Douglass was a man, properly prepared, placed in the perfect time in history. A former slave, Douglass rose to fame in America in the pre-Civil War furor over slavery. In 1841, three years after his escape from servitude, he spoke at an Abolitionist gathering in Massachusetts, recalling his experiences of the institution. Soon Douglass was engaged to speak at many such meetings. When his autobiography was published in 1845, the subsequent publicity launched him on his own path of glory.

Douglass was an impressive orator. His imposing physique and rich, booming voice impressed those who heard him, but the message of freedom he preached perhaps had the greater impact. Douglass published a weekly paper in 1847, helped free slaves through the underground railroad, sent money from his speaking tours to assist runaways, and persuaded voters in political rallies to take up the cause of abolition. He sympathized with and befriended John Brown in his unsuccessful effort to invade Virginia, and fled to Canada to avoid arrest for participation in the scheme.

Though Douglass was impatient with Abraham Lincoln's unhurried approach toward the South, he was won to friendship with the President by the Emancipation Proclamation and Lincoln's personal assurances. After the war, Douglass' support of the Radical Republicans won him political power and position. He became the chief spokesman and guide to Black Americans in their struggle to build a new world of freedom. His major role in history is the sympathetic critic of injustice, not the promulgator of new political thought.

Douglass' writings are voluminous. His story of slavery is often unpleasant and painful to read but the truth that emerges from his own experience should burn a permanent mark in Christian hearts to show us how, indeed, to love one another.

NARRATIVE OF THE LIFE OF FREDERICK DOUGLASS AN AMERICAN SLAVE

WRITTEN BY HIMSELF

Chapter X

I left Master Thomas's house, and went to live with Mr. Covey, on the 1st of January, 1833. I was now, for the first time in my life, a field hand. In my new employment, I found myself even more awkward than a country boy appeared to be in a large city. I had been at my new home but one week before Mr. Covey gave me a very severe whipping, cutting my back causing the blood to run, and raising ridges on my flesh as large as my little finger. The details of this affair are as follows: Mr. Covey sent me, very early in the morning of one of our coldest days in the month of January, to the woods, to get a load of wood. He gave me a team of unbroken oxen. He told me which was the in-hand ox, and which the off-hand one. He then tied the end of a large rope around the horns of the in-hand ox, and gave me the other end of it, and told me, if the oxen started to run, that I must hold on upon the rope. I had never driven oxen before, and of course I was very awkward. I, however, succeeded in getting to the edge of the woods with little difficulty; but I had got a very few rods into the woods, when the oxen took fright, and started full tilt, carrying the cart against trees, and over stumps, in the most frightful manner. I expected every moment that my brains would be dashed out against the trees. After running thus for a considerable distance, they finally upset the cart, dashing it with great force against a tree, and threw themselves into a dense thicket. How I escaped death, I do not know. There I was, entirely alone, in a thick wood, in a place new to me. My cart was upset and shattered, my oxen were entangled among the young trees, and there was none to help me. After a long spell of effort, I succeeded in getting my cart righted, my oxen disentangled, and again yoked to the cart. I now proceeded with my team to the place where I had, the day before, been chopping wood, and loaded my cart pretty heavily, thinking in this way to tame my oxen. I then proceeded on my way home. I had now consumed one half of the day. I got out of the woods safely, and now felt out of danger. I stopped my oxen to open the woods gate; and just as I did so, before I could get hold of my ox-rope, the oxen again started, rushed through the gate, catching it between the wheel and the body of the cart, tearing it to pieces, and coming within a few inches of crushing me against the gatepost. Thus twice, in one short day, I escaped death by the merest chance. On my return, I told Mr. Covey what had happened, and how it happened. He ordered me to return to the woods again immediately. I did so, and he followed on after me. Just as I got into the woods, he came up and told me to stop my cart, and that he would teach me how to trifle away my time and break gates. He then went to a large gum-tree, and with his axe cut three large switches, and, after trimming them up neatly with his pocket-knife, he ordered me to take off my clothes. I made him no answer, but stood with my clothes on. He repeated his order. I still made him no answer, nor did I move to strip myself. Upon this he rushed at me with the fierceness of a tiger, tore off my clothes, and lashed me till he had worn out his switches, cutting me so savagely as to leave the marks visible for a long time after. This whipping was the first of a number just like it, and for similar offences.

I lived with Mr. Covey one year. During the first six months, of that year, scarce a week passed without his whipping me. I was seldom free from a sore back. My awkwardness was almost always his excuse for whipping me. We were worked fully up to the point of endurance. Long before day we were up, our horses fed, and by the first approach of day we were off to the field with our hoes and ploughing teams. Mr. Covey gave us enough to eat, but scarce time to eat it. We were often less than five minutes taking our meals. We were often in the field from the first approach of day till its last lingering ray had left us; and at saving-fodder time, midnight often caught us in the field binding blades.

Covey would be out with us. The way he used to stand it, was this. He would spend the most of his afternoons in bed. He would then come out fresh in the evening, ready to urge us on with his words, example, and frequently with the whip. Mr. Covey was one of the few slaveholders who could and did work with his hands. He was a hard-working man. He knew by himself just what a man or boy could do. There was no deceiving him. His work went on in his absence almost as well as in his presence; and he had the faculty of making us feel that he was ever present with us. This he did by surprising us. He seldom approached the spot where we were at work openly, if he could do it secretly. He always aimed at taking us by surprise. Such was his cunning, that we used to call him, among ourselves, "the snake." When we were at work in the cornfield, he would sometimes crawl on his hands and knees to avoid detection, and all at once he would rise nearly in our midst, and scream out, "Ha, ha! Come, come! Dash on, dash on!" This being his mode of attack, it was never safe to stop a single minute. His comings were like a thief in the night. He appeared to us as being ever at hand. He was under every tree, behind every stump, in every bush, and at every window, on the plantation. He would sometimes mount his horse, as if bound to St. Michael's, a distance of seven miles, and in half an hour afterwards you would see him coiled up in the corner of the wood-fence, watching every motion of the slaves. He would, for this purpose, leave his horse tied up in the woods. Again, he would sometimes walk up to us, and give us orders as though he was upon the point of starting on a long journey, turn his back upon us, and make as though he was going to the house to get ready; and, before he would get half way thither, he would turn short and crawl into a fence-corner, or behind some tree, and there watch us till the going down of the sun.

Mr. Covey's *forte* consisted in his power to deceive. His life was devoted to planning and perpetrating the grossest deceptions. Every thing he possessed in the shape of learning or religion, he made conform to his disposition to deceive. He seemed to think himself equal to deceiving the Almighty. He would make a short prayer in the morning, and a long prayer at night; and, strange as it may seem, few men would at times appear more devotional than he. The exercises of his family devotions were always commenced with singing; and, as he was a very poor singer himself, the duty of raising the hymn generally came upon me. He would read his hymn, and nod at me to commence. I would at times do so; at others, I would not. My non-compliance would almost always produce much confusion. To show himself independent of me, he would start and stagger through with his hymn in the most discordant manner. In this state of mind, he prayed with more than ordinary spirit. Poor man! such was his disposition, and success at deceiving, I do verily believe that he some-times deceived himself into the solemn belief, that he was a sincere worshipper of the most high God; and this, too, at a time when he may be said to have been guilty of compelling his woman slave to commit the sin of adultery. The facts in the case are these: Mr. Covey was a poor man; he was just commencing in life; he was only able to buy one slave; and, shocking as is the fact, he bought her, as he said, for a *breeder*. This woman was named Caroline. Mr. Covey bought her from Mr. Thomas Lowe, about six miles from St. Michael's. She was a large, able-bodied woman, about twenty years old. She had already given birth to one child, which proved her to be just what he wanted. After buying her, he hired a married man of Mr. Samuel Harrison, to live with him one year; and him he used to fasten up with her every night! The result was, that, at the end of the year, the miserable woman gave birth to twins. At the result Mr. Covey seemed to be highly pleased, both with the man and the wretched woman. Such was his joy, and that of his wife, that nothing they could do for Caroline during her confinement was too good, or too hard, to be done. The children were regarded as being quite an addition to his wealth.

If at any one time of my life more than another, I was made to drink the bitterest dregs of slavery, that time was during the first six months of my stay with Mr. Covey. We were worked in all weathers. It was never too hot or too cold; it could never rain, blow, hail, or snow, too hard for us to work in the field. Work, work, work, was scarcely more the order of the day than of the night. The longest days were too short for him, and the shortest nights too long for him. I was somewhat unmanageable when I first went there, but a few months of this discipline tamed me. Mr. Covey succeeded in breaking me. I was broken in body, soul, and spirit. My natural elasticity was crushed, my intellect languished, the disposition to read departed, the cheerful spark that lingered about my eye died; the dark night of slavery closed in upon me; and behold a man transformed into a brute!

Sunday was my only leisure time. I spent this in a sort of beast-like stupor, between sleep and wake, under some large tree. At times I would rise up, a flash of energetic freedom would dart through my soul, accompanied with a faint beam of hope, that flickered for a moment, and then vanished. I sank down again, mourning over my wretched condition. I was sometimes prompted to take my life, and that of Covey, but was prevented by a combination of hope and fear. My sufferings on this plantation seem now like a dream rather than a stern reality.

Our house stood within a few rods of the Chesapeake Bay, whose broad bosom was ever white with sails from every quarter of the habitable globe. Those beautiful vessels, robed in purest white, so delightful to the eye of freemen, were to me so many shrouded ghosts, to terrify and torment me with thoughts of my wretched condition. I have often, in the deep stillness of a summer's Sabbath, stood all alone upon the lofty banks of that noble bay, and traced, with saddened heart and tearful eye, the countless number of sails moving off to the mighty ocean. The sight of these always affected me powerfully. My thoughts would compel utterance; and there, with no audience but the Almighty, I would pour out of my soul's complaint, in my rude way, with an apostrophe to the moving multitude of ships:--

"You are loosed from your moorings, and so free; I am fast in my chains, and am a slave! You move merrily before the gentle gale, and I sadly before the bloody whip! You are freedom's swift-winged angels, that fly round the world; I am confined in bands of iron! O that I were free! O, that I were on one of your gallant decks, and under your protecting wing! Alas! betwixt me and you, the turbid waters roll. Go on, go on. O that I could also go! Could I but swim! If I could fly! O, why was I born a man, of whom to make a brute! The glad ship is gone; she hides in the dim distance. I am left in the hottest hell of unending slavery. O God, save me! God, deliver me! Let me be free! Is there any God? Why am I a slave? I will run away. I will not stand it. Get caught, or get clear, I'll try it. I had as well die with ague as the fever. I have only one life to lose. I had as well be killed running as die standing. Only think of it; one hundred miles straight north, and I am free! Try it? Yes! God helping me, I will. It cannot be that I shall live and die a slave. I will take to the water. This very bay shall yet bear me into freedom. The steamboats steered in a north-east course from North Point. I will do the same; and when I get to the head of the bay, I will turn my canoe adrift, and walk straight through Delaware into Pennsylvania. When I get there, I shall not be required to have a pass; I can travel without being disturbed. Let but the first opportunity offer, and, come what will, I am off. Meanwhile, I will try to bear up under the yoke. I am not the only slave in the world. Why should I fret? I can bear as much as any of them. Besides, I am but a boy, and all boys are bound to some one. It may be that my misery in slavery will only increase my happiness when I get free. There is a better day coming."

Thus I used to think, and thus I used to speak to myself; goaded almost to madness at one moment, and the next reconciling myself to my wretched lot.

I have already intimated that my condition was much worse, during the first six months of my stay at Mr. Covey's, than in the last six. The circumstances leading to the change in Mr. Covey's course toward me form an epoch in my humble history. You have seen how a man was made a slave; you shall see how a slave was made a man. On one of the hottest days of the month of August, 1833, Bill Smith, William Hughes, a slave named Eli, and myself, were engaged in fanning wheat. Hughes was clearing the fanned wheat from before the fan, Eli was turning, Smith was feeding, and I was carrying wheat to the fan. The work was simple, requiring strength rather than intellect; yet, to one entirely unused to such work, it came very hard. About three o'clock of that day, I broke down; my strength failed me; I was seized with a violent aching of the head, attended with extreme dizziness; I trembled in every limb. Finding what was coming, I nerved myself up, feeling it would never do to stop work. I stood as long as I could stagger to the hopper with grain. When I could stand no longer, I fell, and felt as if held down by an immense weight. The fan of course stopped; every one had his own work to do; and no one could do the work of the other, and have his own go on at the same time.

Mr. Covey was at the house, about one hundred yards from the treading-yard where we were fanning. On hearing the fan stop, he left immediately, and came to the spot where we were.   He hastily inquired what the matter was.   Bill answered that I was sick, and there was no one to bring wheat to the fan. I had by this time crawled away under the side of the post and rail-fence by which the yard was enclosed, hoping to find relief by getting out of the sun. He then asked where I was. He was told by one of the hands. He came to the spot, and, after looking at me awhile, asked me what was the matter. I told him as well as I could, for I scarce had strength to speak. He then gave me a savage kick in the side, and told me to get up. I tried to do so, but fell back in the attempt. He gave me another kick, and again told me to rise. I again tried, and succeeded in gaining my feet; but, stooping to get the tub with which I was feeding the fan, I again staggered and fell. While down in this situation, Mr. Covey took up the hickory slat with which Hughes had been striking off the half-bushel measure, and with it gave me a heavy blow upon the head, making a large wound, and the blood ran freely; and with this again told me to get up. I made no effort to comply, having now made up my mind to let him do his worst. In a short time after receiving this blow, my head grew better. Mr. Covey had now left me to my fate. At this moment I resolved, for the first time, to go to my master, enter a complaint, and ask his protection. In order to [do] this, I must that afternoon walk seven miles; and this, under the circumstances, was truly a severe undertaking. I was exceedingly feeble; made so as much by the kicks and blows which I received, as by the severe fit of sickness to which I had been subjected. I, however, watched my chance, while Covey was looking in an opposite direction, and started for St. Michael's. I succeeded in getting a considerable distance on my way to the woods, when Covey discovered me, and called after me to come back, threatening what he would do if I did not come. I disregarded both his calls and his threats, and made my way to the woods as fast as my feeble state would allow; and thinking I might be overhauled by him if I kept the road, I walked through the woods, keeping far enough from the road to avoid detection, and near enough to prevent losing my way I had not gone far before my little strength again failed me. I could go no farther. I fell down, and lay for a considerable time. The blood was yet oozing from the wound on my head. For a time I thought I should bleed to death; and think now that I should have done so, but that the blood so matted my hair as to stop the wound. After lying there about three quarters of an hour, I nerved myself up again, and started on my way, through bogs and briers, barefooted and bareheaded, tearing my feet sometimes at nearly every step; and after a journey of about seven miles, occupying some five hours to perform it, I arrived at master's store. I then presented an appearance enough to affect any but a heart of iron. From the crown of my head to my feet, I was covered with blood. My hair was all clotted with dust and blood; my shirt was stiff with blood. My legs and feet were torn in sundry places with briers and thorns, and were also covered with blood. I suppose I looked like a man who had escaped a den of wild beasts, and barely escaped them. In this state I appeared before my master, humbly entreating him to interpose his authority for my protection. I told him all the circumstances as well as I could, and it seemed, as I spoke, at times to affect him. He would then walk the floor, and seek to justify Covey by saying he expected I deserved it. He asked me what I wanted. I told him, to let me get a new home; that as sure as I lived with Mr. Covey again, I should live with but to die with him; that Covey would surely kill me; he was in a fair way for it. Master Thomas ridiculed the idea that there was any danger of Mr. Covey's killing me, and said that he knew Mr. Covey; that he was a good man, and that he could not think of taking me from him; that, should he do so, he would lose the whole year's wages; that I belonged to Mr. Covey for one year, and that I must go back to him, come what might; and that I must not trouble him with any more stories, or that he would himself *get hold of me*. After threatening me thus, he gave me a very large dose of salts, telling me that I might remain in St. Michael's that night, (it being quite late,) but that I must be off back to Mr. Covey's early in the morning; and that if I did not, he would *get hold of me*, which meant that he would whip me. I remained all night, and, according to his orders, I started off to Covey's in the morning, (Saturday morning,) wearied in body and broken in spirit. I got no supper that night, or breakfast that morning. I reached Covey's about nine o'clock; and just as I was getting over the fence that divided Mrs. Kemp's fields from ours, out ran Covey with his cowskin, to give me another whipping. Before he could reach me, I succeeded in getting to the cornfield; and as the corn was very high, it afforded me the means of hiding. He seemed very angry, and searched for me a long time. My behavior was altogether unaccountable. He finally gave up the chase, thinking, I suppose, that I must come home for something to eat; he would give himself no further trouble in looking for me. I spent that day mostly in the woods, having the alternative before me,--to go home and be whipped to death, or stay in the woods and be starved to death. That night, I fell in with Sandy Jenkins, a slave with whom I was somewhat acquainted. Sandy had a free wife who lived about four miles from Mr. Covey's; and it being Saturday, he was on his way to see her. I told him my circumstances, and he very kindly invited me to go home with him. I went home with him, and talked this whole matter over, and got his advice as to what course it was best for me to pursue. I found Sandy an old adviser. He told me with great solemnity, I must go back to Covey; but that before I went, I must go with him into another part of the woods, where there was a certain *root*, which, if I would take some of it with me, carrying it *always on my right side*, would render it impossible for Mr. Covey, or any other white man, to whip me. He said he had carried it for years; and since he had done so, he had never received a blow, and never expected to while he carried it. I at first rejected the idea, that the simple carrying of a root in my pocket would have any such effect as he had said, and was not disposed to take it; but Sandy impressed the necessity with much earnestness, telling me it could do no harm, if it did no good. To please him, I at length took the root, and, according to his direction, carried it upon my right side. This was Sunday morning. I immediately started for home; and upon entering the yard gate, out came Mr. Covey on his way to meeting. He spoke to me very kindly, made me drive the pigs from a lot near by, and passed on towards the church. Now, this singular conduct of Mr. Covey really made me begin to think that there was something in the *root* which Sandy had given me; and had it been on any other day than Sunday, I could have attributed the conduct to no other cause than the influence of that root; and as it was, I was half inclined to think the *root* to be something more than I at first had taken it to be. All went well till Monday morning. On this morning, the virtue of the *root* was fully tested. Long before daylight, I was called to go and rub, curry, and feed, the horses. I obeyed, and was glad to obey. But whilst thus engaged, whilst in the act of throwing down some blades from the loft, Mr. Covey entered the stable with a long rope; and just as I was half out of the loft, he caught hold of my legs, and was about tying me. As soon as I found what he was up to, I gave a sudden spring, and as I did so, he holding to my legs, I was brought sprawling on the stable floor. Mr. Covey seemed now to think he had me, and could do what he pleased; but at this moment--from whence came the spirit I don't know--I resolved to fight; and, suiting my action to the resolution, I seized Covey hard by the throat; and as I did so, I rose. He held on to me, and I to him. My resistance was so entirely unexpected, that Covey seemed taken all aback. He trembled like a leaf. This gave me assurance, and I held him uneasy, causing the blood to run where I touched him with the ends of my fingers. Mr. Covey soon called out to Hughes for help. Hughes came, and, while Covey held me, attempted to tie my right hand. While he was in the act of doing so, I watched my chance, and gave him a heavy kick close under the ribs. This kick fairly sickened Hughes, so that he left me in the hands of Mr. Covey. This kick had the effect of not only weakening Hughes, but Covey also. When he saw Hughes bending over with pain, his courage quailed. He asked me if I meant to persist in my resistence. I told him I did, come what might; that he had used me like a brute for six months, and that I was determined to be used so no longer. With that, he strove to drag me to a stick that was lying just out of the stable door. He meant to knock me down. But just as he was leaning over to get the stick, I seized him with both hands by his collar, and brought him by a sudden snatch to the ground. By this time, Bill came. Covey called upon him for assistance. Bill wanted to know what he could do. Covey said, "Take hold of him, take hold of him!" Bill said his master hired him out to work, not to help him whip me; so he left Covey and myself to fight our own battle out. We were at it for nearly two hours. Covey at length let me go, puffing and blowing at a great rate, saying that if I had not resisted he would not have whipped me half so much. The truth was, that he had not whipped me at all. I considered him as getting entirely the worst end of the bargain; for he had drawn no blood from me, but I had from him. The whole six months afterwards, that I spent with Mr. Covey, he never laid the weight of his finger upon me in anger. He would occasionally say, he didn't want to get hold of me again. "No, thought I, "you need not; for you will come off worse than you did before."

This battle with Mr. Covey was the turning-point in my career as a slave. It rekindled the few expiring embers of freedom, and revived within me a sense of my own manhood. It recalled the departed self-confidence, and inspired me again with a determination to be free. The gratification afforded by the triumph was a full compensation for whatever else might follow, even death itself. He only can understand the deep satisfaction which I experienced, who has himself repelled by force the bloody arm of slavery. I felt as I never felt before. It was a glorious resurrection, from the tomb of slavery, to the heaven of freedom. My long-crushed spirit rose, cowardice departed, bold defiance took its place; and I now resolved that, however long I might remain a slave in form, the day had passed forever when I could be a slave in fact. I did not hesitate to let it be known of me, that the white man who expected to succeed in whipping, must also succeed in killing me.

From this time I was never again what might be called fairly whipped, though I remained a slave four years afterwards. I had several fights, but was never whipped.

It was for a long time a matter of surprise to me why Mr. Covey did not immediately have me taken by the constable to the whipping-post, and there regularly whipped for the crime of raising my hand against a white man in defense of myself. And the only explanation I can now think of does not entirely satisfy me; but such as it is, I will give it. Mr. Covey enjoyed the most unbounded reputation for being a first-rate overseer and negro-breaker. It was of considerable importance to him. That reputation was at stake; and had he sent me--a boy about sixteen years old--to the public whipping-post, his reputation would have been lost; so, to save his reputation, he suffered me to go unpunished.

My term of actual service to Mr. Edward Covey ended on Christmas day, 1833. The days between Christmas and New Year's day are allowed as holidays; and, accordingly, we were not required to perform any labor, more than to feed and take care of the stock. This time we regarded as our own, by the grace of our masters; and we therefore used or abused it nearly as we pleased. Those of us who had families at a distance, were generally allowed to spend the whole six days in their society. This time, however, was spent in various ways. The staid, sober, thinking and industrious ones of our number would employ themselves in making corn-brooms, mats, horse-collars, and baskets; and another class of us would spend the time in hunting opposums, hares, and coons. But by far the larger part engaged in such sports and merriments as playing ball, wrestling, running foot-races, fiddling, dancing, and drinking whisky; and this latter mode of spending the time was by far the most agreeable to the feelings of our masters. A slave who would work during the holidays was considered by our masters as scarcely deserving them. He was regarded as one who rejected the favor of his master. It was deemed a disgrace not to get drunk at Christmas; and he was regarded as lazy indeed, who had not provided himself with the necessary means, during the year, to get whisky enough to last him through Christmas.

From what I know of the effect of these holidays upon the slave, I believe them to be among the most effective means in the hands of the slaveholder in keeping down the spirit of insurrection. Were the slaveholders at once to abandon this practice, I have not the slightest doubt it would lead to an immediate insurrection among the slaves. These holidays serve as conductors, or safety-valves, to carry off the rebellious spirit of enslaved humanity. But for these, the slave would be forced up to the wildest desperation; and woe betide the slaveholder, the day he ventures to remove or hinder the operation of those conductors! I warn him that, in such an event, a spirit will go forth in their midst, more to be dreaded than the most appalling earthquake.

The holidays are part and parcel of the gross fraud, wrong, and inhumanity of slavery. They are professedly a custom established by the benevolence of the slaveholders; but I undertake to say, it is the result of selfishness, and one of the grossest frauds committed upon the down-trodden slave. They do not give the slaves this time because they would not like to have their work during its continuance, but because they know it would be unsafe to deprive them of it. This will be seen by the fact, that the slaveholders like to have their slaves spend those days just in such a manner as to make them as glad of their ending as of their beginning. Their object seems to be, to disgust their slaves with freedom, by plunging them into the lowest depths of dissipation. For instance, the slaveholders not only like to see the slave drink of his own accord, but will adopt various plans to make him drunk. One plan is, to make bets on their slaves, as to who can drink the most whisky without getting drunk; and in this way they succeed in getting whole multitudes to drink to excess. Thus, when the slave asks for virtuous freedom, the cunning slaveholder, knowing his ignorance, cheats him with a dose of vicious dissipation, artfully labelled with the name of liberty. The most of us used to drink it down, and the result was just what might be supposed: many of us were led to think that there was little to choose between liberty and slavery. We felt, and very properly too, that we had almost as well be slaves to man as to rum. So, when the holidays ended, we staggered up from the filth of our wallowing, took a long breath, and marched to the field--feeling, upon the whole, rather glad to go, from what our master had deceived us into a belief was freedom, back to the arms of slavery.

I have said that this mode of treatment is a part of the whole system of fraud and inhumanity of slavery. It is so. The mode here adopted to disgust the slave with freedom, by allowing him to see only the abuse of it, is carried out in other things. For instance, a slave loves molasses; he steals some. His master, in many cases, goes off to town, and buys a large quantity; he returns, takes his whip, and commands the slave to eat the molasses, until the poor fellow is made sick at the very mention of it. The same mode is sometimes adopted to make the slaves refrain from asking for more food than their regular allowance. A slave runs through his allowance, and applies for more. His master is enraged at him; but, not willing to send him off without food, gives him more than is necessary, and compels him to eat it within a given time. Then, if he complains that he cannot eat it, he is said to be satisfied neither full or fasting, and is whipped for being hard to please! I have an abundance of such illustrations of the same principle, drawn from my own observation, but think the cases I have cited sufficient. The practice is a very common one.

On the first of January, 1834, I left Mr. Covey, and went to live with Mr. William Freeland, who lived about three miles from St. Michael's. I soon found Mr. Freeland a very different man from Mr. Covey. Though not rich, he was what would be called an educated southern gentleman. Mr. Covey, as I have shown, was a well-trained negro-breaker and slave-driver. The former (slaveholder though he was) seemed to possess some regard for honor, some reverence for justice, and some respect for humanity. The latter seemed totally insensible to all such sentiments. Mr. Freeland had many of the faults peculiar to slaveholders, such as being very passionate and fretful; but I must do him the justice to say, that he was exceedingly free from those degrading vices to which Mr. Covey was constantly addicted. The one was open and frank, and we always knew where to find him. The other was a most artful deceiver, and could be understood only by such as were skillful enough to detect his cunningly-devised frauds. Another advantage I gained in my new master was, he made no pretensions to, or profession of, religion; and this, in my opinion, was truly a great advantage. I assert most unhesitatingly, that the religion of the south is a mere covering for the most horrid crimes,--a justifier of the most appalling barbarity,--a sanctifier of the most hateful frauds,--and a dark shelter under, which the darkest, foulest, grossest, and most infernal deeds of slaveholders find the strongest protection. Were I to be again reduced to the chains of slavery, next to that enslavement, I should regard being the slave of a religious master the greatest calamity that could befall me. For of all slaveholders with whom I have ever met, religious slaveholders are the worst. I have ever found them the meanest and basest, the most cruel and cowardly, of all others. It was my unhappy lot not only to belong to a religious slaveholder, but to live in a community of such religionists. Very near Mr. Freeland lived the Rev. Daniel Weeden, and in the same neighborhood lived the Rev. Rigby Hopkins. These were members and ministers in the Reformed Methodist Church. Mr. Weeden owned, among others, a woman slave, whose name I have forgotten. This woman's back, for weeks, was kept literally raw, made so by the lash of this merciless, *religious* wretch. He used to hire hands. His maxim was, Behave well or behave ill, it is the duty of a master occasionally to whip a slave, to remind him of his master's authority. Such was his theory, and such his practice.

Mr. Hopkins was even worse than Mr. Weeden. His chief boast was his ability to manage slaves. The peculiar feature of his government was that of whipping slaves in advance of deserving it. He always managed to have one or more of his slaves to whip every Monday morning. He did this to alarm their fears, and strike terror into those who escaped. His plan was to whip for the smallest offences, to prevent the commission of large ones. Mr. Hopkins could always find some excuse for whipping a slave. It would astonish one, unaccustomed to a slaveholding life, to see with what wonderful ease a slaveholder can find things, of which to make occasion to whip a slave. A mere look, word, or motion,--a mistake, accident, or want of power,--are all matters for which a slave may be whipped at any time. Does a slave look dissatisfied? It is said, he has the devil in him, and it must be whipped out. Does he speak loudly when spoken to by his master? Then he is getting highminded, and should be taken down a button-hole lower. Does he forget to pull off his hat at the approach of a white person? Then he is wanting in reverence, and should be whipped for it. Does he ever venture to vindicate his conduct, when censured for it? Then he is guilty of impudence,--one of the greatest crimes of which a slave can be guilty. Does he ever venture to suggest a different mode of doing things from that pointed out by his master? He is indeed presumptuous, and getting above himself; and nothin less than a flogging will do for him. Does he, while ploughing, break a plough,--or, while hoeing, break a hoe? It is owing to his carelessness, and for it a slave must always be whipped. Mr. Hopkins could always find something of this sort to justify the use of the lash, and he seldom failed to embrace such opportunities. There was not a man in the whole county, with whom the slaves who had the getting their own home, would not prefer to live, rather than with this Rev. Mr. Hopkins. And yet there was not a man any where round, who made higher professions of religion, or was more active in revivals,--more attentive to the class, love-feast, prayer and teaching meetings, or more devotional in his family,--that prayed earlier, later, louder, and longer,--than this same reverend slave-driver, Rigby Hopkins.

But to return to Mr. Freeland, and to my experience while in his employment. He, like Mr. Covey, gave us enough to eat; but, unlike Mr. Covey, he also gave us sufficient time to take our meals. He worked us hard, but always between sunrise and sunset. He required a good deal of work to be done, but gave us good tools with which to work. His farm was large, but he employed hands enough to work it, and with ease, compared with many of his neighbors. My treatment, while in his employment, was heavenly, compared with what I experienced at the hands of Mr. Edward Covey.

Mr. Freeland was himself the owner of but two slaves. Their names were Henry Harris and John Harris. The rest of his hands he hired. These consisted of myself, Sandy Jenkins,* and Handy Caldwell. Henry and John were quite intelligent, and in a very little while after I went there, I

---

* This is the same man who gave me the roots to prevent my being whipped by Mr. Covey. He was "a clever soul." We used frequently to talk about the fight with Covey, and as often as we did so, he would claim my success as the result of the roots which he gave me. This superstition is very common among the more ignorant slaves. A slave seldom dies but that his death is attributed to trickery.

succeeded in creating in them a strong desire to learn how to read. This desire soon sprang up in the others also. They very soon mustered up some old spelling-books, and nothing would do but that I must keep a Sabbath school. I agreed to do so, and accordingly devoted my Sundays to teaching these my loved fellow-slaves how to read. Neither of them knew his letters when I went there. Some of the slaves of the neighboring farms found what was going on, and also availed themselves of this little opportunity to learn to read. It was understood, among all who came, that there must be as little display about it as possible. It was necessary to keep our religious masters at St. Michael's unacquainted with the fact, that, instead of spending the Sabbath in wrestling, boxing, and drinking whisky, we were trying to learn how to read the will of God; for they had much rather see us engaged in those degrading sports, than to see us behaving like intellectual, moral, and accountable beings. My blood boils as I think of the bloody manner in which Messrs. Wright Fairbanks and Garrison West, both class-leaders, in connection with many others, rushed in upon us with sticks and stones, and broke up our virtuous little Sabbath school, at St. Michael's--all calling themselves Christians! humble followers of the Lord Jesus Christ! But I am again digressing.

I held my Sabbath school at the house of a free colored man, whose name I deem it imprudent to mention; for should it be known, it might embarrass him greatly, though the crime of holding the school was committed ten years ago. I had at one time over forty scholars, and those of the right sort, ardently desiring to learn. They were of all ages, though mostly men and women. I look back to those Sundays with an amount of pleasure not to be expressed. They were great days to my soul. The work of instructing my dear fellow-slaves was the sweetest engagement with which I was ever blessed. We loved each other, and to leave them at the close of the Sabbath was a severe cross indeed. When I think that these precious souls are today shut up in the prison-house of slavery, my feelings overcome me, and I am almost ready to ask, "Does a righteous God govern the universe? and for what does he hold the thunders in his right hand, if not to smite the oppressor, and deliver the spoiled out of the hand of the spoiler?" These dear souls came not to Sabbath school because it was popular to do so, nor did I teach them because it was reputable to be thus engaged. Every moment they spent in that school, they were liable to be taken up, and given thirty-nine lashes. They came because they wished to learn. Their minds had been starved by their cruel masters. They had been shut up in mental darkness. I taught them, because it was the delight of my soul to be doing something that looked like bettering the condition of my race. I kept up my school nearly the whole year I lived with Mr. Freeland;

and, beside my Sabbath school, I devoted three evenings in the week, during the winter, to teaching the slaves at home. And I have the happiness to know, that several of those who came to Sabbath school learned how to read; and that one, at least, is now free through my agency.

The year passed off smoothly. It seemed only about half as long as the year which preceded it. I went through it without receiving a single blow. I will give Mr. Freeland the credit of being the best master I ever had, *till I became my own master.* For the ease with which I passed the year, I was, however, somewhat indebted to the society of my fellow-slaves. They were noble souls; they not only possessed loving hearts, but brave ones. We were linked and interlinked with each other. I loved them with a love stronger than anything I have experienced since. It is sometimes said that we slaves do not love and confide in each other. In answer to this assertion, I can say, I never loved any or confided in any people more than my fellow-slaves, and especially those with whom I lived at Mr. Freeland's. I believe we would have died for each other. We never undertook to do anything, of any importance, without a mutual consultation. We never moved separately. We were one; and as much so by our tempers and dispositions, as by the mutual hardships to which we were necessarily subjected by our condition as slaves.

At the close of the year 1834, Mr. Freeland again hired me of my master, for the year 1835. But by this time, I began to want to live *upon free land* as well as *with Freeland;* and I was no longer content, therefore, to live with him or any other slaveholder. I began, with the commencement of the year, to prepare myself for a final struggle, which should decide my fate one way or the other. My tendency was upward. I was fast approaching manhood, and year after year had passed, and I was still a slave. These thoughts roused me--I must do something. I therefore resolved that 1835 should not pass without witnessing an attempt, on my part, to secure my liberty. But I was not willing to cherish this determination alone. My fellow-slaves were dear to me. I was anxious to have them participate with me in this, my life-giving determination. I therefore, though with great prudence, commenced early to ascertain their views and feelings in regard to their condition, and to imbue their minds with thought of freedom. I bent myself to devising ways and means for our escape, and meanwhile strove, on all fitting occasions, to impress them with the gross fraud and inhumanity of slavery. I went first to Henry, next to John, then to the others. I found, in them all, warm hearts and noble spirits. They were ready to hear, and ready to act when a feasible plan should be proposed. This was what I wanted. I talked to them of our want of manhood, if we submitted to our enslavement without at least one noble effort to be

100

free. We met often, and consulted frequently, and told our hopes and fears, recounted the difficulties, real and imagined, which we should be called on to meet. At times we were almost disposed to give up, and try to content ourselves with our wretched lot; at others, we were firm and unbending in our determination to go. Whenever we suggested any plan, there was shrinking--the odds were fearful. Our path was beset with the greatest obstacles; and if we succeeded in gaining the end of it, our right to be free was yet questionable--we were yet liable to be returned to bondage. We could see no spot this side of the ocean, where we could be free. We knew nothing about Canada. Our knowledge of the north did not extend farther than New York; and to go there, and be forever harassed with the frightful liability of being returned to slavery--with the certainty of being treated tenfold worse than before--the thought was a horrible one, and one which it was not easy to overcome. The case sometimes stood thus: At every gate through which we were to pass, we saw a watchman--at every ferry a guard--on every bridge a sentinel--and in every wood a patrol. We were hemmed in upon every side. Here were the difficulties, real or imagined--the good to be sought, and the evil to be shunned. On the one hand, there stood slavery, a stern reality, glaring frightfully upon us,--its robes already crimsoned with the blood of millions, and even now feasting itself greedily upon our own flesh. On the other hand, away back in the dim distance, under the flickering light of the north star, behind some craggy hill or snow-covered mountain, stood a doubtful freedom--half frozen--beckoning us to come and share its hospitality. This in itself was sometimes enough to stagger us; but when we permitted ourselves to survey the road, we were frequently appalled. Upon either side we saw grim death, assuming the most horrid shapes. Now it was starvation, causing us to eat our own flesh;--now we were contending with the waves, and were drowned;--now we were overtaken, and torn to pieces by the fangs of the terrible bloodhound. We were stung by scorpions, chased by wild beasts, bitten by snakes, and finally, after having nearly reached the desired spot,--after swimming rivers, encountering wild beasts, sleeping in the woods, suffering hunger and nakedness,--we were overtaken by our pursuers, and, in our resistance, we were shot dead upon the spot! I say, this picture sometimes appalled us, and made us

"rather bear those ills we had,
Than fly to others, that we knew not of."

In coming to a fixed determination to run away, we did more than Patrick Henry, when he resolved upon liberty or death. With us it was a doubtful liberty at most, and almost certain death if we failed. For my part, I should prefer death to hopeless bondage.

Sandy, one of our number, gave up the notion, but still encouraged us. Our company then consisted of Henry Harris, John Harris, Henry Bailey, Charles Roberts, and myself. Henry Bailey was my uncle, and belonged to my master. Charles married my aunt: he belonged to my master's father-in-law, Mr. William Hamilton.

The plan we finally concluded upon was, to get a large canoe belonging to Mr. Hamilton, and upon the Saturday night previous to Easter holidays, paddle directly up the Chesapeake Bay. On our arrival at the head of the bay, a distance of seventy or eighty miles from where we lived, it was our purpose to turn our canoe adrift, and follow the guidance of the north star till we got beyond the limits of Maryland. Our reason for taking the water route was, that we were less liable to be suspected as runaways; we hoped to be regarded as fishermen; whereas, if we should take the land route, we should be subjected to interruptions of almost every kind. Any one having a white face, and being so disposed, could stop us, and subject us to examination.

The week before our intended start, I wrote several protections, one for each of us. As well as I can remember, they were in the following words, to wit:--

"This is to certify that I, the undersigned, have given the bearer, my servant, full liberty to go to Baltimore, and spend the Easter holidays. Written with mine own hand, &c., 1835.

"WILLIAM HAMILTON,
"Near St. Michael's, in Talbot county, Maryland."

We were not going to Baltimore; but, in going up the bay, we went toward Baltimore, and these protections were only intended to protect us while on the bay.

As the time drew near for our departure, our anxiety became more and more intense. It was truly a matter of life and death with us. The strength of our determination was about to be fully tested. At this time, I was very active in explaining every difficulty, removing every doubt, dispelling every fear, and inspiring all with the firmness indispensable to success in our undertaking; assuring them that half was gained the instant we made the move; if not now, we never should be; and if we did not intend to move now, we had as well fold our arms, sit down, and acknowledge ourselves fit only to be slaves. This, none of us were prepared to acknowledge. Every man stood firm; and at our last meeting, we pledged ourselves afresh, in the most solemn manner, that, at the time appointed, we would certainly start in pursuit of freedom. This was a middle of the week, at the end of which we were to be off. We went, as usual, to our several fields of labor, but with bosoms highly agitated with thoughts of our truly hazardous undertaking. We tried to conceal our feelings as much as possible; and I think we succeeded very well.

After a painful waiting, the Saturday morning, whose night was to witness our departure, came. I hailed it with joy, bring what of sadness it might. Friday night was a sleepless one for me. I probably felt more anxious than the rest, because I was, by common consent, at the head of the whole affair. The responsibility of success or failure lay heavily upon me. The glory of the one, and the confusion of the other, were unlike mine. The first two hours of that morning were such as I never experienced before, and hope never to again. Early in the morning, we went, as usual, to the field. We were spreading manure: and all at once, while thus engaged, I was overwhelmed with an indescribable feeling, in the fulness of which I turned to Sandy, who was near by, and said, "We are betrayed!" "Well," said he, "that thought has this moment struck me." We said no more. I was never more certain of anything.

The horn was blown as usual, and we went up from the field to the house for breakfast. I went for the form, more than for want of anything to eat that morning. Just as I got to the house, in looking out at the lane gate, I saw four white men, with two colored men. The white men were on horseback, and the colored ones were walking behind, as if tied. I watched them a few moments till they got up to our lane gate. Here they halted, and tied the colored men to the gatepost. I was not yet certain as to what the matter was. In a few moments, in rode Mr. Hamilton, with a speed betokening great excitement. He came to the door, and inquired if Master William was in. He was told he was at the barn. Mr. Hamilton, without dismounting, rode up to the barn with extraordinary speed. In a few moments, he and Mr. Freeland returned to the house. By this time, the three constables rode up, and in great haste dismounted, tied their horses, and met Master William and Mr. Hamilton returning from the barn; and after talking awhile, they all walked up to the kitchen door. There was no one in the kitchen but myself and John. Henry and Sandy were up at the barn. Mr. Freeland put his head in at the door, and called me by name, saying, there were some gentlemen at the door who wished to see me. I stepped to the door, and inquired what they wanted. They at once seized me, and, without giving me any satisfaction, tied me--lashing my hands closely together. I insisted upon knowing what the matter was. They at length said, that they had learned I had been in a "scrape," and that I was to be examined before my master; and if their information proved false, I should not be hurt.

In a few moments, they succeeded in tying John. They then turned to Henry, who had by this time returned, and commanded him to cross his hands. "I won't!" said Henry, in a firm tone, indicating his readiness to meet the consequences of his refusal. "Won't you?" said Tom Graham, the constable. "No. I won't!" said Henry, in a still stronger tone. With this, two of the constables pulled out their shining pistols, and swore, by their Creator, that they would make him cross his hands or kill him. Each cocked his pistol, and, with fingers on the trigger, walked up to Henry, saying, at the same time, if he did not cross his hands, they would blow his damned heart out. "Shoot me! shoot me!" said Henry; "you can't kill me but once. Shoot, shoot,--and be damned! *I won't be tied!*" This he said in a tone of loud defiance; and at the same time, with a motion as quick as lightning, he with one single stroke dashed the pistols from the hand of each constable. As he did this, all hands fell upon him, and, after beating him some time, they finally overpowered him, and got him tied.

During the scuffle, I managed, I know not how, to get my pass out, and, without being discovered, put it into the fire. We were all now tied; and just as we were to leave for Easton jail, Betsy Freeland, mother of William Freeland, came to the door with her hands full of biscuits, and divided them between Henry and John. She then delivered herself of a speech, to the following effect:--addressing herself to me, she said, *"You devil! You yellow devil!"* it was you that put it into the heads of Henry and John to run away. But for you, you long-legged mulatto devil! Henry nor John would never have thought of such a thing." I made no reply, and was immediately hurried off towards St. Michael's. Just a moment previous to the scuffle with Henry, Mr. Hamilton suggested the propriety of making a search for the protections which he had understood Frederick had written for himself and the rest. But, just at the moment he was about carrying his proposal into effect, his aid was needed in helping to tie Henry; and the excitement attending the scuffle caused them either to forget, or to deem it unsafe, under the circumstances, to search. So we were not yet convicted of the intention to run away.

When we got about half way to St. Michael's, while the constables having us in charge were looking ahead, Henry inquired of me what he should do with his pass. I told him to eat it with his biscuit, and own nothing; and we passed the word around, *"Own nothing;"* and *"Own nothing!"* said we all. Our confidence in each other was unshaken. We were resolved to succeed or fail together, after the calamity had befallen us as much as before. We were now prepared for anything. We were to be dragged that morning fifteen miles behind horses, and then to be placed in the Easton jail. When we reached St. Michael's, we underwent a sort of examination. We all denied that we ever intended to run away. We did this more to bring out the evidence against us, than from any hope of getting clear of being sold; for, as I have said, we were ready for that. The fact was, we cared but little where we went, so we went together. Our greatest concern was about separation. We dreaded that more than anything this side of death. We found the evidence against us to be the testimony of one person; our master would not tell who it was; but we came to a unanimous decision among ourselves as to who their informant was. We were sent off to the jail at Easton. When we got there, we were delivered up to the sheriff, Mr. Joseph Graham, and by him placed in jail. Henry, John, and myself, were placed in one room together--Charles, and Henry Bailey, in another. Their object in separating us was to hinder concert.

We had been in jail scarcely twenty minutes, when a swarm of slave traders, and agents for slave traders, flocked into jail to look at us, and to ascertain if we were for sale. Such a set of beings I never saw before! I felt myself surrounded by so many fiends from perdition. A band of pirates never looked more like their father, the devil. They laughed and grinned over us, saying, "Ah, my boys! we have got you, haven't we" and after taunting us in various ways, they one by one went into an examination of us, with intent to ascertain our value. They would impudently ask us if we would not like to have them for our masters. We would make them no answer, and leave them to find out as best they could. Then they would curse and swear at us, telling us that they could take the devil out of us in a very little while, if we were only in their hands.

While in jail, we found ourselves in much more comfortable quarters than we expected when we went there. We did not get much to eat, nor that which was very good; but we had a good clean room, from the windows of which we could see what was going on in the street, which was very much better than though we had been placed in one of the dark, damp cells. Upon the whole, we got along very well, so far as the jail and its keeper were concerned. Immediately after the holidays were over, contrary to all our expectations, Mr. Hamilton and Mr. Freeland came up to Easton, and took Charles, the two Henrys, and John, out of jail, and carried them home, leaving me alone. I regarded this separation as a final one. It caused me more pain than anything else in the whole transaction. I was ready for anything rather than separation. I supposed that they had consulted together, and had decided that, as I was the whole cause of the intention of the others to run away, it was hard to make the innocent suffer with the guilty; and that they had, therefore, concluded to take the others home, and sell me, as a warning to the others that remained. It is due to the noble Henry to say, he seemed almost as reluctant at leaving the prison as at leaving home to come to the prison. But we knew we should, in all probability, be separated, if we were sold; and since he was in their hands, he concluded to go peaceably home.

I was now left to my fate. I was all alone, and within the walls of a stone prison. But a few days before, and I was full of hope. I expected to have been safe in a land of freedom; but now I was covered with gloom, sunk down to the utmost despair. I thought the possibility of freedom was gone. I was kept in this way about one week, at the end of which, Captain Auld, my master, to my surprise and utter astonishment, came up, and took me out, with the intention of sending me, with a gentleman of his acquaintance, into Alabama. But, from some cause or other, he did not send me to Alabama, but concluded to send me back to Baltimore, to live again with his brother Hugh, and to learn a trade.

Thus, after an absence of three years and one month, I was once more permitted to return to my old home at Baltimore. My master sent me away, because there existed against me a very great prejudice in the community, and he feared I might be killed.

In a few weeks after I went to Baltimore, Master Hugh hired me to Mr. William Gardner, an extensive ship-builder, on Fell's Point. I was put there to learn how to calk. It, however, proved a very unfavorable place for the accomplishment of this object. Mr. Gardner was engaged that spring in building two large man-of-war brigs, professedly for the Mexican government. The vessels were to be launched in the July of that year, and in failure thereof, Mr. Gardner was to lose a considerable sum; so that when I entered, all was hurry. There was no time to learn anything. Every man had to do that which he knew how to do. In entering the ship-yard, my orders from Mr. Gardner were, to do whatever the carpenters commanded me to do. This was placing me at the beck and call of about seventy-five men. I was to regard all these as masters. Their word was to be my law. My situation was a most trying one. At times I needed a dozen pair of hands. I was called a dozen ways in the space of a single minute. Three or four voices would strike my ear at the same moment. It was--"Fred., come help me to cant this lumber here."--"Fred., come carry this timber yonder."--"Fred., bring that roller here."--"Fred., go get a fresh can of water."--"Fred., come help saw off the end of this timber."--"Fred., go quick, and get the crowbar."--"Fred., hold on the end of this fall."--"Fred., go to the blacksmith's shop, and get a new punch."--"Hurra, Fred! run and bring me a cold chisel."--"I say, Fred, bear a hand, and get up a fire as quick as lightning under that steam-box."--"Hallo, nigger! come, turn this grind-stone."--"Come, come! move, move! and *bowse* this timber forward."--"I say, darky, blast your eyes, why don't you heat up some pitch?"--"Halloo! halloo! halloo! (Three voices at the same time.) "Come here!--Go there!--Hold on where you are! Damn you, if you move, I'll knock your brains out!"

This was my school for eight months; and I might have remained there longer, but for a most horrid fight I had with four of the white apprentices, in which my left eye was nearly knocked out, and I was horribly mangled in other respects. The facts in the case were these: Until a very little while after I went there, white and black ship-carpenters worked side by side, and no one seemed to see any impropriety in it. All hands seemed to be very well satisfied. Many of the black carpenters were freemen. Things seemed to be going on very well. All at once, the white carpenters knocked off, and said they would not work with free colored workmen. Their reason for this, as alleged, was, that if free colored carpenters were encouraged, they would soon take the trade into their own hands, and poor white men would be thrown out of employment. They therefore felt called upon at once to put a stop to it. And, taking advantage of Mr. Gardner's necessities, they broke off, swearing they would work no longer, unless he would discharge his black carpenters. Now, though this did not extend to me in form, it did reach me in fact. My fellow-apprentices very soon began to feel it degrading to them to work with me. They began to put on airs, and talk about the "niggers" taking the country, saying we all ought to be killed; and, being encouraged by the journeymen, they commenced making my condition as hard as they could, by hectoring me around, and sometimes striking me. I, of course, kept the vow I made after the fight with Mr. Covey, and struck back again, regardless of consequences; and while I kept them from combining, I succeeded very well, for I could whip the whole of them, taking them separately. They, however, at length combined, and came upon me, armed with sticks, stones, and heavy handspikes. One came in front with a half brick. There was one at each side of me, and one behind me. While I was attending to those in front, and on either side, the one behind ran up with the handspike, and struck me a heavy blow upon the head. It stunned me. I fell, and with this they all ran upon me, and fell to beating me with their fists. I let them lay on for a while, gathering strength. In an instant, I gave a sudden surge, and rose to my hands and knees. Just as I did that, one of their number gave me, with his heavy boot, a powerful kick in the left eye. My eyeball seemed to have burst. When they saw my eye closed, and badly swollen, they left me. With this I seized the handspike, and for a time pursued them. But here the carpenters interfered, and I thought I might as well give it up. It was impossible to stand my hand against so many. All this took place in sight of not less than fifty white ship-carpenters, and not one interposed a friendly word; but some cried, "Kill the damned nigger! Kill him! kill him! He struck a white person." I found my only chance for life was in flight. I succeeded in getting away without an additional blow, and barely so; for to strike a white man is death by Lynch law,--and that was the law in Mr. Gardner's ship-yard; nor is there much of any other out of Mr. Gardner's ship-yard.

I went directly home, and told the story of my wrongs to Master Hugh; and I am happy to say of him, irreligious as he was, his conduct was heavenly, compared with that of his brother Thomas under similar circumstances. He listened attentively to my narration of the circumstances leading to the savage outrage, and gave many proofs of his strong indignation at it. The heart of my once overkind mistress was again melted into pity. My puffed-out eye and blood-covered face moved her to tears. She took a chair by me, washed the blood from my face, and, with a mother's tenderness, bound up my head, covering the wounded eye with a lean piece of fresh beef. It was almost compensation for my suffering to witness, once more, a manifestation of kindness from this, my once affectionate old mistress. Master Hugh was very much outraged. He gave expression to his feelings by pouring out curses upon the heads of those who did the deed. As soon as I got a little the better of my bruises, he took me with him to Esquire Watson's, on Bond Street, to see what could be done about the matter. Mr. Watson inquired who saw the assault committed. Master Hugh told him it was done in Mr. Gardner's ship-yard, at midday, where there were a large company of men at work. "As to that," he said, "the deed was done, and there was no question as to who did it." His answer was, he could do nothing in the case, unless some white man would come forward and testify. He could issue no warrant on my word. If I had been killed in the presence of a thousand colored people, their testimony combined would have been insufficient to have arrested one of the murderers. Master Hugh, for once, was compelled to say this state of things was too bad. Of course, it was impossible to get any white man to volunteer his testimony in my behalf, and against the white young men. Even those who may have sympathized with me were not prepared to do this. It required a degree of courage unknown to them to do so; for just at that time, the slightest manifestation of humanity toward a colored person was denounced as abolitionism, and that name subjected its bearer to frightful liabilities. The watchwords of the bloody-minded in that region, and in those days, were "Damn the abolitionists!" and "Damn the niggers!" There was nothing done, and probably nothing would have been done if I had been killed. Such was, and such remains, the state of things in the Christian city of Baltimore.

Master Hugh, finding he could get no redress, refused to let me go back again to Mr. Gardner. He kept me himself, and his wife dressed my wound till I was again restored to health. He then took me into the ship-yard of which he was foreman, in the employment of Mr. Walter Price. There I was immediately set to calking, and very soon learned the art of using my mallet and irons. In the course of one year from the time I left Mr. Gardner's, I was able to command the highest wages given to the most inexperienced calkers. I was now of some importance to my master. I was bringing him from six to seven dollars per week. I sometimes brought him nine dollars per week: my wages were a dollar and a half a day. After learning how to calk, I sought my own employment, made my own contracts, and collected the money which I earned. My pathway became much more smooth than before; my condition was now much more comfortable. When I could get no calking to do, I did nothing. During these leisure times, those old notions about freedom would steal over me again. When in Mr. Gardner's employment, I was kept in such a perpetual whirl of excitement, I could think of nothing, scarcely, but my life; and in thinking of my life, I almost forgot my liberty. I have observed this in my experience of slavery,--that whenever my condition was improved, instead of its increasing my contentment, it only increased my desire to be free, and set me to thinking of plans to gain my freedom. I have found that, to make a contented slave, it is necessary to make a thoughtless one. It is necessary to darken his moral and mental vision, and, as far as possible, to annihilate the power of reason. He must be able to detect no inconsistencies in slavery; he must be made to feel that slavery is right; and he can be brought to that only when he ceases to be a man.

I was now getting, as I have said, one dollar and fifty cents per day. I contracted for it; I earned it; it was paid to me; it was rightfully my own; yet, upon each returning Saturday night, I was compelled to deliver every cent of that money to Master Hugh. And why? Not because he earned it,--not because he had any hand in earning it,--not because I owed it to him,--not because he possessed the slightest shadow of a right to it; but solely because he had the power to compel me to give it up. The right of the grim-visaged pirate upon the high seas is exactly the same.

SIR ARTHUR CONAN DOYLE
(1859-1930)

"Elementary, my dear Watson!" The renowned Sherlock Holmes is the creation of A. Conan Doyle, a Scottish physician who found writing more exciting and lucrative than the practice of medicine. Holmes, and his own physician friend Watson, have become so alive by the hand of Doyle that the detective stories have never lost their immense popularity. Movies, television, and all sorts of publications have arisen to retell the adventures of the world's most famous sleuth.

Doyle also wrote successful romantic novels and served Great Britain as a soldier in the Boer War. His fame, however, will undoubtedly always be connected to the great detective Holmes. Doyle's skill with English is very obvious. The Holmes mysteries breathe the smog of London, bleed the blood of the murdered victims, shake with the fear of the hunted, and boil with Holmes' anger with evil. Readers return again and again to the experience of the mysteries and drama into which Holmes constantly delves.

Not so hidden in Holmes' escapades is the realization of the necessity of victory for the forces of right and justice. Even in stories where Holmes must act as judge and implementor of right without the usual chain of legal command, Doyle reveals the hero's abilities to "do the right thing," to see the end of the matter put fairly, and exercise mercy and grace where needed. Holmes is believable. He is also extraordinary.

$$\$$$

THE ADVENTURE OF THE DYING DETECTIVE

Mrs. Hudson, the landlady of Sherlock Holmes, was a long-suffering woman. Not only was her first-floor flat invaded at all hours by throngs of singular and often undesirable characters but her remarkable lodger showed an eccentricity and irregularity in his life which must have sorely tried her patience. His incredible untidiness, his addiction to music at strange hours, his occasional revolver practice within doors, his weird and often malodorous scientific experiments, and the atmosphere of violence and danger which hung around him made him the very worst tenant in London. On the other hand, his payments were princely. I have no doubt that the house might have been purchased at the price which Holmes paid for his rooms during the years that I was with him.

The landlady stood in the deepest awe of him and never dared to interfere with him, however outrageous his proceedings might seem. She was fond of him, too, for he had a remarkable gentleness and courtesy in his dealings with women. He disliked and distrusted the sex, but he was always a chivalrous opponent. Knowing how genuine was her regard for him, I listened earnestly to her story when she came to my rooms in the second year of my married life and told me of the sad condition to which my poor friend was reduced.

"He's dying, Dr. Watson," said she. "For three days he has been sinking, and I doubt if he will last the day. He would not let me get a doctor. This morning when I saw his bones sticking out of his face and his great bright eyes looking at me I could stand no more of it. 'With your leave or without it, Mr. Holmes, I am going for a doctor this very hour,' said I. 'Let it be Watson, then,' said he. I wouldn't waste an hour in coming to him sir, or you may not see him alive."

I was horrified for I had heard nothing of his illness. I need not say that I rushed for my coat and my hat. As we drove back I asked for the details.

"There is little I can tell you, sir. He has been working at a case down at Rotherhithe, in an alley near the river, and he has brought this illness back with him. He took to his bed on Wednesday afternoon and has never moved since. For these three days neither food nor drink has passed his lips."

"Good God! Why did you not call in a doctor?"

"He wouldn't have it, sir. You know how masterful he is. I didn't dare to disobey him. But he's not long for this world, as you'll see for yourself the moment that you set eyes on him."

He was indeed a deplorable spectacle. In the dim light of a foggy November day the sick room was a gloomy spot, but it was that gaunt, wasted face staring at me from the bed which sent a chill to my heart. His eyes had the brightness of fever, there was a hectic flush upon either cheek, and dark crusts clung to his lips; the thin hands upon the coverlet twitched incessantly, his voice was croaking and spasmodic. He lay listlessly as I entered the room, but the sight of me brought a gleam of recognition to his eyes.

"Well, Watson, we seem to have fallen upon evil days," said he in a feeble voice, but with something of his old carelessness of manner.

"My dear fellow!" I cried, approaching him.

"Stand back! Stand right back!" said he with the sharp imperiousness which I had associated only with moments of crisis. "If you approach me, Watson, I shall order you out of the house."

"But why?"

"Because it is my desire. Is that not enough?"

Yes, Mrs. Hudson was right. He was more masterful than ever. It was pitiful, however, to see his exhaustion.

"I only wished to help," I explained.

"Exactly! You will help best by doing what you are told."

"Certainly, Holmes."

He relaxed the austerity of his manner.

"You are not angry?" he asked, gasping for breath.

Poor devil, how could I be angry when I saw him lying in such a plight before me?

"It's for your own sake, Watson," he croaked.

"For *my* sake?"

"I know what is the matter with me. It is a coolie disease from Sumatra--a thing that the Dutch know more about than we, though they have made little of it up to date. One thing only is certain. It is infallibly deadly, and it is horribly contagious."

He spoke now with a feverish energy, the long hands twitching and jerking as he motioned me away.

"Contagious by touch, Watson--that's it, by touch. Keep your distance and all is well."

"Good heavens, Holmes! Do you suppose that such a consideration weighs with me for an instant? It would not affect me in the case of a stranger. Do you imagine it would prevent me from doing my duty to so old a friend?"

Again I advanced, but he repulsed me with a look of furious anger.

"If you will stand there I will talk. If you do not you must leave the room."

I have so deep a respect for the extraordinary qualities of Holmes that I have always deferred to his wishes, even when I least understood them. But now all my professional instincts were aroused. Let him be my master elsewhere, I at least was his in a sick room.

"Holmes," said I, "you are not yourself. A sick man is but a child, and so I will treat you. Whether you like it or not, I will examine your symptoms and treat you for them."

He looked at me with venomous eyes.

"If I am to have a doctor whether I will or not, let me at least have someone in whom I have confidence," said he.

"Then you have none in me?"

"In your friendship, certainly. But facts are facts, Watson, and, after all, you are only a general practitioner with very limited experience and mediocre qualifications. It is painful to have to say these things, but you leave me no choice."

I was bitterly hurt.

"Such a remark is unworthy of you, Holmes. It shows me very clearly the state of your own nerves. But if you have no confidence in me I would not intrude my services. Let me bring Sir Jasper Meek or Penrose Fisher, or any of the best men in London. But someone you *must* have, and that is final. If you think that I am going to stand here and see you die without either helping you myself or bringing anyone else to help you, then you have mistaken your man."

"You mean well, Watson," said the sick man with something between a sob and a groan. "Shall I demonstrate your own ignorance? What do you know, pray, of Tapanuli fever? What do you know of the black Formosa corruption?"

"I have never heard of either."

"There are many problems of disease, many strange pathological possibilities, in the East, Watson." He paused after each sentence to collect his failing strength. "I have learned so much during some recent researches which have a medico-criminal aspect. It was in the course of them that I contracted this complaint. You can do nothing."

"Possibly not. But I happen to know that Dr. Ainstree, the greatest living authority upon tropical disease, is now in London. All remonstrance is useless, Holmes, I am going this instant to fetch him." I turned resolutely to the door.

Never have I had such a shock! In an instant, with a tiger-spring, the dying man had intercepted me. I heard the sharp snap of a twisted key. The next moment he had staggered back to his bed, exhausted and panting after his one tremendous outflame of energy.

"You won't take the key from me by force, Watson. I've got you, my friend. Here you are, and here you will stay until I will otherwise. But I'll humour you." (All this in little gasps, with terrible struggles for breath between.) "You've only my own good at heart. Of course I know that very well. You shall have your way, but give me time to get my strength. Not now, Watson, not now. It's four o'clock. At six you can go."

"This is insanity, Holmes."

"Only two hours, Watson. I promise you will go at six. Are you content to wait?"

"I seem to have no choice."

"None in the world, Watson. Thank you, I need no help in arranging the clothes. You will please keep your distance. Now, Watson, there is one other condition that I would make. You will seek help, not from the man you mention, but from the one that I choose."

"By all means."

"The first three sensible words that you uttered since you entered this room, Watson. You will find some books over there. I am somewhat exhausted; I wonder how a battery feels when it pours electricity into a non-conductor? At six, Watson, we resume our conversation."

But it was destined to be resumed long before that hour, and in circumstances which gave me a shock hardly second to that caused by his spring to the door. I had stood for some minutes looking at the silent figure in the bed. His face was almost covered by the clothes and he appeared to be asleep. Then, unable to settle down to reading, I walked slowly round the room, examining the pictures of celebrated criminals with

which every wall was adorned. Finally, in my aimless per-
ambulation, I came to the mantelpiece. A litter of pipes,
tobacco-pouches, syringes, penknives, revolver-cartridges,
and other débris was scattered over it. In the midst of these
was a small black and white ivory box with a sliding lid. It
was a neat little thing, and I had stretched out my hand to
examine it more closely when--

It was a dreadful cry that he gave--a yell which might
have been heard down the street. My skin went cold and my
hair bristled at that horrible scream. As I turned I caught a
glimpse of a convulsed face and frantic eyes. I stood para-
lyzed, with the little box in my hand.

"Put it down! Down, this instant, Watson--this instant, I
say!" His head sank back upon the pillow and he gave a deep
sigh of relief as I replaced the box upon the mantelpiece. "I
hate to have my things touched, Watson. You know that I
hate it. You fidget me beyond endurance. You, a doctor--
you are enough to drive a patient into an asylum. Sit down,
man, and let me have my rest!"

The incident left a most unpleasant impression upon my
mind. The violent and causeless excitement, followed by this
brutality of speech, so far removed from his usual suavity,
showed me how deep was the disorganization of his mind. Of
all ruins, that of a noble mind is the most deplorable. I sat in
silent dejection until the stipulated time had passed. He
seemed to have been watching the clock as well as I, for it
was hardly six before he began to talk with the same feverish
animation as before.

"Now, Watson," said he. "Have you any change in your
pocket?"

"Yes."

"Any silver?"

"A good deal."

"How many half-crowns?"

"I have five."

"Ah, too few! Too few! How very unfortunate, Watson!
However, such as they are you can put them in your watch-
pocket. And all the rest of your money in your left trouser-
pocket. Thank you. It will balance you so much better like
that."

This was raving insanity. He shuddered, and again made a
sound between a cough and a sob.

"You will now light the gas, Watson, but you will be very
careful that not for one instant shall it be more than half
on. I implore you to be careful, Watson. Thank you, that is
excellent. No, you need not draw the blind. Now you will
have the kindness to place some letters and papers upon this
table within my reach. Thank you. Now some of that litter
from the mantelpiece. Excellent, Watson! There is a sugar-
tongs there. Kindly raise that small ivory box with its

assistance. Place it here among the papers. Good! You can go now and fetch Mr. Culverton Smith, of 13 Lower Burke Street."

To tell the truth, my desire to fetch a doctor had somewhat weakened, for poor Holmes was so obviously delirious that it seemed dangerous to leave him. However, he was as eager now to consult the person named as he had been obstinate in refusing.

"I never heard the name," said I.

"Possibly not, my good Watson. It may surprise you to know that the man upon earth who is best versed in this disease is not a medical man, but a planter. Mr. Culverton Smith is a well-known resident of Sumatra, now visiting London. An outbreak of the disease upon his plantation, which was distant from medical aid, caused him to study it himself, with some rather far-reaching consequences. He is a very methodical person, and I did not desire you to start before six, because I was well aware that you would not find him in his study. If you could persuade him to come here and give us the benefit of his unique experience of this disease, the investigation of which has been his dearest hobby, I cannot doubt that he could help me."

I give Holmes's remarks as a consecutive whole and will not attempt to indicate how they were interrupted by gaspings for breath and those clutchings of his hands which indicated the pain from which he was suffering. His appearance had changed for the worse during the few hours that I had been with him. Those hectic spots were more pronounced, the eyes shone more brightly out of darker hollows, and a cold sweat glimmered upon his brow. He still retained, however, the jaunty gallantry of his speech. To the last gasp he would always be the master.

"You will tell him exactly how you have left me," said he. "You will convey the very impression which is in your own mind--a dying man--a dying and delirious man. Indeed, I cannot think why the whole bed of the ocean is not one solid mass of oysters, so prolific the creatures seem. Ah, I am wandering! Strange how the brain controls the brain! What was I saying, Watson?"

"My directions for Mr. Culverton Smith."

"Ah, yes, I remember. My life depends upon it. Plead with him, Watson. There is no good feeling between us. His nephew, Watson--I had suspicions of foul play and I allowed him to see it. The boy died horribly. He has a grudge against me. You will soften him, Watson. Beg him, pray him, get him here by any means. He can save me--only he!"

"I will bring him in a cab, if I have to carry him down to it."

"You will do nothing of the sort. You will persuade him to come. And then you will return in front of him. Make any excuse so as not to come with him. Don't forget, Watson. You won't fail me. You never did fail me. No doubt there are natural enemies which limit the increase of the creatures. You and I, Watson, we have done our part. Shall the world, then, be overrun by oysters? No, no; horrible! You'll convey all that is in your mind."

I left him full of the image of this magnificent intellect babbling like a foolish child. He had handed me the key, and with a happy thought I took it with me lest he should lock himself in. Mrs. Hudson was waiting, trembling and weeping, in the passage. Behind me as I passed from the flat I heard Holmes's high, thin voice in some delirious chant. Below, as I stood whistling for a cab, a man came on me through the fog.

"How is Mr. Holmes, sir?" he asked.

It was an old acquaintance, Inspector Morton, of Scotland Yard, dressed in unofficial tweeds.

"He is very ill," I answered.

He looked at me in a most singular fashion. Had it not been too fiendish, I could have imagined that the gleam of the fanlight showed exultation in his face.

"I heard some rumour of it," said he.

The cab had driven up, and I left him.

Lower Burke Street proved to be a line of fine houses lying in the vague borderland between Notting Hill and Kensington. The particular one at which my cabman pulled up had an air of smug and demure respectability in its old-fashioned iron railings, its massive folding-door, and its shining brasswork. All was in keeping with a solemn butler who appeared framed in the pink radiance of a tinted electric light behind him.

"Yes, Mr. Culverton Smith is in. Dr. Watson! Very good, sir, I will take up your card."

My humble name and title did not appear to impress Mr. Culverton Smith. Through the half-open door I heard a high, petulant, penetrating voice.

"Who is this person? What does he want? Dear me, Staples, how often have I said that I am not to be disturbed in my hours of study?"

There came a gentle flow of soothing explanation from the butler.

"Well, I won't see him, Staples. I can't have my work interrupted like this. I am not at home. Say so. Tell him to come in the morning if he really must see me."

Again the gentle murmur.

"Well, well, give him that message. He can come in the morning, or he can stay away. My work must not be hindered."

I thought of Holmes tossing upon his bed of sickness and counting the minutes, perhaps, until I could bring help to him. It was not a time to stand upon ceremony. His life depended upon my promptness. Before the apologetic butler had delivered his message I had pushed past him and was in the room.

With a shrill cry of anger a man rose from a reclining chair beside the fire. I saw a great yellow face, coarse-grained and greasy, with heavy, double-chin, and two sullen, menacing gray eyes which glared at me from under tufted and sandy brows. A high bald head had a small velvet smoking-cap poised coquettishly upon one side of its pink curve. The skull was of enormous capacity, and yet as I looked down I saw to my amazement that the figure of the man was small and frail, twisted in the shoulders and back like one who has suffered from rickets in his childhood.

"What's this?" he cried in a high, screaming voice. "What is the meaning of this intrusion? Didn't I send you word that I would see you tomorrow morning?"

"I am sorry," said I, "but the matter cannot be delayed. Mr. Sherlock Holmes--"

The mention of my friend's name had an extraordinary effect upon the little man. The look of anger passed in an instant from his face. His features became tense and alert.

"Have you come from Holmes?" he asked.

"I have just left him."

"What about Holmes? How is he?"

"He is desperately ill. That is why I have come."

The man motioned me to a chair, and turned to resume his own. As he did so I caught a glimpse of his face in the mirror over the mantelpiece. I could have sworn that it was set in a malicious and abominable smile. Yet I persuaded myself that it must have been some nervous contraction which I had surprised, for he turned to me an instant later with genuine concern upon his features.

"I am sorry to hear this," said he.   "I only know Mr. Holmes through some business dealings which we have had, but I have every respect for his talents and his character. He is an amateur of crime, as I am of disease. For him the villain, for me the microbe. There are my prisons," he continued, pointing to a row of bottles and jars which stood upon a side table. "Among those gelatine cultivations some of the very worst offenders in the world are now doing time."

"It was on account of your special knowledge that Mr. Holmes desired to see you. He has a high opinion of you and thought that you were the one man in London who could help him."

The little man started, and the jaunty smoking-cap slid to the floor.

"Why?" he asked.   "Why should Mr. Holmes think that I could help him in his trouble?"

"Because of your knowledge of Eastern diseases."

"But why should he think that this disease which he has contracted is Eastern?"

"Because, in some professional inquiry, he has been working among Chinese sailors down in the docks."

Mr. Culverton Smith smiled pleasantly and picked up his smoking-cap.

"Oh, that's it--is it?" said he. "I trust the matter is not so grave as you suppose. How long has he been ill?"

"About three days."

"Is he delirious?"

"Occasionally."

"Tut, tut! This sounds serious. It would be inhuman not to answer his call. I very much resent any interruption to my work, Dr. Watson, but this case is certainly exceptional. I will come with you at once."

I remembered Holmes's injunction.

"I have another appointment," said I.

"Very good. I will go alone. I have a note of Mr. Holmes's address. You can rely upon my being there within half an hour at most."

It was with a sinking heart that I reentered Holmes's bedroom. For all that I knew the worst might have happened in my absence. To my enormous relief, he had improved greatly in the interval. His appearance was as ghastly as ever, but all trace of delirium had left him and he spoke in a feeble voice, it is true, but with even more than his usual crispness and lucidity.

"Well, did you see him, Watson?"

"Yes; he is coming."

"Admirable, Watson! Admirable! You are the best of messengers."

"He wished to return with me."

"That would never do, Watson. That would be obviously impossible. Did he ask what ailed me?"

"I told him about the Chinese in the East End."

"Exactly! Well, Watson, you have done all that a good friend could. You can now disappear from the scene."

"I must wait and hear his opinion, Holmes."

"Of course you must. But I have reasons to suppose that this opinion would be very much more frank and valuable if he imagines that we are alone. There is just room behind the head of my bed, Watson."

"My dear Holmes!"

"I fear there is no alternative, Watson. The room does not lend itself to concealment, which is as well, as it is the less likely to arouse suspicion. But just there, Watson, I fancy that it could be done." Suddenly he sat up with a rigid intentness upon his haggard face. "There are the wheels, Watson. Quick, man, if you love me! And don't budge, whatever happens--whatever happens, do you hear? Don't speak! Don't

118

move! Just listen with all your ears." Then in an instant his sudden access of strength departed, and his masterful, purposeful talk droned away into the low, vague murmurings of a semi-delirious man.

From the hiding-place into which I had been so swiftly hustled I heard the footfalls upon the stair, with the opening and the closing of the bedroom door. Then, to my surprise, there came a long silence, broken only by the heavy breathings and gaspings of the sick man. I could imagine that our visitor was standing by the bedside and looking down at the sufferer. At last that strange hush was broken.

"Holmes!" he cried. "Holmes!" in the insistent tone of one who awakens a sleeper. "Can't you hear me, Holmes?" There was a rustling, as if he had shaken the sick man roughly by the shoulder.

"Is that you, Mr. Smith?" Holmes whispered. "I hardly dared hope that you would come."

The other laughed.

"I should imagine not," he said. "And yet, you see, I am here. Coals of fire, Holmes--coals of fire!"

"It is very good of you--very noble of you. I appreciate your special knowledge."

Our visitor sniggered.

"You do. You are, fortunately, the only man in London who does. Do you know what is the matter with you?"

"The same," said Holmes.

"Ah! You recognize the symptoms?"

"Only too well."

"Well, I shouldn't be surprised, Holmes. I shouldn't be surprised if it were the same. A bad lookout for you if it is. Poor Victor was a dead man on the fourth day--a strong, hearty young fellow. It was certainly, as you said, very surprising that he should have contracted an out-of-the-way Asiatic disease in the heart of London--a disease, too, of which I had made such a very special study. Singular coincidence, Holmes. Very smart of you to notice it, but rather uncharitable to suggest that it was cause and effect."

"I knew that you did it."

"Oh, you did, did you? Well, you couldn't prove it, anyhow. But what do you think of yourself spreading reports about me like that, and then crawling to me for help the moment you are in trouble? What sort of a game is that--eh?"

I heard the rasping, laboured breathing of the sick man. "Give me the water!" he gasped.

"You're precious near your end, my friend, but I don't want you to go till I have had a word with you. That's why I give you water. There, don't slop it about! That's right. Can you understand what I say?"

Holmes groaned.

"Do what you can for me. Let bygones be bygones," he whispered. "I'll put the words out of my head--I swear I will. Only cure me, and I'll forget it."

"Forget what?"

"Well, about Victor Savage's death. You as good as admitted just now that you had done it. I'll forget it."

"You can forget it or remember it, just as you like. I don't see you in the witness-box. Quite another shaped box, my good Holmes, I assure you. It matters nothing to me that you should know how my nephew died. It's not him we are talking about. It's you."

"Yes, yes."

"The fellow who came for me--I've forgotten his name-- said that you contracted it down in the East End among the sailors."

"I could only account for it so."

"You are proud of your brains, Holmes, are you not? Think yourself smart, don't you? You came across someone who was smarter this time. Now cast your mind back, Holmes. Can you think of no other way you could have got this thing?"

"I can't think. My mind is gone. For heaven's sake help me!"

"Yes, I will help you. I'll help you to understand just where you are and how you got there. I'd like you to know before you die."

"Give me something to ease my pain."

"Painful, is it? Yes, the coolies used to do some squealing towards the end. Takes you as cramp, I fancy."

"Yes, yes; it is cramp."

"Well, you can hear what I say, anyhow. Listen now! Can you remember any unusual incident in your life just about the time your symptoms began?"

"No, no; nothing."

"Think again."

"I'm too ill to think."

"Well, then, I'll help you. Did anything come by post?"

"By post?"

"A box by chance?"

"I'm fainting--I'm gone!"

"Listen, Holmes!" There was a sound as if he was shaking the dying man, and it was all that I could do to hold myself quiet in my hiding-place. "You must hear me. You *shall* hear me. Do you remember a box--an ivory box? It came on Wednesday. You opened it--do you remember?"

"Yes, yes. I opened it. There was a sharp spring inside it. Some joke--"

"It was no joke, as you will find to your cost. You fool, you would have it and you have got it. Who asked you to

120

cross my path? If you had left me alone I would not have hurt you."

"I remember," Holmes gasped. "The spring! It drew blood. This box--this on the table."

"The very one, by George! And it may as well leave the room in my pocket. There goes your last shred of evidence. But you have the truth now, Holmes, and you can die with the knowledge that I killed you. You knew too much of the fate of Victor Savage, so I have sent you to share it. You are very near your end, Holmes. I will sit here and I will watch you die."

Holmes's voice had sunk to an almost inaudible whisper.

"What is that?" said Smith. "Turn up the gas? Ah, the shadows begin to fall, do they? Yes, I will turn it up, that I may see you the better." He crossed the room and the light suddenly brightened. "Is there any other little service that I can do you, my friend?"

"A match and a cigarette."

I nearly called out in my joy and my amazement. He was speaking in his natural voice--a little weak, perhaps, but the very voice I knew. There was a long pause, and I felt that Culverton Smith was standing in silent amazement looking down at his companion.

"What's the meaning of this?" I heard him say at last in a dry, rasping tone.

"The best way of successfully acting a part is to be it," said Holmes. "I give you my word that for three days I have tasted neither food nor drink until you were good enough to pour out that glass of water. But it is the tobacco which I find most irksome. Ah, here *are* some cigarettes." I heard the striking of a match. "That is very much better. Halloa! halloa! Do I hear the step of a friend?"

There were footfalls outside, the door opened, and Inspector Morton appeared.

"All is in order and this is your man," said Holmes.

The officer gave the usual cautions.

"I arrest you on the charge of the murder of one Victor Savage," he concluded.

"And you might add of the attempted murder of one Sherlock Holmes," remarked my friend with a chuckle. "To save an invalid trouble, Inspector, Mr. Culverton Smith was good enough to give our signal by turning up the gas. By the way, the prisoner has a small box in the right-hand pocket of his coat which it would be as well to remove. Thank you. I would handle it gingerly if I were you. Put it down here. It may play its part in the trial."

There was a sudden rush and a scuffle, followed by the clash of iron and a cry of pain.

"You'll only get yourself hurt," said the inspector. "Stand still, will you?" There was the click of the closing handcuffs.

"A nice trap!" cried the high, snarling voice. "It will bring *you* into the dock, Holmes, not me. He asked me to come here to cure him. I was sorry for him and I came. Now he will pretend, no doubt, that I have said anything which he may invent which will corroborate his insane suspicions. You can lie as you like, Holmes. My word is always as good as yours."

"Good heavens!" cried Holmes. "I had totally forgotten him. My dear Watson, I owe you a thousand apologies. To think that I should have overlooked you! I need not introduce you to Mr. Culverton Smith, since I understand that you met somewhat earlier in the evening. Have you the cab below? I will follow you when I am dressed, for I may be of some use at the station."

"I never needed it more," said Holmes as he refreshed himself with a glass of claret and some biscuits in the intervals of his toilet. "However, as you know, my habits are irregular, and such a feat means less to me than to most men. It was very essential that I should impress Mrs. Hudson with the reality of my condition, since she was to convey it to you, and you in turn to him. You won't be offended, Watson? You will realize that among your many talents dissimulation finds no place, and that if you had shared my secret you would never have been able to impress Smith with the urgent necessity of his presence, which was the vital point of the whole scheme. Knowing his vindictive nature, I was perfectly certain that he would come to look upon his handiwork."

"But your appearance, Holmes--your ghastly face?"

"Three days of absolute fast does not improve one's beauty, Watson. For the rest, there is nothing which a sponge may not cure. With vaseline upon one's forehead, belladonna in one's eyes, rouge over the cheekbones, and crusts of beeswax round one's lips, a very satisfying effect can be produced. Malingering is a subject upon which I have sometimes thought of writing a monograph. A little occasional talk about half-crowns, oysters, or any other extraneous subject produces a pleasing effect of delirium."

"But why would you not let me near you, since there was in truth no infection?"

"Can you ask, my dear Watson? Do you imagine that I have no respect for your medical talents? Could I fancy that your astute judgement would pass a dying man who, however weak, had no rise of pulse or temperature? At four yards, I could deceive you. If I failed to do so, who would bring my Smith within my grasp? No, Watson, I would not touch that box. You can just see if you look at it sideways where the sharp spring like a viper's tooth emerges as you open it. I dare say it was by some such device that poor Savage, who stood between this monster and a reversion, was done to death. My correspondence, however, is, as you know, a varied one, and I am somewhat upon my guard against any packages which reach me. It was clear to me, however, that by pretending that he had really succeeded in his design I might surprise a confession. That pretense I have carried out with the thoroughness of the true artist. Thank you, Watson, you must help me on with my coat. When we have finished at the police-station I think that something nutritious at Simpson's would not be out of place."

FRANCIS THOMPSON
(1859-1907)

Francis had been wandering the streets of London for nearly three years, ravaged by his drug habit and the despicable living conditions of his poverty. Worse yet, the guilt that often overwhelmed him had not abated. How could God love me, he thought. He had failed in his seven-year effort to become a priest; he was so lazy by nature, physically weak and impractical. What else could he have expected? But he had so loved God, the Church, the hymns, the ritual. Wasn't that enough?

Now he was receiving what he deserved for his sinfulness, especially since he had also failed to become a physician. What else is left but degradation for such a lowly, sinful creative? Francis hadn't become immoral though, and he tried to work at odd jobs, even a little writing now and then.

One day, however, Francis was rescued from his hideous nightmare. Two very zealous evangelical Christians, Mr. and Mrs. Wilfrid Meynell, fulfilled the roles of delivering angels for Francis. In 1887, Thompson had written some poems and essays on some dirty, bedraggled paper and sent them to Meynell for possible publication in the evangelical magazine Merry England. For almost a year's time, Meynell ignored the writings, but when he did read them, he recognized a hidden talent, a brilliant poet entrenched in the abyss of urban squalor. Meynell had to labor with difficulty to get Francis to write more works for the magazine. Thompson's guilt and self-depreciation were severe, his despair nearly complete.

But the Meynells proved worthy rescuers. Francis was restored to health in a hospital where his benefactors provided for him. He lived in Catholic cloisters at times after that, but remained close to the Meynell family. His poems reflect much of his restored new life, especially The Hound of Heaven, a deeply moving account of God's relentless perseverance of the restoration of an injured soul. The Meynells, have been repaid; in fact, they have left a great man who loved God, learned to love himself and other creatures of God, and put powerful expression to the deepest needs of those creatures.

THE HOUND OF HEAVEN

I fled Him, down the nights and down the days;
I fled Him, down the arches of the years;
I fled Him, down the labyrinthine ways
    Of my own mind; and in the midst of tears
I hid from Him, and under running laughter.
        Up vistaed hopes I sped;
        And shot, precipitated,
Adown Titanic glooms of chasmèd fears,
    From those strong Feet that followed, followed after.
        But with unhurrying chase,
        And unperturbèd pace,
      Deliberate speed, majestic instancy,
        They beat--and a Voice beat
        More instant than the Feet--
      'All things betray thee, who betrayest Me.'

        I pleaded, outlaw-wise,
By many a hearted casement, curtained red,
    Trellised with intertwining charities;
(For, though I knew His love Who followèd,
        Yet was I sore adread
Lest, having Him, I must have naught beside.)
But, if one little casement parted wide,
    The gust of His approach would clash it to:
    Fear wist not to evade, as Love wist to pursue.
Across the margent of the world I fled,
    And troubled the gold gateways of the stars,
    Smiting for shelter on their clangèd bars;
        Fretted to dulcet jars
And silvern chatter the pale ports o' the moon.
I said to Dawn: Be sudden--to Eve: Be soon;
    With thy young skiey blossoms heap me over
        From this tremendous Lover--
Float thy vague veil about me, lest He see!
    I tempted all His servitors, but to find
My own betrayal in their constancy,
In faith to Him their fickleness to me,
    Their traitorous trueness, and their loyal deceit.
To all swift things for swiftness did I sue;
    Clung to the whistling mane of every wind.
      But whether they swept, smoothly fleet,
    The long savannahs of the blue;
        Or whether, Thunder-driven,
      They clanged his chariot 'thwart a heaven,
Plashy with flying lightnings round the spurn o' their feet:--
    Fear wist not to evade as Love wist to pursue.
        Still with unhurrying chase,
        And unperturbèd pace,

Deliberate speed, majestic instancy,
　　　Came on the following Feet
　　　And a Voice above their beat--
'Naught shelters thee, who wilt not shelter Me.'

I sought no more that after which I strayed
　　　In face of man or maid;
But still within the little children's eyes
　　　Seems something, something that replies,
They at least are for me, surely for me!
I turned me to them very wistfully;
But just as their young eyes grew sudden fair
　　　With dawning answers there,
Their angel plucked them from me by the hair.
'Come then, ye other children, Nature's--share
With me' (said I) 'your delicate fellowship;
　　　Let me greet you lip to lip,
　　　Let me twine with you caresses,
　　　　　Wantoning
　　　With our Lady-Mother's vagrant tresses,
　　　　　Banqueting
　　　With her in her wind-walled palace,
　　　Underneath her azured daïs,
　　　Quaffing, as your taintless way is,
　　　From a chalice
Lucent-weeping out of the dayspring.'
　　　So it was done:
I in their delicate fellowship was one--
Drew the bolt of Nature's secrecies.
　　　I knew all the swift importings
　　　On the wilful face of skies;
　　　I knew how the clouds arise
　　　Spumèd of the wild sea-snortings;
　　　　　All that's born or dies
　　　Rose and drooped with; made them shapers
Of mine own moods, or wailful or divine;
　　　With them joyed and was bereaven.
　　　I was heavy with the even,
　　　When she lit her glimmering tapers
　　　Round the day's dead sanctities.
　　　I laughed in the morning's eyes.
I triumphed and I saddened with all weather,
　　　Heaven and I wept together,
And it sweet tears were salt with mortal mine;
Against the red throb of its sunset-heart
　　　I laid my own to beat,
　　　And share commingling heat;
But not by that, by that, was eased my human smart.
In vain my tears were wet on Heaven's grey cheek.

For ah! we know not what each other says,
These things and I; in sound *I* speak--
Their sound is but their stir, they speak by silences.
Nature, poor stepdame, cannot slake my drouth;
Let her, if she would owe me,
Drop yon blue bosom-veil of sky, and show me
The breasts o' her tenderness:
Never did any milk of hers once bless
My thirsting mouth.
Nigh and nigh draws the chase,
With unperturbèd pace,
Deliberate speed, majestic instancy;
And past those noisèd Feet
A voice comes yet more fleet--
'Lo! naught contents thee, who content'st not Me.'
Naked I wait Thy love's uplifted stroke!
My harness piece by piece Thou hast hewn from me,
And smitten me to my knee;
I am defenceless utterly.
I slept, methinks, and woke,
And slowly gazing, find me stripped in sleep.
In the rash lustihead of my young powers,
I shook the pillaring hours
And pulled my life upon me; grimed with smears,
I stand amid the dust o' the mounded years--
My mangled youth lies dead beneath the heap.
My days have crackled and gone up in smoke,
Have puffed and burst as sun-starts on a stream.
Yea, faileth now even dream
The dreamer, and the lute the lutanist;
Even the linked fantasies, in whose blossomy twist
I swung the earth a trinket at my wrist,
Are yielding; cords of all too weak account
For earth with heavy griefs so overplussed.
Ah! is Thy love indeed
A weed, albeit an amaranthine weed,
Suffering no flowers except its own to mount?
Ah! must--
Designer infinite!--
Ah! must Thou char the wood ere Thou canst limn with it?
My freshness spent its wavering shower i' the dust;
And now my heart is as a broken fount,
Wherein tear-drippings stagnate, spilt down ever
From the dank thoughts that shiver
Upon the sighful branches of my mind.
Such is; what is to be?
The pulp so bitter, how shall taste the rind?
I dimly guess what Time in mists confounds;
Yet ever and anon a trumpet sounds
From the hid battlements of Eternity;

127

Those shaken mists a space unsettle, then
Round the half-glimpsed turrets slowly wash again.
        But not ere him who summoneth
        I first have seen, enwound
With glooming robes purpureal, cypress-crowned;
His name I know, and what his trumpet saith.
Whether man's heart or life it be which yields
        Thee harvest, must Thy harvest-fields
        Be dunged with rotten death?

        Now of that long pursuit
        Comes on at hand the bruit;
    That Voice is round me like a bursting sea;
        'And is thy earth so marred,
        Shattered in shard on shard?
    Lo, all things fly thee, for thou fliest Me!
    Strange, piteous, futile thing!
Wherefore should any set thee love apart?
Seeing none but I makes much of naught' (He said),
'And human love needs human meriting:
        How hast thou merited--
Of all man's clotted clay the dingiest clot?
        Alack, thou knowest not
How little worthy of any love thou art!
Whom wilt thou find to love ignoble thee,
        Save Me, save only Me?
All which I took from thee I did but take,
        Not for thy harms,
But just that thou might'st seek it in My arms.
        All which thy child's mistake
Fancies as lost, I have stored for thee at home:
        Rise, clasp My hand, and come!'
    Halts by me that footfall:
    Is my gloom, after all,
Shade of His hand, outstretched caressingly?
    'Ah, fondest, blindest, weakest,
    I am He Whom thou seekest!
Thou dravest love from thee, who dravest Me.'

G. K. CHESTERTON
(1874-1936)

Tremendous Trifles (1909) contains several of Chesterton's greatest essays, two of which are reprinted here. Chesterton was one of the profound apologists for the Christian faith, one who influenced C. S. Lewis and many other intellectual and thoughtful people. His wit, as well as his paradoxical thought, made him famous and enjoyable. People like him certainly see the world differently, which provides the rest of us with refreshing alternatives to many issues.

Chesterton wrote many volumes of essays and criticisms, but he was also a novelist, best known for his Father Brown mysteries. His theological treatises, especially Orthodoxy and The Everlasting Man, compete successfully with the greatest Christian apologetic works of all time. His humor opens the mind, creates receptivity to his arguments, and makes his writing pleasantly appreciated. Such an example, taken from The Everlasting Man, pokes fun at rationalism's critique of religious thought.

But the poems did not exist before the poets. The poetry did not arise out of the poetic forms. . . . It needed a certain sort of mind to see that there was anything mystical about the dreams or the dead, as it needed a particular sort of mind to see that there was anything poetical about the skylark or the spring. . . . But there is not the faintest hint to suggest that anything short of the human mind we know feels any of these mystical associations at all. A cow in a field seems to derive no lyrical impulse or instruction from her unrivalled opportunities for listening to the skylark. And similarly there is no reason to suppose that live sheep will ever begin to use dead sheep as the basis of a system of elaborate ancestor-worship (page 48).

Never let Chesterton's humor, however, diminish the profundity of his depth of thought. He has the terrific ability to get to the heart of an issue, make realistic analyses of the inherent problems, and persuasively present a devastating solution. Whether the reader agrees with Chesterton on all issues or opposes his views, his writing style evokes great joy with the reading.

A PIECE OF CHALK

I remember one splendid morning, all blue and silver, in the summer holidays, when I reluctantly tore myself away from the task of doing nothing in particular, and put on a hat of some sort and picked up a walking-stick, and put six very bright-coloured chalks in my pocket. I then went into the kitchen (which, along with the rest of the house, belonged to a very square and sensible old woman in a Sussex village), and asked the owner and occupant of the kitchen if she had any brown paper. She had a great deal; in fact, she had too much; and she mistook the purpose and the rationale of the existence of brown paper. She seemed to have an idea that if a person wanted brown paper he must be wanting to tie up parcels; which was the last thing I wanted to do; indeed, it is a thing which I have found to be beyond my mental capacity. Hence she dwelt very much on the varying qualities of toughness and endurance in the material. I explained to her that I only wanted to draw pictures on it, and I did not want them to endure in the least; and that from my point of view, therefore, it was a question not of tough consistency, but of responsive surface, a thing comparatively irrelevant in a parcel. When she understood that I wanted to draw she offered to overwhelm me with note-paper, apparently supposing that I did my notes and correspondence on old brown paper wrappers from motives of economy.

I then tried to explain the rather delicate logical shade, that I not only liked brown paper, but liked the quality of brownness in paper, just as I liked the quality of brownness in October woods, or in beer, or in the peat-streams of the North. Brown paper represents the primal twilight of the first toil of creation, and with a bright-coloured chalk or two you can pick out points of fire in it, sparks of gold, and blood-red, and seagreen, like the first fierce stars that sprang out of divine darkness. All this I said (in an off-hand way) to the old woman; and I put the brown paper in my pocket along with the chalks, and possibly other things. I suppose everyone must have reflected how primeval and how poetical are the things that one carries in one's pocket; the pocket-knife, for instance, the type of all human tools, the infant of the sword. Once I planned to write a book of poems entirely about the things in my pocket. But I found it would be too long; and the age of the great epics is past.

With my stick and my knife, my chalks and my brown paper, I went out on to the great downs. I crawled across those colossal contours that express the best quality of England, because they are at the same time soft and strong.

The smoothness of them has the same meaning as smoothness of great cart-horses, or the smoothness of the beech-tree; it declares in the teeth of our timid and cruel theories that the mighty are merciful. As my eye swept the landscape, the landscape was as kindly as any of its cottages, but for power it was like an earthquake. The villages in the immense valley were safe, one could see, for centuries; yet the lifting of the whole land was like the lifting of one enormous wave to wash them all away.

I crossed one swell of living turf after another, looking for a place to sit down and draw. Do not for heaven's sake, imagine I was going to sketch from Nature. I was going to draw devils and seraphim, and blind old gods that men worshipped before the dawn of right, and saints in robes of angry crimson, and seas of strange green, and all the sacred or monstrous symbols that look so well in bright colours on brown paper. They are much better worth drawing than Nature; also they are much easier to draw. When a cow came slouching by in the field next to me, a mere artist might have drawn it; but I always get wrong in the hind legs of quadrupeds. So I drew the soul of the cow; which I saw there plainly walking before me in the sunlight; and the soul was all purple and silver, and had seven horns and the mystery that belongs to all the beasts. But though I could not with a crayon get the best out of the landscape, it does not follow that the landscape was not getting the best out of me. And this, I think, is the mistake that people make about the old poets who lived before Wordsworth, and were supposed not to care very much about Nature because they did not describe it much.

They preferred writing about great men to writing about great hills; but they sat on the great hills to write it. They gave out much less about Nature, but they drank in, perhaps, much more. They painted the white robes of their holy virgins with the blinding snow, at which they had stared all day. They blazoned the shields of their paladins with the purple and gold of many heraldic sunsets. The greenness of a thousand green leaves clustered into the live green figure of Robin Hood. The blueness of a score of forgotten skies became the blue robes of the Virgin. The inspiration went in like sunbeams and came out like Apollo.

But as I sat scrawling these silly figures on the brown paper, it began to dawn on me, to my great disgust, that I had left one chalk, and that a most exquisite and essential chalk, behind. I searched all my pockets, but I could not find any white chalk. Now, those who are acquainted with all the philosophy (nay, religion) which is typified in the art of drawing on brown paper, know that white is positive and essential. I cannot avoid remarking here upon a moral significance. One of the wise and awful truths which this brown-paper art reveals, is this, that white is a colour. It is not a mere absence of colour; it is a shining and affirmative thing, as fierce as red, as definite as black. When (so to speak) your pencil grows red-hot, it draws roses; when it grows white-hot, it draws stars. And one of the two or three defiant verities of the best religious morality, of real Christianity for example, is exactly this same thing; the chief assertion of religious morality is that white is a colour. Virtue is not the absence of vices or the avoidance of moral dangers; virtue is a vivid and separate thing, like pain or a particular smell. Mercy does not mean not being cruel or sparing people revenge or punishment; it means a plain and positive thing like the sun, which one has either seen or not seen. Chastity does not mean abstention from sexual wrong; it means something flaming, like Joan of Arc. In a word, God paints in many colours; but He never paints so gorgeously, I had almost said so gaudily, as when He paints in white. In a sense our age has realized this fact, and expressed it in our sullen costume. For if it were really true that white was a blank and colourless thing, negative and noncommittal, then white would be used instead of black and grey for the funeral dress of this pessimistic period. We should see city gentlemen in frock coats of spotless silver satin, with top hats as white as wonderful arum lilies. Which is not the case.

Meanwhile, I could not find my chalk.

I sat on the hill in a sort of despair. There was no town nearer than Chichester at which it was even remotely probable that there would be such a thing as an artist's colourman. And yet, without white, my absurd little pictures would be as pointless as the world would be if there were no good people in it. I stared stupidly round, racking my brain for expedients. Then I suddenly stood up and roared with laughter, again and again, so that the cows stared at me and called a committee. Imagine a man in the Sahara regretting that he had no sand for his hour-glass. Imagine a gentleman in mid-ocean wishing that he had brought some salt water with him for his chemical experiments. I was sitting on an immense warehouse of white chalk. The landscape was made entirely out of white chalk. White chalk was piled mere miles until it met the sky. I stopped and broke a piece off the rock I sat on: it did not mark so well as the shop chalks do; but it gave the effect. And I stood there in a trance of pleasure, realizing that this Southern England is not only a grand peninsula, and a tradition and a civilization; it is something even more admirable. It is a piece of chalk.

ON LYING IN BED

Lying in bed would be an altogether perfect and supreme experience if only one had a coloured pencil long enough to draw on the ceiling. This, however, is not generally a part of the domestic apparatus on the premises. I think myself that the thing might be managed with several pails of Aspinall and a broom. Only if one worked in a really sweeping and masterly way, and laid on the colour in great washes, it might drip down again on one's face in floods of rich and mingled colour like some strange fairy rain; and that would have its disadvantages. I am afraid it would be necessary to stick to black and white in this form of artistic composition. To that purpose, indeed, the white ceiling would be of the greatest possible use; in fact it is the only use I think of a white ceiling being put to.

But for the beautiful experiment of lying in bed I might never have discovered it. For years I have been looking for some blank spaces in a modern house to draw on. Paper is much too small for any really allegorical design; as Cyrano de Bergerac says: "Il me fauts des géants." But when I tried to find these fine clear spaces in the modern rooms such as we all live in I was continually disappointed. I found an endless pattern and complication of small objects hung like a curtain of fine links between me and my desire. I examined the walls; I found them to my surprise to be already covered with wallpaper, and I found the wallpaper to be already covered with very uninteresting images, all bearing a ridiculous resemblance to each other. I could not understand why one arbitrary symbol (a symbol apparently entirely devoid of any religious or philosophical significance) should thus be sprinkled all over my nice walls like a sort of small-pox. The Bible must be referring to wallpapers, I think, when it says "Use not vain repetitions, as the Gentiles do." I found the Turkey carpet a mass of unmeaning colours, rather like the Turkish Empire, or like the sweetmeat called Turkish Delight. I do not exactly know what Turkish Delight really is; but I suppose it is Macedonian Massacres. Everywhere that I went forlornly, with my pencil or my paint brush, I found that others had unaccountably been before me, spoiling the walls, the curtains, and the furniture with their childish and barbaric designs.

Nowhere did I find a really clear space for sketching until this occasion when I prolonged beyond the proper limit the process of lying on my back in bed. Then the light of that white heaven broke upon my vision, that breadth of mere white which is indeed almost the definition of Paradise, since it means purity and also means freedom. But alas! like all heavens now that it is seen it is found to be unattainable; it

133

looks more austere and more distant than the blue sky outside the window. For my proposal to paint on it with the bristly end of a broom has been discouraged--never mind by whom; by a person debarred from all political rights--and even my minor proposal to put the other end of the broom into the kitchen fire and turn it into charcoal has not been conceded. Yet I am certain that it was from persons in my position that all the original inspiration came for covering the ceilings of palaces and cathedrals with a riot of fallen angels or victorious gods. I am sure that it was only because Michelangelo was engaged in the ancient and honourable occupation of lying in bed that he ever realized how the roof of the Sistine Chapel might be made into an awful imitation of a divine drama that could only be acted in the heavens.

The tone now commonly taken towards the practice of lying in bed is hypocritical and unhealthy. Of all the marks of modernity that seem to mean a kind of decadence, there is none more menacing and dangerous than the exaltation of very small and secondary matters of conduct at the expense of very great and primary ones, at the expense of eternal ties and tragic human morality. If there is one thing worse than the modern weakening of major morals it is the modern strengthening of minor morals. Thus it is considered more withering to accuse a man of bad taste than of bad ethics. Cleanliness is not next to godliness nowadays, for cleanliness is made an essential and godliness is regarded as an offence. A playwright can attack the institution of marriage so long as he does not misrepresent the manners of society, and I have met Ibsenite pessimists who thought it wrong to take beer but right to take prussic acid. Especially this is so in matters of hygiene; notably such matters as lying in bed. Instead of being regarded, as it ought to be, as a matter of personal convenience and adjustment, it has come to be regarded by many as if it were a part of essential morals to get up early in the morning. It is upon the whole part of practical wisdom; but there is nothing good about it or bad about its opposite.

Misers get up early in the morning; and burglars, I am informed, get up the night before. It is the great peril of our society that all its mechanism may grow more fixed while its spirit grows more fickle. A man's minor actions and arrangements ought to be free, flexible, creative; the things that should be unchangeable are his principles, his ideals. But with us the reverse is true; our views change constantly; but our lunch does not change. Now, I should like men to have strong and rooted conceptions, but as for their lunch, let them have it sometimes in the garden, sometimes in bed, sometimes on the roof, sometimes in the top of a tree. Let them argue from the same first principles, but let them do it in a bed, or a boat, or a balloon. This alarming growth of

134

good habits really means a too great emphasis on those virtues which mere custom can ensure, it means too little emphasis on those virtues which custom can never quite ensure, sudden and splendid virtues of inspired pity or of inspired candour. If ever that abrupt appeal is made to us we may fail. A man can get used to getting up at five o'clock in the morning. A man cannot very well get used to being burnt for his opinions; the first experiment is commonly fatal. Let us pay a little more attention to these possibilities of the heroic and the unexpected. I dare say that when I get out of this bed I shall do some deed of an almost terrible virtue.

For those who study the great art of lying in bed there is one emphatic caution to be added. Even for those who can do their work in bed (like journalists), still more for those whose work cannot be done in bed (as, for example, the professional harpooners of whales), it is obvious that the indulgence must be very occasional. But that is not the caution I mean. The caution is this: if you do lie in bed, be sure you do it without any reason or justification at all. I do not speak, of course, of the seriously sick. But if a healthy man lies in bed, let him do it without a rag of excuse; then he will get up a healthy man. If he does it for some secondary hygienic reason, if he has some scientific explanation, he may get up a hypocondriac.

THE WIND AND THE TREES

I am sitting under tall trees, with a great wind boiling like surf about the tops of them, so that their living load of leaves rocks and roars in something that is at once exultation and agony. I feel, in fact, as if I were actually sitting at the bottom of the sea among mere anchors and ropes, while over my head and over the green twilight of water sounded the everlasting rush of waves and the toil and crash and shipwreck of tremendous ships. The wind tugs at the trees as if it might pluck them root and all out of the earth like tufts of grass. Or, to try yet another desperate figure of speech for this unspeakable energy, the trees are straining and tearing and lashing as if they were a tribe of dragons each tied by the tail.

As I look at these top-heavy giants tortured by an invisible and violent witchcraft, a phrase comes back into my mind. I remember a little boy of my acquaintance who was once walking in Battersea Park under just such torn skies and tossing trees. He did not like the wind at all; it blew in his face too much; it made him shut his eyes; and it blew off his hat, of which he was very proud. He was, as far as I remember, about four. After complaining repeatedly of the atmospheric unrest, he said at last to his mother, "Well, why don't you take away the trees, and then it wouldn't wind."

135

Nothing could be more intelligent or natural than this mistake. Anyone looking for the first time at the trees might fancy that they were indeed vast and titanic fans, which by their mere waving agitated the air around them for miles. Nothing, I say, could be more human and excusable than the belief that it is the trees which make the wind. Indeed, the belief is so human and excusable that it is, as a matter of fact, the belief of about ninety-nine out of a hundred of the philosophers, reformers, sociologists, and politicians of the great age in which we live. My small friend was, in fact, very like the principal modern thinkers; only much nicer.

In the little apologue or parable which he has thus the honour of inventing, the trees stand for all visible things and the wind for the invisible. The wind is the spirit which bloweth where it listeth; the trees are the material things of the world which are blown where the spirit lists. The wind is philosophy, religion; revolution; the trees are cities and civilizations. We only know that there is a wind because the trees on some distant hill suddenly go mad. We only know that there is a real revolution because all the chimney-pots go mad on the whole sky-line of the city.

Just as the ragged outline of a tree grows suddenly more ragged and rises into fantastic crests or tattered tails, so the human city rises under the wind of the spirit into toppling temples or sudden spires. No man has ever seen a revolution. Mobs pouring through the palaces, blood pouring down the gutters, the guillotine lifted higher than the throne, a prison in ruins, a people in arms--these things are not revolution, but the results of revolution.

You cannot see a wind; you can only see that there is a wind. So, also, you cannot see a revolution; you can only see that there is a revolution. And there never has been in the history of the world a real revolution, brutally active and decisive, which was not preceded by unrest and new dogma in the region of invisible things. All revolutions began by being abstract. Most revolutions began by being quite pedantically abstract.

The wind is up above the world before a twig on the tree has moved. So there must always be a battle in the sky before there is a battle on the earth. Since it is lawful to pray for the coming of the kingdom, it is lawful also to pray for the coming of the revolution that shall restore the kingdom. It is lawful to pray "Thine anger come on earth as it is in heaven."

The great human dogma, then, is that the wind moves the trees. The great human heresy is that the trees move the wind. When people begin to say that the material circumstances have alone created the moral circumstances, then they have prevented all possibility of serious change. For if my circumstances have made me wholly stupid, how can I be certain even that I am right in altering these circumstances?

The man who represents all thought as an accident of environment is simply smashing and discrediting all his own thoughts--including that one. To treat the human mind as having an ultimate authority is necessary to any kind of thinking, even free thinking. And nothing will ever be reformed in this age or country unless we realize that the moral fact comes first.

For example, most of us, I suppose, have seen in print and heard in debating clubs an endless discussion that goes on between Socialists and total abstainers. The latter say that drink leads to poverty; the former say that poverty leads to drink. I can only wonder at either of them being content with such simple physical explanations. Surely it is obvious that the thing which among the English proletariat leads to poverty is the same as the thing which leads to drink; the absence of strong civic dignity, the absence of an instinct that resists degradation.

When you have discovered why the enormous English estates were not long ago cut up into small holdings like the land of France, you will have discovered why the Englishman is more drunken than the Frenchman. The Englishman, among his million delightful virtues, really has this quality, which may strictly be called 'hand to mouth', because under its influence a man's hand automatically seeks his own mouth, instead of seeking (as it sometimes should do) his oppressor's nose. And a man who says that the English inequality in land is due only to economic causes, is saying something so absurd that he cannot really have thought what he was saying.

Yet things as preposterous as this are said and written under the influence of that great spectacle of babyish helplessness, the economic theory of history. We have people who represent that all great historic motives were economic, and then have to howl at the top of their voices in order to induce the modern democracy to act on economic motives. The extreme Marxian politicians in England exhibit themselves as a small, heroic minority, trying vainly to induce the world to do what, according to their theory, the world always does. The truth is, of course, that there will be a social revolution the moment the thing has ceased to be purely economic. You can never have a revolution in order to establish a democracy. You must have a democracy in order to have a revolution.

I get up from under the trees, for the wind and the slight rain have ceased. The trees stand up like golden pillars in a clear sunlight. The tossing of the trees and the blowing of the wind have ceased simultaneously. So I suppose there are still modern philosophers who will maintain that the trees make the wind.

MARY WEBB
(1881-1927)

She passed this meadow every day, on her way to Shrewsbury. The larks seemed to understand her life: simple, peaceful, full of love as well as hard work. Work was normal. She always had work, though none of it, nor any from her dear husband, Henry, had ever produced an abundance of income. Mary wouldn't complain, her life was full though her body often suffered under the strain. The daily nine-mile walk to the town market where she sold her flowers tired her at times, probably because she awoke so early to get there.

People in the neighborhood spoke well of Mary and Henry. They were so generous, to a fault, said some. "That's why they're so eternally poor," said others. But Mary couldn't bear the suffering of those poorer than she. If only the writings would sell better. Mary thought perhaps the publishers hadn't promoted her work successfully. Her first three books (The Golden Arrows, Gone to Earth, and The House in Dormer Forest) really had little success, and the advances she received from the publishers were not enough to relieve her physical necessities.

Finally, in 1921, Mary and her schoolteacher husband, Henry, moved to a small home in London. The trips to the market, the back-breaking labor was not over. Mary could write now in some comfort, though the strength of her body was never completely restored.

Precious Bane was published in 1924 and received some literary awards, but Mary never really knew how well her book was received. She died in 1927.

Mary Gladys Meredith Webb was an unique person who wrote unusually well, especially about the Shropshire country of western England which she deeply loved. Love itself is the emotion she captured so exquisitely, clearly, deeply. She knew the intricacies of nature and the diversities in human character. Such profound understanding seems unlikely in a common rural woman of little education or opportunity. However, readers of her work are always astounded by the beauty and strength of her insight, experience, and perception. In Precious Bane, Mary Webb presents the reader with many expressions common to Western rural England but uncommon to most Americans. The inclusion of these vocabulary add richness and character, perhaps even charm, to her work but we do need to be familiar with their meanings.

VOCABULARY FOR PRECIOUS BANE

a power	-	a lot, bunch
ah	-	yes
argle	-	argue
bain't	-	aren't
binna	-	being
blow	-	bloom, blossom
clem	-	hunger
dun	-	do
dunna	-	do not
frommet	-	from
good sadness	-	true or deep feelings
inna	-	isn't
lanthorn	-	lantern
lief	-	rather
liefer	-	like, likely
met	-	might
mommet	-	child
mun	-	must
na	-	not
ool	-	will
oot	-	will you
raught	-	arrived
rid	-	would
seesta	-	sister
shanna	-	should not
summat	-	something
toerts	-	towards
un	-	him
wanna	-	wasn't

Foreword

To conjure, even for a moment, the wistfulness which is the past is like trying to gather in one's arms the hyacinthine colour of the distance. But if it is once achieved, what sweetness!--like the gentle, fugitive fragrance of spring flowers, dried with bergamot and bay. How the tears will spring in the reading of some old parchment--'to my dear child, my tablets and my ring'--or of yellow letters, with the love still fresh and fair in them though the ink is faded--'and so good night, my dearest heart, and God send you happy.' That vivid present of theirs, how faint it grows! The past is only the present become invisible and mute; and because it is invisible and mute, its memoried glances and its murmurs are infinitely precious. We are to-morrow's past. Even now we slip away like those pictures painted on the moving dials of antique clocks--a ship, a cottage, sun and moon, a nosegay. The dial turns, the ship rides up and sinks again, the yellow painted sun has set, and we, that were the new thing, gather magic as we go. The whirr of the spinning-wheels has ceased in our parlours, and we hear no more the treadles of the loom, the swift, silken noise of the flung shuttle, the intermittent thud of the batten. But the imagination hears them, and theirs is the melody of romance.

When antique things are also country things, they are easier to write about, for there is a permanence, a continuity in country life which makes the lapse of centuries seem of little moment.

Shropshire is a county where the dignity and beauty of ancient things lingers long, and I have been fortunate not only in being born and brought up in its magical atmosphere, and in having many friends in farm and cottage who, by pleasant talk and reminiscence have fired the imagination, but also in having the companionship of such a mind as was my father's-- a mind stored with old tales and legends that did not come from books, and rich with an abiding love for the beauty of forest and harvest field, all the more intense, perhaps, because it found little opportunity for expression.

In treating of the old subject of sin-eating I am aware that William Sharpe has forestalled me and has written with consummate art. But sin-eaters were as well known on the Welsh border as in Scotland, and John Aubrey tells of one who lived 'in a cottage on Rosse highway,' and was a 'lamentable poore raskell.'

My thanks are due to the authors of *Shropshire Folk Lore* for the rhymes of 'Green Gravel' and 'Barley Bridge,' and for the verification of various customs which I had otherwise only known by hearsay, and to the Somerset weavers, who recently let me see both hand looms and spinning wheels in use.

Mary Webb, May 1924

Contents

Book One

1.	Sarn Mere	142
2.	Telling the Bees	145
3.	Prue takes the Bidding Letters	153
4.	Torches and Rosemary	155
5.	The First Swath Falls	160
6.	'Saddle Your Dreams Before You Ride 'Em'	166
7.	Pippins and Jargonelles	172

Book Two

1.	Riding to Market	177
2.	The *Mug of Cider*	185
3.	'Or Die In 'Tempting It'	191
4.	The Wizard of Plash	196
5.	The Love-Spinning	200
6.	The Game of Costly Colours	204
7.	'The Maister Be Come'	211
8.	Raising Venus	215
9.	The Game of Conquer	218

Book Three

1.	The Hiring Fair	228
2.	The Baiting	235
3.	'The Best Tall Script, Flourished'	242
4.	Jancis Runs Away	251
5.	Dragon-Flies	267

Book Four

1.	Harvest Home	274
2.	Beguildy Seeks a Seventh Child	286
3.	The Deathly Bane	300
4.	All on a May Morning	308
5.	The Last Game of Conquer	320
6.	The Breaking of the Mere	328
7.	'Open the Gates as wide as the sky'	336

Book One

Chapter One
Sarn Mere

It was at a love-spinning that I saw Kester first. And if, in these new-fangled days, when strange inventions crowd upon us, when I hear tell there is even a machine coming into use in some parts of the country for reaping and mowing, if those that may happen will read this don't know what a love-spinning was, they shall hear in good time. But though it was Jancis Beguildy's love-spinning, she being three-and-twenty at that time and I being two years less, yet it is not the beginning of the story I have set out to tell.

Kester says that all tales, true tales or romancings, go farther back than the days of the child; aye, farther even than the little babe in its cot of rushes. Maybe you never slept in a cot of rushes; but all of us did at Sarn. There is such a plenty of rushes at Sarn, and old Beguildy's missus was a great one for plaiting them on rounded barrel-hoops. They they'd be set on rockers, and a nice clean cradle they made, soft and green, so that the babe could feel as big-sorted as a little caterpillar (painted butterflies-as-is-to-be, Kester calls them) sleeping in its cocoon. Kester's very set about such things. Never will he say caterpillars. He'll say, 'There's a lot of butterflies-as-is-to-be on our cabbages, Prue.' He won't say 'It's winter.' He'll say, 'Summer's sleeping.' And there's no bud little enough nor sad-coloured enough for Kester not to callen it the beginnings of the blow.

But the time is not yet come for speaking of Kester. It is the story of us all at Sarn, of Mother and Gideon and me, and Jancis (that was so beautiful), and Wizard Beguildy, and the two or three other folk that lived in those parts, that I did set out to tell. There were but a few, and maybe always will be, for there's a discouragement about the place. It may be the water lapping, year in and year out--everywhere you look and listen, water; or the big trees waiting and considering on your right hand and on your left; or the unbreathing quiet of the place, as if it was created but an hour gone, and not created for us. Or it may be that the soil is very poor and marshy, with little nature or goodness in the grass, which is ever so where reeds and rushes grow in plenty, and the flower of the paigle. Happen you call it cowslip, but we always named it the paigle, or keys of heaven. It was a wonderful thing to see our meadows at Sarn when the cowslip was in blow. Gold-over they were, so that you would think not even an angel's feet were good enough to walk there. You could make a tossy-ball before a thrush had gone over his song twice, for you'd only got to sit down and gather with both hands. Every way you looked, there was nought but gold, saving towards

Sarn, where the woods began, and the great stretch of grey water, gleaming and wincing in the sun. Neither woods nor water looked darksome in that fine spring weather, with the leaves coming new, and buds the colour of corn in the birch-tops. Only in our oak wood there was always a look of the back-end of the year, their young leaves being so brown. So there was always a breath of October in our May. But it was a pleasant thing to sit in the meadows and look away to the far hills. The larches spired up in their quick green, and the cowslip gold seemed to get into your heart, and even Sarn Mere was nothing but a blue mist in a yellow mist of birch-tops. And there was such a dream on the place that if a wild bee came by, let alone a bumble, it startled you like a shout. If a bee comes in at the window now to my jar of gillyflowers, I can see it all in clear colours, with Plash lying under the sunset, beyond the woods, looking like a jagged piece of bottle glass. Plash Mere was bigger than Sarn, and there wasn't a tree by it, so where there were no hills beyond it you could see the clouds rooted in it on the far side, and I used to think they looked like the white water-lilies that lay round the margins of Sarn half the summer through. There was nothing about Plash that was different from any other lake or pool. There was no troubling of the waters, as at Sarn, nor any village sounding its bells beneath the furthest deeps. It was true, what folks said of Sarn, that there was summat to be felt there.

It was at Plash that the Beguildys lived, and it was at their dwelling, that was part stone house and part cave, that I got my book learning. It may seem a strange thing to you that a woman of my humble station should be able to write and spell, and put all these things into a book. And indeed when I was a young wench there were not many great ladies, even, that could do much more scribing than to write a love-letter, and some could but just write such things as 'This be quince and apple' on their jellies, and others had ado to put their names in the marriage register. Many have come to me, time and again, to write their love-letters for them, and a bitter old task it is, to write other women's love-letters out of your own burning heart.

If it hadna been for Mister Beguildy I never could have written down all these things. He learned me to read and write, and reckon up figures. And though he was a preached-against man, and said he could do a deal that I don't believe he ever could do, and though he dabbled in things that are not good for us to interfere with, yet I shall never forget to thank God for him. It seems to me now a very uncommon working of His power, to put it into Beguildy's heart to learn me. For a wizard could not rightly be called a servant of His, but one of Lucifer's men. Not that Beguildy was wicked, but only empty of good, as if all righteousness was burnt out by the flame of his fiery mind, which must know and intermeddle with mysteries. As for love, he did not know the word. He could read the stars, and tell the future, and he claimed to have laid spirits. Once I asked him where the future was, that he could see it so plain. And he said, 'It lies with the past, child, at the back of Time.' You couldn't ever get the better of Mister Beguildy. But when I told Kester what he said, Kester would not have it so. He said the past and the future were two shuttles in the hands of the Lord, weaving Eternity. Kester was a weaver himself, which may have made him think of it thus. But I think we cannot know what the past and the future are. We are so small and helpless on the earth that is like a green rush cradle where mankind lies, looking up at the stars, but not knowing what they be.

As soon as I could write, I made a little book with a calico cover, and every Sunday I wrote in it any merry time or good fortune we had had in the week, and so kept them. And if times had been troublous and bitter for me, I wrote that down too, and was eased. So when our parson, knowing of the lies that were told of me, bade me write all I could remember in a book, and set down the whole truth and nothing else, I was able to freshen my memory with the things I had put down Sunday by Sunday.

Well, it is all gone over now, the trouble and the struggling. It be quiet weather now, like a still evening with the snow all down, and a green sky, and lambs calling. I sit here by the fire with my Bible to hand, a very old woman and a tired woman, with a task to do before she says good night to this world. When I look out of my window and see the plain and the big sky with clouds standing up on the mountains, I call to mind the thick, blotting woods of Sarn, and the crying of the mere when the ice was on it, and the way the water would come into the cupboard under the stairs when it rose at the time of the snow melting. There was but little sky to see there, saving that which was reflected in the mere; but the sky that is in the mere is not the proper heavens. You see it in a glass darkly, and the long shadows of rushes go thin and sharp across the sliding stars, and even the sun and moon might be put out down there, for, times, the moon would get lost in lily leaves, and, times, a heron might stand before the sun.

Chapter Two
Telling the Bees

My brother Gideon was born in the year when the war with the French began. That was why Father would have him called Gideon, it being a warlike name. Jancis used to say it was a very good name for him, because it was one you couldn't shorten. You can make most names into little love-names, like you can cut down a cloak or a gown for children's wearing. But Gideon you could do nought with. And the name was like the man. I was more set on my brother than most are, but I couldna help seeing that about him. If nobody calls you out of your name, your name's like to be soon out of mind. And most people never even called him by his Christen name at all. They called him Sarn. In Father's life it was old Sarn and young Sarn. But after Father died, Gideon seemed to take the place to himself. I remember how he went out that summer night, and seemed to eat and drink the place, devouring it with his eyes. Yet it was not for love of it, but for what he could get out of it. He was very like Father then, and more like every year, both to look at and in his mind. Saving that he was less tempersome and more set in his ways, he was Father's very marrow. Father's temper got up despert quick, and when it was up he was a ravening lion. Maybe that was what gave Mother that married-all-o'er look. But Gideon I only saw angered, to call angered, three times. Mostly, a look was enough. He'd give you a look like murder, and you'd let him take the way he wanted. I've seen a dog cringing and whimpering because he'd given it one of those looks. Sarns mostly have grey eyes--cold grey like the mere in winter--and the Sarn men are mainly dark and sullen. 'Sullen as a Sarn,' they say about these parts. And they say there's been something queer in the family ever since Timothy Sarn was struck by forkit lightning in the times of the religious wars. There were Sarns about here then, and always have been, ever since there was anybody. Well, Timothy went against his folk and the counsels of a man of God, and took up the wrong side, whichever that was, but it's no matter now. So he was struck by lightning and lay for dead. Being after awhile recovered, he was counselled by the man of God to espouse the safe side and avoid the lightning. But Sarns were ever obstinate men. He kept his side, and as he was coming home under the oak wood he was struck again. And seemingly the lightning got into his blood. He could tell when tempest brewed, long afore it came, and it is said that when a storm broke, the wildfire played about him so none could come near him. Sarns have the lightning in their blood since his day. I wonder sometimes whether it be a true tale, or whether it's too old to be true. It used to seem to me sometimes as if Sarn was too old to be true. The woods and the farm and the church at the other end of the mere were all so old, as if they were in somebody's dream. There was frittening about the place, too, and what with folk being afraid to come there after dusk, and the quiet noise of the fish jumping far out in the water, and Gideon's boat knocking on the steps with little knocks like somebody tapping at the door, and the causeway that ran down into the mere as far as you could see, from just outside our garden gate, being lost in the water, it was a very lonesome old place. Many a time, on Sunday evenings, there came over the water a thin sound of bells. We thought they were the bells of the village down under, but I believe now they were nought but echo bells from our own church. They say that in some places a sound will knock against a wall of trees and come back like a ball.

It was on one of those Sunday evenings, when the thin chimes were sounding along with our own four bells, that we played truant from church for the second time. It being such a beautiful evening, and Father and Mother being busy with the bees swarming, we made it up between us to take dog's leave, and to wait by the lych-gate for Jancis and get her to come with us. For old Beguildy never werrited much about her church-going, not being the best of friends with the parson himself. He sent her off when the dial made it five o'clock every fourth Sunday—for we had service only once a month, the parson having a church at Bramton, where he lived, and another as well, which made it the more wicked of us to play truant—but whether she got there early or late, or got there at all, he'd never ask, let alone catechize her about the sermon. Our Father would catechize us last thing in the evening when our night-rails were on. Father would sit down in the settle with the birch-rod to his hand, and the settle, that had looked such a great piece of furniture all the week, suddenly looked little, like a settle made for a mommet. Whatever Father sat in, he made it look little. We stood barefoot in front of him on the cold quarries, in our unbleached homespun gowns that mother had spun and the journeyman weaver had woven up in the attic at the loom among the apples. Then he'd question us, and when we answered wrongly he made a mark on the settle, and every mark was a stroke with the birch at the end of the cate-chizing. Though Father couldn't read, he never forgot anything. It seemed as if he turned things over in his head all the while he was working. I think he was a very clever man with not enow of things to employ his mind. If he'd had one of the new-fangled weaving machines I hear tell of to look after, it would have kept him content, but there was no talk of such things then. We were all the machines he had, and we wished very heartily every fourth Sunday, and Christmas and Easter, that we were the children of Beguildy, though he was thought so ill of by our parson, and often preached against, even by name.

146

I mind once, when Father leathered us very bad, after the long preaching on Easter Sunday, Gideon being seven and me five, how Gideon stood up in the middle of the kitchen and said, 'I do will and wish to be Maister Beguildy's son, and the devil shall have my soul. Amen.'

Father got his temper up that night, no danger! He shouted at Mother terrible, saying she'd done very poorly with her children, for the girl had the devil's mark on her, and now it seemed as if the boy came from the same smithy. This I know, because Mother told it to me. All I mind is that she went to look very small, and being only little to begin with, she seemed like one of the fairy folk. And she said--'Could I help it if the hare crossed my path? Could I help it?' It seemed so strange to hear her saying that over and over. I can see the room now if I shut my eyes, and most especially if there's a bunch of cowslips by me. For Easter fell late, or in a spell of warm weather that year, and the cowslips were very forrard in sheltered places, so we'd pulled some. The room was all dim like a cave, and the red fire burning still and watchful seemed like the eye of the Lord. There was a little red eye in every bit of ware on the dresser too, where it caught the gleam. Often and often in after years I looked at those red lights, which were echoes of the fire, just as the ghostly bells were reflections of the chime, and I've thought they were like a deal of the outer show of this world. Rows and rows of red, gledy fires, but all shadows of fires. Many a chime of merry bells ringing, and yet only the shadows of bells; only a sigh of sound coming back from a wall of leaves or from the glassy water. Father's eyes caught the gleam too, and Gideon's: but Mother's didna, for she was standing with her back to the fire by the table where the cowslips were, gathering the mugs and plates together from supper. And if it seem strange that so young a child should remember the past so clearly, you must call to mind that Time engraves his pictures on our memory like a boy cutting letters with his knife, and the fewer the letters the deeper he cuts. So few things ever happened to us at Sarn that we could never forget them. Mother's voice clings to my heart like trails of bed-straw that catch you in the lanes. She'd got a very plaintive voice, and soft. Everything she said seemed to mean a deal more than the words, and times it was like a person fumbling in the dark, or going a long way down black passages with a hand held out on this side, and a hand held out on that side, and no light. That was how she said, 'Could I help it if the hare crossed my path--could I help it?'

Everything she said, though it might not have anything merry in it, she smiled a bit, in the way you smile to take the edge off somebody's anger, or if you hurt yourself and won't show it. A very grievous smile it was, and always there. So when Father gave Gideon another hiding for wishing he was Beguildy's boy, Mother stood by the table saying, 'Oh, dunna, Sarn! Hold thy hand, Sarn!' and smiling all the while, seeming to catch at Father's hands with her soft boice. Poor Mother! Oh, my poor Mother! Shall we meet you in the other world, dear soul, and atone to you for our heedlessness?

I'd never forgotten that Easter, but Gideon had, seemingly, for when I remembered him of it, saying we surely durstn't take dog's leave, he said, 'It's nought. We'll make Sexton's Tivvy listen to the sermon for us, so as we can answer well. And I dunna care much if I *am* leathered, so long as I can find some good conkers and beat Jancis, for last time she beat me.'

Conkers, maybe you know, are snail shells, and children put the empty ones on strings, and play like you play with chestnut cobs. Our woods were a grand place for snails, and Gideon had conker matches with lads from as far away as five miles the other side of Plash. He was famous all about, because he played so fiercely, and not like a game at all.

All the bells were sounding when we started that Sunday in June--the four metal bells in the church and the four ghost bells from nowhere. Mother was helping Father with the bees, getting a new skep ready, down where the big chestnut tree was, to put the play of bees in. They'd swarmed in a dead gooseberry bush, and Mother said, with her peculiar smile, 'It be a sign of death.'

But Gideon shouted out-

'A play of bees in May is worth a noble that same day.
A play in June's pretty soon.'

And he said-

'So long as we've got the bees, Mother, we're the better of it, die who may.'

Eh, dear! I'm afraid Gideon had a very *having* spirit, even then. But Father thought he was a sensible lad, and he laughed and said--

'Well, we've got such a mort of bees now, I'm in behopes it wunna be me as has the telling of 'em if anybody does die.'

'Where be your sprigs of rosemary and your Prayer Books and your clean handkerchers?' says Mother.

Gideon had been in behopes to leave them behind, but now he ran to fetch them, and Mother began setting my kerchief to rights over my shoulders. She put in her big brooch with the black stone, that she had when George the Second died, and while she was putting it in she kept saying to herself-- 'Not as it matters what the poor child wears. Dreary, dreary me! But could I help it if the hare crossed my path? Could I help it?'

Whenever she said that, her voice went very mournful and I thought again of somebody in a dark passage, groping.

'Now then, Mother! Hold the skep whilst I keep the bough up,' said Father; 'they've knit so low down.'

I'd lief have stayed, for I dearly loved to see the great tossy-ball of bees' bodies, as rich as a brown Christmas cake, and to hear the heavy sound of them.

We went through the wicket and along the top path, because it was the nighest way to the church, and we wanted to catch Tivvy afore she went in. The coots were out on the mere, and the water was the colour of light, with spears in it.

'Now,' said Gideon, 'we'll run for our lives!'

'What's after us?'

'The people out of the water.'

So we ran for our lives, and got to the church just as the two last bells began their snabbing '*Ting* tong! *Ting* tong!' that always minded me of the birch-rod.

We sat on the flat grave where we mostly sat to play *Conquer*, and the church being on a little hill we could watch the tuthree folks coming along the fields. There was Tivvy with her father, coming from the East Coppy, and Jancis in the flat water-meadows where the big thorn hedges were all in blow. Jancis was a little thing, not tall like me, but you always saw her before you saw other people, for it seemed that the light gathered round her. She'd got golden hair, and all the shadows on her face seemed to be stained with the pale colour of it. I was used to think she was like a white water-lily full of yellow pollen or honey. She'd got a very white skin, creamy white, without any colour unless she was excited or shy, and her face was dimpled and soft, and just the right plumpness. She'd got a red, cool, smiling mouth, and when she smiled the dimples ran each into other. Times I could almost have strangled her for that smile.

She came up to us, very demure, in her flowered bodice and blue skirt and a bunch of blossom in her kerchief.

Although she was only two years older than I was, being of an age with Gideon, she seemed a deal older, for she'd begun to smile at the lads already, and folks said, 'Beguildy's Jancis will soon be courting.' But I know old Beguildy never meant her to get married. He meant to keep her as a bait to draw the young fellows in, for mostly the people that came to him were either young maids with no money or old men who wanted somebody cursed cheap. So at this time, when he saw what a white, blossomy piece Jancis was growing, he encouraged her to dizen herself and sit in the window of the Cave House in case anybody went by up the lane. It was only once in a month of Sundays that anybody did, for Plash was nearly as lonesome as Sarn. He made a lanthorn of coloured glass, too, the colour of red roses, and while Jancis sat in the stone frame of the window he hung it up above her with a great candle in it from foreign parts, not a rushlight such as we used. He had it in mind that if some great gentleman came by to a fair or a cockfight beyond the mountains he might fall in love with her, and then Beguildy planned to bring him in and give him strong ale and talk about charms and spells, and offer at long last to work the charm of raising Venus. It was all written in one of his books: how you went into a dark room and gave the wise man five pound, and he said a charm, and after awhile there was a pink light and a scent of roses, and Venus rose naked in the middle of the room. Only it wouldna have been Venus, but Jancis. The great gentleman, howsoever, was a long while coming, and the only man that saw her in the window was Gideon one winter evening when he was coming back that way from market, because the other road was flooded. He was fair comic-struck about her, and talked of her till I was aweary, he being nineteen at the time, which is a foolish age in lads. Before that, he never took any account of her, but just to tell her this and that as he did with me. But afterwards he was nought but a gauby about her. I could never have believed that such a determined lad, so set in his ways and so clever, could have been thus soft about a girl. But on this evening he was only seventeen, and he just said, 'Take dog's leave oot, Jancis, and come with us after conkers.'

'O' said Jancis, 'I wanted to play "Green Gravel, Green Gravel." '

She'd got a way of saying 'O' afore everything, and it made her mouth look like a rose. But whether she did it for that, or whether she did it because she was slow-witted and timid, I never could tell.

'There's nought to win in Green Gravel,' said Gideon, 'we'll play Conquer.'

'O I wanted Green Gravel! You'll beat me if we play Conquer.'

'Ah. That's why we'll play.'

Tivvy came through the lych-gate then, and we told her what she'd got to do. She was a poor, foolish creature, and she could hardly mind her own name, times, for all its outlandishness, let alone a sermon. But Gideon said, so long as she got an inkling of it he could make up the rest. And he said if she didna remember enough of it he'd twist her arm proper. So she began to cry.

Then we saw Sexton coming across the ploughed field, very solemn, with his long staff, black and white in bands, and we could hear Parson's piebald pony clop-clopping up the lane, so we made off, and left Tivvy with her round chin trembling, and her mouth all crooked with crying, because she knew she'd never remember a word of the sermon. Tivvy at a sermon always used to make me think of our dog being washed. He'd lie down and let the water souse over him, and

she did the same with a sermon. So I knew trouble was brewing.

It was a beautiful evening, with swallows high in the air,
and a powerful smell of may-blossom. When the bells
stopped, ours and the others, we went and looked down into
the water, to see if we could get a sight of the village there,
as we did most Sundays. But there was only our own church
upside down, and two or three stones and crosses the same,
and Parson's pony grazing on its head.

Times, on summer evenings, when the sun was low, the
shadow of the spire came right across the water to our dwelling, and I was used to think it was like the finger of the Lord
pointing at us. We went down into the marshy places and
found plenty of conkers, and Gideon beat Jancis every time,
which was a good thing, for at the end he said he'd play *Green
Gravel*, and they were both pleased. Only we were terrible
late, and nearly missed Tivvy.

'Now, tell!' says Gideon. So she began to cry, and said she
knew nought about it. Then he twisted her arm, and she
screamed out, 'Burning and fuel of fire!'

She must have said that because it was one of the texts
the Sexton was very fond of saying over, keeping time with
tapping his staff the while.

'What else?'

'Nought.'

'I'll twist your arm till it comes off if you dunna think of
any more.'

Tivvy looked artful, like Pussy in the dairy, and said—

'Parson told about Adam and Eve and Noah and
Shemamanjaphet and Jesus in the manger and thirty pieces of
silver.'

Gideon's face went dark.

'There's no sense in it,' he said.

'But she's told you, anyway. You must let her go now.'

So we went home, with the shadow of the spire stretching
all across the water.

Father said—

'What was the text?'

'Burning and fuel of fire.'

'What was the sarmon about?'

Poor Gideon made out a tale of all the things Tivvy had
said. You never heard such a tale! Father sat quite quiet,
and Mother was smiling very painful, standing by the fire,
cooking a rasher.

Suddenly Father shouted out—

'Liar! Liar! Parson called but now, to say was there sickness, there being nobody at church. You've not only taken
dog's leave and lied, but you've made game of *me*.'

His face went from red to purple, and all veined, like raw
meat. It was awful to see. Then he reached for the horsewhip and said—

'I'll give you the best hiding ever you had, my boy!'

He came across the kitchen towards Gideon.

But suddenly Gideon ran at him and bunted into him, and taking him by surprise he knocked him clean over.

Now whether it was that Father had eaten a very hearty supper, after a big day's work with the bees, or whether it was him being in such a rage, and then the surprise of the fall, we never knew. However it was, he was taken with a fit. He never stirred, but lay on his back on the red quarries, breathing so loud and strong that it filled the house, like somebody snoring in the night. Mother undid his Sunday neckcloth, and lifted him up, and put cold water on his face, but it was no manner of use.

The awful snoring went on, and seemed to eat up all other sounds. They went out like rushlights in the wind. There was no more ticking from the clock, nor purring from the cat, nor sizzling from the rasher, nor buzzing from the bee in the window. It seemed to eat up the light, too, and the smell of the white bush-roses outside, and the feeling in my body, and the thoughts I had afore. We'd all come to be just a part of a dark snoring.

'Sarn, Sarn!' cried Mother. 'Oh, Sarn, poor soul, come to thyself!'

She tried to put some Hollands between his lips, but they were set. Then the snore changed to a rattle, very awful to hear, and in a little while it stopped, and there was a dreadful silence, as if all the earth had gone dumb. All the while, Gideon stood like stone, remembering the horsewhip Father meant to beat him with, so he said after. And though he'd never seen anyone die afore, when Father went quiet, and the place dumb, he said in an everyday voice, only with a bit of a tremble--

'He's dead, Mother. I'll go and tell the bees, or we met lose 'em.'

We cried a long while, Mother and me, and when we couldna cry any more, the little sounds came creeping back-- the clock ticking, bits of wood falling out of the fire, and the cat breathing in its sleep.

When Gideon came in again, the three of us managed to get Father on to a mattress, and lap him in a clean sheet. He looked a fine, good-featured man, now that the purple colour was gone from his face.

Gideon locked up, and went round to look the beasts and see all well.

'Best go to bed now, Mother,' he said. 'All's safe, and the beasts in their housen. I told every skep of bees, and I can see they're content, and willing for me to be maister.'

Chapter Three
Prue takes the Bidding Letters

In those days there was little time for the mourners to think of their sorrow till after the funeral. There was a deal to do. There was the mourning to make, and before that, if a family hadn't had the weaver lately, there was the cloth to weave and dye. We hadn't had the weaver for a good while, so we were very short of stuff.

Mother told Gideon he must go and fetch the old weaver, who lived at Lullingford, by the mountains, and went out weaving by the day or the week. Gideon saddled Bendigo, Father's horse, and picked up the riding whip with a queer kind of smile. As soon as he was gone, Mother and I began to bake. For it wasn't only the weaver that must be fed, but the women we were going to bid to the funeral sewing-bee. They would come for love, as was the custom, but we must feed them.

It seemed lonesome that night without Gideon. He had to bait and sleep in Lullingford, but he came back in good time next day, and I heard the sound of the hoofs on the yard cobbles through my spinning. We were hard at it, getting yarn ready for the old man. He came riding after Gideon on a great white horse, very bony, which put me in mind of the rider on a white horse in the Bible. He was the oldest man you could see in a month of Sundays. He hopped about like a magpie, prying here and there over the loom, looking at his shuttle for all the world like a pie that's pleased with some bright thing it's found. I had to take his meals up to the attic, for he wouldna waste time leaving off for them. It was a good thing the apples were all done, so he could hop about the loft without let or hindrance.

'Now you must take the bidding letters for the sewing, Prue.' Mother told me.

'Can I take one to Jancis, Mother?'

'No. We munna spend money paying for a bidding letter to Jancis. But she can come, and welcome.'

'I'll go and tell her. She sews very nice.'

'But not so well as you, my dear. Whatsoever's wrong, thee sews a beautiful straight seam, Prue.'

I ran off, mighty pleased with praise, which came seldom my way. I met Gideon by the lake.

'Taking the biddings?' he said.

'Ah.'

'Jancis coming?'

'Ah.'

'Well, when you be there, ask Beguildy to lend us the white oxen for the funeral, oot?'

'To lug Father to the church?'

'Ah. And when we've buried Father, you and me must talk a bit. There's a deal to think of for the future. All these bidding letters, now, you met as well have written 'em and saved a crown.'

I wondered what he meant, seeing he knew I couldna write a word, but I knew he'd say in his own time, and not afore, that being his way. Nobody would have thought he was but seventeen; he seemed five-and-twenty by the way he spoke, so choppy and quick, but ever so quiet.

When I got to Plash, Jancis was sitting in the garden, spinning. She said we could borrow the beasts, that were hers by right, being a present from her Granny, though she never had the strength to control them in a waggon nor to drive plough with 'em like I had in the years after. But she got a bit of pin money by hiring them out for wakes, when Beguildy didna pocket it. They dressed up beautiful with flowers and ribbons after they'd been scrubbed.

I went in to speak to Beguildy.

'Father's dead, Mister Beguildy,' I said.

'So, so! What's that to me, dear soul?'

He was a very strange man, always, was Beguildy.

'Tell me what I knew not, child,' he said.

'Did you know, then?'

'Ah, I knew thy feyther was gone. Didna he go by me on a blast of air last Sunday evening, crying out, thin and spiteful, "You owe me a crown, Beguildy!" Tell me sommat fresh, girl--strange things. Now if you could say that the leaves be all fallen this day of June, and my damsons ripe for market; or that the mere hath dried; or that man lusteth no more to hurt his love; or that Jancis looketh no more at her own face in Plash Pool, there would be telling, yes! But for your dad, it is nought. I cared not for the man.'

And taking up his little hammer, he beat on a row of flints that he had, till the room was all in a charm. Every flint had its own voice, and he knew them as a shepherd the sheep, and it was his custom when the talk was not to his mind to beat out a chime upon them.

'I came to see if we could borrow the beasts for our waggon. Jancis said yes.'

'You mun pay.'

'How much, mister?'

'The same as for wakes, a penny a head. So you be taking the biddings? Now who did your mam pay to write 'em?'

'Parson wrote 'em for us, and Mother put a crown in the poorbox.'

'Dear soul! The bitter waste! I'd have wrote 'em very clear and fine for half the money. I can write the tall script and the dwarf, round or square, red or black. Parson can only do the sarmon script, and a very poor script it be.'

'I wish I could write, Mister Beguildy.'

'Oh, you!'

He laughed in a very peculiar way he had, soft and light, at the top of his head.

'It's not for children,' he said.

But I thought about it a deal. I thought it would be a fine thing to sit by the fire, in the settle corner, and write bidding letters and love-letters and market bills, or even a verse for a tombstone, and to do the round or the square, tall or little, red or black, and sermon script too if I'd a mind. I thought when anybody like Jancis angered me by being so pretty, I'd do her letters very crabbed, and with no red at all. But I knew that was wicked of me, for poor Jancis couldna help being pretty.

Then Beguildy went off to cure an old man's corns, and Jancis and I played lovers, but Jancis said I did it very bad, and she thought Gideon would do it a deal better.

Chapter Four
Torches and Rosemary

It was a still, dewy summer night when we buried Father. In our time there was still a custom round about Sarn to bury people at night. In our family it had been done for hundreds of years. I was busy all day decking the waggon with yew and the white flowering laurel, that has such a heavy, sweet smell. I pulled all the white roses and a tuthree pinks that were in blow, and made up with daisies out of the hay grass. While I pulled them, I thought how angered Father would have been to see me there, trampling it, and I could scarcely help looking round now and again to see if he was coming.

After we'd milked, Gideon went for the beasts, and I put black streamers round their necks, and tied yew boughs to their horns. It had to be done carefully, for they were the Long-horn breed, and if you angered them, they'd hike you to death in a minute.

The miller was one bearer, and Mister Callard, of Callard's Dingle, who farmed all the land between Sarn and Plash, was another. Then there were our two uncles from beyond the mountains.

Gideon, being chief mourner, had a tall hat with black streamers and black gloves and a twisted black stick with streamers on it. They took a long while getting the coffin out, for the doors were very narrow and it was a big, heavy coffin. It had always been the same at all the Sarn funerals, yet nobody ever seemed to think of making the doors bigger.

Sexton went first with his hat off and a great torch in his hand. Then came the cart, with Miller's lad and another to lead the beasts. The waggon was mounded up with leaves and branches, and they all said it was a credit to me. But I could only mind how poor Father was used to tell me to take away

155

all those nasty weeds out of the house. And now we were taking him away, jolting over the stones, from the place where he was maister. I was all of a puzzle with it. It did seem so unkind, and disrespectful, as well, leaving the poor soul all by his lonesome at the other end of the mere. I was glad it was sweet June weather, and not dark.

We were bound to go the long way round, the other being only a foot road. When we were come out of the fold-yard, past the mixen and were in the road, we took our places--Gideon behind the coffin by himself, then Mother and me in our black poke bonnets and shawls, with Prayer Books and branches of rosemary in our hands. Uncles and Miller and Mister Callard came next, all with torches and boughs of rosemary.

It was a good road, and smoother than most--the road to Lullingford. Parson used to say it was made by folk who lived in the days when the Redeemer lived. Romans, the name was. They could make roads right well, whatever their name was. It went along above the water, close by the lake; and as we walked solemnly onwards, I looked into the water and saw us there. It was a dim picture, for the only light there was came from the waning, clouded moon, and from the torches. But you could see, in the dark water, something stirring, and gleams and flashes, and when the moon came clear we had our shapes, like the shadows of fish gliding in the deep. There was a great heap of black, that was the waggon, and the oxen were like clouds moving far down, and the torches were flung into the water as if we wanted to dout them.

All the time, as we went, we could hear the bells ringing the corpse home. They sounded very strange over the water in the waste of night, and the echoes sounded yet stranger. Once a white owl came by, like a blown feather for lightness and softness. Mother said it was Father's spirit looking for its body. There was no sound but the bells and the creaking of the wheels, till Parson's pony, grazing in the glebe, saw the dim shapes of the oxen a long way off, and whinnied, not knowing, I suppose, but what they were ponies too, and being glad to think, in the lonesomeness of the night, of others like herself near by.

At last the creaking stopped at the lych-gate. They took out the coffin, resting it on trestles, and in the midst of the heavy breathing of the bearers came the promising words--

'I am the resurrection and the life.'

They were like quiet rain after drought. Only I began to wonder, how should we come again in the resurrection? Should we come clear, or dim, like in the water? Would Father come in a fit of anger, as he'd died, or as a little boy running to Grandma with a bunch of primmy-roses? Would Mother smile the same smile, or would she have found a light in the dark passage? Should I still be fast in a body I'd no

156

mind for, or would they give us leave to weave ourselves bodies to our own liking out of the spinnings of our souls?

The coffin was moved to another trestle, by the graveside, and a white cloth put over it. Our best tablecloth, it was. On the cloth stood the big pewter tankard full of elderberry wine. It was the only thing Mother could provide, and it was by good fortune that she had plenty of it, enough for the funeral feast and all, since there had been such a power of elderberries the year afore. It looked strange in the doubtful moonlight, standing there on the coffin, when we were used to see it on the table, with the colour of the Christmas Brand reflected in it.

Parson came forrard and took it up, saying--

'I drink to the peace of him that's gone.'

Then everybody came in turn, and drank good health to Father's spirit.

At the coffin foot was our little pewter measure full of wine, and a crust of bread with it, but nobody touched them.

The Sexton stepped forrard and said--

'Be there a Sin Eater?'

And Mother cried out--

'Alas no! Woe's me! There is no Sin Eater for poor Sarn. Gideon gainsayed it.'

Now it was still the custom at that time, in our part of the country, to give a fee to some poor man after a death, and then he would take bread and wine handed to him across the coffin, and eat and drink, saying--

'I give easement and rest now to thee, dear man, that ye walk not over the fields nor down the by-ways. And for thy peace I pawn my own soul.'

And with a calm and grievous look he would go to his own place. Mostly, my Grandad used to say, Sin Eaters were such as had been Wise Men or layers of spirits, and had fallen on evil days. Or they were poor folk that had come, through some dark deed, out of the kindly life of men, and with whom none would trade, whose only food might oftentimes be the bread and wine that had crossed the coffin. In our time there were none left around Sarn. They had nearly died out, and they had to be sent for to the mountains. It was a long way to send, and they asked a big price, instead of doing it for nothing as in the old days. So Gideon said--

'We'll save the money. What good would the man do?'

But Mother cried and moaned all night after. And when the Sexton said 'Be there a Sin Eater?' she cried again very pitifully, because Father had died in his wrath, with all his sins upon him, and besides, he had died in his boots, which is a very unket thing and bodes no good. So she thought he had great need of a Sin Eater, and she would not be comforted.

Then a strange, heart-shaking thing came to pass.
Gideon stepped up to the coffin and said--
'There *is* a Sin Eater.'
'Who then? I see none,' said Sexton.
'I ool be the Sin Eater.'
He took up the little pewter measure full of darkness, and
he looked at Mother.
'Oot turn over the farm and all to me if I be the Sin Eater,
Mother?' he said.
'No, no! Sin Eaters be accurst!'
'What harm, to drink a sup of your own wine and chumble
a crust of your own bread? But if you dunna care, let be. He
can go with the sin on him.'
'No, no! Sin Eaters be accurst!'
'What harm, to drink a sup of your own wine and chumble
a crust of your own bread? But if you dunna care, let be. He
can go with the sin on him.'
'No, no! Leave un go free, Gideon! Let un rest, poor
soul! You be in life and young, but he'm cold and helpless, in
the power of Satan. He went with all his sins upon him, in his
boots, poor soul! If there's none else to help, let his own lad
take pity.'
'And you'll give me the farm, Mother?'
'Yes, yes, my dear! What be the farm to me? You can
take all, and welcome.'
Then Gideon drank the wine all of a gulp, and swallowed
the crust. There was no sound in all the place but the sound
of his teeth biting it up.
Then he put his hand on the coffin, standing up tall in the
high black hat, with a gleaming pale face, and he said--

'I give easement and rest now to thee, dear man. Come
not down the lanes nor in our meadows. And for thy peace I
pawn my own soul. *Amen.*'

There was a sigh from everybody then, like the wind in dry
bents. Even the oxen by the gate, it seemed to me, sighed as
they chewed the cud.
But when Gideon said, 'Come not down the lanes nor in our
meadows,' I thought he said it like somebody warning off a
trespasser.
Now it was time to throw the rosemary into the grave.
Then they lowered the coffin in, and all threw their burning
torches down upon it, and douted them.
It was over at long last, and we went home by the shortest
way, only Gideon going by the road with the waggon. We
were a tidy few, for all that had been at the church came
back for the funeral feast. There was the smith, and the ox-
driver from Plash Farm, and the shepherd from the Mountain,

and the miller's man and a good few women, as well as those I spoke of afore.

Mother had asked Tivvy to mind the fire and see to the kettles for making spiced ale and posset, for the air struck chill along the water at that time of night.

When we raught home there was Missus Beguildy as well, and Jancis. They had a nice gledy fire, and the horn of ale set upon it all ready. She was a kind soul, Missus Beguildy, but sorely misliked through being the wife of a wizard, a preached-against man. She was never invited to weddings nor baptisms. But at a burying, when the harm's on the house already, what ill can anybody do? Missus Beguildy dearly loved an outing. She'd have liked to live in Lullingford and keep a shop, and go to church twice of a Sunday, and sing in the choir. She'd no faith at all in her goodman's spells, though she never said so, except to me and a tuthree she knew well. Once, a long while after this, when there'd been trouble at the Stone House, which you'll hear of in good time, when she quarrelled with Beguildy, I went in by chance and found her with Lady Camperdine's bottle (in which he said he'd got the old lady's ghost), shaking it as if it was an ill-mixed sauce, so that I thought the cork would come out, and shouting, 'I'll learn ye! I'll learn ye! Lady Camperdine indeed! Plash water! That's what's in this here bottle. Plash water and nought else.'

It was seldom anybody saw Missus Beguildy. She was always out with the fowl or the ducks, or digging the garden, or fishing. She was a good fisherwoman. If it hadna been for her, they'd have clemmed, for Beguildy never reckoned to do anything but wizardry. She'd baked us a batch of funeral cakes in case we hadna enough, and she was so kind and comely, being fair, like Jancis, and plump, and the posset she made was so good, that everybody forgot she was the wizard's wife, even Parson.

'I'm to take back the cattle, my dear,' she said to Mother; 'hay harvest, we use 'em a deal.'

'Bin you started?'

'Ah. Bin you?'

'I start to-morrow,' said Gideon.

Everybody looked at him, tall in the doorway, with a kind of power in him. And it seemed to me that everybody drew away a bit, as if from summat untoert.

Parson got up to go.

'It's to-morrow now, young Sarn,' he said. 'See you do well in it, and in all the to-morrows.'

'To-morrow! O to-morrow!' said Jancis. 'It be a word of promise.'

She yawned, and all in a minute her mouth was a rose, and I knew I couldna abide her.

'One song!' Sexton spoke very solemn. 'One holy song afore we part.'

So we stood up about the table, where the twelve candles were guttering low, and we sang--

> With a turf all at your head, dear man,
> An another at your feet,
> Your good deeds and your bad ones all
> Before the Lord shall meet.

There being a sign more men than women, the song sounded deep, like bees in a lime-tree. Jancis and Tivvy sang very clear and high, and cold too, as if they didna mind at all that the poor corpse lay out yonder with only turfs for company.

Then there was a trampling and a traversing, and they all went out, Mother standing by the door the while, doling out the funeral cakes. These were made of good sponge, with plenty of eggs, coffin-shaped and lapped up in black-edged paper.

By this the birds were singing very loud and clear, with a ringing, echoing noise. Our chimneys lay in the mere, which meant that it was sunrise. There was a cuckoo in the oak wood, and the first corncrake spoke up from the hay grass, very masterful.

Gideon said--

'It be too late for sleep now. To-morrow be come. Let's go down into the orchard. I want to tell you what I've planned out.'

Little did I think, as I followed him down into the orchard, where was neither blossom nor fruit, what those plans were to mean for us all.

Chapter Five
The First Swath Falls

We climbed up into the old pippin tree, where we had a favourite place between the boughs. Looking at Gideon's face among the bright leaves, I thought it was very queer to think of all those sins being on him. Ever since Father was a little baby, roaring and beating on his cot of rushes, on through the time when he was a lad, taking dog's leave from church, and after, when he went cockfighting and courting, all the evil he did, Gideon had got to carry. All his rages were Gideon's rages.

'Now, Prue,' says Gideon, 'listen what I be going to tell ye. You and me has got to get on.'

'And Mother?'

'Oh, well, Mother too. But she's old.'

'She'd like to get on though, sure.'

'That be neither here nor there. If we get on, she will. You and me ha' got to work, Prue.'

'I amna afeered of work,' I said.

'Well, there'll be a plenty. I want to make money on the place--a mort of money. Then, when the time's ripe, we'll sell it. Then we'll go to Lullingford and buy a house, and you shall hold up your head with the best, and be a rich lady.'

'I dunna mind all that about being rich and holding up my head.'

'Well, you *must* mind. And I'll be churchwarden and tell the Rector what to do, and say who's to go in the stocks, and who's to go in the almshousen, and vote for the parliament men. And when any wench has a baby that's a love-child, you'll go and scold her.'

'I'd liefer play with the baby.'

'Anybody can play with a baby. None but a great lady can scold. And we'll buy a grand house. I hanna put my eye on one yet, but there be time enow. And a garden with a man to see to it, and serving-wenches, and the place full of grand furniture and silver plate and china.'

'I dearly like pretty china,' I said. 'Can we get some of them new cups and saucers from Staffordshire, with little people on 'em?'

'You can get anything you like, and a gold thimble and a press full of gowns into the bargain. Only you mun help me first. It'll take years and years.'

'But couldna we stop at Sarn, and get just a little bit of new furniture and china, and do without so many maids and men?'

'No. There's not enow of folks at Sarn, saving at the Wake, and that's only once a year. What's once a year? And what use being chief if there's nobody to be chief of? "Chief among ten thousand." That's a good sounding text. I'd lief be chief among ten thousand.'

'I wonder if it be the lightning in you,' I said, 'makes you feel like that?'

I always used to think he looked as if he'd got it in him when there was anything out of the common going on. His eyes would be all of a blaze, but cold too. And he'd make you feel as if you wanted what he wanted, though you didna. Times, when he wanted to look for badger-earths in the woods, he made me think I did too. And all the while, what I wanted in my own self was to go and gather primmyroses.

'Well, it'll take a deal of lightning in the blood to do what I'm set to do,' he said. 'The place never did more than keep us, Mother says. And Father left nought--not but just enough to pay the weaver and Sexton and buy the wax candles and gloves and that for the burying.'

'Whatever shall we do, if we'd only just enough afore,' I wondered, 'and Father to work for us? We can never put by money, lad.'

'I shall do what he did and a deal more beside.'

'You never can.'

'I can do all as I've a mind to do. I've got such a power in me that nought but death can bind it. And with you to give a hand--'

He stopped a bit there, and pulled a leaf, and tore it.

'Being as how things are, you'll never marry, Prue.'

My heart beat soft and sad. It seemed such a terrible thing never to marry. All girls got married. Jancis would. Tivvy would. Even Miller's Polly, that always had a rash or a hoost or the ringworm or summat, would get married. And when girls got married, they had a cottage, and a lamp, maybe, to light when their man came home, or if it was only candles it was all one, for they could put them in the window, and he'd think 'There's my missus now, lit the candles!' And then one day Mrs. Beguildy would be making a cot of rushes for 'em, and one day there'd be a babe in it, grand and solemn, and bidding letters sent round for the christening, and the neighbours coming round the babe's mother like bees round the queen. Often, when things went wrong, I'd say to myself, 'Ne'er mind, Prue Sarn! There'll come a day when you'll be queen in your own skep.' So I said--

'Not wed, Gideon? Oh, ah! I'll wed for sure.'

'I'm afeered nobody'll ask you, Prue.'

'Not ask me? What for not?'

'Because--oh, well, you'll soon find out. But you can have a house and furniture and all just the same, if you give a hand in the earning of 'em.'

'But not a 'usband, nor a babe in a cot of rushes?'

'No.'

'For why?'

'Best ask Mother for why. Maybe she can tell you why the hare crossed her path. But I'm main sorry for ye, Prue, and I be going to make you a rich lady, and maybe when we've gotten a deal of gold, we'll send away for some doctor's stuff for a cure. But it'll cost a deal, and you must work well and do all I tell you. You're a tidy, upstanding girl enough, Prue, and but for that one thing the fellows ud come round like they will round Jancis.'

I thought about it a bit, while the water lapped on the banks at the foot of the orchard. Then I said I'd do all Gideon wanted.

'You mun swear it, Prue, a solemn oath on the Book. Maybe, if you didna, you'd tire and give over soon. And I'll swear what I promised, too.'

He went into the house to fetch the Book. I sat still and listened to the rooks going over to the rookery at the back of the house, beyond the garden and the rickyard. They were coming back from their breakfast in the fields away towards Plash. I wanted my breakfast, too; for whoever's dead, we poor mortals clem. And as I listened to the sleepy sound of

162

the cawing, and the flapping of their wings when they came over low down, I thought it seemed a criss-cross sort of world, where you bury your Father at night, and straightway begin to think of breakfast and housen and gold with the first light of dawn; where you've got to go cursed all your life long because a poor silly hare looked at your Mother afore you were born; where a son, eating his Mother's batch-cake and drinking of her brewing, loads his poor soul with all his Father's sins.

Gideon came running back with the great Book in his hands, very heavy, and fastened with a silver clasp.

'Come down, Prue, and swear,' he said. 'Now hold the Book.'

I asked him if he was sure Mother would give us leave to do it.

'Give us leave? It's not for her to give us leave. She canna hinder me. The farm be mine. Didna you hear her say so when I took the sin upon me?'

'But will you make Mother abide by that?'

'Will folk pawn their souls for nought? Is another's sin sweet in the mouth that I should eat it save at a price? The farm be mine for ever and ever, until I choose to sell it. Now swear! Say--

> "I promise and vow to obey my brother Gideon Sarn and to hire myself out to him as a sarvant, for no money, until all that he wills be done. And I'll be as biddable as a prentice, a wife, and a dog, I swear it on the Holy Book. Amen.'"

So I said it. Then Gideon said--

> 'I swear to keep faith with my sister, Prue Sarn, and share all with her when we've won through, and give her money up to fifty pound, when we've sold Sarn, to cure her. Amen.'

After we'd done, I felt as if Sarn Mere was flowing right over us, and I shivered as if I'd got an ague.

'What ails you?' says Gideon. 'Best go and light the fire if you be cold, and get the breakfast. We can talk while we eat. Mother's asleep. There's a deal to say yet.'

So I went in and lit the fire, and set the table as nice as I could, for it seemed a bit of comfort in a dark place. I wondered if it would be unfeeling to pull a few rosebuds to put in the middle. And seeing that it wasna unfeeling to eat and drink, I thought it wouldna hurt to pull a rose or two.

When Gideon came in from the milking, we sat down, and he told me all that was in his mind. First, I was to learn to make cheeses as well as butter. Then he was going to make some withy panniers for Bendigo, and every market day he'd ride to Lullingford with butter and eggs, cheeses and honey-comb, fruit and vegetables, and even flowers.

'Them roses, now,' he said, 'you could bunch 'em up, and they'd bring in a bit.'

Times there'd be dressed poultry and ducks, rabbits, fish, and mushrooms.

'You'll see, Prue, we'll make a deal,' he said.

'But what a journey! Thirty mile in the day.'

'I'll plough a bit of land to grow corn for Bendigo. As for me, I'm never tired.'

When we'd saved a bit, we were to buy another cow. She'd calve in the spring, and then there'd be two cows milking when one was dry. That ud mean more market butter. After that, we were to buy two oxen to plough and turn the flail and lug manure, and save hiring Beguildy's beasts. When our sow farrowed, we were to keep all the piglets and turn them loose in the oakwoods, and Mother was to take her knitting and mind them. Then there'd be a deal of bacon for market, over and above what we could eat. We'd only got five sheep, but Gideon said we'd mend that by keeping all the lambs, and so have wool to sell and a big flock of sheep next year. Mother and me were to spin yarn all winter, and he'd sell it at the draper's or change it for things we were bound to have at the grocer's, such as salt for curing, yeast and sugar. Soap we made ourselves out of lye. Rushlights we made too, out of fat and large dry rushes. Rye we had, and one small field of wheat. Father used to take a few sacks at a time to be ground at the mill where Tivvy's uncle lived.

'I shall grow more corn, acres of corn,' he said, 'and take it to the mill in the ox-wain. Whatsoever the French do, corn wunna come amiss. And though it's cheap now, it wunna be if they tax it, which I hear tell is more than likely. It'll be better, a power, to have one acre under wheat then than to be coddling about with twenty acres under ought else. We'll grow hops as well, and never be short of a drop of good ale, for though I mean to work you, Prue, I wunna clem you. Good plain food, as much as you can eat, but no fallals. The rough honey after we've put by the best for market, fruit when it's cheap, bacon and taters and bread, and eggs and butter when the roads are too bad for market.'

'I shall put up a prayer for bad roads,' I said.

Gideon looked at me very sharp, but seeing it was only my fun, he laughed.

'A' right, but it'll take the Devil's own weather to stop me.'

He'd got a plan that I should learn to do sums and keep accounts and write. I was glad, for I dearly loved the thought of being able to read books, and especially the Bible. It always werrited me in church when Sexton read out of the

Bible, for no matter what he read, it all sounded like a bee in a bottle. It didna matter when he was reading--'And he took unto him a wife and begat Aminadab . . .' for it was nought to me if he did. But when there were things to be read with a sound in 'em like wind in the aspen tree, it seemed a pitiful thing that he should mouth it over so, being very big-sorted at being able to read at all. I wanted to be able to read

'Or ever the silver cord be loosed'

for myself, and savour it. It would be grand to be able to write, too, and put down all such things as I wanted to keep in mind. So when Gideon said I was to learn, I was joyfully willing.

'But if Mister Beguildy learns me, how can I pay?' I said.

'You can dig taters for 'em, and give a hand in the hay, and drive plough for 'em now and again. Beguildy's so mortal lazy, and so big-sorted with being a wise man, there's not a hand's turn of work in the man. Mooning, mooning! A salve for every sore, he's got, saving for idleness. You be strong. You can pretty near dig spade for spade with me. Pay that way. And if you've a mind, you can put on your black and go and ask him this evening.'

He went off to the hay meadow with his scythe, and I set about my work with a will, and should have sung a bit, but called poor Father to mind. It made me gladsome to be getting some education, it being like a big window opening. And out of that window who knows what you metna see?

When I took Gideon's nooning, going through the rookery, I called to mind that we'd never told the rooks about a death in the place. It's an old ancient custom to tell them. Folk say if you dunna, a discontent comes over them, and they fall into a melancholoy and forget to come home. So in a little while there are your ellums with the nests still like dark fruit on the sky, but all silent and deserted. And though rooks do a deal of mischief, it's very unlucky to lose them, and the house they leave never has any prosperation after. So I remembered Gideon of this, and we went to the rookery.

They were the biggest ellum trees I've ever seen, both common and wych ellums. Under them it was all dimmery with summer leaves. The ground was green with celandine, that had just left blowing, and enchanter's nightshade, not quite in blow. The leaves were white with droppings. It was a very still, hot day, with only a little breeze rocking the very tops of the trees, and a sleepy caw coming down to us time and again. I used to like to come to the rookery on days like this, after tea, when I'd cleaned myself. And on Ascension Day in special I liked to come and watch if they worked. For they say no rook'll work on Ascension Day. And sure enough I never saw them bring even a stick on that day, but they seemed very thoughtful and holy in their minds, sitting each in his tree like Parson in pulpit.

'Ho, rooks!' shouted Gideon. 'Father's dead, and I be maister, and I've come to say as you shall keep your housen in peace, and I'll keep you safe from all but my own gun, and you're kindly welcome to bide.'

The rooks peered down at him over their nests, and when he'd done there was a sudden clatter of wings, and they all swept up into the blue sky with a great clary, as if they were considering what was said. In a while they came back, and settled down very serious and quiet. So we knew they meant to bide.

When we were back in the field, Gideon laughed a bit, while he was whetting his scythe on the hone, and he said--

'I'm glad they mean stopping. I be despert fond of rooky-pie.'

With that, he swept the scythe through the grass, thinnish and full of ox-eye daisies, and sighing with a dry sound. And because the grass was so thin, you could watch the scythe, like a flash of steely light, through the standing crop before the swath fell. And it seems to me now that it was like the deathly will of God, which is ever waiting behind us till the hour comes to mow us down; yet not in unkindness, but because it is best for us that we leave growing in the meadow, and be brought into His safe rickyard, and thatched over warm with His everlasting loving-kindness.

Chapter Six
'Saddle Your Dreams Before You Ride 'Em'

So soon as I'd milked, Gideon being still hard at it in the meadow, I went upstairs and put on my black, and my mob-cap. I never wore it to work in, to save washing, and folk thought I was a heathen, pretty near, what with no mob-cap and no shoes or stockings most of the time, but bare feet or clogs. Gideon could whittle a clog right well, and they be grand for doing mucky work like I did. I'd made me a sacking gown, too, short to the knee, for cleaning the beast-housen in. I know everybody called me the barn-door savage of Sarn. But I remembered the beautiful house at Lullingford that was to be, and the flowered gowns and dimity curtains and china, I didna take it to heart much.

I was very choice of my homespun gown with the cross-over, with a new mob-cap trimmed with little sausages made of sarsnet, very new-fangled. So I did my hair in ringlets-- one on each side and two at the back, down to my waist.

I was comfortable in my mind, thinking how we were going to send away for simples to make me as beautiful as a fairy. While I milked, I thought about it, and while I cleaned the sties, and while I scrubbed the kitchen quarries.

Mother winnocked a bit, to hear I was off to Plash, for she was low and melancholy from abiding under the shadow of death. She'd been so used to humouring a tempersome man that she felt as restless as you do when you've just cast off the second stocking-toe of a pair. She'd sit quiet a bit in the chimney corner, and you'd hear the wheel whirring softly, like a little lych-fowl. Then suddenly she'd give over spinning, and wring her hands, that always made me think of a mole's little hands, lifted up to God when it be trapped. And she'd say, 'Sunday was a week, he had no bacon to his tea! Sunday was a fortnit, he didna like the dumplings, and no wonder, for they were terrible sad, Prue. Twice I o'er-boiled his eggs in that last week, and the new smock, Prue--'

At that, she'd cry a long while.

'I hivered and hovered over it, Prue, so he died afore it was done. Oh, my dear, to think on it! It wanted but the shoulder-pieces and the cuffs and it would ha' been the best smock ever I made. But I hivered and hovered, and he couldna bide any longer. He heard the mighty voice, child, calling among the ellums out yonder, and he couldna tarry for his smock, poor soul. All my stitches for nought.'

'Now, Mother, you mun finish it for Gideon,' I said. 'It'll fit Gideon right well, for he's a fine big man, though not so broad as Father. But he'll fill out. Come his eighteenth birthday, I shouldna wonder but he'll look right well in it. So you'd best hurry up.'

'Well,' she said, 'well, there's sense in that, child. He took the sin, to wear all his life long. He shall have the smock.'

She fetched Gideon's Sunday coat, and took the smock out of the dresser drawer, to measure it.

I sent up a wish that they might be enough of a size to content her. And so they were, and she quieted down again, and set off once more, whirring like a little lych-fowl.

But it wunna for long. She gave me a look, time and again, while I was putting on my mittens, and said--

'The ringlets be right nice, Prue.' And then: 'You've got a very tidy figure, child.'

And all in a minute she bent two-double over the wheel and began the old weariful cry--

'Could I help it if the hare crossed my path; could I help it?'

'Oh, Mother, Mother!' I beseeched her, 'give over crying for what we canna mend. I canna bear to hear you cry, my dear. Mother! Look ye! I dunna mind at all. There, there now, my lamb!' (I was used to called her that, because she seemed so little and so lost.) 'There, dunna take it to heart. Listen what I'll tell you! *I'd as lief have a hare-shotten lip as not!*' With that, I ran out of the house and through the wicket and up the wood path, roaring-crying.

I cried so loud that there was a whirr of wings on this side and on that, and far up the glade a coney heard me, and sat up in the middle of the path like a Christian, with one paw held up, just as Parson does, giving the blessing. Only it was a curse that his cousin, the hare, gave me.

I wondered why it cursed me so. Was it of its own free will and wish, or did the devil drive it? Did God begrutch me an 'usband and a cot of rushes, that He'd let it be so? In the years after, it did seem a queer thing that I should be obliged to work weekdays and Sundays so as to earn enough money to put straight what a silly hare had put crooked. And I knew it would take a great deal of money to cure a hare-shotten lip. There was a kind of sour laughter in the thought of it. It called to mind the blackish autumn evenings, when grouse rise from the bitter marsh and fly betwixt the withered heather and the freezing sky, and laugh. Old harsh men laugh that way at the falling down of an enemy. And the good ladies of a town, big with stiff flowered silks and babes righteously begotten, laughed so behind their fans when they went to the prison to see a lovely harlot whipped. With that kind of bitterness a man might laugh when he was dying of a wound gotten in the king's cause, and one came busily in while the Parson was reading the prayer for the dying, and cried out, 'The king doth give you an earldom, and sends you a bidding letter to his palace.'

Ah! Those be the ways grouse laugh, and that was how I laughed in those days. But now I sit here between the hearth and the window, with the tea brewing for one that will be home afore sundown, and the clouds standing upon the mountains, and when I laugh, I laugh easy, like the woodpecker in spring. He was ever a laugher, was the woodpecker, and a right merry laugher too. He'll fly into an ellum tree, and laugh to see it so green. And he'll fly into an ash, and laugh to see it so bare, with only the black buds and no leaves. And then he'll fly into an oak, and laugh fit to burst to see the young brown leaves. Ah, the woodpecker's a good laugher, and the laughter's sweet as a sound nut. If we can laugh so at the end of long living, we've not lived in vain.

But that evening I laughed like the grouse, and my heart was rebellious within me.

Yet I could not but be pleased to think of the writing. I was glad also because it would give me a hold over Gideon, since if he was too harsh with Mother and me, I could be a bit awkward about the writing. I ran along by the water, feeling light and easy in my best sandal shoes, thinking how I'd work to get the stuff that was to make me as beautiful as a fairy, and how in a while there'd come a lover, and the axings would be put up in church, and in another while I'd sit in my oun houseplace with my foot on a rocker and with a babe, grand

and solemn, on my knee, better than all the French wax dolls they told of, that I'd never seen, but wanted very bad.

I was contented to see the coots swimming about with a trail of coot chickens after them, for all the world as if they were on a string. And I laughed to see the heron that lived on the far side of the water, and had got a missus and a nest there, standing knee-deep among the lilies, fair comic-struck. In after days I saw Gideon look like that, time and again, when he'd lief talk to Jancis and couldna call to mind a single word, or when he'd put his best cravat on and couldna get it to his liking, looking in the glass that he bought out of his second wool money, after he'd seen Jancis under the rosy light.

I met Jancis afore I got to the Stone House. She was bringing the oxen in, because they were ordered for a fair and the people were coming for 'em early in the morning. Betwixt the two white beasts, with a hand on each, with all that gold hair shining, and a face like a white rose, she looked like the ghost of a beautiful lady that died a long while ago and came again every midsummer and fled at cockcrow.

'Oh!' she said, 'you've gotten ringlets, Prue. Shall I have ringlets for Sarn Wake?'

'As you please,' I answered, very snappy. For she was pretty enough without ringlets, and her mouth more a rose than ever. I thought how rich the ringlets would look, hanging down like ripe yellow bunches of white currants when they be traced very thick on the boughs, and she saying 'O!' and the fellows wanting to kiss her.

When she'd fastened the beasts in the trevis, we went indoors. 'Mister Beguildy!' I called out, 'I want you to learn me to read and write and sum, and all you know. I'm to pay in work. Gideon and me's going to get rich, and buy a place in Lullingford, and have maids and men and flowered gowns for me, and china—'

Beguildy looked at me over the rim of a great measure of mead. 'Saddle your dreams afore you ride 'em, my wench,' he said.

'How mean you, Mister Beguildy?'

"The answer's under your mob-cap,' says he. 'If I be to learn ye, there's to be no argling, no questions and no answers. I say the saying, but you mun find the meaning. Now you come back to me a week to-day and tell me what I meant, and then for a bit of a treat I'll show you the bottle with the old Squire in it, old Camperdine, great-grandad to this un, him as came again so bad every Harvest Home, and sang a roaring bawdy song somewhere up in the chancel, only none could see un, so none could catch un.'

'Saving you.'

Beguildy smiled. He'd got a very slow stealing smile, that came like a ripple on the water, and stayed a long while.

'Ah. Saving me. I caught un proper.'

'What way did you?'

'If I told you, Prue Sarn, you'd know as much as me.'

'But do tell how you got him into the bottle!'

'Dear to goodness! You've forgotten the bargain. No questions.' He picked up the hammer and beat upon the row of flints, making out a little tune. And with that, in came Missis Beguildy, like the dancing woman at the fair comes in when they sound the drum. She'd got a basket of trout and a couple of fowl she was going to dress for the Wake the oxen were going to. She'd got on an old bottle-green hat of Beguildy's, tall in the crown, such as gentlemen of the road were partial to then, and it looked very outlandish atop of her frizzy grey hair.

'Did you hear tell?' she said to me.

She'd got a deep solemn voice, and as she was too busy to speak often, everything she said seemed very weighty, as if the Town Crier said it, standing on the steps of the market in his braided coat.

'I heard as the Devil was dead,' said Beguildy, 'but it inna true, for I met un yestreen, and very pleasant spoken he was indeed, and right pleased to have your Feyther's company, Prue.'

'Now hush your gabble,' said Missis Beguildy, pulling the feathers out of the fowl in handfuls, so that the room was like a snowstorm. 'Did you hear tell, Prue, as poor John Weaver strayed off the road going through the woods in the dark of the moon last night, and was drownded in Blackmere? Death's very catching, poor soul.'

'Why, it wanted but an hour to dawn when he left,' I said.

'Time enow, time enow. It's dark as Egypt in the woods down yonder.'

'Who'll take his place?'

'They seyn there's a nephew learning the trade. But he's bound 'prentice for a year or two. They'll make shift with a hired mon, I reckon.'

'And it ud be better, a power,' burst out Missis Beguildy, 'if *you* took that sort of job.'

She took the poker from the fire and singed the fowl very shrewdly, as if it met had been Beguildy.

'Woman, I've better things to think on than weaving weeds to cover the poor dying body. Dunna I snare souls like conies, and keep 'em from troubling the lives of men? Canna I bless, and they are blessed, curse, and they are cursed? Canna I cure warts and the chin-cough and barrenness and the rheumatics, and tell the future and find water, though it be in the depth of the earth? Dunna the fowls I bless beat all other fowls in the cock-fighting? Ah, and if I choose, I could make a waxen man for every man in the parish, and consume them away, wax, men, and all. Canna I do all that, woman?'

'So you say, my dear.'

Missis Beguildy set the fowl's legs to rights and ran a skewer through, to make all safe.

Seeing that the Wizard was becoming very angry, I told his missus how I was going to be his scholar, and he was to learn me to spell and write.

'Will your headpiece stand it, child?' she asked. For she always thought, in common with many people, that if there was anything wrong with a person's outward seeming, there must be summat wrong with their mind as well. By that measure, Jancis, who was so silly that oftentimes she appeared to be well-nigh simple, would be a very clever woman.

'Ah. Prue's headpiece be right enow,' said Beguildy. 'Only I do think there be too many questions in it. But her'll fettle into a good scholar, will Prue. We'll start to-day's a week, Prue. Jancis, you can get the besom and sweep out my room a bit. Put the tuthree books together, gather me some quills, and be very careful of all my bottles, for you never know who's in 'em. We dunna want any frittening about the place. Oh, and you met as well turn them toads out from behind the locker; they be dead.'

'Prue,' says Jancis, when I went out, 'if you'll tell me the way to make ringlets like that, I'll tell you what Feyther's old riddle-me-ree means. I know, because he's said it over and over, and I've heard un tell the answer.'

'I made 'em round and round the poker, my dear,' I said. 'Not too hot, and give it a good clean first. But you needna tell me the answer to the riddle-me-ree, for I'd liefer find it out.'

The dew came showering on to my gown as I went past the bushes of wild roses at the wood gate, spilling out of the hearts of the blossoms. It was so quiet that I could hear the sheep cropping across the corner of the mere in the glebe, and the fish rising out in the middle, and the water lapping against the big, stiff leaves of the bulrushes.

I felt like a lady, walking out in my best on a weekday. It wasna often that I could be spared, and it was to be a deal less often now. So I was glad Gideon wanted me to be a scholar, for once every week I should get the afternoon and evening off.

When a breeze came, the leaves lapped up the silence like the tongues of little creatures drinking. Up in heaven there were clouds like the bit of lace on Mother's wedding-gown, and a setting moon as green as a young beech leaf. And down under the polished water was another moon, not quite so bright, and other clouds, not quite so lacy, and the shadow of the spire, very faint and ghostly, pointing across the water at us.

Chapter Seven
Pippins and Jargonelles

Mother looked up when I went in. She was stitching the smock.

'What a big girl you look, coming in, Prue,' she said. 'And you not near sixteen yet!'

I asked where Gideon was.

'Cutting by moonlight. Such a lad I never saw! Labours and sweats as if summat was after un.'

'Well, the moon's setting down behind the church croft now, mother,' I said, 'so he'll be bound to give over.'

I went to the meadow. He'd got as much cut as a full-grown man could ha' done. He was rubbing the scythe down with a handful of grass, and honing it for putting away, as I came over the field. I thought it sounded nice, coming over the wet, dimmery swaths, and sad as well. When I called to mind all the things he'd taken on shoulder, I was sorry for un.

'Come thy ways in to supper, Gideon,' I said.

'By gun! You look like a ghost, stealing out from under the dark hedge, all in your blacks, with that white face.'

Then he seemed to remember him of all we'd got in hand. He began to cross-waund me about the work.

'Shut the fowl up?'

'No.'

'Be quick about it, then; it should ha' bin done this hour. Looked the traps?'

'No, I thought you would.'

'When I'm mowing, I canna do ought else, saving the jobs that are too heavy for you.'

'There binna many of them.'

'When you've done the fowl and the traps, you can set a tuthree night-lines in the mere. I've got some sawing to do yet.'

'It'll take a terrible long while, and I'm no good at setting the night-lines,' I said, nearly crying, being tired already, and it late, and another day's work beginning, seemingly.

'Did you make a bargain, or didna you?'

'Ah, I did, Gideon.'

'Then abide by it.'

Wandering about the place when Mother was abed and Gideon in the fields, I felt lonesome. I wished there was some shorter way to be as beautiful as a fairy. Then a thought came to me all of a sudden. I wonder it didna come afore, but then I'd never minded having a hare-lip afore. It seems to me that often it's only when you begin to see other folks minding a thing like that for you, that you begin to mind it for yourself. I make no doubt, if Eve had been so unlucky as to have such a thing as a hare-lip, she'd not have minded it till Adam came by, looking doubtfully upon her, and the Lord, frowning on His marred handiwork.

Now my thought was this: why shouldna I, that was in sore need of healing, do as the poor folk did here at Sarn in time past, and even now and again in our own day. Namely, at the troubling of the waters which comes every year in the month of August, to step down into the mere in sight of all the folk at the Wake, dressed in a white smock. It was said that this troubling of the water was the same as that which was at Bethesda, and though it had not the power of that water, which healed every year, and for which no disease was too bad, it being in that marvellous Holy Land where miracles be daily bread, yet every seventh year it was supposed to cure one, if the disease was not too deadly. You must go down into the water fasting, and with many curious ancient prayers. These I could learn, when I could read, for they were in an old book that Parson kept in the vestry. Not that he believed it, nor quite disbelieved it, but only that it was very rare and strange.

The thing I misdoubted most was it being such a public thing. I had need be a very brazen piece to make a show of myself thus, as if I were a harlot in a sheet, or a witch brought to the ducking-stool. And sure enough, when I spoke of it timidly to Mother and Gideon, they liked it not at all.

'What,' says Gideon, 'make yourself a nay-word and a show to three hundred folk? You met as well go for a fat woman at the fair and ha' done with it.'

'Only I amna fat,' I said.

'That's neither here nor there. You'd be making yourself a talked-about wench from Sarn to Lullingford and from Plash to Bramton. Going down into the water the like of any poor plagued 'oman without a farden! Folk ud say, "There's Sarn's sister douked into the water like poor folk was used to do, because Sarn's too *near* to get the Doctor's mon, let alone the Doctor." And when I went to market, they'd laugh, turning their faces aside. Never shall you do such a brassy thing! It ud be better, a power, if you took and made some mint cakes and spiced ale for the fair when the time comes, like Mother was used to do. You'd make a bit that way.'

'Yes, my dear,' said Mother, 'you do as Sarn says. It'll bring in a bit and you'll see all as is to be seen, which you couldna, saving in the way of business, for it'll scarce two months from Father's death. And come to think of it, what an unkind thing it would be for a poor widow to have it flung in her face afore such a mort of people that her girl had got a hare-shotten lip.'

She began to wring her little hands, and I knew she'd go back to the old cry in a minute, so I gave in.

'You've got to promise me you'll never do such a thing, Prue,' ordered Gideon.

'I promise for this year, but no more.'

'You've got a powerful curst will of your own, Prue, but promise or no, you shanna do such a thing, never in life shall you!'

'And in death I shanna mind,' I said. 'For if I do well and go to heaven I shall be made all new, and I shall be as lovely as a lily on the mere. And if I do ill and go to hell, I'll sell my soul a thousand times, but I'll buy a beautiful face, and I shall be gladsome for that though I be damned.'

And I ran away into the attic and cried a long while.

But the quiet of the place, and the loneliness of it comforted me at long last, and I opened the shutter that gave on the orchard and had a great pear tree trained around it, and I took my knitting out of my reticule. For it was on Saturday after tea that I had spoken of the troubling of the water, and the week's work being nearly done, I had my tidy gown on, and the reticule to match. Sitting there looking into the green trees, with the smell of our hay coming freshly on the breeze, mixed with the scent of the wild roses and meadowsweet in the orchard ditch, I hearkened to the blackbirds singing near and far. When they were a long way off you could scarcely disentangle them from all the other birds, for there was a regular charm of them, thrushes and willow-wrens, seven-coloured linnets, canbottlins, finches, and *writing-maisters*. It was a weaving of many threads, with one maister-thread of clear gold, a very comfortable thing to hear.

I thought maybe love was like that--a lot of coloured threads, and one maister thread of pure gold.

The attic was close under the thatch, and there were many nests beneath the eaves, and a continual twittering of swallows. The attic window was in a big gable, and the roof on one side went right down to the ground, with a tall chimney standing up above the roof-tree. Somewhere among the beams of the attic was a wild bees' nest, and you could hear them making a sleepy soft murmuring, and morning and evening you could watch them going in a line to the mere for water. So, it being very still there, with the fair shadows of the apple trees peopling the orchard outside, that was void, as were the near meadows, Gideon being in the far field making hay-cocks, which I also should have been doing, there came to me, I cannot tell whence, a most powerful sweetness that had never come to me afore. It was not religious, like a goodness of a text heard at a preaching. It was beyond that. It was as if some creature made all of light had come on a sudden from a great way off, and nestled in my bosom. On all things there came a fair, lovely look, as if a different air stood over them. It is a look that seems ready to come sometimes on those gleamy mornings after rain, when they say, 'So fair the day, the cuckoo is going to heaven.'

Only this was not of the day, but of summat beyond it. I cared not to ask what it was. For when the nut-hatch comes into her own tree, she dunna ask who planted it, nor what name it bears to men. For the tree is all to the nut-hatch, and this was all to me. Afterwards, when I had mastered the reading of the book, I read--

His banner over me was love.

And it called to mind that evening. But if you should have said, 'Whose banner?' I couldna have answered. And even now, when Parson says, 'It was the power of the Lord working in you,' I'm not sure in my own mind. For there was nought in it of churches nor of folks, praying nor praising, sinning nor repenting. It had to do with such things as bird-song and daffadown-dillies rustling, knocking their heads together in the wind. And it was as wilful in its coming and going as a breeze over the standing corn. It was a queer thing, too, that a woman who spent her days in sacking, cleaning sties and beast-housen, living hard, considering over fardens, should come of a sudden into such a marvel as this. For though it was so quiet, it was a great miracle, and it changed my life; for when I was lost for something to turn to, I'd run to the attic, and it was a core of sweetness in much bitter.

Though the visitation came but seldom, the taste of it was in the attic all the while. I had but to creep in there, and hear the bees making their murmur, and smell the woody, o'er-sweet scent of kept apples, and hear the leaves rasping softly on the window-frame, and watch the twisted grey twigs on the sky, and I'd remember it and forget all else. There was a great wooden bolt on the door, and I was used to fasten it, though there was no need, for the attic was such a lost-and-forgotten place nobody ever came there but the travelling weaver, and Gideon in apple harvest, and me. Nobody would ever think of looking for me there, and it was parlour and church both to me.

The roof came down to the floor all round, and all the beams and rafters were oak, and the floor went up and down like stormy water. The apples and pears had their places according to kind all round the room. There were codlins and golden pippins, brown russets and scarlet crabs, biffins, nonpareils and queanings, big green bakers, pearmains and red-streaks. We had a mort of pears too, for in such an old garden, always in the family, every generation'll put in a few trees. We had Worcester pears and butter pears, jargonelle, bergamot and Good Christian. Just after the last gathering, the attic used to be as bright as a church window, all reds and golds. And the colours of the fruit could always bring my visitation back to me, though there was not an apple or pear in the place at the time, because the colour was wed to the scent, which had been there time out of mind. Every one of those round red cheeks used to smile at poor Prue Sarn, sitting betwixt the weaving-frame and the window, all by her lonesome. I found an old locker, given up to the mice, and scrubbed it, and put a fastening on it, and kept my ink and quills there, and my book, and the Bible, which Mother said I could have, since neither she nor Gideon could read in it.

One evening in October I was sitting there, with a rushlight, practising my writing. The moon blocked the little window, as if you took a salver and held it there. All round the walls the apples crowded, like people at a fair waiting to see a marvel. I thought to myself that they ought to be saying one to another, 'Be still now! Hush your noise! Give over jostling!'

I fell to thinking how all this blessedness of the attic came through me being curst. For I hadna had a hare-lip to frighten me away into my own lonesome soul, this would never have come to me. The apples would have crowded all in vain to see a marvel, for I should never have known the glory that came from the other side of silence.

Even while I was thinking this, out of nowhere suddenly came that lovely thing, and nestled in my heart, like a seed from the core of love.

Book Two

Chapter One
Riding to Market

In telling this story I take little count of time. For when the heart is in stress, what is time? It is nought. Does the bridegroom, that has clemmed for his love a long while, hearken to the watchman's voice telling over the hastening hours? Does he that dies in the dawn care to what hour the dial points when the sun arises, that rises not on him? And when we poor beings take up our stand against all the might of the things that be, striving to win through to our peace, or to what we think is our peace, when we are dumbfounded like a baited creature in the bull-ring, then we forget time. So four years went by, and though a deal happened out in the world, nought happened to us.

Rumours came to us of battles over sea and discontents at home. The French went to Russia and never came back, save a few.

At last, one golden summer evening, there came one riding all in a lather to tell of the great victory of Waterloo. But the news Gideon liked best, which came in the same year, was the news of the corn tax.

'Fetch me a mug of home-brewed, Prue,' he shouted, when he raught home from market and told me. 'It's the best news ever we had. We'll be rich in a tuthree years. We must get more land under corn. I *thought* corn would never come amiss, but I didna hope for anything like this'll be. When Callard came up to my stall with the tidings, I was fair comic-struck. "Dang me!" I says. "What?" I says. "Make the furriners pay to lug their corn to us?" "Ah, that's the size of it," says Callard. "And that'll make it scarce, seesta, and that'll make it dear, seesta!" "Why, mon, I've seen that this long while," I says. "But I never thought they'd do it." And what d'ye think I did then, Prue? Why, I axed un to the *Mug of Cider* and stood un a drink! So you can tell how comic-struck I must ha' bin. And now all we've got to do is to drive plough, both of us.'

So there was a prospect of living harder than we had in the four years gone, when we'd slaved from daybreak to dark, and in the dark too, by the wandering light of the horn lanthorn. It wouldna have come so hard to me, if it hadna been all for the money, if I could have been a bit house-proud, and if Gideon had taken a pride in fettling the farm. But there was none of that. It was just scrat and scrape to get the money out of the place and be off.

I grew as lanky as a clothes prop, and Mother began to show signs of wringing her hands about that too. For being little herself, and Missis Beguildy and Jancis and most of the women about being little, it seemed meet to Mother that a woman should be small. So when I grew and grew, and was very slender also (for indeed, with such a deal of work and little time to eat, anybody would be slender) she said I was like a poplar in a unthinned woodland or an o'er-tall bulrush in the mere, and I got used to being ashamed of my tallness as well as the other trouble, until--but I munna be too forrard with the tale.

Gideon wore his smock and looked right well in it. He was two-and-twenty now, a man grown, very personable, broad in the shoulder, with a firm, well-knit figure. As his body set, his mind set with it, harder than ten-days' ice. He'd no eye for the girls at market, though there was a many looked at him. And once at market when he was wearing Father's blue coat with the brass buttons, Squire Camperdine's daughter (not the squire in the bottle, but his great-grandson) came riding past his booth, and smiled at him. But Gideon would only laugh when I questioned him, and stroke his chin, and look at me warily. There was no doubt he was a very comely man, and it used to seem to me unfair that it was me, and not Gideon, that was born after the hare looked at Mother. For Gideon could have grown what they call a *moustachio* and looked very well, and none need have known he'd got a hare-shotten lip. But with me it was past hiding.

As to the farm, it was doing pretty well. We'd got a big flock of sheep, so that the shearing took us above a week. We'd got a herd of pigs that kept Mother busy all the time the acorns lasted, tending them in the oakwood. The grass-meadow by the orchard was under wheat, but we had no good of it the first year, for the wheat sprouted and ackerspired in the ear, it being a very wet season.

There was enough saved to buy two oxen for ploughing and other heavy work about the place. Being a bit out of fashion, they were not very dear. Gideon said that when he went to buy them I could go too and give a hand driving them back. And I could look in the shop windows while he haggled over the beasts, and then we could look at the house he'd set his mind on buying when it should come into the market. But Mother must know nought about the house, or she'd tell folk. 'And if they thought I had such a thing in mind, they'd bant all my prices and double all their own, and where should we be then?' said Gideon.

You may guess I was glad to be going pleasuring, for I'd scarcely been away from Sarn since Father died, and Lullingford always seemed a wonderful place to me.

I was in the cornfield, leasing, when Gideon said it, he being just back from market, coming across the field in the last light of evening; and the shadows of him and Bendigo stretched away over the grass from the far gate to the orchard as I watched them come.

'But how'll I go?' I asked. 'I canna ride pillion, for there be the panniers.'

'If you'll do a bit extra leasing, I'll hire the mill pony when I take the next corn to be ground. Going to Plash for a lesson tomorrow?'

'Ah.'

'Then fetch back the beasts, oot, and I'll go with corn Saturday.'

'But I've leased till there's scarce an ear left in any part of this field or the other,' I said.

'Ask Beguildy to let you lease his. I saw them lugging their corn.'

'But Jancis and Missis Beguildy--'

'Now you know very well Jancis is too bone-idle to pick up as much as an ear. Though I like her right well, and as for looks--'

He stopped, and stood with his hand on Bendigo's neck, gazing away to where Plash shone like bright honey in the long light, dreaming.

It was but seldom Gideon sat still, and very seldom he gave his mind to any thought but the thought of making money. But the name of Jancis would often quieten him, and when he fell into one of his silences he would make me think of a tranced man that was once brought to Beguildy to be awakened. And he made me think of a brooding summer tree on a windless day, minding its own thoughts above the water. He was like the lychgate yew that dreams the year long, and keeps its dream as secret as it keeps its red fruit under the boughs. Gideon had been used to fall into a dream like this ever since he saw Jancis under the rosy light. Times, he'd mutter 'No, no!' and shift his shoulders as though from a weight, and bestir himself, and be more of a driver than ever. For Gideon was a driver if ever there was one, and what he drove was his own flesh and blood. It seemed a pity to me that a young man should be so set in his ways, and have no pleasant times, for I was mighty fond of Gideon. I knew well where he went of a Sunday, when he took off his smock and put on the bottle-blue coat. He was a deal more regular at Plash than ever he was at church. The rosy light started it, but it would have likely been the same, anyway. Missis Beguildy told me how he'd come and knock, and Jancis would run to the door in her best gown and a ribbon or a flower in her hair, and go red and white by turns. And I saw for myself too, when she came to our place, how she would pant under her kerchief, and I wondered how this might be. For Gideon was just Gideon to me, but to her he was fire and tempest and the very spring, and his voice was as the voice of the mighty God.

He'd come in, Missis Beguildy said, with no word, and he'd sit down, and Beguildy would scowl, having no mind for Jancis

179

to marry. He'd scowl from the innermost chimney corner, for he felt the cold very bad, living in such a damp place and being a very stay-at-home man. And Gideon would scowl back.

Jancis blushed and trembled over her spinning, taking sideways looks at Gideon as a wren will. And Missis Beguildy set her face like a flint, and laid plans to get her good man out of the kitchen. She dearly loved to see a bit of lovering going on, being short of summat to think of and talk of. She wanted to be a granny too. So she'd go to any length, but she'd get Beguildy out of the room. Once, when Gideon was glowering more than common, being very desirous to kiss Jancis because she'd put on some new ribbon or what-not to set her off, and when Missis Beguildy had called her man, and come back and argufied, and gone out and called again, but still he'd only sit there like a goblin in the dark of the fire, she even went so far as to set a light to the thatch on the barn. Ah! She did! She was a very strong-minded woman. And she kept the poor man, who couldn't abide any work with his hands, running to-and-agen with buckets all evening. When he'd nearly douted one place, she set light to another while he was dipping water from the lake.

'I kept the flint and tinder right hot, my dear,' she said to me. And she laughed! I never saw a woman laugh more lungeously over anything than she did over that. She said she took a peep at the window, just to encourage her, and she could see through the clear bits in among the bottle-glass that they were sitting side by side on the settle.

'Very right and proper!' she says, and runs back to her work.

Another time she loosed the sow, and it made straight for our oakwood, she having taken it there afore. Beguildy liked his rasher, and the sow meant many a bacon-pig, so for fear she should come to harm, he took stick and went after her, cursing considerable. After a bit he began to be suspicious, because any ill that came, came on a Sunday, and he liked his day of rest, though he *was* a heathen man. So he said to Gideon, 'There's no luck with you. When you come, harm brews. Keep off.'

So he had to give over going. Then he wiled Jancis into the woods, and I'd see them going up the dim ways, rainy or frosty was no matter, she with her face like a white rose, shining, and he looking down at her, loving, and angered to be loving. When they were in the woods, Missis Beguildy was so interested in the wizard's bottles with the ghosts in them (so he said) that he'd have hard work to answer her questions. And she'd give him such a tea that it lasted nearly to supper. But he found out. He began to wonder why Jancis had taken such an affection for Tivvy, it being Tivvy she said she went to see. And as he couldn't speak to Sexton, being at daggers drawn, he followed her one evening unbeknown. And when she got home, he leathered her so that her eyes were red for weeks, and she came running to Gideon all bedraggled with tears. He was in a rage with Beguildy, and he told Jancis he'd lief wed with her, only not till he'd won through, and was rich. For how could he get along, he said, with a helpless one like Jancis clinging to him, and a tribe of children, very likely? But he was moody and troubled in mind, for he could see Jancis but seldom, Beguildy being so watchful. I thought maybe the plan to show me the house he wanted was to comfort himself and strengthen his will, because he was afraid of giving in. He wanted to give in, mind you, for he was sore set on Jancis, only he was fixed, and when he was fixed he couldna let himself give in, not if it was ever so.

It turned out that we couldna borrow the mill pony for a good few weeks, because she'd gone lame. So the harvest was long over, winter upon us, and Christmas drawing nigh, when they sent a message to say we could have the loan of it for the Christmas market, for they'd just bought one of the old horses from the Lullingford and Silverton coach, and they would drive that to market themselves. I may say I was very pleased to think of the outing, and watched the weather very anxious, for it boded snow.

I was up at four on market day, setting the place to rights for Mother and getting the things together for market. Eggs and dressed fowl we had in plenty, and greens and apples and a bit of butter. Polishing the apples in the attic, peace came upon me, as it ever did up there, since the time I told of. While the rushlight flickered in the cold air, and the mice scuttled, I stood at the open window that was like an oblong of black paper. No sound came in. Nought stirred outside. Even the mere was frozen round the edges, so that the ducks must go skating every morning afore they could come at the water. The world was all so piercing still that it was almost like a voice crying out. It was used to seem to me that when the world was so quiet, it was like being along of somebody as knew you very well, ah! like being with your dear acquaintance.

Down in the dark barn the cock crew, thin and sweet, and I thought it sounded like no earthly bird; but maybe that was because I was in the attic, where things were always new. You may think it strange that a woman like me should think such things, being one that worked with my hands always, at poor harsh tasks, whereas you'd expect such thoughts to come to fine ladies sitting at their tapestry work. But I was so lonesome, and had such a deal of time for thinking, and what with that and the booklearning I was getting, all sorts of thoughts grew up in my mind, like flowering rushes and forget-me-nots coming into blow in a poor marshy place, that else had nought. And I can never see that it did much harm, for the thoughts seldom came but in the attic, and they did never make me dreamy over my work.

So now, hearing the clear sound of our game-cock crying out upon the dawn, that was yet more than two hours away, I ran downstairs all of a lantun-puff to get the breakfast. When Gideon came in, it was all ready, and a great fire roaring, for we need never stint of wood at Sarn, which was much to be thankful for at a time when many poor families in England must herd together six or seven in one cottage to boil their kettles all on one fire. I was always thankful for our plenteous wood, that cost nought, and need not take up too much of Gideon's time neither, for if I burnt more than he cut I could make shift to chop it myself.

We were as snug as could be, sitting in the merry fire-light with a red glow shining on the quarries and the ware and the spinning-wheels in the corner. I was pleased to think Mother wasna to be lonesome, for I'd asked Tivvy to come and keep her company, since I never could enjoy anything if one I loved was lonesome or sad. Shaking the cloth out of the door after it got light, I could see her red cloak coming along under the dark woods; for as Tivvy never did anything nor thought anything, she had all her time to herself, as you met say, and so she had no cause to be late.

Gideon had roughed Bendigo and the mill pony overnight, so all being ready and the sun just risen, we set off.

All the lake was full of red lights, as if our farm was on fire, reflected in the water. The black pines stood with their arms out, dripping with hoar frost, all white-over, so that the tips of their drooping branches were like your fingers when you take them from the suds. The rooks were very contented, cawing soft and pleasant, as if they knew their breakfast was ready so soon as our ploughland thawed a bit, and in the stackyard there was a great murmuration of starlings.

'Bring me a fairing!' screams Tivvy from across the water.

Gideon looked sullen, and I knew the only fairing he'd a mind to bring was one for Jancis. So I called out--

'I will. What shall it be?'

'A bit of cherry-coloured sarsnet to tie up my hair,' she calls. For though she was a foolish piece in most things, she knew very well she'd got pretty curls, bright brown and thick. She'd toss them ever so when Gideon was there, and take every chance to miscall Beguildy, though she durstna say anything against Jancis, for fear Gideon might blaze out. But she was clever enough in this, as oftentimes a stupid girl is when she's in love, and she could always make it seem a very poor, ill-liking sort of thing to be sweet on a wizard's wench, and a grand thing to be in love with the sexton's daughter, whose dad could mouth texts as fast as the wizard could mouth charms.

It was a grand morning, very crispy underfoot, with moor-fowl about, especially widgeon. We were riding to the hills. Across the far woods and the rough moors beyond, and the bits of ploughland here and there, and the frosty stubble where partridges ran from the noise of the trotting, we could see the hills, as blue as pansies. Promising hills, they seemed to me. There was a clatter in the spinney, and a flock of wood-pigeons got up and took their flight, with wings flashing blue in the sun, for the same hills. It was as if some wonderful thing was there, as it might be a healing well, or some other miracle, or a holy person such as there were of old time.

I said as much to Gideon, but he was looking away over shoulder to Plash and the long spire of blue smoke going up from the Stone House. He began to whistle below his breath, for he'd never whistle outright, even at the merriest, but always very quiet and to his mommets. So I said no more, and in a while our old road ended, and we came into the main road where it was bad going, for whatever the weather was, the road the Romans made was good going, and even better than the turnpike. In a little we passed the mill folk going soberly along, and then a tuthree more, and soon we were riding up the hill into the town, with the plovers crying about us in their winter voices.

So we rode to Lullingford to look upon a dream. For the house we were about seeing was woven into the dream of Gideon's life. The house, that is, along with what it meant, the maids and the men, the balls and the dinners with the gentry at the *Mug of Cider* at election time.

When we were going through the ford as you come into the lower part of the place, Gideon said--

'I wish Jancis was riding pillion with me.'

'Why, so she shall,' I said, 'the very next time we come. Why shouldna she come every time?'

'There be Beguildy.'

'Oh, Beguildy! I'll wile un with his own spells and charm un with his own charms,' I said, and I laughed as we went up the narrow street, so that heads came out of windows here and there to see what it might be.

'Husht now, girl!' says Gideon. 'Laugh quiet. Not like a wild curlew.'

'But a curlew's very good company, and a pleasanter voice I seldom heard, and I'm pleased with the compliment, lad.'

And indeed I was pleased with the world and all. For there was summat about Lullingford, as if a different air blew there, and as if there was a brighter sun and a safer daylight. I knew not why it was. It was a quiet place, though not near so quiet as now. Folks go off to the cities these days, but when I was young they gathered together from many miles around into the little market towns. Still, it was quiet, and very peaceful, though not with the stillness of Sarn, that was almost deathly, times. There was one broad street of black and white houses, jutting out above, and gabled, and made into rounded shop windows below. They stood back in little gardens. At the top of the street was the church, long and low, with a tremendous high steeple, well carved and pleasant to see. Under the shadow of the church was the big, comfortable inn, with its red sign painted with a tall blue mug of cider. It had red curtains in the windows, and a glow of firelight in the winter, and it seemed to say, in being so nigh the church, that its landlord's conscience was clear and his ale honest, and that none would get more than was good for him there. But of the last I a little doubt.

Of a Sunday the shops had each a bit of white canvas stuff hung afore the window like an apron, which made it seen very pious and respectable. There were few shops, and only one of each kind, so you could never run from one to another, cheapening goods.

There was the Green Canister, where they kept groceries and spools and pots and pans, and there was the maltster's and the butcher's and the baker's, for Lullingford was well up with the times, since it wasna all towns could boast a baker in days when nearly everybody baked at home. Then there was the leather shop, for boots and harness, and the tailor's, which was only open in winter, for in summer he travelled round the country doing piecework. There was the smithy too, where the little boys crowded after Dame-School every winter dusk, begging to warm their hands and roast chestnuts and taters. It was a pleasant thing to see the sparks go up, roaring, and to feel the hearty glow about you, warming you to the heart's core, with nothing to pay or to do, like love. Near by the smithy was the row of little cottages where was the weaver's. Like the tailor, he went abroad over the country-side in summer, and sometimes to a village in winter, if it was open weather. But in hard weather he stayed in his snug slip of a house and heard the wind roaring over from the mountains north to the mountains south. I never could tell why this cottage drew me, even from a child. It had a narrow garden and a walk of red brick, an oaken paling, and bushes of lavender on either side the walk. Three well-whitened steps led up to the door, and there was a window of many little panes, not bottle-glass. Above was another window. At the back, a patch of garden ran down to the meadows, and there was a second window in the living-room that looked over this garden and the meadows, to the mountains. This I knew, because I went there once with a message in the old weaver's time. Upon the front of the house was a vine, very old and twisted. This was a rare thing in a place of such hard winters, but the town was sheltered by the mountains, and the weaver's house faced south, so the vine throve, and though in cold seasons the grapes didna always ripen, in some years they ripened very well. What with the vine and the lavender and the pleasant shadows on the strip of green lawn, and the lilac tree that stood beside the door, and what with the great weaving frame in the living-room, which was comfortable with fire-light shining on brasses and copper vessels, and very well kept, what with it all, I could never pass it without a look of longing. I was used to envy the fat thrushes hopping on the lawn. It drew me as a heaven draws the poor sinner, weary of his miry wanderings.

So to-day, as we rode by, I said--

'Gideon, what is it makes that house different to the other housen?"

'It inna different.'

'Oh, but it's as different as if it was builded of stone fetched from another world!' I cried out. 'It's as different as if the timbers were falled in the forests of the Better Land.'

'Dear to goodness, girl, you bin raving,' says he. 'Husht, or the beadle'll put you in pound.'

So I hushed, and we came to the *Mug of Cider,* and after turning our beasts in among the rest, we set out our goods in the market.

Chapter Two
The Mug of Cider

The market was in the open, in a paven square by the church. Each had his own booth, and the cheeses stood in mounds between. There were a sight of old women in decent shawls and cotton bonnets selling the same as we had, butter and eggs and poultry. There was a stall for gingerbread and one for mincepies. There was a sunbonnet stall and a toy stall, and one for gewgaws such as strings of coral and china cats, shoe buckles and amulets and beaded reticules. It was a merry scene, with the bright holly and mistletoe, the cheeses yellow in the sun, and the gingerbread as brown and sticky as chestnut buds.

The butcher stood at his door, which gave on to the market-place, shouting his meat, and holding up a long, shining knife, enough to make you think the French were coming. There was a woman selling hot potatoes and pig's fry, and a crockman who put up his wares to auction, and every time the clock chimed he broke summat, keeping some *seconds* in readiness, which served to amuse the people. Then the mummers came along and gave us a treat, and in one corner the beast-leech was pulling teeth out for a penny each, and had a crowd watching. What with them all shout-ing, and the mummers mouthing their parts, and the crash of broken china, and beasts lowing and bleating from the fair

185

ground close by, and the chimes ringing out very sweet at the half-hours, you may think there was a cheerful noise.

When we'd got rid of our goods, we went into the *Mug of Cider* for a snack. Ten or a dozen old men sat without, though the air was so nipping that they must have bin starved. Each one was holding a great pewter tankard, and they were roaring out at the top of their voices--

'The Lord's my shepherd, I'll not fear.'

Each one went his own way and made his own tune, and I thought how angered Mister Beguildy would be if he could hear 'em making such an untuneful sound, for he was very particular over his row of flints, and when he struck them he was troubled if they didna strike the note true.

But when we were come by these old ancients, every one held his mug where it was, and stopped in his singing, and so sat with his mouth open and his eyes fast on me. They were like those new-fangled mommet-shows with the little dolls that stop all together when the showman unhands them. There they sat, with the inn behind them and the frosty sunshine on their old, red, veiny faces, and a kind of frittened look. As we passed the bench, every head of them came round slow, and the score or so of eyes stared slantwise over the rims of their cups, as young owls will stare and turn their heads, watching you over their feathers.

As we went through the dark doorway, with its door studded with nails like a prison, and came into the inn parlour, where sat the more genteel, I saw their looks fasten on me too, but more shyly. The farmers and their ladies and two or three folk that had come by the early coach and were baiting here, and the Squire's son, who was a parson in Silverton and was on the way home for Christmas and was taking some refreshment because his nag had cast a shoe, all of them looked up, quiet and careful but very curious, at me. All on a sudden I knew that all these folk, the grand ones within and the old fellows without, were staring at my hare-shotten lip. They were thinking, according to their station and their learning--

'Here's a queer outlandish creature!'

'This is a woman out of a show, sure to goodness!'

'Here be a wench turns into a hare by night.'

'Her's a witch, an ugly, hare-shotten witch.'

Maybe in the tuthree times I'd come to Lullingford in the past they'd stared so, but then I was but a child and didna see.

I could hear the old men without croaking like a lot of rooks, and one said--

'Dunna drink while she's by. It'll p'ison yer innards.'

Another said--

'Dunna look upon the baigle. Her'll put the evil eye on you. You'll dwine and dwine away.'

The folk inside looked each at other, and I wished I could die.

For all the bitter cold and my thin gown and us being far from the fire, I was all in a swelter. For indeed I loved my kind and would lief they had loved me, and I felt a friendliness for the drovers and for the gentry, and the host and his missus. For they were part of my outing and part of Lullingford and of the world, that ever seized my heart in its hands, as a child will hold a small bird, which is both affrighted and comforted to be so held. I would lief have ridden forth and seen new folk, new roads, new hamlets, children playing on strange village greens, unknown to me as if they were fairies, come there I knew not whence not how, singing their song and running away into the dusk; old folk wending their way along paths in meadows of which I knew not so much as the name of the owner, to churches deep in trees, with all the bells a-ringing, pulled by men I never saw afore. Ah, I should dearly ha' liked that. Only the gist of it must ever be that the old folk looked kind as they saw me go by, and the children smiled or threw me a blossom, and that when I came to inn or tavern they'd say, 'Draw in to the fire now, dear 'eart, for night thickens.' Ah, I'd dearly ha' liked that!

This made it all the more of a shocking thing to me that the real world was thus toward me, for living so apart I had not truly felt my grief afore. But now I knew that I was fast bound in misery and iron, as the Book saith. Ah, prisoned beyond a door to which the great nailed door of the inn was but paper!

As I was bending over my plate so that my bonnet met hide the tears, a lady came in. She was a handsome piece if ever there was one! She was lissom as a wand, dressed in a long scarlet riding coat and a highwayman hat to match, with a great swath of chestnut hair tied in a bow. She'd got black eyes with no human soul in them, but sparkles instead, like a cat's eyes on a frosty night. Gauntlets on her little hands, spurs on her boots, she came in laughing from a talk with the old men on the bench.

'A besom, host!' she says. 'We want a besom here.'

Everybody smiled and sniggered a bit. I knew well what she meant, for once when Mother was talking to me she said that if folk began to speak of besoms I'd best go, since it was their way of saying I was a witch.

But Gideon never noticed, for not being afflicted like me he never thought of such things, and being used to me he didna have it in mind that other folk met not be. And he was very deep in considering over whether Jancis or the big house and the maids and men were best, so it all went by him.

The lady ran to the Squire's son and clapped him on shoulder, which made him frown because of his dignity, and she says--

'So you've come Christmassing like a good lad! Who's the woman with the hare-shotten lip?'

He made a sign to warn her to talk soft, and nodded towards Gideon ever so little.

'Why, if yonder isn't young Sarn of Sarn!' she says, flushing a bit and coming running across to where Gideon sat, very handsome in the blue coat with the brass buttons and the black band for Father on the arm, and his eyes darkling over the thought of Jancis. I nudged him, and he stood up, and looked all the better for it, being such a fine figure.

She held out her hand, for the gentry were always friendly to the farmers, in especial to voters about election time, and she sparkled at him out of her black eyes and said--

'There's to be an election soon, and Father's got some work for you, Sarn. So you'd best come and see us one day, and take bite and sup, if your sweetheart can spare you.'

She looked very spitefully at me. Seemingly she thought Gideon was an only child, and so she chose to take me for his acquaintance, or else she chose to mock him, lashing him into her slavery by making him look a fool.

Now Gideon was altogether with the Squire as to politics, because of the corn tax, but he hadna made up his mind in good sadness whether he meant giving all those things up and settling down contented with Jancis and a crowd of little uns till death them parted. So he hummed and hawed a bit, and not being used to hiver-hover from a common man, she lost her temper.

'So! So! You've no time, Sarn. You've no time, I see,' she says. 'You'll be dancing on Diafoll Mountain next Thomastide no doubt. Oh, fine you'll look, Sarn, with your missus here, and broomsticks all round and the moon shining!'

She laughed like a tinkle of jangled bells, and Gideon came to the knowledge of what she meant. He was ever slow, but sure. Eh, terrible sure.

That was one of the times I spoke of when I saw Gideon angered. His face had gone dark and his eyes had the look as if the mere was running behind them, cold, and bitter cold. He looked down at her so that she blenched, and he said very slow--

'Ma'am, this be my sister. If I've a mind to dance on the Diafoll Mountain along of witches, I ool. And if I've a mind to dance upstairs at the 'unt Ball along of the gentry, I ool. But I wunna ask you for a partner. And I doubt I wunna be able to vote for Squire neither, for can a man govern the land as canna govern his own womankind, but lets his girl go about like a ripstitch-rantipole? He should ha' give you more stick, ma'am.'

'Dorabella!' calls her brother, very much put about at her being in such a brawl.

They went out, and Gideon sat down and went on with his victuals. Nor did he eat a bit less hearty for it all, though I could scarce touch a morsel. So soon as he went off too buy the oxen, I made haste to go from the place. There were plenty of errands to do, what with malt and sugar and tea to buy, and boots for us all, and Tivvy's present, and a bit of baccy for Gideon, for he never bought any himself, since, if he was near with others, he was near with himself also. When I'd finished, and bought a tuthree extras for Christmas, and packed all into the panniers, Gideon was ready to go and see the house. He was pleased with the cattle. Brindled long-horns they were, and very strong. With so few people using oxen for farm work they were cheaper, a power, than they used to be. So he was cheerful, since neither then nor at any other time did he seem cast down by my sorrow. How could he know, indeed, that my heart was bleeding because of Miss Dorabella and the old men on the bench? He was angered because he thought it disgrace to himself that a hare-shotten lip should be cast up against one of his family, and a scent of witchcraft into the bargain. But for me he took no thought, any more than if I was one of the new-bought oxen that some-body prodded in passing by. He whistled under breath as we went along the by-road that led to the house he'd set his mind on. I'd never been along that way, for it lay outside the town on the other road from ours, and when we did come in we hadna much time for gadding about. We soon left the coach road and were in a lane with deep frozen ruts in it, and high hedges white-over with rime.

The evening was closing in a bit, but Gideon said never mind, we'd manage the beasts all right, for it ud be light as day when the moon rose. He was very wrought-up about the house, I could see, so I agreed to all he said, for I never liked to dampen down anybody's pleasure. Lord knows there's little enow in the world, and Gideon was ever one that took life hard. So when it turned out that he'd planned to treat me to a dish of tea after, at the *Mug of Cider*, and have a chat about all we meant to do, seeing we couldna when Mother was by, I said nought agen it, though I thought I'd liefer have gone into Hell's mouth than face it. But Gideon wanted to talk while the holiday feeling was on him, afore the dumbness of Sarn got the better of him agen. For it was a most peculiar thing how you couldna speak your heart out at Sarn, and I never knew whether it was the big trees brooding, or the heavy rheumatikcy feeling of being so close to the water, or the old ancient house full of the remembrances of old ancient people, or that there was summat foreboded. So Gideon kept his thoughts and turned them over and over in his mind like a

189

snowball, till at last the snowball was too much for six strong men to shift, and nigh big enough to bury anybody.

We went through a gate into an avenue like a carriage drive. At the end there was another gate, with balls on posts, very grand. Within was a carriage sweep and flower knots, trimly kept.

We stood there, looking through the wrought-iron gates at the place that Gideon said was to be ours. It was new, built since Queen Anne died, and it was a despert big house, very solid, with four windows each side the door, and over the door a porch of stone. Above the eight windows were eight more, and over them dormer windows that Gideon said would be the windows of the men-servants and maid-servants. There were steps up to the door, and a stone mounting-block with steps also, and a walled garden at one side, and a round pigeon cote.

No light showed, and the place had a melancholy look, so still it was, so dark, in its dark still trees.

'I'd lief there was a light,' I said.

'Dear to goodness, a light? It wunna be dark this hour, to call dark. What do they want with a light? The housekeeper can spin by firelight, I hope, and an old chap can sit in the chimney corner and set his mind on a better world without wasting tallow, let alone wax!'

Gideon had taken over the management already, seemingly, and I was bound to laugh.

'You seem pretty anxious the poor gentleman should set his mind on a better world,' I says.

'Why, so I am, but not too soon. It ud never do for the old chap to go out all of a lantun-puff afore we've got the money together. Say in about ten year.'

'So he's to order his coffin in ten years' time, poor gentleman.'

'You be very sharp to-day, Prue,' says he. 'But he's bound to go some day, no danger. We mun bide our time.'

'He's Miss Dorabella's great-uncle, inna he?'

'Ah.'

"Wunna they want it for young Mister Camperdine?'

'Laws, no! He's after a bishop's palace.'

'Nor yet his cousin?'

'Dear no! He'll never bide long in a place, that lad wunna. A rolling stone, he be, and a caution. No, it'll be put up to auction when the old man goes, and you and me must mind to get the money ready.'

'Why, look ye, a light!' I says.

'Where?'

'Why there, in that lower window on the garden side.'

I saw it as well as could be, a large pale light wandering from window to window downstairs and then sliding up, in a long window that seemed to go down the stairs, and beginning

190

over again in the upper story. One window would shine for a minute and then go black, and another shine. It had a very strange, uncontented look, wandering like that. There's nothing so contented as a steadfast light, but a flickering light going to and agen in a void is a sad thing to see. It went on like that a long time, and the cold strengthened. There was no sound at all. We stood there like beggars outside the gate, and the unquiet light wandered in the dark. All of a sudden it went out.

'Oh, it's gone out!' I says. 'Oh, deary, deary me!'

'What of that?' says Gideon.

'I wanted it to steady and come to rest in a window, and shine out with a heartening glow,' I said. 'But now it's gone out.'

It distressed me mightily that it should go out, so that I wrung my colds hands together, though why it should hurt me thus I couldna say.

'It was but the housekeeper looking for her knitting-needles or old Camperdine seeking his snuff-box. And now they've found it, they've douted the light. Very sensible too.'

'No!' I said. 'No! It was love, lad, wanting to steady and shine. But the house was too much for it. The dark's closed in now. The light's douted.'

And I began to cry, which was a foolish thing to do. But Gideon wasna so angered as he met have been, for he was in a good temper about the oxen and the house. 'You're sickening for summat,' he said, 'for you be no cry-baby, Prue. Come on to your tea now, while I tell you all that's in my mind. I've a deal to say, for that little vixen of Camperdine's has changed my mind for me, so I must tell you the new plans as well as the old.'

We turned away from the shut gate, as dumb as stones, and we left all the twenty-four windows with no light in them, and the dark trees with no breath of air in them, lying there in the vast of night.

Chapter Three
'Or Die In 'Tempting it'

It wasna near so bad as I'd feared at the inn, for the old men were gone with their droves, and the Camperdines were by this at their dinner. It is often so, if you are in heavy dread of summat and yet brave it, and behold! it is nought. The landlord and his missus, thinking little of us, sent the maid-servant to wait on us--a frightened, simple creature, like Miller's Polly, and nothing to be feared of. We had the parlour to ourselves, for folk go home early from Lullingford market in the winter, seeing what the roads are, even too this day. I was glad of the red fire and the steaming tea, after the sadness of that house with its dead light.

Gideon began to talk after a while, very slow, and as if the words cost gold.

'Now, Prue, I've gotten a deal to say, and if we dunna want to be benighted, I'd best start. You know as me and Jancis have taken up together in good sadness?'

'Ah.'

'I didna think to care about any wench like I do about that girl, Prue. Catches at a chap's vitals, she do. I never meant to go furder than a bit of fun. I didna reckon to marry, nor yet I didna mean lawless love. I meant fair by Jancis, and so long as we had our Sunday evenings it was all right. When there's no gainsaying there's no burning in the blood. Gainsay, and the blood's on fire. Afore old Beguildy found us out we were contented enow and as innicent as two pinks on a stem.'

'And still be that last,' I says.

'Ah.'

He looked strangely on me for a while, and said--

'You've got the second sight, seemingly, our Prue.'

'No. Only a bit of sense.'

'Well, now as the old man's given me the go-by, I do hunger and thirst after Jancis pretty near as much as I do after the place yonder, and the money and all as goes with it.'

'Not more?'

'Laws, no!'

'Then you dunna love Jancis in good sadness, Gideon. You do but lust after the girl in carnality.'

'Dear to goodness! It met be Parson preaching. That's what the book-learning does to a woman.'

He laughed a bit, awkward like, and began stuffing baccy into his pipe. But I knew that if I'd got any wisdom it was never book-learning as gave it to me, but just the quietness of the attic.

'Well, big words or not, it's no matter,' he said. 'I want the wench. I want her so bad that I'd very near set my heart to give up all and bring her to Sarn and order one of them rush cradles off Missis Beguildy. So then, to conquer the longing, I planned to bring you to see the place, and talk about it, and maybe begin to buy some bits of things agen we furnish.'

'To harden your heart the more.'

'Ah. And I planned to get some education off you after a while, and gather power to me at election times, and be so well thought of that I could even put my heart on a squire's girl.'

'Miss Dorabella!'

'No less. What be she, after all, but a woman? She hanna got more to give than any other woman, and what would any man, even the Lord of the Manor, do more for a girl than get her with child?'

'Husht! They'll hear in the kitchen and be angered at such wild talk.'

'True talk.'

'Maybe true. But nobody'd like it the better for that.'

'Ever since she threw me that first saucy look I've had it in mind. She angered me and pleased me both. So I thought if so be I could bring myself to give up Jancis--for either I mun give up Jancis or I mun give up all thought of the other-- then Jancis met have taken up with Sexton's Sammy.'

'It would nigh kill the girl, Gideon, and Sammy's no woman's man, and he's pretty well crazed with learning texts, into the bargain.'

'Oh, he'd take her if I'd let un. She stirs him to anger with her flighty ways and being a wizard's wrench and all. I see a look in Sammy's face time and agen. Wed with her and tame her, that's what Sammy ud do.'

'But that would be a cruel thing, Gideon.'

'Well, I'd a mind for it when we set out for market. I thought to throw Jancis at the fellow's yead like I throw a crust to Towser, for it mun be one thing or other. And she'd have been contented enough when the children came. Though, Lord help 'em, they'd ha' had Sammy's scowl and bin born with their mouths full of texes. But she'd have seen nought wrong with 'em. Anyway, that's what I'd settled in my own mind.'

'Dear to goodness, what a God Almighty!' I says, mocking a bit, though I knew he could ha' done it if he'd a mind. He was ever a strong man, which is almost the same, times, as to say, a man with little time for kindness. For if you stop to be kind, you must swerve often from your path. So when folk tell me of this great man and that great man, I think to myself. Who was stinted of joy for his glory? How many old folk and children did his coach wheels go over? What bridal lacked his song, and what mourner his tears, that he found time to climb so high?

'But now,' said Gideon, 'my mind's set, and I shanna change agen. I wunna give up either Jancis or the place at Lullingford here; I'll have both. And I'll lead Jancis out in a gown as would stand of itself, with her bosom bare as a lady's, at the 'unt Ball, in front of Miss Dorabella. Not only that neither. But when you and Jancis be at the grand place, and the gentry calling in their carriages--'

'And Mother! You've missed out Mother.'

'And me a man of standing, more looked up to than Squire, and not yet old, nor near it, then--'

He was quiet a long while, thinking.

'Well, Gideon,' I says, 'what then?'

"Why then, if Dorabella Camperdine comes across my path with them black eyes and that red smile, let her look to herself. I'll take her. Out of wedlock, I ool, for what she said to you and me to-day. And when the poor wizard's wench is my lawful missus, I'll make Squire's girl a w'ore.'

With that word he banged down his fist on the table so that the tankard of ale rolled on the floor.

'If you be so set in your ways,' I says, 'there'll be more than a flagon of ale spilled, my dear.'

'You talk like an old ancient woman, Prue. I be as I was made. None can go widdershins to that.'

I can hear Gideon say that now, gruff and short and with a kind of broken-hearted sound. It was as if he'd give all to be as he could never be; as if his soul in that hour, away from Sarn and all its ancient power, wrostled mightily to be free of itself. Maybe you've seen a dragon-fly coming out of its case? It does so wrostle, it does so wrench, you'd think its life ud go from it. I've seen 'em turn somersets like a mountebank in their agony. For get free they mun, and it cosses 'em a pain like the birth pain, very pitiful to see. But in our Gideon it was worse to watch. There he sat, by the comfortable fire, with the spilled beer gleaming on the quarries like dark blood, and he said no word for above an hour. I know it was that, for when he went into his trance I heard the missus of the inn call to the maid-servant to turn the spit and hasten on the meat, for supper must be served in an hour. Then all was still, and I sat with folded hands, seeing Gideon's dark face there opposite when the fire blazed up. I sat as mum as a winter blackbird. It seemed to me that the mighty hand was upon him, striving with him to make him go widdershins to what he was, to what Father had made him, and Grandad, and all of them, back to Timothy, that had the lightning in his blood. I could see in mind Lullingford New House, and the light wandering, as if it wanted to steady and shine. I wished it might be well with Gideon, and that he met take Jancis, not for vengeance but for love, and because she was the candle of his eye, and his dear acquaintance, and not for lust. And I wished he might take thought for Mother, and even for me, that I be not like his dog or his bought slave.

After a long lapse of time I heard a voice outside say, 'Is all finished?' And another voice answered, 'Ah, all's done.' It had a solemn sound, though I knew it was only the dinner they meant.

Gideon stirred and muttered to himself.

'Or die in 'tempting it,' he said.

So I knew we were all set out on a dark road, Gideon and Mother and me, and now Jancis.

We went out and saddled the nags, and set forth for home through a world as stiff as a rock, driving the oxen afore us. The dumbness had come back upon Gideon. The outing was over. The road puddles were gone beyond crackling-stiff, and were iron. And the hedges were even as the wrought-iron gates of Lullingford New House. It was the middle of the night when we came past Sarn Mere, and saw the ice a deal further out, and the lily leaves frozen under.

'Well, it's bin a very costly day,' says Gideon, 'and I'm in behopes you've enjoyed yourself.'

I knew it hurt the lad sore to spend. It was a crust in pocket and a sup of water mostly on market days. So I put the old men and Miss Dorabella out of mind, and only said—

'Ah, it was grand, and thank you kindly, lad.'

'And you'll agree to all?'

'Ah, didna I vow it?'

'But that was afore Jancis.'

'I agree to Jancis. But it ud be all one if I didna.'

'Not if you wouldna work.'

'Oh, I'll work. I never was afeared of work.'

All of a sudden a sweet scattered whistling came falling from the dim moony sky.

'Hark!' he says. 'The Seven Whistlers!'

But I said I thought it was only some magpie-widgeon we'd disturbed at the end of the mere, being mortally afeared to think of those other ghostly birds.

'No,' he says. 'No. It be the Seven Whistlers, sure enough. It bodes no good.'

This was a strange thing for Gideon to say, for he mostly laughed at signs and bodings, and I could not but think of it, up in the attic after.

Mother and Tivvy were sitting up for us, and seemingly Mother had seen us in the tea leaves, drownded in Sarn. She'd scarce believe in us for a long while, but cried and wrung her hands and said, 'They binna real. It's only the *know* of them.' So I was bound to give her one of my Christmas presents to comfort her. She was ever a child in heart, was poor Mother. She was so simple and trustful that I always thought it would be as wicked to hurt her as to hurt a babe in swaddling clothes, or a poor moth flittering in the dusk. Ah, an evil thing, a devil's trick, to betray such a trusting heart, such trembling, praying little hands!

'I be to lie in your chamber, Prue,' says Tivvy. 'I be glad, for it's cold lying alone in black frost weather.'

She looked slanting at Gideon, and I could see she was nearly wild with jealousy of Jancis. And indeed Gideon did look a proper fine man, with his face all frosty red and his eyes lit up with the day's doings. He'd but to nod, and Tivvy ud follow. But he was never one to chop and change, and his mind was made up, so I knew it was Jancis or none. I didna want Tivvy in my bed, she did so snore and snoffle in her slumber. So I waited till she was fast, and then I took the lanthorn and Father's old sheepskin coat that lapped me up feet and all, and I went to the attic and wrote in my book. It was always my custom, if things grieved me or gladdened me, to write them down in full. Also I had much need of the peace that was in the attic, after such a bitter dose of the world beyond Sarn. Because I had no lover, I would lief have been the world's lover--such world, that is, as I could reach. I was like a maid standing at the meeting of the lane-ends on May Day with a posy-knot as a favour for a rider that should come by. And behold! The horseman rode straight over me, and left me, posy, and all, in the mire.

<h3 align="center">Chapter Four
The Wizard of Plash</h3>

Christmas went by us and nought stirred the quiet, unless you count killing the pig. Nobody came Christmassing, for there was nowhere for them to come from, and nothing for them to come for. Mother was very middling with a cough, and took to her bed, so I didna go for a lesson till the New Year. But on New Year's Day I went, and, as I ever liked to pay first, I took the oxen straight away to the field I was ploughing for Beguildy. He couldna abide ploughing, so for every lesson I did so many furrows. I could plough nearly as well as most men, though not so well as Gideon. He drove the straightest furrow I ever saw. It was impossible to him to do anything ill. What he did, whether it was to be seen or not, whether it was done once in a way or every day, must be done as if his life was on it. He'd have no makeshifts. He'd thatch the ricks, even though they were to be cut into straight away, as well as if he was working for the thatchers' medal. Working by his lonesome in the fields, hedging or binding sheaves, with only the tall clouds for watchers, and the woods, floating on the summer mist, he'd still labour like a man showing his mettle at a hiring fair. Times, I thought it was pitiful, the way he'd give himself no rest. And times I could almost see the crowd of folk, the farmers watching, the judge sitting in his waggon or trotting to and agen on his cob. I could almost hear the muttering of the folks, the jeering when Gideon bungled, the roar of cheering when he did well, and the judge saying in his loud voice, 'I give the prize to Gideon Sarn, best man in the hedging, the binding, and the ploughing.'

Then I'd come to myself and see only the tall clouds, that hadna stirred, the tall hedges with meadowsweet below, the woods and the hills and the sweet blue air with larks hanging in it as if them above had let them down on threads, and shaking so with their joyful song that they threatened to break their threads. Not a bit did they care who won the prize, nor which of them sang best or loudest, so long as all sang, so long as none lacked nest or cropful, drink of dew and space to sing in.

These things I thought while I was ploughing the five-acre field at Plash with the white oxen, that looked yellow in the deathly white of the hoar-frost which lay over the earth like a shroud, though not too hard for ploughing.

As the share went onwards, the reddish, turned earth shone richly, and the rooks followed, for they were sore clemmed, poor things, walking stately in the furrows.

In a while Jancis came running across from the house with her mother, all agog to tell me of the handfasting of her and Gideon and of how angered Beguildy was. Jancis did truly look as lovely as a fairy, with her rosy face and yellow curls. Missis Beguildy came panting after, apron flying, and loaded with news, like one of the French frigates folk tell of.

'But we wunna starve here like crows,' she said. 'Come you in and have a sup of tea. Sarn brought me a pound canister, no less!'

I knew he must be very deep in love to bring more than a quarter, but I said nought, only finished my furrow and unspanned the cattle.

'We can have a nice chat, for Dad's busy in his room, curing Miller's Polly,' says Jancis.

'What's to do with Polly?'

'It's what *inna* to do with the child,' says Missis Beguildy. 'First she got the chin-cough and now she's got the ringworm. She's always got summat. He's put her in a chair with a string of roasted onions round her neck, and I'm sure I cried quarts getting em ready. Dunna you ever be wife to a wizard, Prue. It's like what it says in the good book, and I wish I could go to church Christian and hear it, it be like it says, "I die daily." Ah, it's like that, being wife to a wizard. If it inna onions it's summat else. I'm sure I near broke my neck fetching bletch from the church bells for this very child, to cure the chick-pox, the maister being a deal too bone-idle to fetch it himself.'

'Never you mind, Mother, when I'm married I'll look after you,' says Jancis.

I couldna but sigh to think what a many plans they were all making, and each plan cutting the throats of the others. I put the oxen in the shippen and came in. There was a good fire and a pleasant scent of tea, and I was bound to feel a bit glad that Polly was such a measly child, though it *was* unkind, for I knew Beguildy ud be a long while curing her. Mother always said the mill children were measly because the water-fairy in the pool under the mill-race put her eye on their mother afore they were born, but Gideon said it was because they were fed on the flour the rats got into, and Missis Beguildy said it was because they sent em to Beguildy to be cured.

'A dose of brimstone and treacle, that be what she wants, and some good food. But the mill's no place for good bread, no more than the farm's a place for good butter, seeing it means cash, and the home folk get the leavings.'

Just then Beguildy popped his head in, and looking dreamily at his missus said--

'I want some May butter.'

'May butter! You met as well ask for gold. How dun you think I've got any May butter, nor June nor July butter neither, when we sell every morsel of butter we make almost afore it be out of the churn, and never taste nought but lard?'

'I'm bound to have May butter or the charm wunna work,' says Beguildy in his husky voice.

'What be it for?'

'To fry the mid bark of the elder and cure the chin-cough.'

'Well, for all the butter, May or December, as she'll get in our place, she may die of the chin-cough!' shouts Missis Beguildy. And with that, a loud roaring came from the inner chamber, because poor Polly thought she was at death's door.

'Go and read in your old books, and find summat easier,' says Missis Beguildy. 'I've summat better to think of than charms.'

'You be above yerself, woman. You think to see our Jancis wedded and bedded and rounding to a grandchild all in a lantun-puff. But I tell ye not every troth ends in church, not every ring holds wedlock, not every bridegroom takes his vargin, and I dunna like the match! Owd Sarn still begrutches me that crown, though he be where crowns buy nought. And I tell you young Sarn was born under the threepenny planet and 'll never keep money. Sleeps on his face, too. And them as does that drowns. My gel's not for Sarn. You may ride rough-shod over my wish and will. You may send out bidding letters for a love-spinning, which is all to the good. But still I'll bide for a higher bidder. Why, she be as white as a lady and as sound as a well-grown tater! No squire nor lord even but ud take it kind to be asked to lie beside her.'

'But not to wed with her.'

'What of it? He'd pay, wouldna he?'

By this, Jancis was roaring-crying as well as Polly. Beguildy popped into his room again, and we set to work to comfort her. We drew close in to the fire with our tea and planned for me to write the bidding letters for the love-spinning.

'And a caking into the bargain,' says Missis Beguildy.

'You make money by a caking. And weaver shall come and stop a tuthree days and make up all we've spun.'

Jancis clapped her hands.

'Oh! I dearly love a Do!' she said.

'Ah, so do I.'

'But a caking be the best of all. Oh, I love Gideon dearly for asking me to wed!'

All the while as we talked we could hear poor Polly coughing and whooping sore, and Beguildy shouting--

'Quiet now, hush yer noise, I say! Curse ye! Ye're cured!'

Then Missis Beguildy asked me to write down the biddings for them to see. So I did, and they were mighty pleased, for all they couldna read what I'd written any more than two butterflies in the hedge can read the mile stone.

'Put down,' says Missis Beguildy, 'as Jancis, only daughter of Mister Felix Beguildy and Hepzibah his wife, is promised and trothed to Mister Gideon Sarn, farmer, living on his own land at Sarn. And put down as they'll be wed as soon as maybe, and that Jancis invites em to a love-spinning.'

'And put down,' says Beguildy, popping his head in again, 'that you're a parcel of fools, and that this marriage shall not be till Sarn Mere goeth into the earth whence it came. For I've seen in a glass darkly a young squire that rides this way with his pockets full of gold.'

When Polly was gone, coughing as bad as ever, and I went into the other room for my lesson, I gave Jancis a little pat on shoulder, for I was sorry for the child. She looked more than ever like a petal of the may on a day of cold rain.

'Well, well now,' says Beguildy, 'I make no doubt you've ploughed a tidy bit?'

'Ah.'

'Well, what'll learn ye?'

'Learn me to write "*Marriages be made in heaven,*" Mister, and "*Whom God hath joined together let no man put asunder.*" '

He chuckled a bit.

'Clever wench! Clever wench! But you'll not get the better of me. Rather shall you write, "*Intermeddle not with high matters.*" Dunna a wizard, as knows the fortunes of a parish, know what be best for his own?'

'Leave be, Mister! There's enough agen the poor child, what with Fate and such a pigheaded man as Gideon. If you meddle, maybe you'll do harm as you canna mend.'

'Namore, namore! I've said me say. Dunna weary me.'

He beat lightly on his little music, which was a sign that his patience was over. As the notes tinkled out, I knew it was useless to argle any more. For as there was no power or sweetness in his flinty music, such as there is from harp and fiddle, so there was none in his soul. It gave a small and flinty music because it was a small and flinty thing. He'd got no pity because he'd got no strength. For it inna weaklings and women that pity best, but the strong, mastering men. They may put it from them as my brother Sarn did. But even so it will come upon them some day, and the longer they deny it the stronger it will be when it comes. Ah! It met even be such an agony as will make a man hate his life.

Chapter Five
The Love-Spinning

It took a long while to get ready for the Do, it being a caking as well. A good few of the religious sort held that cakings were wickedness, being in the nature of gambling. But for us women, leading such lost-and-forgotten lives, they were a bit of enjoyment, and even Sexton's wife said she'd come and bring Tivvy. She got Missis Beguildy to fix it on a day when Sexton was going with Parson to a place a long way off to look into the case of a woman taken in adultery. She knew Sexton ud stay till the bitter end, and wouldna be raught back till the small hours. And even if he found out, he'd be so contented at the punishing of a sinner that maybe he'd not be more than grumbling-angry.

The name *caking* was given because we played cards for cakes. To tell the sober truth, it was real gambling. The woman who gave the Do made a big batch of cakes, saffron or rich sponge, and sold them to the guests at a penny each. Cakes were what we played for, and the losers were bound to buy more, whereas a good player could go away with a big basketful, or she could sell them to the losers at twopence each.

Mother was not to hold or to bind, but she must come. Gideon promised to look after our jobs for the day, so we set our early. We were to make a day of it, spinning all the forenoon and then, after the noon-spell, settling down to cards.

It was a fine fresh morning with a damp wind full of the scent of our ricks. There's no scent like it for bringing summer in winter. When I smell it now I see the long gleamy waves of grass like green silk, and the big red clover bobs, and corncrakes running low in the thick grass, dark with dew.

But at that time the first thing it put me in mind of was how hard-got it was, how we'd sweated and laboured by moonlight, and got up agen afore we'd had time for a dream, to sweat and labour once more. Still, it smelled pleasant, and so did Gideon's bonfire of old hedge-brushings, and the deep floor of leaves in the wood, and the pine-trees where there were always canbottlins cheeping and playing.

Mother looked well in her big poke bonnet and frilled tippet, like a bright bird with her quick brown eyes and red cheeks. We only took the little spinning-wheels, seeing we were to spin flax and hemp and not wool, so I could carry them easy. The mere was a bit cruddled with ice at the north side still, but you could tell that spring was afoot though it was but February, by the mating-games of the water-ousels and the nesting caw of our rooks. There were green tongues on the woodwind sprays too, so bright, they minded me of the tongues of flame that came down from heaven. In that dead time, coming so quick and fresh, they always seemed more to me than all the honeysuckle blossoms of the summer.

When we came through the oakwood Mother smoothed her mittens very complaisant and said--

'I binna tending swine this day. I be a lady.'

'Indeed to goodness you be,' I said. For I did dearly like her to enjoy herself. I said I made no doubt she'd win enough of cakes to keep us all for a week of nine days.

'Will Jancis be a good daughter to me, think you, my dear?'

'I make no doubt of it, Mother,' I said.

'Will she leave me my own place by the fire and speak kind?'

'Ah, she ool, I know. But you needna fret, for it'll be many a long day afore those two are shouted in church.'

'I'd lief not. I'd lief be a granny, Prue. Will the babe favour Gideon or her, dun you think?'

I said, not having the second sight I couldna tell, but I thought it ud be the very spit-and-image of its dad.

'Maybe, maybe. It ud be better, a power, that it should favour us than the Beguildys. It's bad for a baby to have a preached-against grandad.'

'Oh, there's not much harm in Beguildy, nor yet good,' I said. 'He be just a pleasant painted show like a blown egg.'

'I be glad he'll be away to-day.'

Missis Beguildy had sent a message by Gideon to her cousin at Lullingford to tell her to send for Beguildy on that day to come and cure her man's toothache. For seemingly he'd had one taken out by the beast-leech, and he parted so hard with it that the beast-leech, being a terrible man when his blood's up, loosened all the others lugging it out. So he got the toothache shouting-bad, and it was a good amusement for Beguildy to go and cure it. He was always very proud of that charm beginning--

'Peter sat a-weeping on a marble stone,'

and he'll go on saying it over and over till the person cries for mercy. Then he claps on a bagful of salt, fire-hot, and whether it's the salt or the charm, the person most always says he's cured.

'They'll keep him late, not to spoil our sport,' says Mother, clapping her hands softly like a child.

We came out into the open fields, and I thought no day had ever looked so fair, yet knew not why. The hills Lullingford way were blue as a summer sky, a deep promising blue, and there was a richness on the world, so it looked what our Parson used to call sumptuous. There were the red plough-lands and the old yellow stubble in the sun, and Plash Pool, glassy blue, and the mill roof in the valley, red. All the grassland was clear green like the green in church windows, or like the green hill far away where no herb grows but the Calvary clover. Even a summery day can seldom match such a day as that, when the snow is but just gone and the waters freed, and when there is a clear shining above and below. You could tell there was summat out of the common at the Stone House, by the great blaze of firelight in the window. Jancis came running to the door and made her obedience to Mother very prettily. We were the first, saving for Miller's Polly and her mother. They were always first everywhere, for they said an hour from home was an hour in heaven. They wouldna explain more, only if you drove them hard and asked them for why, was it the Mill-'us or the water or what? Then they'd say, 'The Miller.' And if you said why, what ailed the man? they'd say, 'Was he ever known to smile, leave alone laugh?' And indeed he never was. He'd got a lattance in the speech as well, and what with the two things he was very disheartening to live with. There was a foolish tale that he'd had a bogy out of the water for sweetheart, and that when he got married she put silence on him for a curse.

Missis Miller was a poor creature, like a mealworm, but very pleasant-spoken. Sexton's missus was just the opposite. She always made me think of a new-painted coach, big and wide, with an open road, and the horn blowing loud and cheerful, and full speed ahead. She was as gay in her dress as a seven-coloured linnet, and if she *could* wear another shawl or flounce or brooch, she would. She wore so many petticoats it was a wonder she could walk, and once Tivvy said to me that to watch her mother undress was like peeling a big onion down to the core. Tivvy wasna one ever to make a joke, so it shows what a great thing it must ha' been to watch. I was used to think myself, seeing her and Sexton together, that she was like a big hank of dyed wool, and he was the thin black distaff it was to be wound off on to. When she and Tivvy were come, we were eight, and our wheels made a pleasant humming in the warm room the while we talked. The ox-driver's wife from Plash Farm came next, with two tall girls, very quiet and meek for all their size. Folk said their father tied them to the ox-trevis every Saturday night and beat them to keep them in mind of their manners. They'd always stand up if their mother spoke to them, and bend their long necks like meek swans. The twelfth was the shepherd's wife from the moors beyond Plash. She was a strange creature, but fair to look upon, enough to make a man's mouth water. She'd got sloping shoulders and long hips, and her hair was like a blackbird's wings. Her eyes were clear green and her face was flushed like a ripe peach, and she'd smile in secret to herself like a fairy. It was said, but whether with any truth I know not, that the shepherd paid no money for the moors, that belonged to a tavern-keeper in Silverton, but that every mid-summer Felena, which was his wife, went up to the rocks at the hilltop and spent the night with the tavern-keeper. There were wilder tales too, about her being seen dancing by moonlight in a ring of cattle and sheep, mother-naked, and how a shaggy creature with ram's horns, that could only have been Satan, came and danced along with her, mopping and mowing, while the ring of beasts made a low moaning. But to me she seemed a pleasant, harmless creature, and very handy in all she did.

I could see that the ox-herd's wife didna care for her girls to be spinning with Felena. She was so respectable and high-minded that she never spoke of anything between banns-up and baptism if she could help it, and took no notice of young couples during that time. She said nought to Felena, and it was Mother, ever kindly, who said--

'You spin like a fairy, Missis Felena.'

'There's nought else to do in the mountain,' said Felena in a low, singing voice, 'but spin and spin and spin, morning noon, and night.'

'Save on Midsummer night, my girl,' raps out Missis Sexton, 'and then I'm told you've enough to do and plenty!'

Felena turned scarlet and hung her head, and suddenly Moll and Sukey burst out, as if they'd wanted to say it for years and years--

'Oh, Missis Felena, is it true as you lie with the tavern-keeper and dance on the yeath mother-naked?'

Never did I see any woman so angered as their mother was. "Sukey and Moll!' she says.

'Honoured ma'am?' says they, all of a twitter.

'Out with yer hands!' says she.

And stooping down she took off her sandal shoe, which she wore because it was a party, and slippered em both on the hands right soundly, till they roared agen.

I heard after that one married a farmer and the other a retired coachman, and both did well: it wasna for lack of correction if they did ill.

They went on with their spinning, meek as mice, snoffling over their wheels. Missis Beguildy was very put-about, for it seemed like being a melancholy party. So I asked Jancis to sing *Green Gravel* to liven us up. We all joined in, even Polly, whooping the while. Felena sang in a cool-sounding voice, and Sexton's missus sang very loud, and Mother quavering, and Missis Miller like a bird new come from the cage.

So what with the singing and the whirring, the kitchen was like a tree full of starlings. It was getting on for time to stop spinning when Mother said should we sing--

'The Lord's my Shepherd,'

and afterwards I spoke for having--

203

'He brought me to His Lordly House,
His Banner it was Love.'

And just as we were singing that, and the wheels going like
churn-owls, there was a quick footfall without, and a rush of
fresh air, and a long ray of sunshine from the door to me, and
he stood there in the light looking upon us.

'He,' I say, as if you'd know him out of the world as I did.

He stood in the doorway, and I rose up from my seat in the
shadows at the back of the room, as if he was my own bidden
guest.

Chapter Six
The Game of Costly Colours

How did he look? What like was he? Was he well-
favoured? It be hard to say. There are no looks in love, no
outward seeming, no telling over of features. When you are
but a moth in the candle of his eye, can you tell his stature,
or if he be dark or fair? Did Magdalene, that was like Felena,
know, when she lay at the feet of the only man she ever loved
yet never loved, whether the carpenter's Son featured His
mother or not, whether He was big or little in stature? Shall
we know, when we be come into His presence that made us,
what outward seeming His majesty has? No. Only our hearts
will tremble in the light. I could never tell you how he looked
as he stood there; but I can tell you how the women looked
that glassed him.

Tivvy and Polly gaped in wonder, finger on lip. Moll and
Sukey leaned forrard as you lean to a fire in winter, and their
mother gathered them to herself jealously. Missis Sexton
spread her flounces, and Jancis coloured up and said 'O!' and
set one of her ringlets straight, and said 'O!' again. Mother
smiled at him, and Felena--well, Felena's eyes settled on him
as a brown owl drops to its prey.

I sat down farther back in my corner, and a faintness
came over me. For here was my lover and my lord, and
behold! I was hare-shotten.

The room was all so still, you could hear the drip of water
off the roof.

All of a sudden he laughed out, and indeed it must have
been a comical thing to see us all like mice when Pussy goes
by, and to hear us one minute making such a to-do, and the
next making no to-do at all.

He off with his hat and made us a little bow and said--
'Sarvant, ladies! The weaver, if you please.'

If we pleased! As if we wouldna be pleased with anything
he met say! So he was the weaver! Well, it made no manner
difference to me. If he'd said he was the king of Fairyland or

204

a murderer with the bloodhounds after un, it would ha' been all one to me.

'Kester Woodseaves, if you please, missus,' he says in a kind of merry mockery, looking towards Missis Sexton, she being the biggest, both in tallness and roundness.

Then Missis Beguildy brought him to the fire and made him take bite and sup. But I kept out of sight.

'Be you from far, sir?' asks Felena in her lingering way. Her lips were red and pleasant, though not kind.

'Lullingford, missus,' he made answer, with a measuring look. 'Neither very near nor very far.'

'As the crow flies, near,' she said, as if she pleaded.

'Only we bain't crows, missus.'

'I live on the mountain over yonder,' she says; 'and I'm nigher to Lullingford, a power, than these.'

'A longish ride.'

'Not far! It be on your road to—a'most everywhere.'

I thought, 'She says all I'd like to say.'

'By gum, missus, I doubt it's on the way to hell,' he made answer.

They were like folk wrestling, but we did not know their quarrel.

'Oh, I be glad it's you that's to weave my wedding linen, and not the ugly hired man,' said Jancis.

'So you're to be wed, child?'

'Ah. To Gideon Sarn, sir. Dun you know Gideon?'

'I've heard tell of him.'

I wondered what he'd heard of Gideon. All in a minute it was more to me that he should like Gideon and Mother and me than that I should master the reading of Revelations, which beat me still, because of the strange words and the roundabout way of the telling. I'd laboured over it a long while, and labour brings a thing near the heart's core. Above and beyond that, I wanted to know the mind of John, he being lonesome on his bylet in the sea as we were at Sarn, and having many thoughts in his mind, both deep and bright. Now one like Tivvy had no thoughts at all, and you soon tire of looing in an empty porringer. And Mother had two thoughts or three, and Gideon two. So the mind of John had drawn me as none other did afore; but now the book of Revelations was but a windlestraw to this man's whim.

'Oh, Mister Woodseaves, will you come to my wedding if Prue writes you a bidding-letter?' asked Jancis.

'Maybe I ool,' he made answer, looking at her mother as much as to say that she could give him the go-by if she would. 'And who's Prue, that can write bidding-letters?'

I was in a swelter, but just as Jancis was going to rush on me and drag me out of hiding, Sukey and Moll, who could never be quiet for long, burst out—

'Please, mister, ool you come to our weddings too?'

Then they giggled mightily, and put their heads together, shaking their curls and bending their long necks. Then they put their hands afore their mouths and ran across the kitchen to him, and one whispered in this ear and one whispered in that, and then they ran back, to their bench, two-double with laughter. Jancis, being near, heard Sukey whisper, 'I'd lief you were bridegroom!' I hoped their mother wouldna get to know, and slipper them again, for they'd saved me from being seen. I couldna bear that he should see me, for fear of a cold look, or scorn. I'd liefer stay down-under, like the daffadilly, lest the weather be winterly. For if she too eagerly comes up, desirous of the sun, she can but stand and shudder in the bitter frost, torn by the fangs of the winds. So she has lost her warmship, and yet hanna won through to summer.

'Sir! Be you wed?' asked Felena, and her voice was pretty and slippery like a grass snake.

'Why, no to that, missus.'

'Nor handfasted?'

'I'm thinking you were an attorney once,' he says, 'and stuck questions into poor men like skewers before you put em out of their misery.'

She took no notice, but only said—

'You be not of this country. You come from afar.'

'Oh, indeed to goodness, he is of this country, Missis Felena,' Mother chirped up like a little bird. 'He came back from being 'prenticed after his uncle was drownded. It was his uncle wove the mourning when my poor maister died, falling down in a fit and dying in his boots on the sabbath the bees did play.'

'And now he's dead and your A'ntie's dead, you live by your lonesome, I suppose,' says Jancis.

'Well, I do and I don't.'

'Dear to goodness, Mister, have you got a kept 'oman?'

This was Felena.

'Your thoughts be all beaded on one string,' says Kester.

Then Sukey and Moll burst out—

'Who cooks for ye?'

'Who sweeps for ye?'

'Who sews yer buttons on?'

'Who knits yer stockings?'

'I do for myself, my dears, and my thoughts be my company.'

He looked round very contented, and I could see he was thankfull that none of all these women had a right to come over his door-sill.

'Well, thank you for me, Missus,' he said, putting down his mug and plate. 'And now for work. The loom's in the attic, I suppose?'

'Ah, I'll show you. There's a bed there too. You wunna finish for two days or three. There's plenty for you to do.

But come down and get your supper along with us, for it inna every day we have a randy.'

By the time she came back every tongue was at it. Sukey and Moll were quarreling as to which of them, if they could do as they willed and go and work for him, should pour his supper ale and fill his pipe. It was enough to make an owl laugh.

'A nice young fellow,' says Missis Sexton, 'and a God-fearing, I'll lay, if the women let un alone.'

She looked very meaningly at Felena.

But Felena was fallen into a muse.

'I like him better than Gideon, a power, though Gideon be your brother, Prue,' said Tivvy.

Missis Miller spoke for the first time.

'He's as different,' she said, 'as different as mortal man could be, from the Miller!'

It was the greatest praise she could give.

Polly gave a loud whoop, as if to say that she agreed.

'Well, time goes by, and even a toothache must be cured some day,' said Missis Beguildy. 'So we'd best set to at the caking afore my maister comes back. Thank you kindly for the spinning. We've done enough to keep that young man busy for above a bit.'

She brought out a big willow-pattern dish stacked with cakes, saffron and sponge fingers and gingerbread babies. These last are little men of gingerbread, with currants for eyes.

Sukey and Moll screamed with joy to see them.

'I dunna care about the others, if so be I can win a ginger bread man!' says Sukey.

'I'll win six,' says Moll. 'Six curranty babies for me!'

'You'll need more gumption than you've got then,' says Missis Sexton, 'for there's no game so hard as the game of Costly Colours. I've played it at every randy since I was a maid, and I'll lay that your Ma has too, and Missis Sarn and Missis Miller. Yet it's a difficult game to us still. And for you that have played it seldom or never, it'll go hard, but you'll lose every cake.'

'Tell 'em the way of it,' says Missis Beguildy, 'you've got such a head.'

Though she meant it in good sadness, it made me laugh. For indeed Missis Sexton's head was marvellous to see, with oiled hair in rolls and bobs and bands, and a high comb, and ribbons, and a vasty cap on top of all.

She went across the kitchen like a coach and six, and stood by the fire, telling us about the game of Costly Colours--how you counted, and of the trumps, and how three of a suit was a *prial*, and four of a suit was *Costly*, and how you could *mog*, or change, your cards, and of the deuces and Jacks, and 'Two for his heels,' and how if you made nought of your hand it was called a cock's nest, and you were bound to give a cake all round.

'I canna mind a word!' says poor Tivvy.

'Nor me,' says Polly.

So they stood out and left us ten, and it was only eight we wanted for two tables. So I offered to stand out.

'Why, you be the best player of all,' says Jancis. And the mother of Sukey and Moll settled it, saying--

'Stand out, girls. You can play turn-the-trencher with Polly and Tivvy. But no noise!'

They burst out crying, wanting to win the cakes. But their mother said did they want more slipper, so they hushed. Then she bought them each a gingerbread man, and promised them some more at the end.

Felena drew at the same table with me. That is to say, it was the pig-killing bench with a board and a white cloth on it, for they had but one table.

'There's not one of us women but ud like a gingerbread man, is there, Prue Sarn?' she says. 'So, us being too old for cakes, shall us make-beleive to be playing for the soul of the weaver?'

'As you please,' I says. 'But it seems to me to be none of our business.'

'Why, Prue Sarn, you're as white as a shroud one minute, and as red as a peony the next, and such burning eyes! What ails you?'

I was angry, yet there was a warmship in this one thing, that she seemed to be counting me as one like herself, and not as one that was set aside from the game of love. I suppose, being under suspicion of dancing with the devil, she had a fellow-feeling with me for being mixed up with tales of witchcraft. For they'd even begun to say of me that I took shape as a hare on dark moonless nights, and went loping across the hills, and had a muse running under the churchyard. Such things were first said in idleness or mischief or to scare children, and then, in the loneliness of old farms, full of creakings and moanings on windy nights, they grew. And none can tell what such things will grow into at long last, nor what harm they may do. I didna like it much when Felena took his name on her lips, for all on a sudden it was a precious name to me. And it seemed to me then, as it ever has, that he was not a man to speak of lightly. Watching him out of my darkness beyond the settle, I had thought his wrath would be like a cloud-burst, though his smile was a spring day full of warm gilly-flowers.

Felena drew me farther from the rest.

'A man,' she said, 'whose like I've not seen afore, neither on the roads nor at market. The others are gaubies to him. Did you see the colour of his eyes?'

'No.'

'Nor could I see. His eyelids cut across them so straight, and the candle of his eye is so big and black, you canna see the colour. I'd lief be nigh him, to see.'

Her glass-green eyes misted, and a rich, swooning look came over her.

'A man to gamble for,' she said.

'Take your places! Take your places! Cut for first deal in the game of Costly Colours!' cries Missis Sexton.

As I sat down I twisted the words of Felena in my mind, and said in the deeps of myself--

'Not a man to gamble for. A man to die for.'

We gave our minds to the game, and the four girls having been sent into the yard, the room was as silent as a dream.

I could hear them singing *Barley Bridge* out there.

> Shift your feet in nimble flight,
> You'll be home by candlelight,
> Open the gates as wide as the sky,
> And let the king come riding by.

After a while the singing died away, and I wondered what mischief was brewing. But I'd enough to do, for I was determined to beat Felena, and as Missis Sexton was her partner and Missis Miller was mine, I knew I should have my work cut out.

The fire, mended with pine wood, gave a good, sweet smell and a warm light, enough to play by. It lit up the walls, and the sticky gingerbread men on the blue dish, and Jancis, as fair to see as if she'd been made out of solid gold in old time, for an altar. In the quietness, with *Barley Bridge* in my mind, a sort of waking dream came to me.

I saw a great crowd of people beside the troubled water of Sarn. They were dressed in holiday colours, but their faces were evil. Then one came riding through them on a tall horse, and his face was the face of the weaver. A woman stood forth from the crowd. She had a necklace of green glass beads and green blazing eyes. She cried out--

'My body, my body, for a ride on your saddle!'

But he turned aside from her to one who stood hidden, in a torn, sad-coloured dress, with a hare-shotten lip.

He stooped to her, saying--

'Ah, my dear acquaintance!'

And she gave him a sprig of rosemary. She said no word, and she supposed he would go by her. But he set his arms about her and gathered her up before him on the saddle, and his right arm was strong around her. So they rode away, and the sound of the people died till it was less than the hum of a midge, and there was nothing but a scent of rosemary, and warm sun, and the horse lengthening its stride towards the mountains, whence came the air of morning.

'Two for his nob!' called Missis Sexton. 'Your deal, Prue.'

So I tucked my legs under the bench as well as I could for her furbelows, and went at it with a will. And I may say that Missis Miller and I won, out and out, to her everlasting astonishment. For she seemed to think it an impertinence on her part to beat Missis Sexton.

'You played like a demon, Prue Sarn,' Said Felena.

It was late, so Jancis opened the door and called, 'Supper!' and in rushed the four hoydens, who seemed children to me, though I was nearly of an age with them. They burst out with their doings, though they had better have kept them to themselves.

'We've bin in the attic.'

'We sat on the bed!'

'He can whistle like a throstle.'

'He weaves as quick as ninepence!'

'He's got a green coat for Sundays and a Bible with pictures in it, and he can read the Bible.'

'He's got a watch, and a pipe with a silver band, and he won the wrestlers' medal at Silverton.'

'He canna abide bull-baiting nor cock-fighting nor shameless women.'

'He likes a good song and home-brewed in reason, and a dance in the meadow, and the sound of bells.'

'He's got a great lump of muscle on his arm, like a frozen snowball.'

'We measured un on the attic door, and found the inches with the weaver's measure.'

'He be thirty-eight inches round the middle and five foot ten inches high!'

He's got a pair of Wellington boots, but he dunna wear 'em much, being above his station and a dommed lot of trouble to clean.'

'*He* said dommed, *we* didna.'

'He likes children and dogs and a quiet life.'

'He wouldna mind a missus of his own if she was biddable. Only he's never seen the woman he'd lief have yet.'

'His eyes be watchet blue, what you can see of 'em for the black middles and the lids and the lashes.'

'And if so be he'd got any sisters he'd like 'em too favour Sukey and me!'

'God bless me!' says the mother of Sukey and Moll, and I could see the slipper threatening, 'God bless me, not a thousand starlings in the reeds make such a din.'

It was lucky for the girls that their mother happened to have won.

'Get your tippets on now, this instant minute!' she said.

'Call un down, Jancis!' they pleaded.

So she called him to supper. The sound of the treadles and the thud of the batten stopped, and he came down.

Sukey ran to him and put summat into his hand. Then they made their curtsies and said--

'Thank you for me,' and followed their mother.

But Sukey put her head in at the door again, and gave a bit of a giggle and whispered--

'I gid him my gingerbread baby!'

'Out, girls!' ordered their mother, and off they went, with a lanthorn to light them, and the ox-goad in case of gentlemen of the road.

I went out to the barn, that Kester Woodseaves might not see me, and when I came back he was gone to the attic again. Felena had gone early, with a luring smile and a word for him.

'If you come our way, Mister, I'll learn you the story of Adam and Eve.'

The two from the mill were very unwilling to part, but at last they went, and we made ready to go also.

'A right good caking!' says Missis Beguildy. 'I've made enough on the cakes to pay weaver, and we've spun a deal. A Love Spinning's a great salvation. So now you can tell your son, Missis Sarn, as we shall be ready with the bride and the linen as well, when he gives the word to make the bed.'

Beguildy raught back as we set out. He was a bit peart, but not drunk. He said he'd met Miss Dorabella's cousin, and that he wouldna believe Beguildy could raise Venus. So he'd told him to come and see for himself.

'Venus? Where is the baggage?' says his wife. 'How can you raise her if she inna here?'

But he'd only sing--
'Peter sat a-weeping,'

and play, very dot-and-go-one, on his little flints.

Chapter Seven
'The Maister Be Come'

'Well, Sarn,' says Mother when we raught back, 'we've spun a deal and had a good randy, and now your wedding sheets be on the loom.'

Gideon looked bashful and said it ud be many a long day afore enough of money was gotten together for that.

'Our Prue won at her table!'

'Eh, did she now?' Well done!'

He could understand that and respect it, for it was what he liked to do.

'Cakes enough to keep us a week of nine days!' says Mother.

'She was thinking of the salvation, I make no doubt.'

'No, I wunna, Mother,' I said.

'Why, what was it then?'

'I dunno. I just wanted--Costly Colours, Mother,' I says, in a foolish way.

'But what use be they if you get no cakes with them?' I said I supposed they were no use, but all the same I wanted them--the Costly Colours.

'She's sleepy,' says Gideon, 'that's what she is, else she'd talk sense. Best go to bed both.'

'Shanna I bide for the lambs?'

For at lambing-time I was used to sit up part of the nights, to let Gideon get a wink of sleep. But he said no, I'd had a day of it, and I might as well finish in style with a good night.

'I've bin as lazy as a lord all day,' he says, 'being obliged to be about the place to do the little jobs.'

He was a good-hearted lad, in spite of all, and if he missed to do a kindness it was only because he didna think of it, or because his mind was so set on one thing. And times if he'd been callous and it was brought home to him, he'd take it very hard, though often it was a long while after.

'Well, bed then, Prue!'

Mother hopped about with her stick like a robin with the rheumatics.

'It's been a grand day. A day to think on and talk over. Not wrong neither, for if we *be* still in our blacks, it was a kindess we were doing. None can blame for a kindness. Did I demean myself well, Prue?'

'Why, yes, Mother, no danger!'

'Did I spin well?'

'You spun grand.'

She ever had this way of asking, like a child, and she wound herself round your heart like a child, too.

'And such a nice young man, the weaver be, Sarn! A man any woman ud like for a son.'

'Be that Woodseaves?'

'Ah.'

'A fine wrostler, they say. A deal of booklarning for one of our class too. Squire offered un a clerking job at the Hall, but he wouldna take it. Said he'd liefer work with his hands and that he couldna abide politics, for they were all lies and he'd sooner keep clear. "I'll weave white linen rather than black lies," he says, and the owd Squire was very huffy. He'd like to have given Woodseaves warning to leave the place, only the house is hisn, willed by his uncle.'

Mother wanted to know if I liked the weaver.

'I thought you didna, my dear, for you never spoke, but went beyond the settle.'

'Like him?' I said. 'Oh . . . like him?'

'Why, lookye, Prue, you be asleep on your feet,' says Gideon. 'Off to bed now, or you'll do no work to-morrow.'

But indeed I was not asleep, but moithered. For it is a strange thing, and very strange, when the maister is come, and you would lief fetch him in and bring out the best, fresh butter and cheese in large dishes, and new milk, even to the top of the big stean, and when you'd put on your Sabbath gown and a posy, and smile at him with a yes for all his askings, and behold! all is nothing, for you have a hare-shotten lip, being under the ban of witchcraft.

'The Maister be come, and calleth for thee. The Maister be come . . . '

All night, in the attic, I could hear those words, very triumphing and yet sad. And when the dark thinned and shapes began to steal out from the blackness, and the smell of dawn came in, and our game-cock crowed loud and sweet because it was the beginning of spring, I still heard those words, with kindness in them and a shiver of dread--

'The Maister be come.'

The words made such a murmuration, and were so piercing-sweet that I wrote them in my book. Of all I had thought to write of the Love-Spinning and the game of Costly Colours, and of his coming, I wrote little. Yet when I open the book and see those four words in the very best tall script I could do, it all comes back to me so clear, as if it was to-day.

I looked at the loom, and saw him there, weaving. I looked at my copy book and wondered if he could do the tall script and the short, red and black, plain and flourished. And I was very sure that he could do them all, and more.

Next morning Jancis came running down the path, and I wanted to say, 'Is he well?' For it seemed to me that any-thing might have come to him in the dark hours. But I could only say, 'When does the weaver go?'

'Oh, to-morrow,' she said, as if it was no matter.

Then she cried and begged me to help her, for Beguildy was determined to raise Venus to confound the young squire, come what might.

'And it be me as is to be Venus! Oh dear! Oh dear! And it's the day after to-morrow. And I'm feared, Prue. For if Sarn knew that I'd stood up in a rom all naked with a pink light a-shining on me, and a strange man there, never would he speak to me agen.'

'No,' I said, for I knew Gideon pretty well.

'And he'd be bound to find out.'

'Ah, he met.'

'But Feyther's mad about it. Raise Venus he ool. He says young Mister Camperdine laughed so, and clapped him on shoulder and said he'd give un five pound to do it, *whatever* he raised. Five pound, Prue! And when I said no, he beat me. And he says if I wunna do it, he'll put me to the field work, and beat me every Saturday for a year. Oh, Prue, whatever is to be done?'

'How's he going to set about it?'

'Oh, I'm to be in the cellar under his room, and the trap door's to be open, and I'm to have a rope under armpits on a pulley to the roof, and Mother's to be in cellar to light the smoky stuff and put the rope round me proper. Then Feyther'll pull the rope in the kitchen, under the door, and I shall come up slow under the red light. He says it ull be too dimmery to see my face, but that's poor comfort. It wouldna be any excuse to Sarn's mind.'

'No. Be you very fond of Gideon, Jancis?'

'Ah, I be.'

'Do ye mind that text, "The Maister be come"?'

'In the Bible? Ah, I mind it.'

'Do ye feel that way about Gideon?'

The pretty colour came in her face.

'Oh, yes, indeed, Sarn be maister.'

'And the other . . . goes to-morrow, you say?'

'What other?'

'Why, Mister Woodseaves.'

'Oh, he goes to-morrow.'

'Well, look ye, Jancis, I'll do it for you.'

'*You?*'

Her mouth was so round and so red in her astonishment that I could have hit the girl.

'Yes, me! I know it's a funny thing for me to be Venus,' I said bitterly.

'But Feyther ud know.'

'You say he's to be in the kitchen.'

'And the young man!'

'You say he inna to see your face. It'll be dark and I'll turn aside. And I'll put the muslin off the currant bushes over my head, so as he wunna see my dark hair. He'll see what he's come to see, the gallus young wretch, a naked woman. Then he'll pay the money and you'll go free.'

'Oh, Prue, you be good! I love you, Prue! I'll make it up to you some way. The best of it is that it wunna matter for you, seeing you'll never have a lover.'

So cruel can folk be, and mean nothing. This was the reward for my kind act. But those that say good doings are rewarded are wrong.

I'd like to have strangled her for that saying. The angry blood was roaring in my ears.

'Go away now,' I said. 'We'll talk of it to-morrow. But go quick now out of my sight!'

And with a puzzled and frightened look she went.

Chapter Eight
Raising Venus

Serious-minded folk will need to pass over this raising of Venus, but I will shorten it as well as I can.

It seemed a dreadful thing to me, as I set forth when the evening came, that I should be going to show myself stark naked. For though I knew that Miss Dorabella and other grand ladies did take off the tops of their gowns, evenings, and come forth half bare, and think it no shame, yet women of our sort have more chariness of themselves.

As I went in by the garden way, through the door on the low level, not to be seen, I was all of a tremble, and it was only the pitifulness of poor Jancis that made me go through with it. We could hear Beguildy moving about up above, opening the trapdoor and putting all ready. I thought what a silly old man he was, to think anybody believed in his May-games. Then we heard young Mister Camperdine's horse, and there was a shuffling of feet above, and Beguildy pulled on the rope to show all was ready.

Oftentimes it is easier to die for love's sake than to be made a fool of for love's sake. So I thought as I was lugged up into the dark room in a cloud of smoke that made me gasp, holding out my hands to keep me from knocking against the sides of the trap, and not knowing whether to laugh at the foolishness of it all, or to cry at the sorrowfulness of this play-acting, which so mocked me. For here I was pretending to be the most beautiful woman that ever was, and a goddess into the bargain, and yet I was cursed as you know.

All was dimmery in the room. I could but just make out a figure at the far side. Beguildy was singing some queer kind of spell in the kitchen, and the young man's horse was stamping and shaking its bridle outside.

As I came up clear of the trap, and hung there in the rosy light, the young squire started forrard in his chair, and held out his hands like a child at a pastry shop. But I knew he was under solemn oath not to stir from his chair. I thought it must be a strange thing to go through life with men holding out their hands on this side and on that, to be always the pastry cake in the window with hungry eyes upon it. Then all of a sudden I heard a movement on the other side of the room, and turning that way I could have cried aloud, for there sat Kester Woodseaves.

Did ever Fate play such a trick? Here was the one man out of all the world that I must hide from, since already I loved him so dear, and so must never hurt him with my grief.

And there he was, so close in the small place that two strides would have fetched him to me. He was leaning forrard like the young squire, and he made to hold his arms out and then drew back and gave a sigh, and I know now that the desire of woman was stirring within him. It came on me then with a great joy that it was my own self and no other that had made him hold out his arms. For in that place he could not see my curse, he could only see me gleaming pale as any woman would. Often since, I have wondered if he'd have been so stirred if it had been Jancis hanging there, crucified in nakedness, instead of me. Was it all of the flesh as it was with the young squire, or did my soul, that was twin to his, draw him and wile him, succour his heart and summon his love, even then? For I do think that the spirit makes herself busy about the body, and breathes through it, and throws a veil over it to make it more fair than it is of itself. For what is flesh alone? You may see flesh alone and feel nought but loathing. You may see it in the butcher's shop cut up, or in the gutter, drunken, or in the coffin, dead. For the world is full of flesh as the chandler's shelf is full of lanthorns at the beginning of winter. But it inna till you take the lanthorn home and light it that you have any comfort of it. And I have ever seen that the women with fair mounded cheeks, and breasts like the round pyatt where Felena danced, yet lacking any soul to laugh or weep in them, be not the ones that draw men. The ones that lure men to them by the tuthree, the score, and the hundred, as folk draw towards a lighted church when the Easter Supper is ready, be often those that care not much for their bodies.

This is a strange thing, as true things are often, but not so strange as this willing and summoning of a man by a woman flawed and cursed, a woman to whom it was said, 'You'll never have a lover.' Two men would have been my lovers that night if I'd willed it so. And as I saw the squire's shoulders stooped forrard with the weight of his longing I knew for that first time that, whatever my face might be, my body was fair enough. From foot to shoulder I was as passable as any woman could be. Under the red light my flesh was like rose petals, and the shape of me was such as the water-fairies were said to have, lissom and lovesome.

I hadna cared so much, nor been so dismayed, at playing this foolish game afore a stranger. But now I was all one blush from head to foot, and cold as ice as well. Every second was an hour, and I was shamed as if I had gone whoring. Yet I couldna but rejoice to have given my body in this wise to the eyes of him who was maister in the house of me for ever and ever.

I pulled the muslin over my face and looked slanting through it towards this wonder. For indeed he was a wonder to me then and always, not for his looks nor for anything that he did, but for the silent power of what he was, the power gathered up in him, as tremendous as a great mountain on the sky, that you couldna measure nor name, but only feel.

In the thinning smoke I could see him, with his face set beneath the shock of bodily love, for whether or not he loved me after, he did in that hour, and with the wounded look that is ever on the faces of men between the coming of the lust of the eye and its satisfying.

It takes a long while to write down, but I was only in the room as long as Missis Beguildy could count sixty. Beguildy was afraid they'd find him out if he allowed them too long, never dreaming, poor simple fool, that neither of them believed a word of his tales. While I was still fainty from the shock of seeing Kester Woodseaves, Beguildy called from the kitchen--

'Well, well, gentlemen, have I yearned my five pound?'

'Aye, aye!' says Mister Camperdine, with his look heavy on me, 'and more, and more!'

Beguildy began to sing another foolish rhyme, which was the sign for me to be ready to go down. Never was any woman so glad of a cellar as I was when I raught back there. I got into my clothes as quick as might be, for we could hear the squire argufying with Beguildy in the kitchen.

'What now? What now? Speak with a body?' Beguildy was saying. 'Now how can ye speak with Missis Venus, and she dead and gone this thousand year? I fetched her back for ye, through the grave and gate of death, for five pound in cash, but I canna keep her. She comes a-walking on the air, in a cloud, for the time you can count sixty, and then she's gone. For she is but a beautiful bogy, seesta! and she mun be raught home by candlelight.'

There was a great burst of laughter at that, and as Mister Camperdine went out to his horse, he called back--

'I'll have another look at Venus one day, Beguildy. She's got a very tidy figure, by Gad, *wherever* she's from!'

As I crept home under the close net of winter boughs, my heart was all dumbfounded, even as the heart of a bride when first her lover looks upon her great beauty. Only there was shame in this, and a great distress, being that I was no bride, and that I had been stared-upon and longed-after by a strange man as well as by him that was the world and all to me, though I had seen him but once afore.

It was strange to think that while I went about my house-work and out-door work to-morrow, slaving like a man, at men's jobs, I should be in my own soul the bride of the weaver. While I ploughed with Gideon, turning up the frosty earth, while I cleaned the shippen in my sacking and clogs, while I stood in the mucky fold giving the ducks and fowls their meat, looking more like a man than a woman, and more like a mawkin than a man, all this time I should be woman to him, dwelling beneath the light of his eyes, warmed by his smile, his banner over me being love. While I strode but half a furrow or so behind Gideon, I should be lying trembling in my lover's arms, fainty as I was at Beguildy's. Though my hands were hard and chapped and my face red and coarsened with weather, I should be, while I thought upon him I loved, a flower and the petal of a flower. For love is a May-dew that can turn the swartest woman to a Jancis. And though I had but the shadow of it, yes! the shadow of a shadow, as when you see the reflection of a water-lily in the mere, not still, but in ripples, so that even the reflection is all distraught and is not wholly yours, yet it had made the world all anew.

I wondered if aught would have happened to me in my outward life by the time the water-lilies came again, lying along the edges of the mere like great gouts of pale wax. There was but a mockery of them now, for amid the frozen leaves lay lilies of ice. Yet as I thought of Kester Woodseaves and what he had come to mean, I seemed to hear and see, on this side and on that, in the dark woods, a sound and a gleam of the gathering of spring. There was a piping call in the oak wood, a bursting of purple in the tree-tops, a soft yellowing of celandine in the rookery. When I was come into the attic, spring was there afore me, though it was so cold that my hands could scarce write. None the less, I put down in my book the words, 'The first day of spring.' And I wrote it in the best tall script, flourished. So I should ever call to mind the second time of seeing him I loved, and the first time of his seeing me. Not only had he looked at me, but he had looked with favour and longing, and though I knew it was only because the truth was hidden from him, yet I was glad of what I had, as a winter bird is, that will come to your hand for a little crumb, though in plenteous times she would but mock you from the topmost bough.

I took my crumb, and behold! it was the Lord's Supper.

Chapter Nine
The Game of Conquer

In the morning, ploughing one of the far meadows with Gideon, I saw yellow nut catkins in the hedge, and brought them home and set them in a jug on my locker in the attic. I plucked them early, and tied a bunch to each of the ox's horns, so all that day of sad-coloured weather the white cattle went up and down the red field, which was white-over in parts, so that they looked yellow, with nodding gold plumes on their heads, as if it was a fair. When we unspanned, Gideon said--

'What'n you been after, bedizening the cattle?'

'It's May Day,' I says.

Gideon looked bepuzzled, but he said, well, he supposed I liked my jokes, and he didna complain so I worked well. 'When'll this weary old ploughing be done, Gideon?' I says, for of all things I hated it, not for itself, but because it spread out over our lives till there was no room for anything else. He was in a fever to plough. Dawn and dark, frost and rain, he'd be on the land, hard at it, and often when it did the land more harm than good. All the farm was to be corn. All the rickyard was to be full of corn. Only grow enow of corn, he said, and we should be rich afore we knew it. I couldna abide the new law, which made it pay so well.

'As soon as we've got enow, off we'll go, Prue, and never see the place again,' he said.

'I canna understand that Gideon,' I told un. 'If you were land-proud, I could. But it do seem so queer to spend every bit of time and strength on the land, like a mother with a child, and then not love it. It's as if the mother cared nought for the child, but only cared to sell it.'

'Ah, that's the size of it, Prue. I dunna care a domm for the land. Nor yet I dunna care for the money. Not *as* money.'

'Well, what is it you *do* care for?'

'To get me teeth into summat hard and chaw it. To play Conquer till there inna a cob nor a conker left but mine. To be king-o'-the-wik and the only apple on the bough.'

'But for why, Gideon?'

'You be always asking me for why. Because I was made like that and I canna go agen it.'

We always came back to that.

'The thing is, to keep the right men in, so as they canna change the law afore we've made our money,' he said.

It was just as if the country was his mommet, to do his will and put crowns in his pocket.

'Which be the right men?'

'Them as keeps up the price of corn.'

'But the poor folk, that clem, would lief have prices down.'

'They mun grin and abide. Let 'em work. I work, dunna I?'

Indeed to goodness, he did work! He was nought but bone and muscle, and if he was a merciless man, he was merciless to his own self first. I said would he side with Squire, at elections, in spite of what Miss Dorabella said. 'Ah, I doubt I mun. He's got a deal of corn land, he'll never let prices down.'

'And when'll you leave ploughing?'

'Not till we've bought the place, and there's money in bank into the bargain.'

'But when we've ploughed up all the farm, save what grass we're bound to keep for the beasts, then you'll be bound to stop.'

'No. If we hanna got enough money, I shall start on the woods.'

'Oh, deary, deary me!' I said, for I was like to cry. It was the unkindest thing that he should think of the woods. For now there'd never be any rest for any of us, since the woods were ours all round the farm, and there was work in them world without end. The tears rolled down my face, and I could feel them, cold and slow as the cold evening light.

'Why, what ails ye?' says Gideon. 'Crying? bless me, what a wench! Look ye, girl, we be working for the future.'

'I mislike the future,' I said. 'It's like the bran pie they give the Lullingford children, Christmas. You may get summat, but most likely you'll only get a motto. And if you get summat, ten to one it inna what you want, for what you want inna in the pie.'

'Dear to goodness, what a mort of idle words! The future's as you make it.'

'Why, no,' I says. 'It be like the blue country a traveller sees at dawn, and he dunna know if it'll be a kind country with farms sending up a trail of smoke in the sunset, and a meal for the asking, or if it'll be a wild, savage moor where he'll starve to death with cold afore morning.'

'Why there now,' says Gideon, 'you're starved with cold, that's what's the matter. You want a cup o' strong tea and a good plate of taters and bacon. And hark ye! If that inna Mother banging the tray I'll be dommed.'

Poor Mother set store by the evening time, being one that like company. She said the days dragged so in the silent place, and she was timid, startled at the fall of a leaf or the creaking of a door. She was used to plead with me, time and agen, to leave ploughing and bide with her a bit. But I was bound to do Gideon's will, so I made up comfortable tales for her of the day when we'd be well-to-do, with men and maids and a kitchen girl and no pigs. She's brighten up a bit, but soon she'd sigh and shake her head.

'A far cry, a far cry, Prue. Maybe I wunna last. I'd lief things were a bit easier now, my dear. I canna abide tending pigs in the 'oods. My poor legs do ache, and if I set down I get the rheumatics. And the pigs do go daggling about down by the water, so my feet be always wet. I'd liefer less maids and men in the years to come, and less pigs now. I'd liefer less company then and a bit more now. All that's a long way off, and no more satisfying than the many mansions of Paradise. Tell un that, Prue. Tell Sarn, my son, I'd liefer have a few things now, and not so many in the years to come.'

'Ah, I'll tell un, Mother. And you must think of the time when we'll leave ploughing.'

'Sarn'll never leave ploughing. Or if he does he'll do summat else. It's this-a-way with un, he canna rest. He's like a man I heard tell of, riding post across the land with dreadful news, foundering nags and buying fresh uns, with no thought but to get there. So when he got there and told the news he was so fixed in mind he couldna stop, but rode and rode, with no rest, crouching down and cutting the horse by day and by dark, going with no news to nowhere. They seyn he rides still. I tell you, Prue, it ud have been better, a power, for us and for him too, if my son Sarn had bin born an idiot boy, to play with coloured stones and put daisies on a string.'

She look so strange, standing there in the fold, with her long staff and red cross-over shawl, with her mouth a-tremble and her eyes shining like a prophet's and the great lean pigs gruntling and snouting around her, and Sarn Mere standing up beyond her like the blue glass round a figure in a church window. I wondered if ever they put pigs in church windows, in pictures of the Prodigal Son, and I couldna help but laugh a bit in a kind of pitiful way, thinking that this here was the prodigal mother, and how glad we'd be if Gideon was a bit prodigal too.

'What ails you, laughing?' she says.

'Only to think as you be the prodigal mother.'

'I dunna understand. I canna understand ever-a-one of my two chillun. Oh, deary me! But I take it unkind in you, Prue, to laugh when I be crying.'

Poor Mother! She said true things, times. She'd put words to my own complaint about the world, that laughed though I cried.

'There, there, I'll tell Gideon,' I said.

It was one of the queer things in our lives that I was the go-between, taking messages from Mother to son. She could never get courage to begin, nor to face his cold, steely look.

Next morning I spoke to Gideon. He was in the field afore me, as always. It was frosty and misty, so the ploughed land looked like tarnished mirrors, or like the mere in overcast weather, sheeny and not solid. Where the frost held and the sun shone, the fields were polished like lake water with a gleam on it.

Gideon and the oxen came on slow, making a little solid dark picture in the lonesome fields. It put me in mind of the black oak figures carved on the peak of the gables on some of the Lullingford houses, and always looking very dark on the sky. The breath of the oxen and the steam from their bodies stood up about them and hemmed them in, so as they went up and down they seemed like a picture, round and all to itself, that somebody was moving about in the waste of fields.

'Gideon,' I says, 'Mother be very middling. She wants rest. Get a lad to mind pigs in the woods.'

'A lad! Dear to goodness, what lad?'

'There's Miller's Tim. He's not but seven, but he could mind pigs and I'd give un his tea.'

'What! Feed a great lad of seven every day of the week save Sunday? Be you mad, Prue?'

'Mother's very moped and middling. She wants rest and she wants company in the going down of the years, and a bit of comfort.'

'Amna I working for that? Inna she going to have maids and men, the best of good things, a pew in church, and real chaney to eat off?'

'Ah! In the years to come, if she lasts. But she met not. It be now that matters.'

'There nought ails Mother. She can go on very well. She gets good air minding pigs, and she can croodle over the fire after dark, to ease the rheumatics.'

'And she's moped, lad. She wants me at home more.'

'Well, you will be when we leave ploughing.'

'That's a long day. Any road, you mun get a boy to mind pigs.'

'Mun, mun? Who be you to say that to me? I be maister of Sarn.'

'You've no right to drive Mother to death when she's old and ailing.'

Gideon gave me that withering look.

'Maybe,' he says, very slow and bitter, 'maybe you'd like to get wed and bring a lad to Sarn that-a-way, to tend pigs. That is, if anybody'll have ye.'

He picked up the plough handles and went on down the furrow. It needed a long while in the attic to wash out those words, but the power that was there washed them away in a while. I made allowance for Gideon since he lost so many nights of rest, it being still lambing time. For lambing time is the shepherd's trial. In the black of night, in the dead of the year, at goblin time, he must be up and about by his lonesome. With mist like a shroud on him, and frosty winds like the chill of death, and snow whispering, and a shriek on this side of the forest and a howl on that side, the shepherd must be waking, though the pleasant things of day are folded up and put by, and the comforting gabble and busyness of the house and the fold are still, and the ghosts are strong, thronging in on the east wind and on the north with none to gainsay them. So when Gideon was short with me I only took a bit more time in the attic. It was pleasant there when spring drew on, with a dish of primmy-roses on the table and a warm wind blowing in. When April came we were still ploughing, and I was so used to it that I'd given over being tired, and enjoyed it, and sang to myself the while. It was grand to go down the red furrow with the share cutting strong into the stiff earth and shining like silver. It was fine to look away to the blue hills by Lullingford, and see the woods of oak and larch and willow all in bud between, as if a warm wind blew from there and called the leaves. It was pleasant too, seeing the rooks follow in a string at my heels, looking as if they'd been polished with the andiron brush, and to see the birds again that had been away, and to hear the waterousel sing wild and sweet, and the lapwings change their winter cry for summat warmer. There were violets now to pull for market, and daffodillies in the corner under the ivy hedge, and tight pink buds like babies' little fists in the apple trees.

Mother cheered up a bit, and one day when we were having our tea by the window, with a bunch of gilly flowers on table, she said,--

'We'll have the weaver.'

I gave a gasp and a choke, and Mother wanted to know what ailed me.

'Nought, nought, but why not the weaver's man? It ud be cheaper.'

'I like the best weaving.'

I feel into a dream, for if Kester was going to weave for us he'd have to come into the attic, walking to and agen round the weaving frame, looking out of my little window, making the place his place, so I should have him there for ever after. Yet still I couldna abide the thought of him seeing me, and I argufied for having the weaver's man till Gideon thought I was in love with the fellow, though he was said to be simple and had got fourteen children into the bargain. But Mother put on her spectacles and looked at me, and pushed them up and looked again, and settled them in place to look a third time.

'We'll have the weaver,' she said, and that was all.

It was the day after this that Jancis came rushing in, all wild, to say that Beguildy was going to take her to the hiring fair on May Day, unless Gideon could stop it. She came into the dairy where I was churning, and she said--

'Oh, Prue, the young gentleman's been again, and have me he will, leastways you!'

She gave a giggle in the midst of her crying.

'And Father says it's that or the hiring fair. It'll be three years, Prue. I'll be bound for a dairymaid or a kitchen wench for three years, that is, unless Gideon offers to wed with me now.'

'Gideon wunna, my dear, he's fixed in mind about the ploughing. Nought'll turn him from that.'

'But I shouldna stop it.'

'You'd be another mouth to feed. And if you ailed--'

'I shouldna. I be stronger than I look.'

'You canna tell, Jancis. When you wed, you begin a game of Blind Man's Buff that ends you canna tell where. And if little uns came, what about all that money Gideon's set on making?'

'Oh, deary me! Oh, I canna bear it, Prue. I do love Gideon right well, and once parted may be as bad as never met.'

'Well, you talk to Gideon.'

'And will you put in a word wiselike?'

'Ah, I'll put in a word. But what he wunna do for you, that be his dear acquaintance, he wunna do for me, that be nought but his hard-drove sister.'

Just then Gideon came across the fold to fetch the buttermilk for the pigs.

He stood in the dairy door, and I thought it small wonder she was sweet on him, for in his smock and leather breeches, with his black head bare and his eyes blazing on Jancis, he was as well favoured a man as you could meet in ten parishes. And I thought, as I looked around the dairy, that it was as good a place as anybody could wish for asking to wed. The sun shone slanting in, though it was off the dairy most of the day. The damp red quarries and the big brown steans made a deal of colour in the place, and the yellow cream and butter and the piles of cheeses were as bright as buttercups and primmyroses. Jancis matched well with them, with her pretty yellow hair and her face all flushed at the sight of Gideon. She was like a rose in her pink gown. Outside the window, in the pink budded may tree, a thrush was singing. I mind it all so clear, and should, even if it wasna written in my book.

'You be early,' says Gideon.

'And welcome?'

'Oh, ah! You be surely welcome.'

She looked at me mischievously as if she was asking me if I did mind, and stood tiptoe for Gideon to kiss her.

'I've got news,' she says. 'Good news or bad, as you do make it.'

'Me?'

"Ah, it's this-a-way, Sarn. Feyther says I mun--'

She looked at me, helpless like.

'Beguildy wants to sell the child, Gideon. What's the use of mincing words? He wants to sell her to young Camperdine for his pleasure.'

Jancis hid her face in her hands.

'And if so be she says no, she's to go as a kitchen wench to the May Fair and be prenticed for three years.'

'What! Sell my girl? Beguildy'll sell my girl? Dang me, I could drown him dead for that!'

'He's not sold her yet, Gideon.'

'The better for un.'

'But she'll be bound prentice for three years away somewhere beyond Lullingford.'

Gideon stooped and pulled away her hands, looking firecely on her face.

'Be you a true wench to me?' he says. 'Dang me, if you've lost your maiden'ead to young Camperdine. I'll lay un out with the pole-axe. Ah! And you I'll strangle.'

'No, no, Sarn, I hanna, I hanna,' she cried out. 'I be a good maid to you, Sarn, indeed I be.'

'But what's she to do, Gideon? For unless she'll be the young man's light-o'-love she's bound to go away.'

'I canna abear to go away.'

She burst out crying again. I waited for Gideon to speak, but he said nought.

'There's one other way, Gideon.'

I said it coaxing, for I knew it was his hour of choice for the two of them. The good road for both was in their power to take this day. It was one of the times in Gideon's life when he might choose his blessing, the path of love and merry days where the pretty paigle grew, the keys of heaven, or the path of strange twists and turns, where the thing of dread, the bane, the precious bane, that feeds on life-blood.

Jancis seemed to know also that their lives in some fashion hung upon this hour. She stooped down and kissed his hand, and she said in a soft hoarse voice--

'O, be my sweetheart, Sarn!'

Gideon gave a kind of groan.

'I know where you be dragging me, Prue,' he said, 'with your eyes so strongly upon me. You be pulling me down to poverty and the loss of all I've dreamt of.'

'I'd work double, lad,' I said.

'What use? You know right well what would happen. Could any man do other with a pretty piece like that for missus? Mouths to feed, mouths to feed. Never no grand house nor maids and men, nor pew in church. No money for you. No 'unt Ball for Jancis. No hail-fellow-well-met with the gentry for me. If ever we make any money it wunna be for years and years. We shall lose the house and go pottering on, eating up all we make. A man with a wife and family never gets on. He mun make his money first.'

'But wouldna you work better if you were happy, lad, with Jancis happy too?'

'Why, no. Happiness and idleness be twins. If you want to work, you munna be happy nor miserable. You mun just think of work and nought else. Another thing, if I take Jancis now, in the teeth of young Camperdine's longing after her, he'll be agen me himself and he'll set all the gentry agen me. Whatever's made the man so mad in love, it's done now, and we mun take care.'

He looked at Jancis suspiciously, and she prayed me with her eyes to explain all. But that I couldna do. I'd done a deal for Jancis, but that was too much. For I was afraid that if I spoke at all it would get round to Kester Woodseaves. Jancis was under promise that none should know, saving only, in the utmost need, Gideon. So I kept silence, and I canna see that it made any difference, for speaking would only have put it off, and Beguildy had made his mind up about Jancis, and if it wasna the young squire then it ud be somebody else. It was best for Gideon to decide once for all, then if he chose right he and Jancis could be wed, and it would be out of Beguildy's power to make any more plans.

'It'll only put off the riches for a bit, Gideon,' I said.

'No. It ud put em off for ever and ever. The best thing to put off is getting wed. We'll wait three year. That'll give us time to turn round. Not as I want to put it off.'

He fell silent, looking at Jancis. I could see the longing in his face, and he was all of a tremble. It was strange to see such a great strong fellow shaking like a woman that's seen frittening.

He took a step towards Jancis, and I made to go out, for I thought he'd take her in arms and all be well. But all of a sudden he muttered--

'No, no!' and drew back. Then he said--

'There'd be no satin gown for ye to dance Sir Roger in at the 'Unt Ball then, Jancis. You'd be sorry for that.'

'Ah.'

'Well, if you go for a dairymaid or summat you'll be yearning for it as well as me. Three year inna long. By the end of three year all the ploughland should be bearing well, andus'll be reaping what we've sown.'

'Dear Lord forbid,' I says.

Gideon fell into a rage, though why I never could think, and burst out--

'Why that, now? Why that? I'm well content to reap what I sow.'

'But not if it's the bane, Gideon? Not if it's the precious bane as I read about in the book the Vicar lent me? You dunna want *that* amid the corn, lad, what grows in hell?'

'*Whatever* it is,' he says, 'if I sow it and it brings me the thing I'd lief have, I'll welcome it.'

There came a little sobbing sound from Jancis, and when I looked at her I saw beyond her golden head the spring day all o'ercast and the thorn tree lashing in a sudden wind.

'You'd best be going home-along, my dear,' I says. 'There's tempest brewing.'

'I shall come on Sunday, and tell your dad what I think on him,' said Gideon.

'No, no, dunna anger him!'

'What do I care for his anger?'

'Oh!' she cried out, 'everything's all as I wouldna have it. Why canna folk live quiet and peaceful? Why must you be so fixed in your mind, Sarn? Hark at the wind rising! There's summat foreboded.'

She began to cry again, hiding her face in her apron. 'O, I wanted to send out the biddings and be shouted in church,' she said, just as she used to say, 'O, I wanted to play *Green Gravel*.'

Gideon snatched her to himself and kissed her, but he didna change his mind. Once he'd made it up, nothing ever would turn him.

'I mun go,' she said. "Come and send me, Sarn.'

As they went, I saw her wring her hands and heard her say--

'O, I see a dark road going down into the water. And the sun's gone out. O, Sarn, dunna make me walk that road!'

All in a minute she'd faded away like a ghost in the wild, dark, stormy woods.

Book Three

Chapter One
The Hiring Fair

On May Day, there being a deal of stuff for market, I borrowed the Mill pony again and set out with Gideon very early, while yet the purple blossom and the green leaves of the lilac trees were all of a grey blur. I'd pulled some lilac overnight for market, so we rode with the sighing of it and the good smell of it all about us. It was a very still morning. Not a breath stirred the young red oak leaves, and even the silver birches, that will shift and shiver in any breeze, like water-weeds at the lake-side, were all becalmed like weeds far down where not a ripple comes. Save for our horse-hoofs on the wet flinty road there was no sound, neither from the grey fields on either side, nor from the water, the woods or the sky. So still! It seemed to me some miracle might come to pass on such a day. The dawn could not hold its breath more if Judgment was to break that eve, and the dead rise. When the colour came in the hedges, the bird's eye, that was in great plenty, looked upon us, very simple and innocent, as if thousands of blue-eyed children watched us go by. The ollern trees that fringed the road dripped with yellow catkins. Beyond stood the hills, mounded out of sapphire stones like the new Jerusalem, and all becalmed under a sky without so much as a cloud. Not a bird nor a trail of mist or smoke stirred in all the plain. It seemed to me, as I rode alongside of Gideon without a word, while he frowned and darkened, thinking of Beguildy, that it was like a great open book with fair pages in which all might read. Only it was written in a secret script like some of Beguildy's books that he never locked away, knowing they were safe. For indeed every tree and bush and little flower and sprig of moss, every least herb, sweet or bitter, bird that furrows the air and worm that furrows the soil, every beast going heavily about its task of living be to us a riddle with no answer. We know not what they do. And all this great universe that seems so still is but like a sleeping top, that looks still from very swiftness. But why it turns, and what we and all creatures do in the giddy steadfastness of it, we know not.

I said to Gideon that it was like a book.

'Book?' he says. 'Why, no, I see no book. But I see a plenty of good land running to waste, as might be under corn.'

So we see in the script of God what we've a mind to see, and nought else.

We came beneath a wild pear tree in early blow, and it put me in mind of Jancis.

'Now I wonder,' I said, 'where Jancis'll sleep this night?'

'At Grimbles'.'

'How can you tell?'

'I can tell because I say it is to be. Missis Grimble is for ever changing dairymaids, and I hear tell she's after one this year.'

'It's a long ways off, Gideon.'

'None the worse for that, she'll be out of young Camperdine's way.'

'She'll be terrible lonesome.'

'You can write me a letter to her now and again.'

'And welcome. But how'll she answer?'

'I thought of that.'

Gideon spoke triumphing-like.

'It's such a great big place that they have the weaver every month or two. Weaver can write for Jancis.'

'What?' I says, with my breath very short, knowing I was going to say that name, 'what, Mister Woodseaves?'

'No other.'

Why, dear to goodness, here was a queer trick of fortune for me! I was to write love-letters for him I loved to read, and he was to write letters back for me to read, once in every few weeks. I let the pony go her own pace, and we fell behind, for Mill pony was like Mill folk, and took everything sad and quiet, as if she'd been discouraged above a bit.

There'd be letters coming in the summer days, written in his own script, with his own wording and turns of speech. His hand would ha' moved slow along every page, over and over, while he looked down at the lettering with those long-shapen blue eyes that pierced to the heart's core. Of course they'd be letters to somebody else from somebody else, and it ud be all the wrong way round, for his would be in the name of Jancis, to Gideon, and mine would be in the name of Gideon, to Jancis. It would all be moithered and twisted and topsy-turvy like the water-lily shadows in the mere, when I'd lief it met be clear and real. Still, I could speak my heart out. I could say the things I'd thought never to say. I could lay my soul as naked afore him as I myself had been, for no eyes but hisn would read my letters. Not that my soul was anything to show, but yet I greatly desired to show it. This is a very strange thing, and ever to be found in lovers. I couldna help but laugh to think what a figure of fun Gideon would look dizened out in my soul, and how dumbfounded Jancis would be, hearing things read out of Gideon's letters that no power of angel nor devil would ever make Gideon say, and how she'd pucker up her face and wonder if weaver was making game of her, and then think, 'Oh, well, folks inna themselves when they're writing.' I was laughing over it all when I heard Gideon shouting—

'Hi! Hi! Where bin 'e going, Pony'll put fut in the ditch in a minute and break her leg and all the eggs in your basket into the bargain. What ails you, dreaming?'

It was but just in time. Pony and I got out of the ditch as best we might and went on, a bit crestfallen and very mim and careful. Then it came over me on a sudden that I should see the mind of Kester Woodseaves in those letters as open as the sky. I should know him as if I lived along of him. For it inna by the deal that's said, but by what's in the things said, that you can know a person. Just as it inna the extra length or breadth of a gown that keeps you warm, but the quality of the stuff. In all he wrote, I'd find him. For you canna write a word, even, but you show yourself--in the word you choose, and the shape of the letters, and whether you write tall or short, plain or flourished. It's a game of *I spy* and there's nowhere to hide. I thought how Mister Woodseaves would go tramping home, pleased to ha' done a kindness, and very pleased to be unlocking his own door, lighting his own fire, and keeping himself to himself. And all the while he'd have showed himself to me, let me into the house of his mind, bid me to sit down by the fire of his great kindness.

> 'He brought me to his noble house.
> His banner it was love.'

'Prue!' shouted Gideon. 'Dang the girl! Oh, dang the girl! Pony's got her foot in the reins and her teeth in the grass, and here I've been obleeged to come back half a mile. Market day and all! Whatever ails you? Be you sickening for summat? Dear to goodness! Anybody ud think you were in love!'

After that, pony and I were very careful. We kept our thoughts on the road and the market, and as you always come, at long last, where your thoughts are, so we came to Lullingford and found the Hiring Fair just beginning.

The long row of young folks, and some not so young, who were there to be hired, began near our stall. Each one carried the sign of his trade or hers. A cook had a big wooden spoon, and if the young fellows were too gallus she'd smack them over the head with the flat of it. Men that went with the teams had whips, hedgers a brummock, gardeners a spade. Cowmen carried a bright tin milk pail, thatchers a bundle of straw. A blacksmith wore a horseshoe in his hat, and there were a tuthree of them, for a few big farms would club together and hire a blacksmith by the year. Shepherds had a crook and bailiffs a lanthorn, to show how late they'd be out and about after robbers. Though, as Gideon said, having a lanthorn is no more promise that a man'll so much as put his nose out his bedclothes after dark than it's promise when a chap agrees to the text, 'Thou shalt not covet thy neighbour's house,' of a Sunday that he wunna spend all the week trying to compass it. Which was just what Gideon did himself.

There were tailors and weavers, wool carders and cobblers too, for the farmers clubbed together for them also. The carders had a hank of coloured wool, and the tailors made great game running up and down the line of young women and threatening to cut their petticoats short.

Jancis laughed with the rest, but I could see she'd been crying. She looked a real picture in her print gown and bonnet, with the dairymaid's milking stool. They were a tidy set of young women, the housemaids with broom on shoulder, the laundrymaids with dollies. It was no wonder that many a young farmer, who wanted neither cook nor dairymaid, should linger a bit, and that it should come into his mind that he wanted a wife.

'There's Grimble,' said Gideon. 'I made sure he'd come, because of the bull-baiting. He's just got a new dog, I hear tell, as fierce as fire.'

There was most always a bull-baiting after May Fair, and it was a thing I couldna abide. I looked where Gideon pointed and saw Mister Grimble, a man with a long nose that looked as if he poked it into everybody's business and stirred up trouble.

'Be that his missus?' I said.

Gideon looked at the woman, like a gingerbread doll, flat and baked pale, with curranty eyes, and said it was.

'Very near, and a driver,' I said.

'Well, Jancis'll take a deal of driving. The pretty ones be always the idle ones. And she's used to being clemmed at home. She'll see she dunna clem to much.'

He seemed quite unconsarned.

'She'd be better, a power, at a small place with nice folk that ud treat her kind,' I said. 'What for do you want her to go to Grimbles'?'

'More money. They give a better wage than smaller folk. We mun think of that first.'

'The bane!' I whispered. 'The precious bane!'

For indeed this talk of money was beginning to wear on me like a song sung over and over, and a song misliked to start with. Gideon had spoken to Farmer Grimble about Jancis, so, as she never dared to go against his word, she beckoned to Beguildy and said—

'Mister Grimble's missus'll hire me, Feyther, if you please.'

'Oh, 'er will, will 'er? And what'll you give me for the wench, for dree year?'

'Eighteen pound.'

'Make it twenty and you shall take her.'

'Nay, nay, it's too much.'

'She can work if she's a mind. She's strong. I give you leave if you make it twenty, to drive if she wunna be led.'

'If you lay finger on my girl it'll be the worse for ye,' said Gideon. 'And *she's* to have the money, not you, Beguildy.'

'Hearken, hearken! Did ever you hear the like! A fellow that was born under the threepenny planet and sleeps on face and'll come to be drowned!

Gideon fell into a sudden rage and gave him a great clout with the flat of his hand, and Beguildy screamed out--

'I'll pay ye! I'll pay ye for this! Curse ye! The very spit of your dad you be. You owe me a crown,' he says, going by me on a blast of air. 'And you canna leave me and mine alone. Curse ye! In sowing and harvesting. In meadows and housen. By fire and by water. A waxen man! I'll make a waxen man this night, and call it Sarn. Slow, slow, it'll consume away--Sarn, the sin-eater!'

Gideon looked at him, making no sign. The people drew back a bit, fearing they knew not what. Just then, elbowing through the crowd, came the young squire, Mister Camperdine's nephew.

'I heard,' he says to Beguildy, 'that Venus was come to the Hiring Fair. My aunt wants a still-room maid, and I came to see if Venus--'

'If you mean Jancis Beguildy, sir,' says Gideon, speaking quick, 'she's prenticed already.'

'What, so soon?'

'Ah, to a farmer a great way off.'

He looked hard at Mister Camperdine, and Mister Camperdine looked hard back.

'It's a great disappointment,' says Mister Camperdine, 'for my good aunt.'

'Your lady-aunt, sir,' says Gideon very dry-like, 'will soon find another maid. Never faithful to one long, if I may make so bold, your lady-aunt inna, sir!'

The young squire frowned, but looking around and seeing nobody but Jancis, short and plump, he supposed the one he was after had gone already, and so thought further argling but waste of time. He sighed and said to himself--

'So Venus vanishes!' and went away. And very glad I was to see the last of him.

Beguildy and Jancis went to the inn with the Grimbles to sign the prentice paper binding Jancis for three years. She was to drive back with them that night. She was free till then, and Gideon said seeing she was going to work for Lullingford New House, she ought to have a look at it. So off they went, while I minded the stall.

I'd all but done, for the place being fuller than ordinary, the things went off pretty quick. The lines of young people had shrunken till there were only a few left that were wanted by none. These were such as were known to be over-fond of the bottle or have a base-born child, or to be incurables of some crippling disease, or not to know rightly what was their own and what was other people's. I used to wonder how they felt, poor folk, going jogging along in the evening, back where they came from. I was glad I worked at whome, and had no need to go and be hired, for certain sure nobody ud have taken me. It was a bitter thought, that.

The marketplace was emptying fast, for the people were getting some refreshment afore the bull-baiting. But I'd still got some daffodillies to sell, and Gideon didna like anything to go back. So I sat still, in the quiet afternoon, looking down the empty street where the shadows and the lilacs and seynty trees lay very dark and pleasant. I noticed that Missis Grimble was there too. She was packing up, and as she put each pat of butter into the basket she gave it a look as much as to say that she'd give it a bit of her mind after, for not being sold. In a while she came across to me.

'You be sister to my new dairymaid's young man, binna you?'

'Ah.'

'I'm in behopes they're serious?'

'Oh, ah!'

'That's right. I like my wenches to be walking out afore they come, and with a chap at a distance. I've got sons, and it's a deal safer. And so long as the chap's at a distance and canna be got at, it dunna hinder the work. Well, I'll be going now. They loose the first dog on the bull in an hour, and I must get a cup of tea first. I never can enjoy anything proper, nor take notice, if I'm clemmed. Whether it's a wedding or a confinement, a baiting or the Lord's Supper, I canna truly enjoy it as it should be enjoyed unless I've got a pint or two of good strong tea inside me. Well, good day. It's a great affliction for ye.'

She went back to her stall to gather her baskets.

There now! Never could I be left in peace. Never could I be let to get away from my misfortune. Here I sat, as peaceful as could be, till she must come and say that. 'A great affliction.' But afore she said it I'd forgotten it, so I hadna got it. I was out of the cage till she put me in again. I was vexed, and the tears stood in my eyes.

Suddenly, along the quiet road, through the shadows, and through the mist of my own eyelashes, I saw somebody coming. A man, it was. And if there be any meaning in that word as I hanna thought on, let them that read put it in. Let them put the strength and the power, the kindness and the patience, the sternness and the stately righteousness of all good men into that word and let him wear it. For it was himself, Kester Woodseaves, the maister.

He came along without haste, yet as if he had some great business to attend. I saw that he was in his best—the black beaver hat, green coat, flowered weskit, and the Wellington boots.

'Weaver, weaver!' called Missis Grimble. 'When'll you work for me next?'

He looked up, and came our way.

What did I do, I, that knew his smile was my summer? Why, I got up so hasty that I upset the daffodillies. I left all our baskets and butter-cloths, and the jam-pots for flowers, and I ran from the place as if summat was after me. But, being that the market was at the end of the road, and only open in front, there was nowhere for me to go but into the market-keeper's office, which was a dark room at the back of the market, and had a small window with no glass, looking on the stalls. So I couldna help but hear all they said.

'Why, lookye!' Missie Grimble screamed out like a cackling hen, 'her's fled away as if you were the murrain or the Lord or the bailiffs. What ails the wench? Mostly I see em run to and not *from* when a young chap comes along.'

'Who be she?' asked Kester.

He had ever a very out-of-the-ornary voice. It was like as if, when he spoke, the sound of the speaking made the world new for itself, not caring about the old world. It was like a wide, blossomy thorn-tree on a sweltering day in early June. You could sit down under it and rest you. And it was like the still hearth-fire on a winter night, when wild Edric's out in the forest, and the curtains be close, candles snuffed, all fast, and the master of the hourse raught whome.

'Who *be* she?' he says. And even though it be only a passing thought and three words, I'm a flower that knows the sun.

'Why, her be Sarn's sister from away yonder at the mere. Prue Sarn. The woman with the hare-shotten lip. A very queer creature. But it make 'em queer, you mind, to be born the like of that. Some say she's a bit of a witch.'

He said nought, but he went across and picked up my flowers, setting them in the jam-pots man's fashiuon, a bit clumsy and all thumbs, enough to make you cry with love. I could see from the dark at the back of the office.

'A very neat, tidy figure she's got,' he said. And in a minute I knew that he knew I'd heard, and so would ease the wound. Oh, most kind maister, the very marrow of Him that loved the world so dear!

'Be you going to the baiting, Mister Woodseaves?' asked Missis Grimble.

'Why, yes and no to that.'

'Eh?'

'You'll see in good time, Missis Grimble.'

With that he went on his way. And what did I do? I did a thing I never thought to do for any man, so forrard it was. I came out of the dark room, straight into the sunlight, and step by step along the road I followed him, as if I'd no bash-fulness at all, such as every girl should have. I kept a long way back, for fear he might turn about and see me, but I never let him out of my sight. It seemed as if I couldna. I

234

was drawn on and on. If I lost sight of his green coat round a
turn of the road, I was all distraught till I'd got sight of it
again.

The bull-ring was well beyond the town, in a green
meadow where a brook ran. And though if you'd gone a-
walking in that green meadow any other day in the year, to
gather lilies or forget-me-nots, or to walk beside the water,
folk would have thought it a soft thing to do, it was all right
and proper to-day, because they were going to kill a creature
there.

The people in the road never noticed me, in my plain
black, with my face hid in my bonnet. From a good way off I
could see the ring, and the bright colours of the gowns and
coats all jumbled together, and a deal of sad-colour from the
coats of the working men who could seldom afford a best coat
save the funeral coat of the family. I could see the bull, a
little white one, tied to a staple in the wall of the bull-ring,
which was a semi-circle built of rough grey stones. The
bright yellow sunshine held them all, as if they were bees in
the mid of the honeycombs, and the blue air, the brown
water, the green meadow were all so fair, I could not believe
blood must be shed on such a day. I wonder to myself, times,
if it was fair, clear weather on Golgotha when Mary looked up
at the cross, and whether there was some small bird singing,
and the bees busy in the clover. Ah! I think it was glass-clear
weather, and bright. For no bitter lacked in that cup, and
surely one of the bitterest things is to see the cruelty of man
on some fair morning with blessing in it.

Chapter Two
The Baiting

As I came nearer I saw that, as the custom was, not only
all the women of Lullingford were there, but all the children
as well. I thought it shame to bring these poor things, that
would soon enough know the evil of the world, to see the dogs
torn to ribbons and the hapless beast killed. I said so after to
Gideon, but he thought nothing of it.

'Why, you'd make 'em as soft as 'ool,' he said. 'They mun
be brave and well-plucked.'

I said I couldna see that it was soft not to like to see a
cruel deed, and that it seemed to me to be braver not to like
seeing another's pain.

'Well, well, we canna make the world, for it's made
already,' says Gideon.

There it all was, then, the crowd, the shouting, and bet-
ting, the yapping and snarling of the dogs, people elbowing
and pushing, men crying hot taters and chestnuts, apples,
spiced ale, and gingerbread, children in their white pinnies
watching the bull, very skeered, for it was grumbling to

itself. Poor thing, it was thinking of its own big blackberry pasture at the back of Callard's Dingle, I make no doubt. It hated neither men nor dogs, and had no grudge against any if only it could be back there, roving the meadows in the dew. There they all were, and there was Kester. I lost sight of him in the crowd, and hastened my steps, with a wonder in my heart the while what he could be doing in such a place. For I thought him to be a different kind of man from all these. Yet such faith I had in him that I was sure, if he was here, that he was here for good. And something drove me on, so that I must seek him in the crowd, and keep nigh him, as if I was his angel for that day. A poor angel, but God minds not much, I think, what like His angels be, so that they do His work proper. The shepherd's collie that runs home to warn the missus that her man has fallen down the rock, is his angel sure enough, though he may be a mongrel of the very worst, with ears as flat as a spaniel.

Blindly and without reason, like the shepherd's dog, I kept close to Kester Woodseaves, yet not so close that he might see me. So it was that I heard all he said to the men who stood round about the ring with their dogs, a bit apart from the crowd. And though they were men of my own country-side, and some of them known to me, yet I must say that there were among them a tuthree very evil faces. The dogs were fierce and ugly, many of em with great jowls, snarling and slavering and showing the red of their eyes. Yet if I had been bound to choose between men and dogs, I'd have chosen the dogs. Mostly they were terriers, but there were a good few bulldogs, and of these Grimbles' new one was far the worst, with a grin that sent me cold. There were one or two with a lot of mastiff in them, and there were a mort of mongrels.

The men all turned towards Kester when he came up, and Farmer Huglet, the chief of them, called out--

'Where's your dawg?'

Mister Huglet was a great raw-looking man who seemed as if he'd come together accidental and was made up of two or three other people's bodies. He was a giant, very nearly, and clumsy, with tremendous long arms, and so big round the mid-dle that tailors who brought their own stuff always charged extra for his clothes. He'd got a mouth like a frog, and a round red snub nose, and such little eyes that they were lost in the mountains of flesh that made up his face. Whenever he couldna understand anything, he laughed, and his laugh was enough to frighten you. It came pretty often too. Grimble was hand-in-glove with him, and while Huglet stuck his red snub nose in the air, Grimble kept his long pale one down, so between them they didna miss much. They'd each got two dogs.

'Why, it's the weaver,' says Grimble. "Dunna you know weaver, Huglet?'

'Why, no, we hanna crossed paths afore. My brother-law weaves for me, you mind. Well, weaver, where's your dawg?'

'I've got none.'

'No dawg? Stand aside, then.'

But he stood where he was. It so happed that he was about at the mid of the half-moon of grey stone that made the bull-ring, and the men with the dogs fell away a bit on either hand, so he was alone. Standing there so slim and straight in his green coat, with the airs blowing his hair a bit, so that a lock of it fell o'er his brow, his hat being under arm, he seemed to have nought to do with any there, but to be a part of the fair meadow, that matched his coat. He wore no beard nor whiskers, so you could see the shape and colour and the lines of all his face, which seemed to me to be a face you could never tire of looking on. Times I wonder if heaven will be thus, a long gazing on a face you canna tire of, but must ever have one more glimpse. He had a kind of arrowy look, so that though Huglet towered over him, he seemed to tower over Huglet. He looked round about and said--

'Chaps, I've come to ask ye to stop this.'

There was a long, bepuzzled silence. Then Huglet laughed and slapped his thigh, and roared again. Grimble looked at his boots and gave a snigger.

'Well, that's a good un!' shouted Huglet. 'Stop the bull-baiting, oot, young fellow?'

'Ah. I'd lief stop it.'

'And what for would you stop it, dear 'eart?' asked Grimble in a soft, sing-song voice.

'Stop it?' roars Huglet 'he *canna* stop it.'

'I'd lief it was stopped over all England.'

'You'd lief a deal, young man. Why, I tell ye there's bin bull-baiting in England ever since it *was* England! Take away the good old sport and it wouldna *be* England!'

All this he said in the same loud roaring voice.

'I asked ye, what for would ye stop it?' repeated Grimble, soft and obstinate.

'Because it's a cruel, miserable business.'

'It inna cruel. The dawgs like it. They enjoy it. And the bull likes it right well.'

Mister Grimble looked down at the trampled grass for all the world as if he was reading the words there.

'What's it matter if they enjoy it or not? *I* enjoy it!' says Huglet. 'That's enough, inna it?'

The other men drew round. For though it was the ordinary thing to hear Mister Huglet shouting fit to burst, it was out of the common to hear him shouting so long at one person. When Huglet shouted like he was doing now, folk said that the person he was shouting at always gave in and went away quiet.

'What be trouble?' asked Mister Callard, the owner of the bull. Mister Huglet turned around and spluttered out--

'This here borsted fellow wants to stop the baiting. The baiting, mind, as we all come a many weary mile to see.'

'Rising up a great while afore day,' puts in Mister Grimble.

'Dear now! And missus and me at such trouble to bring the beast along bright and early. Whatever ails the mon?'

He looked at Kester as the apothecary will look at a man a long while sick.

'Ah,' says the landlord of the *Mug of Cider*, 'I've heard tell of folks as wanted to stop the long kneeling. I've even heard of a tuthree as wanted to stop wars and rumours of wars, but bull-baiting? Never in life! Whoever, save a few fratchety parsons, did ever want to stop a baiting?'

'He must be going a bit simple, poor fellow,' says Grimble. 'Feel well, weaver?'

The miller came up and had a look, shook his head, and went away, which was a great deal for the miller to do.

'But what *for* do ye want to stop it, like?' says Mister Callard, very puzzled.

'I've told em why. Never mind all that. Look ye, Mister Callard, ool ye sell the bull to me?'

'Sell un?'

'Ah, I wunna argle and bargle over the price.'

'But it wouldna be worth my while. I'll get more, a power, by letting un fight. Win, and I'll be a rich mon. Lose, and I get best butcher's price from the ring owners, seesta?'

'What ud you make if he won?'

'Twenty pound.'

'I'll give you twenty pound, and you can take the beast away.'

'God bless me!' says Mister Callard. 'Oh, God bless me, I'm sure.'

He stared at Kester as if he was spirit-struck.

'Bargain?' says Kester.

Missis Callard, who never spoke but after Callard spoke, and then said the same thing, and never did ought but what she was told to do, came up all in a flusker, leading the bull.

'Take the gentleman's offer, Father! Take it, my dear!' she said, all out of breath. 'Take the twenty pound and us'll lead the darling whome.'

Callard was so astounded at her daring to speak that he could only keep on saying--

'God bless me!'

'God bless ye, is it?' says Huglet, beginning to roar again. 'I'll give ye God bless ye if you do any such thing, Callard. Dang me! Spoil all our sport for twenty pound! I'll larn ye! And you too, young man!'

'Oh, but he mun be worse than sawft or simple, he mun be stark raving mad to offer twenty pound for the little beast and then give back what he's bought,' says Grimble. 'Oh, I could cry! Yet the poor chap was all right Monday was a fornit, weaving for us as nice as nice. But he's gone wrong in the yead since, surely to goodness! Oh, dear me!'

He wiped his face and seemed quite taken-to.

Kester pulled out his wallet and offered Callard the money. It was pretty well all his uncle left him, I doubt.

By this, Missis Callard had called all the children to her, for they had five children as well as the baby, and she whispered em, and all of a sudden they cried out together, 'Take it, Feyther! Take it, honoured Feyther! We beseech thee to hear us!'

At the surprise of that, Mister Callard seemed to be quite moithered, and he reached out his hand to Kester for the money. But Mister Huglet struck it down.

'I wunna be robbed of my sport!' he said. 'Dunna you dare take it, Callard. We want our sport, I tell ye!'

All the men with dogs looked black and muttered—

'Ah, that's righteous! That's gospel! We want our sport!'

'Chaps,' says Kester, very pleading, 'it be pity on so fine a day to set one poor creature to tear another. Devil's work, it be. If it's fighting you want, why canna you wrostle, or box man to man? Look ye! To make a bit of sport, I'll take any six of ye on, one after other, to wrostle. The one that beats me by most shall take my coat, and the next shall take my hat and weskit. Now then!'

Nobody said anything, only they shuffled a bit, and looked here and there. Everybody seemed to know that Kester was a very good wrostler, and nobody seemed to take to the job. Mister Grimble looked at Kester as if he hated him. And it was plain, by what came next, that he did, in very truth. For now, having made up his mind not to play second any more to Mister Huglet, he up and said—

'The young man speaks well. Now, I'll fall in with all he says and agree to the stopping of the baiting this day, on one condition.'

'Out with it,' says Kester.

'That you take on the dawgs yerself.'

Mister Grimble gave a spiteful cackling laugh, and Mister Huglet roared agen.

'Got ye there, me lad!' he shouted. And Grimble said—

'You may love the dumb creatures ooth yer purse, but ye wunna go so far as to love em ooth yer own blood!'

'Go on with the baiting!' orders Mister Huglet.

'Tie the beast up agen,' says Mister Callard to his missus, who was standing by, eager to hand it over to Kester, so as he could give it back as he said.

'Whose dawg drew first?'

Mister Huglet took no more notice of Kester, but went on with the arrangements.

'Mister Towler's dawg drew first, and *Mug o' Cider* second,' said one of the owners of the bull-ring.

'Come forrard, Towler.'

Kester stood very still, eyeing Mister Grimble till he got quite put about. For he didna seem to want to meet Kester's eye.

'That ud be the best bit of sport ever you had, eh, Mister Grimble?' says Kester at last. 'To see a man baited like a bull.'

'Why, nobody ud be such a fool.'

Kester looked around.

'Chaps!' he says, 'if so be as I agree to Mister Grimble's plan and take on the the dogs one by one, not to kill 'em, but to put 'em on chain with nought but my bare hands, and they as savage as you like, if I do this at my own risk, will ye give it me in writing as there wunna be another baiting in Lullingford for ten years? And if I fail to put any dog on chain, I've lost and the baiting goes on.'

Everybody's tongue was loosed at that.

'God bless me!'

'Dear to goodness!'

'Domm it!'

'Well, that beats all, dang it!'

'Daze my 'ouns!'

There was a regular clack of voices.

One or two called out that they wouldna agree to it. But mostly they were very curious to see what would come of it, and as it was known that the parson didna like the baitings and had been werriting the squire to put a stop to them, everybody thought they might be stopped soon anyway, and so they might as well have the fun, for this was a chance of rare sport, and the like of it had never been seen in the place.

When Mister Huglet could speak for laughing, he explained to all the people what was doing.

'Hands up for it!' he called out.

All but about a dozen held up their hands.

'Done!' says Mister Huglet. 'And done *for*, my fine feller!'

I caught hold of Miller's Tim and told him to go to Kester and whisper as Grimble's dog was a new one, and extra bad in temper. But indeed I felt that neither this nor anything was any manner of use, and I couldna think of ought to do. But one thing I was determined on, I'd keep nigh him, and when he was down I'd rush in and drag him away, and if Grimble interfered it ud be the worse for un. There's none so fierce as a loving woman, and it always seemed a strange thing to me that the Mother of Jesus could keep her hands off the centurion, and it could only have been because her Son had given orders afore. But indeed if it had been me, I think I should have forgot the orders.

Tim came running back, and I saw those strong blue eyes follow and settle on me for a breath. Then I hid behind Missis Callard.

'He knowed it,' says Tim. 'But obleeged all the same.'

I went to the refreshment booth and stole the carving-knife. But almost afore it was hidden under my flounced skirt I saw that there was to be no need of it, anyway for a while. There was to be summat more like a miracle than anything I've seen afore. This was the way of it.

'Go to the mid of the wall,' says Huglet, 'and fasten the dawgs to the bull chain. And if you fasten either of mine, I'll give ye five shilling, me lad! Oh, I could bust a-laughing to see anybody be such fool!'

'Mister Towler's dawg!' says the head of the ring.

'Ready!'

They loosed Towler's terrier, the savagest little beast in the place.

'At 'im! Bite 'im!' shouts Towler, and I was like to faint. And then it came to pass.

Kester stepped forward.

'Well, Bingo!' he says. 'Good dog!'

Bingo stopped, looked at Towler as much as to say he'd made a mistake, and ran to Kester as pleased as Punch, wagging tail and fawning round.

'We be friends, binna we?' says Kester.

Towler gave a curse, and Huglet looked as black as night. But nobody could say it wunna fair and square, and some of the better sort laughed and said, 'Good for you, lad!'

It was the same with the *Mug o' Cider* dog, and the next. As the owners came up to fetch them when they were on the chain, they looked very old-fashioned and taken aback.

Kester laughed.

'I like a dog,' he says. 'Dumb things be my fancy. You couldna know it, but so it is, and I can only see one dog here as inna friend to me, being new-come to these parts.'

'Ah,' says Grimble, 'you wunna play yer May-games with Toby. Indeed to goodness, if you get off with your life you'll do well.'

All in a minute I thought of a better thing than the carving-knife, though I kept that in case of need. I'd run to the town for the apothecary, there being no doctor in the place, to have him there in case of harm. There were a sight more dogs yet, for they wouldna let him off any. There met be time if I was quick. So, with the carving-knife still under my dress, I edged out of the crowd, got into the road and ran for dear life. But afore I went, I took one look at him I did love, since if I wasna quick enough I might never see him alive again.

He was laughing, and Huglet was leading one of his dogs away. Though Kester didna weave for Huglet, he'd made friends with his dogs on market days, outside the *Mug o' Cider*, seemingly. He's such a way with animals that a tuthree minutes was enough, and they were friends to him for ever.

And as I looked back, it seemed to me, though I told myself it must be fancy, that those eyes, so live and bright, dwelt on me, and smiled atme, friended me and pled with me, being as are the eyes of a man when he looks long upon his dear acquaintance, who has given her peace for his, her soul to his keeping, and her body for his joy.

But as I ran I said to myself--

'Nay, Prue Sarn, you be nought but his angel, and a poor daggly sort of angel, too.'

And all the blue bird's eye in the hedge banks went into a mist of tears as I ran, and looked no more like flowers, but like a blue tide of sorrow to drown me.

Chapter Three
'The Best Tall Script, Flourished

I may say I went over the distance to the town quicker than it's been done this long while. I hid the carving-knife in the hedge, for fear of tripping over it. The apothecary's was open, as I thought, for he was churchwarden, and couldna go agen the parson. I never saw the big green and red bottles look so beautiful, as if they were full of water from Paradise river. Inside there was a pleasant dusk, for the little window was so close-set with liniments and medicines, drenches for horses, simples for cows, plaisters, cordials, and bunches of yarbs that you couldna see at all. It smelt very pleasantly of peppermint, yarbs and soap, and the apothecary looked at me kindly over his spectacles and asked what the matter was.

'Why, sir, it's murder, pretty nigh,' I says. 'I do beseech you to shut up the shop and come, or such a man as this town never saw afore, nor will again, will be done to death.'

He pulled on his boots, good man, at that.

'What remedies must I bring?' he says. 'You can tell me the rest as we run.'

So I told him summat for dog-bites and summat to bring a man round when he was near death. In a minute he clapped his hat on, and off we went.

'Take a sup of brandy,' he says. 'You're nigh done.'

But I told him, no, only if I fell behind he must hasten on to the bull-ring.

I fell back just afore we got to the carving-knife, and caught up again at the field gate. As we came in I could see an awful struggle going on, for we were only just in time. He'd finished but for Grimble's dog.

As we came up there was a roar. He'd got the dog chained. Then there was another roar, and I saw (oh, my dear love!) that the dog had got him by the throat.

I caught Grimble's shoulder.

'Take yer dog off!' I said.

Grimble never stirred.

A second of that grip and he as I loved so dear ud be dead and cold.

I rushed forrard, I, that had never wilfully hurt any living creature, and as the great beast stood reared with his teeth in my maister's throat, I ran him through the heart.

The blood spurted, and the heavy body fell down all of a heap, and Kester with it.

I pulled him away and dragged the dog's jaws apart. There seemed to be no life in Kester.

'Water!' I says to Huglet, who chanced to be nighest. 'Fetch water, you murderer! Brandy, Mister Camlet, please!'

He stooped over Kester.

'I mun burn the bite,' he said. 'Best do it afore we bring him round. But how to heat the iron?'

I stood up. I cared for nobody. They couldna have been more feared if I'd been a savage queen.

'Six men pick up sticks!' I says. 'And quick about it! And you, Grimble, find flint and tinder.'

'I hanna got one,' he muttered.

'Find one!' I screamed like a wild thing, holding up the knife. "Find one, or--'

The fire was blazing quicker than it takes to tell it. We poured a little brandy down Kester's throat, to keep the spark of life in, then Mister Camlet burnt the bite, and Kester awoke with a shout of agony, for being in a dead swound he hadna been ready for the pain.

'There, there, my dear!' I says. For the shriek went through my heart. 'There, there. It be done now! None shall touch you now.'

Mister Camlet bound him up, and washed his face with cold water and gave him more brandy.

'Not a deep wound,' says Mister Camlet. 'We were only just in time, though.'

'We couldna help but be in time,' I says, 'I be his angel for today.'

And with that the green field swam up afore me and I swounded clean away. When I came to myself there were Gideon and Jancis sitting by me on the grass, and all the folks were gone.

'Where be he?' I says.

'Who? Weaver?' says Jancis. 'He be all right and cared for. They've took him back to Lullingford, and Missis Callard'll stop with him.'

'She's mighty pleased with the little bull,' said Gideon. 'You saved that chap's life, and no mistake, Prue. I never saw the like! We were just coming in at the field gate, and I looked across and say you. "By gum!" I says. And that was all I did say. I ran, and Jancis run, but you'd done for the owd dog afore we could come at you. You take the medal, Prue!'

'You canna ride home, Prue. Shall I run and ask Miller to take her, Sarn? And couldna I come back and give her a hand with the work for a day or two?'

'You can ask Miller and welcome. It's a good thought. But as for coming back, you know very well you're Grimble's vessel-maid now, till three years.'

'I didna want to be. It's you and Feyther made me.'

'Well, but you've seen the house, hanna you? You'll be working for that and the 'unt Ball and the silver plate.'

'Ah. I've seen the house, and I think it looks a dark, bitter old place, for all it's new, and I'd liefer never go to no 'unt Ball than lead the life of a driven slave.'

She was crying, but it made no manner of difference to Gideon.

'You've got to go to Grimble's and you've got to go to the 'unt Ball in good time, so why make such a ding-dong?'

'But why must I, Sarn?'

'Because my mind's set.'

It was almost as if he said, 'Because I'm in the stocks.' As if his maid called him to come maying, but, feet and hands, he was fast bound.

When she was gone, they gave me a sup of tea at the *Mug o' Cider*, for I was all of a-tremble still, and then Miller helped me up into the gig, and the old coach horse, that had known the merry sound of the horn tooting, and the sudden light and commotion at the turnpikes, when they rushed out in the dead dark to open, laboured into a trot. For indeed he seemed much of Missis Miller's mind, caring not if he never saw home again. Missis Miller had nought to say, Miller as usual had nought also, and Polly was asleep. After a while Missis Miller and Tim went to sleep too. We drove on sadly in the chilly evening. It was dusk, and then it was dark. Gideon was far ahead, for Bendigo was a good trotter, though aged. The mill pony, tied to the back of the gig, clopped onwards with a sorrowful sound.

It suited me, the quiet and the melancholy, for I was sad and quiet too. He that I loved was hurt, and I couldna get to him. There he lay, as weak as a babe, and only Missis Callard to tend him. I forgot that she, having six, was well knowledged in tending helpless folk, for it is the way of lovers to think that none can bless or succour their love but their own selves. And there is a touch of truth in it, maybe more than a touch. We went on and on, through country that was neither hilly nor flat, in a night neither dark nor gleamy, feeling neither glad nor sorry. I thought we were like people bound for some place beyond the world that was neither hell nor heaven. Our six heads, counting the nag's all nid-nodded, and I think we were all asleep, even the old coach horse, when the miller spoke, out of his sleep, I do believe.

'I canna abide 'em,' he said, with a nod toerts his wife and children. 'I wish they were kit-cats, to drown in mill-pond. I wish the world and all was a kit-cat.'

He said no more. It was like when they say the creed, solemn and choppy. That was all the miller ever said to me, and I do think he said it in his sleep. On we went, till we came to the dark mill, the soundless water, like soft black crape. The others got out and untied the pony, and Miller drove me back to Sarn. The night was full of the smell of water and moss, with a drift of primrose scent now and again. I thought of the weaver's house, that seemed built of a spell, and him, lying there in the kitchen with the loom, his face barred with the shadow of it, cast by the rushlight, his hair all tousled and damp with the sweat of pain.

'If Missis Callard spoke unkind to him, I could slap her babby,' I thought. But I knew she wouldna. She was a good soul, though I always thought she must have had a mind like a shell, hollow, to echo other people as she did.

When we came to our place, there was Mother on the doorsill, very consarned. She said what nobody else had, and what I'd never thought of.

'You met ha' been killed, Prue!'

She sat down and began to cry, so I had to laugh at her and ask for summat to eat, to show I was alive all right. So then she got me such a meal as never was, though she should by rights have been asleep hours. Seemingly Gideon had told her some sort of tale, but she must know more. She wasna to be satisfied, but kept on wanting more. She put on her spectacles and looked at me very attentive, sitting there in the big oak chair. I was quite put-about with her staring so, with that still look of a sitting bird when somebody comes and spies at her, and she never winks nor flinches, but just looks back with sharp brown eyes, as much as to say, 'I'll stand by what's mine.' Mother seemed to be looking past me at summat that threatened me. Maybe it was my Fate, as she thought it to be. It was summat that threatened to do me harm, I'm sure, for after a bit Mother looked very defiant and sat up ever so straight and said--

'We'll have the weaver.'

Just as if somebody forbad her to have him.

She said nought of all I'd told her, never a word about it being a foolish or forrard thing to save a strange young man's life without with your leave or by your leave. She only kept on giving little nods now and again, and saying--

'Ah. Come summer, we'll have weaver.'

Then she said she'd go to bed now, and I went and wrote in my book.

There was no change in our lives, only it was quieter without Jancis coming in of a Sunday. The Stone House seemed very lonesome lacking her, and Missis Beguildy not half the woman she had been. She seemed to cling to me, and kept talking of the little ways and sayings of Jancis as if she was dead. This made Beguildy very angry, for in truth he was sorry Jancis was gone, not only because of the young squire, but because in her unhandy way she'd got through a good bit of work. He'd say, 'Now, hush thy noise, woman. The wench'll be back in no time, with twenty pound in hand, dear me. Now, dunna go to talk of her as if she was dead, fool! A gamesome lusty young woman the like of that! Many's the golden pound her'll put in our pockets, when she's learnt her duty, and given over hankering after a man as was born under the threepenny planet, and'll come to be drowned. No offence meant, Prue, and none taken I'm in behopes. You ploughed the gorsty bit right tidy, Prue, and us'll do words of four synnables this day, if you've a mind.'

Oh, there's no doubt Beguildy was a very queer old man. I was used to think if he'd had a good education he met have been one of these great men we all think so much of. A great scholar he could have been, or a music-man, or a rhymer, or a preacher. And maybe if all of his mind had been used proper, he wouldna have brought ruination on hisself as he did. Ah! And on more than hisself. But that we cannot know. We are His mommets that made us, I do think. He takes us from the box, whiles, and saith, 'Dance now!' or maybe it must bow, or wave a hand or fall down in a swound. Then He puts it back in box, for the part is played. It may be a Mumming, or a Christmas or Easter play, or a tragedy. That is as He pleases. The play is of His making. So the evil mommets do His will as well as the good, since they act the part set for them. How would it be if the play came to the hour when the villainous man must do evilly, and see! he is on his knee-bones at his prayers. Then the play would be in very poor case. There was a mommet once called Judas, and if he had started away from his set part in fear, we should none of us have been saved. Which is all a very strange mystery, and so we must leave it. But it being so, I think we do wrongly to blame ill-doers too hardly. It is a dreadful fate to be obleeged to act in a curst, ugly way, when surely none would choose it. 'Needs be that offences come.' How should Gabriel show his skill with a two-edged sword if Lucifer wouldna fight? 'But woe be to him by whom they come.' Ah! So if the play has a murder in it, or if a good maid is brought to shame, a mommet must be found to do the bad work, though very like, if they could choose, never a one but would say, 'Not me, Maister!' Only they know nought. For I think we be not very different from the beasts, that work deathly harms in the dark of their minds, knowing nothing, weltering in blood, crouching and springing on their prey, with a sound of shrieks in the night, and yet all the while as innicent as a babe. And I think we be not very much other than the storms that raven in the forest, and the hungry fire that licks up lives in a moment, and the lips of the water, sucking in our kin. It is all in the Play. But if we be chosen for a pleasant, merry part, how thankful we ought to be, giving great praise, and helping those less fortunate, and even being grateful to that poor mommet which goeth about night and day to work our destruction. For it might have been the other way.

So, in spite of all, I was always sorry for Beguildy, though, dear knows, he was the villain in our story.

We had a very middling crop that summer, both of grass and grain. Our lives went to the same tune, with no change, saving that Mother was as good as her word and did send for Kester.

I thought she seemed very busy all that June, spinning as if it was ever so, till even Gideon gave a word of praise. Then one day she said—

'There's such a deal spun, I shall be obleeged to send for Weaver.'

But I was settled in my mind not to see him, so the day he was coming, about the end of hay harvest, I took the brummock and went hedging in the far fields where none would find me.

'I'm going hedging, Mother,' I says, "i'll take some bread and cheese. Can you see to the young turkeys and tell Gideon he must make shift with the milking, for I shanna be back till dark.'

What must she do but begin to wring her hands and keep on saying under breath—

'Oh, the pity, the pity, to be so curst!'

But go I did. And when I raught home, there in my attic were the bits of wool and thread he'd left, and a very pleasant smell of tobacco. For he liked to smoke a bit while he worked. And just by the corner of the loom what should I find but a blue-and-white handkerchief, which I very dishonestly did put in my locker, and turned the key with great satisfaction. I said to myself in a kind of gloating way that some day I'd launder it, and roll it up with a bit of lavender, and send it back. But not yet.

Mother was full of tales about the weaver. Oh, he was such a kind man, and strong, and so considerate! I thought I could have told her that. Like a son to her, he'd been, she said. I should ha' seen him a-sitting on the settle at his tea. I dare say, I thought, and lose my heart worse than ever!

'Wanted to know if I'd any other family besides Sarn,' she said. 'So I told un.'

'Oh, Mother, what did you tell him?' I said.

'I told un I'd got the best girl in the 'orld, and a good daughter to me, and very jimp and slender, with a long, silky plait to the knees, and dark, meltin' eyes, and such pleasant ways, merry and mocking and pitiful. Ah! I told un! Proper, I did! And I told un you could do the tall script and the short, and that Beguildy was learning you to read, and that you could do words of four synnables now.'

'Dear to goodness, Mother,' I said, 'what a tale you made out!'

'No tale, my dear, for 'tis the truth.'

'Did you say ought of Gideon's letters? I mean, did you say I wrote 'em?'

'Why, no, my dear. Sarn met not ha' like it, nor Jancis, nor you.'

'No. You've got a lot of sense, Mother.'

'It was always said in our family as I had, my dear.'

'So Weaver thinks we're a very well educated family, I make no doubt, Mother, and he'll take it for gospel that Gideon writes the letters.'

After, when I was helping her to bed, I took courage to say--

'Did you tell Weaver I was hare-shotten?'

'No, no, my dear! What for should I do that?'

'Only he met be thinking of me a bit, seeing you said such things, and then if he met me ever--'

'Well, my dear, if he met you, and he's the man I think him, he'd be bound to like you right well,' says Mother roundly.

When I'd tucked her in, she catched my hand.

'Prue, should you care if he'd got but one leg, one arm, or was all pitted with the smallpox?'

'Care, Mother?' I cried out all in a minute and never thinking, 'of course I shouldna care. I should love un the more for it!'

'I knowed you did, my dear,' says Mother, very contented. 'I knowed you loved the man. And I'm right glad of it. Now, dunna you hide from him, Prue. Be well plucked and risk all, like a good player in the game of Costly Colours.'

'No, no! Never will I. Oh, Mother, it was unkind in you to catch me like that!'

'I only wanted to know, Prue. I be getting ancient and old, and the time draws nigh when life'll be a burden. I'd lief know as there was good in store for the best girl ever.'

She looked out and away through the little moony window, with the dark round blots that were red roses pressing on the panes, and the silver sky dim, and not starry, but very kind-seeming, and she seemed to be listening to summat. Then she said--

248

'I do believe all shall be well with you, Prue. It's come to my heart as soft as dew, and as sweet as a red rose, that you'll get love as well as give it. After my time, though, after my time. But no matter for that, so I do know it's to come.'

I felt a shiver of strangeness in the night.

'What is it, my dear?' I asked her. 'Is it the second sight?'

'No. I see nought. But I feel it within me.'

'You be well, be you, Mother?' I said, for I was afraid she might be slipping from me, since the dying are ever so.

But she said, yes, she was in her daily health, and well, and not going to die this many a day, only it came on her at the thought of Weaver, and how he'd said--

'Well, single I am, and single shall stay, I do believe. But if ever I did think of asking to wed, it ud be just such another as that'n.'

At the end of corn harvest Gideon asked me to write his second letter to Jancis.

We were having our suppers on the bench under the dairy window. After, I fetched the ink and said what should I write? So he said I must write that he was well and hope she was, and she was to be a good girl and work hard and not ask for any early money for clo'es or boots, but think of all that was to come, and it was a middling harvest, and her father still in the same mind about the young squire, who was about coming back from the Low Countries next year with his pockets full of money, and the big longhorn cow had calved, but dropped her calf like the gwerian she was, and to tell Mister Grimble he could do with a few lambs when he fetched them off the hills for the winter, but no sign of fut-rot, or home they'd come, dang-swang, and so no more from G. Sarn.

Then he said, 'Put in as I'll see her, Christmas market, if Grimbles ool bring her.'

I said I'd do the best I could, and did it matter if I put in a bit more? And I couldna help but laugh, for it did seem such a peculiar letter for a fellow to write to his sweetheart. And Gideon looked up very sharp and said, why did I want to write more? So I said the pen did run away sometimes, and he said he supposed it wunna easy to know quite what you were at when you started writing, and God save him from such foolishness, and so long as I put in all he'd told me I might put in some as well, if I'd a mind.

So I wrote it.

SARN.

September Twenty-six.

MY DEAR SWEETHEART,

It do seem a long while since your letter, which was a beauty, and I kissed it a good few times. You know very well how to do a love letter. I can see the two of you at it, your golden hair shining and your pretty face bent down, and Weaver smiling a bit, and looking well amused, with those eyes that would 'tice any girl away from her own man, and mind you dunna fall in love with anybody but me, if possible. Maybe I shall see you at the Christmas market. Tell Weaver that all Mother's tales of our Prue be made-ups, for she's very ornary in every way. Tell Mister Grimble I could do with a few lambs. Tell Weaver when he goes nigh Huglet's he might carry a gun as well as not, for Huglet's got an awful dog now, and I hope all's well betwixt Weaver and Grimble. If there's ever any sewing work Weaver wants done, being a lone womanless man, I've got two women in my house, Mother and sister, both glad of a job at a fair price, and red cabbage pickle and damson cheese they maken, which pays them very well to sell at half market price, and a charity to employ them. It's a middling harvest, longhorn's dropped her calf, young Camperdine's expected back next year, and if they've gotten fut-rot, back they'll come, dang-swang, and so good-bye for now, and take all care of self. In the beginning of a cough take a lemon and crushed honeycomb fire-hot, and you be my dearest, dearest love as I'd spend my life for very willing any time, and die for you by bite of dog or any way, my dear, and so good night, from your lover

GIDEON SARN.

That is a nice text, 'The Maister be come.'

I often wondered as the autumn went on, and the cold nights, what they thought of my letter. We knew they had it all right, for one market day Gideon came back with the lambs, that Grimble had put in pen for him at the *Mug o' Cider*, and they were good ones, with no fut-rot. But it was drawing on to Christmas when a letter came from Jancis, and I mind it was a wild night, with a lashing of rain on the window, when I read it to Gideon. But it was warm within. It made a good Christmas for me, in spite of work, and Mother very ailing, so as we had to send for the doctor's man all the way from Silverton, for Gideon wouldna hear of the doctor, saying the expense was more than enough as it was. He kept on grumbling and saying she was a burden, and Mother would ask me: 'Does Sarn think I be a burden?' So it was very awkward for me. But that letter was as heartening as a platter of good hot soup, and lest Gideon should take it to his own keeping, I made a copy of it, and this is it.

250

December 1.

MY DEAREST ACQUAINTANCE,
I am thinking of Sarn as I write this, and of the best of lovers. Mister Woodseaves ud be very glad of the sewing and the pickle and the damson cheese Sarn was so kind as to mention. Perhaps might speak to your sister one day about it. Mister Woodseaves says that is the best cough cure ever, and tried it one foggy night after getting back from here to Lullingford, but thinks it ud take a woman to mix it proper. Sorry about the harvest and the calf, but no need to worry about Huglet's dog, not being afraid of any dog, nor of Huglet neither. But that was a near shave at the Baiting, by gum, and a plucky woman to rush in the like of that and save a poor fellow. For Mister Woodseaves hears tell it was a woman did it, a tall slim woman with beautiful dark eyes, so they do say. It inna for me to say anything, as you know, Sarn. But others will talk. Weaver says if ever he had an acquaintance he'd lief she was that sort. And so good night, and a merry Christmas from

JANCIS BEGUILDY.

I love you already, and if these things be done in the dry tree, what shall be done in the green?

Chapter Four
Jancis Runs Away

It was a Christmas Eve again and year and eight months after Kester stopped the bull-baiting. There's been no letters from Jancis a long while, but Gideon never worried about such things. He said it was only the weather, for the roads were so waidy round about Grimble's that nobody could come at them in bad weather. They came to market seldom in winter, but laid in a store of such things as they needed, and Mister Grimble would send half a score waggons of grain to be ground at the mill, and then they'd settle down, the farm and the two labourers' cottages, with the horses in stable and the cattle in the near pasture and the sheep in the mangold fields close by, all snug for the winter. They were used to keep a lot of simples and cures at such farms, because no apothecary or doctor could get to them, the roads being past all telling bad, not if it was ever so.
'Woodseaves canna go there, and Jancis canna send to Lullingford, but come a bit of fair weather, we shall hear,' said Gideon.
I used to think of Jancis, mewed up with Missis Grimble, a woman I couldna abide, nor could Jancis. I thought of the

251

high mountains and the sleat storms like a wall of ice between her and us, and the snow, thick and soft, whispering, whispering.

'It goes round the house, and round the house, and leaves a white glove in the window.'

That's what they say of the snow at Sarn.

There were two sons, of course, to liven things up, but one of them was going to wed with the labourer's girl, and the other was very religious and didna hold with any kind of May-games, nor pleasuring, nor even much laughing and talking. So she'd only Missis Grimble, that was a driver and a scold, and Mister Grimble, that was very awkward in bad weather, because of the rheumatics. I used to think of her a deal. For if you thought of anybody at Sarn, you thought of them a deal, it being so quiet, especially in the winter, and time standing still, so it seemed.

And whenever I thought of Jancis I called to mind a thing I saw once in June, when we had strange untoërt weather and a deal of tempest and sleat, which one day for about an hour turned to snow. And I saw the wild roses, so tender and nesh, and used to nothing colder than dew, with their pale pink petals all full of snow, and seeming to be frozen through and through, gold hearts and all. I thought of her always like that, for I was fond of her, and she seemed a child to me, though she was older. Even in spite of her making me remember that she was pretty and I was ugly, I was fond of her, and the more so when she was in trouble, for I never love folks quite so well when it's bright weather for them. So I wished I could have sent her summat for Christmas, if it was only a hemmed kerchief of plain linen. I'd asked Gideon to inquire after her at Kester's when he went to market, but Kester was away, and the house shut up. That was uncomfortable news, for I liked to think of him by his own fireside, in the little house I knew by sight. It seemed he was nigher then. But it was his custom to go off for a month at a time in the winter to stay at one village or another and do all the weaving there, to save going to-and-again.

It was very quiet in our kitchen. Mother was in bed, being always bed-ridden now in hard weather, and Gideon was in the woods, getting the Christmas brand. For whatever else we were stinted of, we always had that, since it took only labour to get it, and Gideon never grudged that, poor lad. I went to the door to listen if he'd finished chopping, and I could hear the axe barking, and the echo of it coming from across the mere. The trees were mounded up with snow, and the mere frozen till near the middle. The woods, as white as sugar, stood round the water so still, as if they were spelled, like folk in some old tale of witchcraft, so deep they were in trusses and bales of snow, and not a breath stirring. You couldna call summer to mind. You couldna think of the mere with lilies on it, and ripples. I held my breath, it was so quiet, till a redshank called from the far end of the mere by the church, very sorrowful, with a sound like 'Mute! Mute!' Then some widgeon went over against the darkening sky, and I heard Mother give a little cough, so I knew she'd be wanting her tea. The sound of the axe had stopped, so Gideon ud be coming soon, and I set about getting the meal.

I was baking, a thing I dearly liked. Most of the work I did was men's work, and baking seemed so light and pleasant after it. I liked to see the dough rising afore the big red fire, and to get the oven ready with burning wood, raking out the ash after, and setting the loaves in rows. It was pleasant to be in the warm, glowing kitchen, full of the good smell of bread, and to look out at the grey-white fields and woods, cold and lonesome, and then to draw the curtain, and kindle the rushlight, setting the table and putting the tater pie to get hot on the gledes, and knowing that in a little while all those I cared for would be comfortable for the night. The fowl had been shut up since the first dusk, the cows and sheep were folded, Bendigo littered-up, Pussy by hearth, Mother with a bit of fire in her room and the warming-pan in the bed, and now Gideon was on the way back to his supper. The oven being still hot, I put in a batch of mince-pies, for Gideon liked a bit of good fare as well as anybody, though he'd growl times, and talk about ruination, and where'd our house be and the silver plate and all. But though I did as he said all the year round, with a bit of bread and cheese and a tater for a meal, at Christmas time I went by my own road, and we had our merrymaking almost like other folks. And since, after all that came to pass, I've been more glad of that bit of disobedience to Gideon than of anything in our lives then. For I can say, 'Anyway, they had *that*, whatever else they didna have.'

I was singing to myself a bit, and talking to Pussy, who was almost too comfortable to purr, only if I spoke she'd partly get up, and arch herself very polite, and open her mouth to mew, and then be too bone-idle to make any sound. But she looked at me as much as to say, 'I know you made this nice gledy fire to warm me, missus, and I know you've got summat in larder for I, and thank you kindly.'

All of a sudden there came a soft tap at the door. So tiny and timid it was, it might almost have been a poor redbreast tapping with its beak. There was one would come in hard weather, and if I was too long feeding it, it would tap on the window. I went to the door, and it being dark by now, and nobody coming our way in a month of Sundays, I may say I thought of frittening and fairies and Lob-lie-by-the-fire, and all sorts of queer things that were used to happen in time past.

I opened it.

There against the white, dreary stretch of the frozen mere, all woebegone and white in the light of the fire, was Jancis.

No sooner did I pull her in than she fell down dang-swang in a heap on the floor. The poor girl! Never did I see such a pickle. Her clothes were all torn, boots broken, hands and face scatched as if she'd been through brier hedges, which it turned out after that she had, and everything wringing wet as if she'd been dragged out of the mere. She'd fainted dead away, and I'd enough to do to get her round. When she came to, she told me she'd had no food for nearly two days, and she'd walked all the way from Grimble's in this weather.

To think of it! The long and the short of it was that she'd run away, and she'd no money and no decent boots, and she had to slip away when she could, which chanced to be when she hadna got her shawl.

She cried and cried.

'Oh, I couldna bear it, Prue! Oh, dear Prue, dunna scold! It was more than anybody could bear. And when it came nigh Christmas and there was no news, and all of 'em ten times worse, being mewed up with the hard weather, oh I *couldna* bear it. And the girl at the cottage told me that the last two dairymaids ran away as well. She said why didna I run away, too? Partly she said it because she was sorry for me, and partly because Alf Grimble, that's her young man, was paying me attentions. So she told me the best time to go, and kept 'em all out of the way, and gave me some bread and meat and a bottle of milk, and promised to tell them some tale to keep them from following me.'

She stopped a bit for breath, and there came from outside the sound of Gideon's cart-wheels creaking along in the snow.

'What be you going to say to Gideon?' I asked her.

'Oh, dunna let him be angered with me, Prue! Dunna! I canna bear any more. When I tell you all I've been through, you'll see I canna.'

Gideon came to the door, dragging the great log, that was the Christmas brand, on a chain.

'Dunna turn me out, Prue! Whatever he do say, and however angered he be at me losing the place he settled on, keep me for this night!'

So I said did she think any creature could make me turn her out at any time, let alone in such weather? And I tucked her up on settle, and said she must rest now, and afterwards she should have a sup of tea, and then to bed, and all her troubles were over. Then she smiled and whispered--

'I love ye, Prue! You bin like the Saviour to me this night,' and so fell asleep.

Times, seeing what came to pass, I'm main glad of that smile and that whisper.

Eh, but Gideon was in a rage!

'Why, she'll lose all the money,' he says, the first minute, 'and she'll not only lose the money for the year and four months to come, but she'll lose the wages for the year and eight months she's been there. If they break their time, they get no money. You know that as well as I do.'

I asked how he could think of the money when she'd come to our door the like of that, all draggled and half dead.

'You always were a fool, Prue,' he says, 'and I suppose you always will be.'

But my patience was out, and I talked to Gideon straight.

'I'd thank you to keep your tongue in leash this evening, Gideon! Here's Christmas, and Jancis come to you out of death's arms, very nearly. For it wanted but a little. If she'd lost her way again, so late, she'd have been done. And seeing I've taken her in and she's to have my bed, and I've cossetted her for ye, she being your dear acquaintance, you'd ought to be humble and grateful to me and to them above for the salvation of the poor child.'

'Dear to goodness! What a spitfire all in a minute!' says he. He laughed a bit, being startled, for I wasna used to breaking out like that. Then he went tramping into the kitchen.

'Well!' he says, very loud, for he wunna used to sick folks, and he always seemed to think they were deaf. When Mother was sick, he'd shout at her summat odd, though Mother had kept her hearing very well.

'Good evening, Sarn!' says Jancis, very small and weak.

'So you've raught back.'

'Ah!'

'Broke your time and all.'

She began to cry.

'Now then, dunna do that!' he says, quite taken-to. 'Prue'll give me some more tongue if you cry. I amna to say a word, not to-night. There'll be summat to be said to-morrow, but I'm to leave you be to-night. Well, how bin 'ee?'

He stood in the middle of the kitchen and shouted it at her, so I couldna help but laugh.

'Nicely, thank you kindly, Sarn,' she says.

'You dunna do much credit to your pasture at Grimble's. I'll say that. Seen young Camperdine ever?'

'No.'

'Got an acquaintance over yonder?'

'No, Sarn. You be my acquaintance for ever and ever.'

'Not Alf Grimble?'

'No. But he was sweet on me, a bit, and pestered me. That was why I ran away.'

I never thought Jancis was so clever. But every woman's clever when she's in love, I do believe. She was ever so white against the black settle.

'I ran away because you be the only acquaintance I do want, Sarn.'

'So that was it! I'll break Alf's head for un come cattle-market.'

'No. Dunna, dunna!'

'So you ran away all those miles and miles because you didna like Alf, and because I was your dear acquaintance?'

'Ah.'

'Give us a kiss, wench!'

I ran away into the dairy at that, and Pussy with me, for she was always a bit skeered when Gideon was in. I skimmed and skimmed, and if I cried a bit, who was the worse? For I wished I was on settle with a young man shouting at *me* from the middle of the kitchen, and then saying, 'Give us a kiss, wench!' And if you should ask what manner of young man would I choose, I'd say as he'd wear a coat the colour of a May meadow, and look at you with eyes full of power and knowledge till your soul turned right over.

'I canna have what I want, Pussy," I says. 'But you can, for your wants be easy got.'

And I gave her a great saucer of cream. I did! What would Gideon have said if he'd known? But he'd got his cream in the kitchen.

'I'm giving you this Pussy,' I says, 'because I canna get my own cream. It eases me to see somebody satisfied.'

She looked at me, frittened, thinking she must be going to get slapped in a minute, since it was too good to be true. Then she lapped it up.

With that, I heard Mother calling.

'You've had that, anyway, Pussy,' I says. 'And now, Mother, would ye like some cream with your tea?'

'Why, yes, my dear. I do dearly like a drop of cream with my tea. But what'll Sarn say?'

'He's busy lapping cream hisself, Mother.'

'Eh?'

Mother thought I was comic-struck.

'Well, in a manner of speaking. Jancis be come.'

'Jancis?'

'Ah. Run away.'

'Dear to goodness!'

'Walked all the way, she did.'

'But why didna she go whome?'

I'd never thought of that. It seemed so natural she should come to us, like a clemmed redbreast.

'She was afraid of Beguildy, I make no doubt, Mother.'

'Ah. You'll have to go and tell Missis Beguildy.'

'Boxing Day, I'll go. Let Jancis have her Christmas.'

'Be they, as you met say, lovering at all?'

'Ah. He was took by surprise, and he gave her a kiss afore he knew it.'

We laughed a bit.

'And now for your tea, Mother. There's getting to be a real Christmassy feeling. Cream all round! And after supper I'll trim the house up with holly.'

'Mind you get some cream yourself, my dear.'

As I went down the stair into the kitchen, where the two were sitting very old-fashioned on the settle, I wondered what would be cream for me. All in a minute, as I was scalding the tea, I knew.

'Jancis,' I said. 'You'd ought to write to Mister Woodseaves and say you've run away, or maybe he'll be making shift to go over extra early to write a letter for you.'

'A' right, Prue, seeing it's you and not me as writes, I dunna mind. But he wunna go over there again.'

'Not go? For why?'

'I'll tell you all about it to-morrow-day. I be so tired now.'

'All right,' I said, though I did long to hear about him.

'I'll tell about running away to-night,' she said, but I told her supper first.

'Draw up now and take bite and sup. Then you can tell us all about it, and then I'll write.'

I knew it would do her good to tell it. For when you've come through a bad time, to tell of it takes the thorn out. So she told us how she'd timed it to get to Lullingford on market day and ask Gideon to bring her back, but took the wrong road in the hills, all looking the same in the snow, and wandered far out of the way, and was benighted, and slept in one of the huts that they make of furze for lambing time; and how she heard a breathing under the door, and thought it was the roaring bull of Bagbury, but she cried out upon the Trinity three times, as loud as she could, and it went away. Then she struggled on to Lullingford, going across fields, not being able to find the road. She was chased by a horse, which was worse than the roaring bull of Bagbury, and that was when she crept through the hedge. When she got to Lullingford, Gideon was gone, for he always started back as soon as he could. She went to Kester's but he being away she could get no help there. She was afraid to ask anybody else, for fear they'd send her back to Grimble's so she started off again. But afore she'd gone far, she was so fainty that she had to creep into a barn and wait till morning. Then when she got to the woods, she thought of a short cut, and lost her way again. And indeed it was no wonder, for in the woods about Sarn it inna all that easy to find your way in summer even.

'Dear to goodness!' says Gideon, 'you want a chap to look after you, seemingly. Such a tale of foolishness I never heard.'

'And what Feyther'll say passes me,' she went on. 'He'll be neither to hold nor to bind. He's very set in his ways now, and

257

if you go agen his plans he's very crousty. If Mother knew, maybe she'd think of a way out.'

'I'll go and see your mother, coming Boxing Day,' I said. 'It'll be a funny thing if we canna invent summat to get the better of an old moithered man, hoping you dunna mind me saying it.'

'Mind! You can say the worst you can think of about my dad, and I doubt I shanna think it's too much. And truly he be moithered, book-learning or no.'

'Set your heart at rest now. We'll think of summat to give you time to turn around. Maybe you could get another place. Or maybe Gideon--'

'If you mean, maybe Gideon'll want to get wed, I say, in my own good time and not afore. I've told Jancis if it's a good harvest and we do well I'll be willing to get wed at Harvest Home. And she's willing as well.'

'I'm right glad. Loving's never too early. And if you be fond of a girl, you mun want her to be in your house, by fireside and table, indoors and out.'

I was thinking of a little house not twenty miles away, as different as could be from ours, and one in it as was a very obstinate bachelor, and didna want any woman there, let alone poor Prue Sarn. I thought it was about time I wrote the letter.

'What shall I say in your letter, Jancis?'

She said I was to say what I liked. So I fetched ink and paper and my quill, and wrote it.

Christmas Eve.

SARN.

DEAR MISTER WOODSEAVES,--
I write to acquaint you as I've left Missis Grimble, being very near with the food and a driver, and maister's rheumatics very awkward in sharp weather, and sons awkward also one way or another. I've broke the journey at Sarn. I may say Gideon and me think to be married come Harvest Home. I may say I be very glad, for when you do love anybody you want to be with them and canna rest, nights, wondering where they be, and if all's well, and if they change their stockings when damp, and if they be lonesome ever.

I be more choice of him I love than of all else in the world beside.

He be so kind and so brave, and when he be there I can but say, 'The maister be come.'

I love him past telling, and shall to the end, and so goodnight, Mister Woodseaves, and a merry Christmas, from

JANCIS BEGUILDY.

'You write a pretty tidy letter, Jancis,' I says. 'Would you like me to read it?'

'Laws, no! What for should ye? You know what's to be said.'

'Ah. I know right well what's to be said. Only I munna say it,' I thought. 'That's the trouble.'

I fastened the letter up and put it on the chimney-piece ready for Gideon to take next market day.

There was a strangeness about the place all that Christmas. It was the best Christmas ever we had, and there was more singing and laughing than there'd bin for many a year. And yet it was in a manner of speaking sad. It seemed to me as if the singing came from a great way off, under the water. And when Jancis sat by the window, with the light falling on her pale gold hair and pale face through the greenish bottle-glass, it made her look as if the water flowed over her.

'Green gravel, green gravel, the grass is so green!
The fairest young lady that ever was seen.
I'll wash you in milk, and clothe you in silk,
And write down your name with a gold pen and ink.'

Ah! I can hear Jancis singing that song now, with her sweet shrilly voice, a great way off, ah, me! a great way off.

Mother let me get her up, Christmas morning, and came into the kitchen, sitting snug in the chimney corner, watching the lovers with a pleased, understanding, merry look, such as I've often seen on the faces of old women that have lived their lives and know summat of love. It's as if they said, as they looked at the young lovers--

'Pleased, be ye, my lad? You'll be better pleased yet! . . . All of a twitter, be ye, my girl? Well, I can tell ye, you'll be in more of a twitter later on, a power.'

I could see very well that when we three sang 'As Joseph was a-walking,' and 'Good Christian men, rejoice!' Mother was hearing other voices too, little voices like the Callard children's, lifted up all together, shrilly and sweet. She was seeing other faces, well scrubbed and rosy, lifted up to her as she sat in the dusk of the settle, ready to smile when the solemn carols were done, and shout 'Granma!'

She kept on patting Jancis on shoulder, and saying, 'Pretty thing! Pretty!' and once I heard her cautioning Jancis against hares.

'When your time comes, my dear, dunna you go in the 'oods much, nor yet in the meadows. Keep near whome and you wunna come across one. 'Twould be a sad mischance, so it would.'

'Oh, Missis Sarn!' says Jancis, laughing and colouring up above a bit, 'you do run on so fast! We inna so much as courting yet.'

'And so do time run on, my dear. You munna let the moss grow on the path of love. Dunna give too many nay-words. He's a good lad when you dunna vex him.'

'But it's Sarn more than me as wants to wait,' said Jancis.

'Foolish, foolish lad! What matter for the silver plate? What matter for so many maids and men? I'm sure I'd be content without, so as I needna tend swine again, and can have my feet to the fire and a cup of tay.'

'Sarn wants to take me to the 'unt Ball,' said Jancis. 'And I be to go in afore Miss Dorabella.'

'That's a mischievous thought. For what dun it matter who's first so long as all be in? And what is it to go to one ball more than another?'

'But I'd like it right well, to go in afore Miss Dorabella!'

'And so thee shall!' called out Gideon from the door, where he was knocking the snow and mud off his boots. 'And so thee shall, my girl, and dressed as shameless as a lady!'

He came across the kitchen with the bit of mistletoe he'd clomb the big apple tree to get, and gave her a loud, smacking kiss under it.

Mother clapped hands, as pleased as a child when kitty wakes up and plays. But even when she clapped for joy, her hands still looked like the little praying paws of a trapped mole.

'Not later than Harvest, Sarn?' she pleaded. 'You wunna put it off later than that? I'll last till then, sure. But after-- the winter comes, and who knows? I'd lief see you wed afore winter.'

'Oh, we shanna put off, Mother. No danger! What need? For I shall be a rich mon when I've sold the corn, and it'll cost nought to get it, for we can have a love-carriage, and I can pay back with task-work in the winter. And in another tuthree years we can shift, for the old mon at Lullingford wunna last long, and the money'll be ready when the place comes on the market.'

So they were all merry, and when I said, 'The tea's scalded!' Gideon gave me a very affectionate pat on the shoulder and said I was a good wench.

'A right good wench if ever there was one. Now draw up! Draw up to table all! I want me tea cruel.'

But I couldna be as merry as they were. I felt outside it all. Only I took a bit of comfort, now and again, between cutting bread and frizzling rashers and pouring tea, in looking up at my letter on the mantel, with the address on it in very tall script--

Mister Woodseaves,
The Weaver's House,
Lullingford.

Then Jancis told us about Kester, and of the things that
had come about through Grimble's spite, which couldna be
told in letters. For it seemed that Grimble and Huglet had
misliked Kester ever since he stopped the baiting, and the
mislike had soon grown into black hatred. They tried to set
all the other farmers agen him, saying this and that. They
found fault with his weaving, which was the best in all the
country round. And they said he was slow, and dear. Not
content with that, they must enquire into his religion and his
ways of thinking in the matter of the corn laws and the
Parliament men. They hobnobbed with Squire over that, and
set him agen Kester too, worse than he was, for they said
nought about the baiting, but kept to the corn. Every way
they could, they worked against Kester, and very worried
they must ha' been that he didna drink or go after women, or
do anything that they could have told of to the Parish
Constable. But they did their best to make his life a burden,
for it irked them so sore to think of no bull-baiting for ten
years. So one day when he was weaving at Grimble's and it
came to evening, Mister Grimble looked at the cloth Kester
had done in the day, and couldna find fault with it, neither
with the quality nor the quantity. For he'd worked right well,
and Jancis said it was as smooth as silk, and never a lump nor
a knot in it. He said nought to Kester, and after supper
Jancis fetched the paper and began to write the letter to
Gideon. And it seemed Mister Grimble couldn't abide to see
that, for he couldna read nor write, and he thought Kester
was above hisself. So when he couldna keep any longer, but
mun speak or burst, he says--

'If young Sarn do like damaged goods, he'll get what he
wants, and I doubt he'll have you to thank, Weaver. Very
comfortable and pleasant you be together, I must say, you and
Sarn's girl. It's baby linen you'd best be weaving, young
Woodseaves.'

And with that, Kester snatched up his hat and all his
things in a fury, but saying nought. And when he got to the
door, he turns round and says--

'You may get Huglet's brother-law to weave for ye from
now on, Grimble. You'll go without weaving for all me. You
bin a foul-mouthed toad and disgrace to your parish, which is
situate in hell.'

He flung out, and he never came near the place again.

I was forced to go up to the attic to think about it a bit. I
did love Kester so sore for his rage. I thought I'd like to see
un in a rage, though not with me, for if he was in a proper
rage with me, I'd die.

On Boxing Day I went across to the Stone House, and a windy walk it was, for the snow was drifted deep along the wood path. But it was fair overhead, and a mistletoe thrush was singing, and the cuckoo's beads were very bright on all the may-trees. Beguildy was out, for a wonder. Missis Beguildy and me had a good talk.

'Well, well, poor lamb,' she said, 'to think she couldna come to her own Mother because the mester be such a pig-headed fool! Drat the man! Now what's to do? For go back to Grimble's she never shall. But ours'll be roaring-mad to think of all that money gone. Keep her a bit longer till the worst's worn off, my dear!'

'Oh, she can bide, and welcome, as long as she's a mind.'

'May them above reward ye!' she says. For she was a very religious person, in the manner of the church. And though I've no wish to speak ill of her, yet I partly think she was religious, in a measure at least, to spite Beguildy. But maybe this is a wicked thought of mine.

'Gideon was telling us that Callard's girl ran away afore winter,' I said. 'She's by lonesome there all day with the five little uns and the baby. Maybe if we went at it the right way, and made a favour of it, they'd pay the same rate as Grimbles. They'll get nobody else till the spring, for they're all hired now till May, and besides, Callard's Dingle inna a place the girls like. You go and see Missis Callard, and I'll make shift to have a lesson to keep your maister busy.'

'But you've left learning this long while, my dear, for you know as much as Beguildy does.'

'Ah well, there's summat new I want to learn, but I dunno if it's in the books.'

'What met that be?'

'It's an old ancient charm, Missis Beguildy, and it's called content.'

'Oh, that! It's in no book of hisn.'

'Nor in any book,' I said. But I thought, there's one knows it. Please God, he met learn me. But that he never will.

'Eh, but it be no manner use for me to go, Prue,' she says. 'They'd set the dogs on me, very like. Callard's very religious, you mind. And he canna abide ours. And all *he* thinks, his missus thinks; all *he* says, *she* says, pat like the Sarn echo. Come to that, it'll go hard but they'll take Jancis in at all, whatever, being who her dada is. But maybe if *you* went, and told them on the quiet that Jancis is promised to Sarn, they met think of it, for your brother's beginning to be well spoken of as a man that's bound to be rich.'

So I said I'd go. I couldna abide going, being looked at a bit sideways myself, and spoken ill of time and again. But when I saw Gideon and Jancis so pleasant and merry together in the even, playing beggar-me-neighbour by firelight, I knew I was bound to go.

'Why, Gideon,' I says, 'you're busy at it, I see. Though you canna play conquer with cob-nuts and snail-housen now, being too old, you're beggaring somebody still.'

'Conquer!' says Mother from her corner. 'Ah, what a game that is! He was always very set on it, you mind. He liked to play ooth them big pink-and-white conquers, the Roman snail, they callen it, dunna they, Prue? It was those you went after the night poor Sarn was took in his boots. Poor soul!'

She cried a bit and went to look very small, which she always did when she was vexed.

'There, there, Mother, dunna fret, he's in peace now.'

'Ah, poor soul! And Sarn's took the sin. My son Sarn. Chumbled it up proper, a did. And I can see as there'll be lads to play conquer in our kitchen yet, with the big pink-and-white uns, of an evening.'

She looked across at the settle. Gideon had just beggared Jancis, and was in very good fettle.

'Ah, boys *and* girls,' says Mother. 'For I see well as he'll beggar her of more than cards.'

She began to laugh at the thought of the grandchildren, and at her joke, and she laughed so much that she gave herself a hoost, and I had to put her to bed.

Next day I set off for Callard's Dingle. It was a way nobody would choose to go with snow deep on the ground, for it lay over bleak, high pastures, with northerly slopes, bitter cold and drifted up. But seeing I was on a good errand, I began to sing, out on the bare pastures with none to hear.

'Open the gates as wide as the sky . . .'

And there by the farm, in a little fenced field, what should I see grazing under a dark pine wood but the white bull that Kester saved from the baiting? I stopped and looked at it a bit. There it was, not dead nor maimed, its nice white coat in good case, and looking as contented as if it was just come to heaven, and all because of Kester.

He'd kept his promise and paid the money, and then given the bull back to Callard for his children.

'if you ever come to think bull-baiting's bad, I'd lief you told 'em so,' he said, 'but not agen your conscience.'

Now Callard was a very honest man, and he felt bound to make some return, whether or no, so he took the matter up in good sadness. Jancis said afterwards that it was very amusing to see him gather all the children together round the hearth, sitting on their little stools of an evening, the baby also being there on its mother's knee. And Callard ud say very loud—

'Bull-baiting's bad!'

And his missus in that melancholy voice of hers would repeat—

'Bad!' like the Sarn echo.

Then all the children would sing out, like a nest of birds—

'Bull-baiting's bad!'

And times the baby would give a guggle, and times he'd stay quiet, considering, like. There was only one disagreeing voice, and that was old Granfer Callard's which was very high and trembling. He'd call out--

'No! No! It inna bad. It be a right good merry old sport!'

But nobody listened to him, for he was getting very simple. He came to the door when I knocked and called out to his daughter-law--

'It be that there long thin young 'oman, Maria. The witch woman.'

'Well, bring her in, feyther-law.'

'Come thy ways,' he says. 'Her'll be down when the baby gives over hollering. I do wish I'd got such lungs as hisn. I be very middling. Very middling I be. Can you do cures?'

I said no to that.

'Oh! I thought Beguildy's learnt ye. A very sinful man is that. Soaked in sin like a sheep in raddle. It wunna be any manner use for 'im to yammer at the doors o' Paradise and say, "Wesh me and I shall be whiter than snow." For I tell ye not the Judge of all could clane 'im, even if He could spare the time to it. Ah! A wicked old man is the Wizard. I do believe he lives by sucking folks' life away in the mid of night. Ah! sucks their blood, he does. They seyn he goes to the churchyard and digs folk up to steal their bwones and grind 'em for his spells. They seyn he fetches little children whome in his bag, and makes a meal of 'em. Oh, he be the wickedest man since Punty Pilate, no danger!'

By this, the elder children were roaring with fright, and Missis Callard called out from the top of the stair--

'Feyther-law, what be saying now? Hold thy noise!'

Mister Callard came in then, and said I'd best take pot-luck, seeing it was tea-time. So when we'd had our tea, I told them about Jancis.

'So 'er run away!' says Mister Callard. 'In this weather. Well, by gum!'

'Gum!' says his missus.

'Broke her time!' says Callard.

'Time!' says his missus, sorrowful.

'Nobody ever broke their time when *I* was a lad,' said the old man. 'They darstna. They'd have been put in the stocks.'

'And you be sure it inna anything to do with Weaver?'

'Weaver!' says Missis Callard, grievous.

'Weaver! Weaver!' shouted the children, and it seemed to me as if they praised his name.

'I be as sure of that as I'm sure that I breathe,' I said.

'And she's promised to your brother?'

'Ah. They'll be wed come Harvest Home.'

'Then,' says Mister Callard, 'the missus shall give the girl a trial.'

'Trial!' echoes Missis Callard in a hopeless sort of way, as if she thought that was what Jancis would be.

They agreed to take Jancis for six months, and to give her three pound, which was a deal for them to offer. So I went back in high feather. Next day Gideon said we could have Bendigo, so I drove Jancis to Callard's, stopping at Beguildy's on the way, to break the news to the old man.

Oh, dear me, but he was in a passion! And the worst of it was, that he blamed it all on to Gideon, who had nought to do with it all.

'I'll be even with that brother of yours for this,' he says. 'Ah! A very aggravating man. His dad was the same. I couldna plan out anything or set my hand to any work but he'd come and knock it down, tiddly-bump. And young Sarn's the same. Look at the way he's let and hindered me over the young squire!"

But Missis Beguildy was pleased.

'And you shall come whome at the end of hay harvest, Jancis,' she said, 'to make your wedding clo'es. And the wedding shall be at Michaelmas. The Glory roses'll be in their second blooming then, and you shall have 'em for your nosegay.'

'I tell ye,' says Beguildy, 'as Sarn shanna take her. You can tell un so from me, Prue Sarn. Thwarted I wunna be. I've cursed the man by fire and watter, and cursed he'll surely be. Tell un neither with the ring nor without it shall he take my wench.'

'Well, good day to you, Mister Beguildy,' I said. For I thought it was time to drive on.

'Prue,' said Jancis as we drove through the water meadows between Plash and Callard's Dingle, 'what for did ye knife Grimble's dog and take on the way you did about Weaver?'

She looked up at me with those big blue eyes of hers, and I beat Bendigo cruel so as to be busy about summat. The poor old nag gave a half look round, and my conscience pricked me, but what was I to do?

'Folk be saying it was a very out-of-the-ornary thing for a girl to do for a stranger. Ah! even as far as Grimble's they knew it was you, though neither Grimble nor the missus told 'em, for they didna like to speak of it, being beaten over it. But everybody knows in all the country round by this.'

She kept on looking and looking at me, and the red-scarlet was burning like fire in my cheeks. I kept on thrashing Bendigo, and we went over the tumps and marshy bits at such a wallop as never was.

Jancis gave a little laugh, very knowing and aggravating.

'Poor owd Bendigo's done nought,' she says.

'I want to get there,' I answers, foolish-like.

'Oh, I'll be bound you'll get there,' she says. Then she was quiet for a bit, though she watched me all the while.

'I wonder,' she said for a time, 'what Weaver ud think if he knew?'

'He couldna know,' I said. 'He was in a swound.'

'He met hear tell! And I wonder what he'd think if it came to his ears that Prue Sarn had foughten for un like a tiger?'

'He'd think nought. Everybody do know I'm sorry for the afflicted.'

'Well, but he inna what you'd call one of the afflicted, Mister Woodseaves inna. He's the best wrostler in these parts, and a right proper man.'

'He was afflicted when Grimble's Toby got 'im by the throat, wunna he?'

'Ah. But why must it be Prue Sarn that did save him? And why must she take his yead to her bosom so kind and all? Not but what he's got very nice brown hair, and silky. I was used to notice it when he was writing the letters for me. And that Felena thinks so too. She does fairly tarment him, market days.'

'What a brazen piece! What does she do?'

I was glad to turn Jancis on to summat else.

'O she goes to the house, and leaves a great basket of mushrooms, or a frail of wimberries, or maybe a bit of mutton, if shepherd's killed a sheep. And if she meets him in the road, she'll look at un with them green eyes and smile as sweet as an October nut. And one night when shepherd was drunk and they were late starting whome, what must she do but go in the dusk and sing a wild song outside his window.'

'What did she sing?'

'O she sang--

'A vargin went a-souling in the dark of the moon.
A soul-cake! A soul-cake!
O give it me kindly and give it me soon.
A soul-cake! A soul-cake!
The young man he looks from his window so bright.
He's a vargin come wailing in the dark of the night!
Now what'll you give me for a soul-cake, my maid?
My body, my body for a soul-cake! she said,'

And I call that a right down improper song, dunna you, Prue?'

'What did he think of it?'

'I wouldna demean myself to ask him. But she's a very wild woman, is Felena. She'll 'tice him and tempt him to a fall if somebody dunna keep her off. But I want to know what I be to say to Weaver if he asks me why you were so busy a-saving of him.'

'Say nought.'

'Nought's no answer.'

'It's all he'll get.'

'The way you stood over the fellow like one of the angels at Eden gate, with that great knife!'
'It's none of your business if I did.'
'Ah. It be.'
'For why?'
'Because I love ye, Prue.'
'Thanks be to goodness, we're at Callard's,' I said, as we came into the fold, and the house door burst open and out came the five children, Granfeyther Callard, Missis Callard and the baby, like bees from a skep.
The last thing Jancis said afore I drove away was—
'I shall be bound to send for Weaver soon.'
'Whatever for?'
'To write me a letter to Sarn.'
'Why, you be only a tuthree miles from Gideon now. Whatever do you want to write a letter for?'
'It's none of your business if I do,' says she, very mim, and laughing to herself, 'which is what you did say to me, Prue Sarn!'

Chapter Five
Dragon-Flies

From the time when Jancis went to Callard's Dingle, through the spring and summer, there is nothing written in my book saving of my own special concerns, such as the progress I made in reading hard books and the thoughts that came to me in the attic. These, as they had no bearing on the lives of others at that time, are not of any interest, and I will not weary you with them. Gideon went to Callard's Dingle every Sunday, and worked like three men in between. I ploughed furrow for furrow along of him, and dug spade for spade. Our farm was rich with corn. Never afore or since did I see any fields in our part of the country in such good case, for it was a year of sweet, growing weather, with enough rain to swell the grain and not enough to make it ackerspire. Sunday after Sunday I saw Gideon, on the way to Callard's, stop and lean over the gate at the top of the sloping meadow, where you could look over the whole place, like a miser with his gold. And now and agen I went with him, and was glad to see such a glowing content in anybody's face, but a deal more glad since it was Gideon's, that was seldom what you met call a happy face. When he'd gone striding along, whistling pretty near out loud, I'd sit a while afore going back to Mother. I'd think to myself that when he was wed to Jancis, the corn sold and Fortune knocking at the door, then at long last he'd whistle out loud. I got a great longing to hear that, for it seemed to me an unhealthy sort of thing for folks to whistle or sing or speak to their mommets all the while.

'Come harvest!' I'd think. And I'd begin to dream of being as beautiful as a fairy.

It was a great delight to me, apart from the thought of all this, to look at the standing corn and see it like a great mere under the wind. Times it was still, without a ripple; times it went in little waves, and you could almost think the big bosses of wild oinion flowers under the far hedges were lilies heaving gently on the tide; and times there was a great storm down in those hollows, like the storm in Galilee Mere, that the King of Love did still. So I watched the grain week by week, from the time when it was all one green till it began to take colour, turning raddled or abron or pale, each in his kind. And it shone, nights, as if there was a light behind it, with a kind of soft shining like glow-worms or a marish light. I never knew, nor do I know now, why corn shines thus in the nights of July and August, keeping a moonlight of its own even when there is no moon. But it is a marvellous thing to see, when the great hush of full summer and deep night is upon the land, till even the aspen tree, that will ever be gossiping, durstna speak, but holds breath as if she waited for the coming of the Lord. I make no doubt that if any read this book it will seem strange to them that a farm woman should look at the things about her in this wise, and indeed it is not many do. But when you dwell in a house you mislike, you will look out of window a deal more than those that are content with their dwelling. So I, finding my own person and my own life not to my mind, took my pleasure where I could. There were things I waited for as a wench waits for her sweetheart at her edge of the forest. This rippling and shining of the corn was one, and another which came about the time of the beginning of the troubling of the water, was the marvellous sight of the dragon-flies coming out of their bodies. We had a power of dragon-flies at Sarn, of many kinds and colours, little and big. But every one was bound in due season to climb up out of its watery grave and come out of its body with great labour and pain, and a torment like the torment of child-birth, and a rending like the rending of the tomb. And there was no year, since the first time I saw it, that I missed to see this showing forth of God's power.

I went down by the mere to gather honeysuckle wrathes to bind besoms. And being sad in calling to mind what Miss Dorabella had said, for besoms ever made me think on it, and seeing that the troubling of the water was even now beginning, with a slow gentle simmering all over the mere, I thought I would go to a place I knew where there were always a mort of dragon-flies, and take comfort from seeing them coming out of their bodies. Dragon-fly, I say, because I doubt some wouldna know what our name for them meant. We called the dragon-fly the ether's mon or ether's nild at Sarn, for it was supposed that where the adder, or ether, lay hid in

268

the grass, there above hovered the ether's mon as a warning. One kind, all blue, we called the kingfisher; and another one, with a very thin body, the darning-needle. Mother was used to tell Gideon that if he took dog's leave or did other mischief the devil would take needle to him and use the dragon-flies to sew up his ears, so he couldna hear the comfortable word of God and would come to damnation. But I could never believe that the devil could have power over such a fair thing as a dragon-fly.

That was the best time of year for our lake, when in the still, hot noons the water looked so kind, being of a calm, pale blue, that you would never think it could drown anybody. All round stood the tall trees, thick-leaved with rich summer green, unstirring, caught in a spell, sending down their coloured shadows into the mere, so that the tree-tops almost met in the middle. From either hand the notes of the small birds that had not yet given up singing went ringing out across the water, and so quiet it was that though they were only such thin songs as those of willow wrens and robins, you could hear them all across the mere. Even on such a burning day as this, when I pulled the honeysuckle wrathes, there was a sweet, cool air from the water, very heady and full of life. For though Sarn was an ill place to live, and in the wintry months a very mournful place, at this one time of the year it left dreaming of sorrow and was as other fair stretches of wood and water. All around the lake stood the tall bulrushes with their stout heads of brown plush, just like a long coat Miss Dorabella had. Within the ring of rushes was another ring of lilies, and at this time of the year they were the most beautiful thing at Sarn, and the most beautiful thing I'd ever seen. The big bright leaves lay calm upon the water, and calmer yet upon the leaves lay the lilies, white and yellow. When they were buds, they were like white and gold birds sleeping, head under wing, or like summat carven out of glistering stone, or, as I said afore, they were like gouts of pale wax. But when they were come into full blow they wunna like anything but themselves, and they were so lovely you couldna choose but cry to see them. The yellow ones had more of a spread of petals, having five or six apiece, but the white ones opened their four wider and each petal was bigger. These petals are of a glistering white within, like the raiment of those men who stood with Christ upon the mountain top, and without they are stained with tender green, as if they had taken colour from the green shadows in the water. Some of the dragon-flies look like this also, for their lacy wings without other colour are sometimes touched with shifting green.

So the mere was three times ringed about, as if it had been three times put in a spell. First there was the ring of oaks and larches, willows, ollern trees and beeches, solemn and strong, to keep the world out. Then there was the ring of rushes, sighing thinly, brittle and sparse, but enough, with their long trembling shadows, to keep the spells in.

Then there was the ring of lilies, as I said, lying there as if Jesus, walking upon the water, had laid them down with His cool hands, afore He turned to the multitude saying, 'Behold the lilies!' And as if they were not enough to shake your soul, there beneath every lily, white and green or pale gold, was her bright shadow, as it had been her angel. And through the long, untroubled day the lilies and their angels looked one upon the other and were content.

There were plenty of dragon-flies about, both big and little. There were the big blue ones that are so strong they will fly over top of the tallest tree if you fritten them, and there were the tiny thin ones that seem almost too small to be called dragon-flies at all. There were rich blue kingfisher-flies and those we called damsels, coloured and polished in the manner of lustre ware. There were a good few with clear wings of no colour or of faint green, and a tuthree with a powdery look like you see on the leaves of 'rickluses. Some were tawny, like a fitchet cat, some were rusty or coloured like the copper fruit-kettle. Jewels, they made you think of, precious gems such as be listed in the Bible. And the sound of their wings was loud in the air, sharp and whirring, when they had come to themselves after their agony. Whiles, in some mossy bit of clear ground between the trees, they'd sit about like so many cats round the hearth, very contented in themselves, so you could almost think they were washing their faces and purring.

On a tall rush close by the bank I found one just beginning to come out of its body, and I leaned near, pretty well holding my breath, to see the miracle. Already the skin over its bright, flaming eyes was as thin as glass, so that you could see them shining like coloured lamps. In a little, the old skin split and it got its head out. Then began the wrostling and the travail to get free, first its legs, then its shoulders and soft wrinkled wings. It was like a creature possessed, seeming to fall into a fit, times, and times, to be struck stiff as a corpse. Just afore the end, it stayed a long while still, as if it was wondering whether it durst get quite free in a world all new. Then it gave a great heave and a kind of bursting wrench and it was out. It clomb a little way further up the bulrush, very sleepy and tired, like a child after a long day at the fair, and fell into a doze, while its wings began to grow.

'Well,' I says, with a bit of a laugh and summat near a bit of a sob, 'well, you've done it! It's cost you summat, but you've won free. I'm in behopes you'll have a pleasant time. I suppose this be your Paradise, binna it?'

But of course it couldna make any sign, save to go on growing its wings as fast as might be. So there I stood, with

270

my armful of wrathes, and there it clung, limp on the brown rush, in the golden light that had come upon Sarn like a merciful healer. I was wasting my time, which was deadly sin at our place, and I turned to go. But just as I turned, there was a bit of a rustle, and there stood Kester Woodseaves.

I made to run away, and indeed I'd have jumped into the mere sooner than he should see me. But he put his hand on my shoulder, and for all it was gentle, it was a wrostler's hand, and not to be said no to.

'What? Oot run away? Why, Prue Sarn?' he said.

I hung my head and wished I was the dragon-fly. I said nought.

I gave a despert pull, but it was no manner use. He only laughed.

'I do think,' he said, in the voice that made its own summer, 'that it be a very funny way to treat a chap as comes to thank ye kindly for saving of his life, Prue Sarn, to take off the like of that'n, and try to jump in the lake!'

His hand sent such a throbbing through me that I could scarce stand.

'What were you looking at when I came?' he asked me.

'The damsel fly, coming out of its shroud.'

'Once out,' he says, 'they're out for good. It costs a deal to get free. But once free, they never fold their wings.'

'No,' I said, 'and some of 'em go so high, I think, times, they might flitter right into heaven.'

'We'd all like to do that, I'll be bound, if we could choose our heaven. I'm not very choice of golden streets myself. And I'd like my heaven afore I die.'

'And what ud it be?' I asked him. I was so inteested, I declare I'd clean forgot my curse.

'I'm not quite sure yet,' he says, 'but come a year, maybe, I'll know.'

'There's a long while,' I says, mocking at him, 'to be hiver hovering, choosing your bit of paradise.'

'Could you think of yours sooner, Prue Sarn?' says he.

I looked at his green coat, which made him a very personable man, and I fixed on a place on the left side, just betwixt the sleeve of it and the breast of it, where I'd lief lay my head, and I said—

'Ah. I've thought of mine.'

'Oh! Well, what is it?'

'I said as I'd thought of it, Mister Woodseaves. But my thoughts be my own.'

He laughed. Then he says—

'You can write a dommed good letter, Prue.'

'They were Gideon's letters.'

'I take it very kind in Sarn to tell me change my stockings when they be wet. It inna often you find a man as thinks of such things, and Sarn least of all, I'd have said.'

He let me have the full light of his eyes, and I hung my head and found nothing to answer.

'And the sewing work, and the damson cheese and the pickle at half market price, well, I tell you, it fairly bowled me over, for I'd heard Sarn was a hard man, very near in a bargain, asking nothing and giving nothing. And then for him to offer me those victuals! I must have misjudged the chap cruel.'

But by this I'd remembered that the stockings were in the letter I wrote for Jancis after she ran away. So I said, it was Jancis mentioned stockings.

'Oh, yes, so it was!' he says. 'I liked that letter. A very nice girl, that. For whoever wrote the letter, she made it up, of course!'

He looked at me again, and I found nought to say.

' "I be more choice of him I love than of all else in the world beside!" That's a woman worth summat to a fellow,' he went on. 'And, "I love him past telling, and shall to the end." And in especial that about, "spend my life any time very willing, and die for you by bite of dog or any way, my dear." I liked that. But when I come to think of it, 'twas Sarn said that to Jancis Beguildy. What a lover the man must be! You must be main fond of him, Prue Sarn.'

'Oh, yes,' I said, all in a flush, 'I be.'

'Indeed yes, and only what you should be. Good feeling he has too, about the choice of texts, and Jancis the same. For that text, "The Maister be come," was in the letter Jancis wrote to me, as well as in the one Sarn wrote to Jancis.'

'Only natural,' I said.

'I'm coming to Sarn's love-carriage, and I'll be bound to thank him for his kind thoughts about the sewing and the damson cheese and the pickle,' he said.

'Oh, dunna!' I cried out, knowing how angry Gideon would be.

'There's a grudging girl,' he says, 'not wanting her brother to be thanked.'

He had a look of satisfaction on his face, as if he'd found out what he wanted to know.

'Well, it's no use ifting and anding any more,' he says. 'You wrote the letters, and you made 'em up. And all I can say is, the chap you were thinking of when you said the things you did say is a lucky chap, whoever he is.'

'I hanna got an acquaintance.'

'Dear me! That's pity, to my mind. But anyway, you've got a friend. You write in your book, when you go back, that Kester Woodseaves is your friend till Time stops.'

I thanked him very kindly for that, and then he said, should we go and look for some more dragon-flies coming out of their shrouds? So we did, and had a tidy bit of talk, one way or another, about this and that. We watched the dragon-flies take off from the tops of the rushes, and we saw the water simmering in its troubling, and the lilies looking at their angels.

But it was a long time before I remembered to say, how did he know about my book that I wrote in? For it seemed I couldna remember anything very well when he was by.

'Well,' he says, 'maybe a bird told me. Or an old ancient woman like a little bird.'

'But how did you get to know all the other things you do seem to know about me?'

'Well,' he said, 'there's a tuthree people know you, Prue. And there's few know you and dunna love you. And I expect I've been leasing in their hearts a bit. And I think there's not much that I dunna know about you, Prue.'

There was rest in that saying. And oh, the summer in his voice, then and always! I forgot the time and all. Yes, indeed to goodness, I forgot milking time! But when I saw the light of evening long upon the mere, and heard the evening breezes lifting up the leaves in the forest, I turned to go. Then he said--

'There's a thing I'm bound to ask you.'

He stood looking straight into my eyes, for we were almost of a height, though he was a little the taller.

'What for did you do all you did for me that day at the baiting?' he said. 'What for did you stand above me with the knife, and run to Lullingford and all, to save me?'

There was a deep silence, with only the lifting of the summer boughs, the lapping of the quiet water. How was I to answer? Yet he would have an answer, I could see.

Then I thought, seeing the lilies looking at their angels, how I'd called myself Kester's angel at the baiting.

'Why, it was only that I was your angel for that day,' I said at long last. 'A poor daggly angel, too.'

'If you're ever wanting an angel's situation, you can send to me for a written character,' he said, and though his words were merry, his eyes were as grave as grave could be. And then, as we said good night and I turned home, he called out after me--'Not so daggly, neither!'

And I could hear him laughing in the wood.

Book Four

Chapter One
Harvest Home

Never in all my days did I see a corn harvest like that one. We started swiving, that is reaping, at the beginning of August-month, and we left the stooks standing in the fields till it should be time for the love-carriage, for the weather was so fine that they took no harm. It was the custom, if a farmer hadna much strength about him, that he should fix on a day for the neighbours to come and give a hand in the lugging of the grain. But up to that time, the weather being so good, we worked alone. It was up in the morning early, and no mistake! Such mornings as they were, too, with a strong heady sweetness in the air from the ripened corn, and the sun coming up stately as a swan into the vasty sky that had no cloud. Mother was very peärt and lively, what with the hot weather, which was good for the rheumatics, and the thought of the easing-off of the work which was to come when the harvest was gotten in. She'd be up and about at five, getting us our breakfast, and then off we'd go, with only just enough of clo'es on to be decent, and with our wooden harvest bottles full of small beer. We always had a brewing for the rep, that is, the reaping. This year we brewed a deal more, for there'd be all the neighbours to find in victuals and drink at the love-carriage. Looking back, it always seemed to me that there was a kind of dwelling charm on all that time. Gideon was more contented than I've ever seen him, for there were two things that contented him, namely, to work till he dropped, and to finish what he set out to do. To see all his farm set with these rich stooks, sound and ripe, with never a sign of the weevil nor of mildew nor the smut, was very life to him. He was all of a fever to get it safe in stack, but we were bound to wait till the day fixed. Jancis was to come on that day, to help in the leasing. And it seemed to me as she ought to go atop of the last load with blossoms about her, like the image they used to set up there, for she seemed a part of the harvest, with all that pink and gold.

As for me, I went all dazed and dumb with wonder. To think it was true, 'The Maister be come!' To think as he'd looked at me and hadna hated me! To think as all that time we spent in the midst of the painted dragon-flies by the mere was true, as true as daily bread! When I called to mind the things he'd said, and still more the things he'd looked, I was like to swound. Dear to goodness, how I did sing, those early dawns, when the dews lay heavy after a ketch of frost, and the corn rustled and stirred in the wind of morning!

When we went out, the leaves of the late-blooming white clover would be folded tight, and the shepherd's hour-glass shut. I'd watch them, in the minutes I took for rest, opening soft and slow like timid hearts. Then Mother would come with our nooning, creeping over the fields in her black like a little sad-coloured bird, and sometimes singing *Barley Bridge* in her old, small voice, that yet was sweet. Then, after the noon-spell, through the long, blazing evening (for with us all the time after noon is called evening) I'd watch the shepherd's hour-glass shutting up again, and the white clover leaves, folding as the dews came. We took turns to go whome and milk, then we'd have our tea in the field, and at it again. All the while I thought of Kester, as would soon be working at the coloured weaving in the great city. But when my heart said he was working for me as well as hisself, I hushed it, saying that it was but his flaming look that made me think it, for he hadna said it, and so it was only that the wish fathered the thought. But I did dream of the fifty pounds I was to have, a great fortune, it seemed. And I did plan how I'd get to be cured as quick as might be, so when Kester came back after his time away I'd stand afore him with as proper a face as even Felena, though I hoped not so forrard.

At last the day of the love-carriage came, and a tremendous blue day it was, with a sky like a dark bowl, Worcester china colour. We'd got fifty people coming, no less, counting the women-folk. I was up afore dawn getting all ready, setting the china, both ours and what we'd borrowed, on the trestles in the orchard, helping Gideon to put the casks of beer in the yard, ready for the men to fill their harvest bottles, and fetching water from the well for the tea. The orchard was a sight to see when the trestles were set out (for I could put all ready with no fear of rain on such a day) with the mugs and platters of many colours, and the brown quartern loaves, and the big pats of butter stamped with a swan, and the slabs of honeycomb, dough cakes, gingerbread, cheese, jam and jelly, let alone the ham at one end of each trestle and the round of beef at the other. Even Gideon didna begrutch the food on this day. For it was one of the laws you couldna break, that a love-carriage everybody must have his bellyful.

It was very early when the waggons began to roll into the fold, with a solemn gladsome sound, and each with its own pair of horses or oxen. Each farmer brought his own men and his own waggon, and sometimes he brought two. The teams were decked out with ribbons and flowers, and some had a motto as well, such as, 'Luck to our Day,' or 'God bless the Corn.' It was a fine thing to see the big horses, with great manes on their fetlocks, groomed till they shone like satin, stepping along as proud as Lucifer, knowing very well how long the waggoner had been, a-plaiting their ribbons. The oxen were good to see, also, for their horns were all bedecked, and about their necks were thick chains of Sweet

William and Travellers' Joy and corn. Miller came among the first, with his gig and the old coach horse, the best he had, poor man. And very good work they did, too, for it's surprising what a deal you can get onto a gig if you put a set of wings on top.

It was time for me to go and give the folks welcome, so I got Miller's Tim to mind the trestles, and left him with a big meat patty, sitting at the top of one of the tables, with half the patty in one cheek, ready to drive away birds and cats and dogs, and even goblins out of fairyland, after the patty. The ox-driver from Plash had dizened his beasts up proper, with bulrushes nodding on their horns, and there were Sukey and Moll each riding one. Their mother wasna coming till late, and they were wild as mountain finches. Then came Felena, riding the shepherd's rough pony, with the panniers to put her leasings in. When I saw those green eyes of hers shining like jewels in her brown face, all flushed with summer, and the long, slim shoulders of her, and that red mouth, I almost hoped Kester would forget to come after all. Missis Beguildy and Jancis came, but Beguildy wouldna. The cousin from Lullingford that got the toothache so bad came, and his missus. Then there were Callards, all packed in a great harvest wain, and a net over the five children, so that they looked for all the world like little calves on the way to market. Granfeyther Callard sat by his son, dressed out in his best snuff-coloured coat, and his beaver hat, for all it was so hot. There was a posy in his hat, which he waved like a lad as they came creaking in at the fold gate, shouting--

'Harroost! Harroost! Never was such God A'mighty's weather!'

He always said harroost, it being the old way of saying harvest. Then came Sexton, tall and black, a bit sour, but the best man of his age with a pikel anywhere round. Missis Sexton had a vast apron of blue gingham, with pockets, for leasing, and it made her look bigger than ever. It did seem a blasphemy to speak of her leasing, as if Solomon in all his glory had put on an apron and gathered up the ears.

Tivvy was dressed out very grand, as often was the way of girls at such *'dos'* as this, for a *'do'* was a thing that came but seldom, and where else but church, where all but bonnets was swallowed by the pew, could you show your gown with the flounces, or your gown that was cut low?

Tivvy had a straw bonnet with quilled mislin under, a sprigged gown cut low with a rose at the breast, white stockings and new black sandal-shoes. Jancis was pretty past telling in her blue poplin and a sunbonnet, and Sukey and Moll had tight frocks of white cotton with red roses sprinkled on them.

The Callard children ran about like a clutch of chickens when you empty 'em out of the basket, but Miller's Tim was as mim as a mute, feeling so grand to be trusted with all the feast to mind. Missis Miller and Polly, I may say, came first of all, and there was Miller's man as well, and Sexton's Sammy, a queer, long lad like an eel, with twice as many teeth as he wanted, and a power of texts in his head that ud fly out at you on every excuse, and hit you like a startle-de-buz will on a summer evening. It seemed as if all the texts his dad had ever read had lodged in his big head, and so he'd always got one pat.

'Pray ye therefore the Lord of the harvest to send down labourers into His harvest,' he says. But the publican from the *Mug o' Cider*, whose missus was looking after the bar so he could come, Gideon being like to be a good customer in the future, catched him up very quick.

'Dunna begin the prayers till I've had a quart, lad,' he says, 'for they might be answered, you being Sexton's lad, and I'm welly parched.'

The men gathered together by the beer barrels, and as more came, they went and got their beer. Towler came, and shepherd, Felena's maister, a tall, brown man, all bones, striding with his long kibba, which is a stick of six foot or so, to walk with, held about the middle.

'Well, shepherd!' pipes up Granfeyther Callard, 'han you seed the sun dance yet, Easter morning, on thy mountain?'

Shepherd took no notice, for being with the dumb sheep so much, he was pretty near as silent as the miller, thought not quite, for nobody could be. But the father of Moll and Sukey said--

'Nay, but 'tis his missus sees the moon dance, mid-summer, as we know well.'

'When she dances with the devil!' screeched Sukey.

'And not the devil only,' says Missis Sexton.

Felena didna seem to care. She was standing by me, and she whispered that she'd liefer dance, whoever it was with, and be jimp and souple, than be as stiff as a tombstone like Missis Sexton.

'She brought him up into the high place of Baal, Numbers twenty-two,' said Sammy. And after that there didna seem anything more to say about it.

Gideon came up to settle each man's work, and he looked right well in his nice clean smock, well broidered, with the sleeves rolled up to show his great arms, and a pikel over shoulder.

'Now Gaffer!' pipes up old Callard. 'What bit 'e going to give I to do?'

'You shall go atop of the waggon I sarve,' says Sexton, 'if ye promise to take as quick as I chuck.'

There was a laugh, for nobody ever liked the job of settling the sheaves Sexton heaved, he being the quickest heaver anywhere round, and never tiring.

'Oh,' says Mug o' Cider, 'we'll put you on the leader of the foremost waggon for a lucky image, wunna we, lads? You can holler *Haw-woop!* and *Jiggin!* and be a sight more use than any of us.'

The old man took this as a great compliment, and nought would do but his son must help him up there and then.

'Well, lads,' says Gideon, 'we'd best be shifting if we're to bring the harvest whome this day.'

'Harroost! Harroost!' calls out old Callard. *'Haw-whoop!'*

Obedient to the word, the lead-horse went forrard, and all the waggons and carts moved slow past the house. Mother stood on the door-sill, nodding and smiling, and saying—

'Thank you for us, I'm sure. My son Sarn'll be obleeged to ye.'

So we went out under the blue sky to lug home the corn, the big waggons with solid wheels rolling over the stubble, Granfeyther Callard shouting *'Jiggin!'* when he meant *'Haw-woop!'* being quite tipsy with enjoyment, and causing a great confusion, the horses not knowing what to do. The rest of us followed on, strung out over the fields in bright colours, children and dogs running hither and thither, while in the rickyard the men told off to make the stacks put the logs in place ready for the stacks to be built on, got all prepared against the first waggon came back loaded high with grain, and then stood leaning on their pikels, talking over the work of the coming day, each man as busy about the planning of it all as if the harvest was his'n, and each man as glad of the grain as if he was to have the selling of it. For that was the manner of the love-carriages in time past.

In the noon-spell I went up to the high pasture, to see if there was any sign of Kester. He was coming across the far meadows, by a field path, and I stayed so long watching him, who was all the world to me, that they'd started work again afore I went back. It was a pretty thing to see, in such a place, on such a day. The farm being all under corn now, it looked like a boss of gold in the dark woods and meadows around. And all the bright colours of the women's gowns, the creamy smocks and a tuthree coloured shirts of the men, the shining horses and deep-coloured oxen, the yellow stooks with blue shadows under, the towering yellow loads on the wains, made up such a picture as you wunna often see in a lifetime, anyway in these days.

It was merry to hear, also. The voices rang so sweet in the thin, still air. I could hear old Callard's *'Haw-woop!'* and *'Jiggin!'* and the other men's shouts, and Jancis laughing out high and sweet at summat Gideon did say, and the children crying out, 'Mother, I've gotten two pinnies full now!' 'Mam, I've found six ears together!' From the rickyard came the far calls of the rickmakers, and, times, a pigeon cooed in the deep woods, where the mere lay like glass, and, times, a jay would scold, or a woodpecker laugh out. Never a cloud was in the sky, nor any hint of trouble in the little airs that stirred in the leavy hedges. And there, two fields off, one field off, and now in the same field, was the man I could never think about but in those words, 'The Maister be come.'

From a long way off he saw me, and waved his hat, so that the well-shapen head I did love was bare, with the dark hair just so upon it, that you must long to stroke it.

I came down from the high pasture and stood beside Gideon's waggon, knowing that Kester would come to get his orders from the maister of the day.

There was some chaff, Kester being so late.

'Weaver's forgot the day and come to-morrow instead!'

'Dunna be so forrard, Weaver, come on Plough Monday!'

'He bin late, but he bin full of power and might and young blood,' said old Callard, for nobody of that family would ever hear a word against Kester.

'The last shall be fust, and the fust last, Matthew twenty,' says Sammy.

'Luck to the day, Gaffer!' Kester called to Gideon.

'And thank you kind for coming,' answers Gideon.

'What be I to do?'

'Ever done any harvesting?'

'Ah.'

'Can ye pitch?'

'Ah.'

'Well then, you take my place a bit while I go the rounds, oot? Sexton's tother side from you, and he's a terrible quick pitcher. But you cana be too quick for young Callard and Towler.'

'But mind not to push pikel too fur when the load be low,' called old Callard, 'for I mind once a fellow did that, and he stuck it right into the chap atop. Ah! like a piece of toast on toasting-fork he was, poor fellow, and hollered so that the team bolted, ooth the pikel still in.'

But Kester did very well and made toast of none. His eyes would laugh at me now and again, and once, when the empty waggon tarried, he came where I was leasing, and said--

'You still go frommet me a bit, I see, Prue Sarn. It mun be toërts, not frommet.'

I put the ears this way and that, but no words came.

Then he said, slow, with a laugh at the back of his voice, but with a cosseting sound as well--

'There, there, my dear! None shall touch you now!'

All the strong life of the man was gathered in his eyes, and blazing full on me. So he'd heard! Folk do sometimes when they seem nigh dead. He'd heard and remembered the words I'd said when his head was on my bosom and my heart was all rent with love. What could I say? Nought. Where could I hide my burning face, that his eyes did so dwell on? Nowhere at all.

'Hi, Weaver!' they called. 'Waggon be come and we be hindered for ye!'

'I never knew a mother's love, nor yet a sister's, not yet a sweetheart's.' He said it ever so softly, but despert earnest, so that the words burnt in. 'But if I had, I should have forgot 'em all three when you said those words to me, Prue Sarn!'

With that, he turned sharp and went back to the waggon.

What a day that was! Gold? I should think it *was* gold! I leased and leased, and it was just as if every armful was some precious, heavenly treasure. Nearly all the fields were clean and bare when we had our tea under the hedge shade, for it grew no cooler as the shadows lengthened, being one of those mid-September days when all the gathered warmship of the summer seems to be spent and squandered in love of the golden grain.

The sun was low in heaven and the harvest-beer low in cask when Mother banged the tray for me to come and help with the urns for supper. They were loading the last waggon, and I told Tim, who'd been a good, faithful watcher, that he could go to the field and ride home atop along with the other children, in the triumph. Then we brought out the urns, and the cask of home-brewed, very strong and good, and set about cutting up the meat and bread.

We heard 'em shouting from the fields, and in a while there it came, the biggest waggon, with Jancis's white oxen and the oxen from Plash lugging it, Granfeyther Callard driving, all the children on top, and Jancis with them, waving green boughs and bunches of poppies, and Gideon, looking taller than customary in his smock, walking glad and solemn beside the load.

Deary me, how the tears do spring! Tears like Mother and I shed then, for the joy of it all, and other tears, for what came to pass after. For if in the mid of that great golden day you'd sent a sough of wind, and a mutter, and black clouds running up the sky, and darkness and thunder and forkit lightning, it couldna have been worse nor less expected than the storm that broke on us so soon.

The waggon came on, and all the people followed, singing and shouting, till they came to the gate of the rickyard.

There stood Parson, with Mother and me close by, to bless the corn.

'People!' he said, 'let us give thanks for daily bread!'

And all the people said—

'We give thanks unto the Lord.'

'God bless the corn and the master of Sarn,' says Parson, 'and may his good deeds return unto him as doves to their mountains.'

'Amen!' said the people.

'Missis Sarn bids me say that the feast is spread in the orchard, and all are welcome,' said Parson.

Gideon stepped forrard.

'The harvest's whome, friends, and thank ye kindly,' he said. 'Let every man who's lent a hand claim task work of me from this on, till I've paid my debt.'

We sate at the trestles in the long light of sunset. At least, the company did, but we at the urns were kept busy enough and hadna much time to sit down.

'Well, Weaver,' says Mug o' Cider, 'I hear tell as they're making it pretty warm for ye, for stopping the bull-baiting. But I bear no grutch, I'm sure.'

'Nor yet me. I like a man that likes a dawg,' says Towler.

'Nor yet me,' says Mister Callard from the next table.

'But there's some not to hold nor to bind,' said Mug o' Cider. 'I hear 'em in the bar, nights. Oh, I say nought! Landlord's a dumb dog with pricket ears. Ah! That's landlord. But they mean ye no good, Weaver. It'll go hard but they'll take thy work away if they can. And if they can do a spite to you and yours, they ool. They've worked on Squire, too.'

'I know, thank ye kindly all the same,' said Kester. 'It was Squire I was hindered for to-day. He wanted to buy my cottage. Nothing would do but he must buy it. He knows very well that if he did he'd soon turn me out of the place, for all the rest belong to him or friends of his'n. Offered me a deal of money, did Squire.'

'Shall you consider it over?'

'Dear to goodness, no! I shall bide.'

There was something very pleasant to me in the way he said that. It was as if he builded a tower of refuge afore my eyes. He met go for a little while, a year even, but for his life-long he'd abide. And it was only fifteen mile away, and less as the crow flies.

'And you'd best look out, too, Prue Sarn,' says Mug o' Cider. 'Grimble took it very ill, you knifing his dawg. Not but what you did it well, I must say. I'm sure any farmer as kills his own meat ud be glad of ye, or you met go for a doctor's mon and do right well.'

'Mine said she couldna believe it when Prue Sarn drave the knife in,' went on the landlord. 'Thought she'd seen a ghostly vision, her did. Said a feather would have knocked her down, her did. Which shows it must have bin pretty bad, for it inna easy to knock the missus down, she's like a bouncing ball.'

'I do wish I'd been there,' said Sukey. 'I'd have knifed the dog for ye in a minute, Mister Woodseaves. What did I give ye at the Beguildy's love-spinning, Mister Woodseaves?'

'Play kiss in the ring with us after, Mister Woodseaves!' says Moll. 'You kiss right well, I know!'

Felena leant forrard across the narrow table.

281

'Oot play?' she said. 'Oot play, Weaver?'

Just then there was a call from the next table.

'Husht, husht! Sexton's going to say a few words.'

When Sexton spoke, the four walls of the church seemed to grow up round you, and you could smell the damp, musty smell of it, and hear the flies plaining in the windows. For whether he was reading, 'He took unto him and wife and begat Aminadab,' or 'The golden bowl be broken,' or speaking at a harvest supper, it was all the same.

'Friends,' says Sexton, 'we've had a good day. I'm sartin there's not a man among us as hanna sweated proper, even Granfeyther Callard, I'll be bound.'

'Oh, ah! I sweated right well!' calls out the old man, very pleased.

'And now we be enjoying good victuals and drink, and after that a game or two--'

'The people sat down to eat and to drink, and rose up to play, Exodus thirty-two.'

This was Sammy.

Sexton looked very angrily at his missus, as much as to say--

'Stop Sammy!' and she said--

'Husht, Sammy! Feyther's speaking. Dunna you forget as you can only call to mind other folks' words, but Feyther makes it all up new as he goes on.'

She settled down again to watching Sexton, for all the world like a cat watching a whirring wheel.

'I say we've had a good day, and Sarn's had a good harvest, and I ask ye for why? Because he's industrious, people, and his sister's industrious, and his mother's industrious. You couldna find in ten parishes a more industrious family. Not like some I could mention, as never do a hand's turn, coddling about with old ancient wicked books. Ah! There's some I could mention, as I dunna see the face of here to-day, that a bit of work would be the saving of. Well, neighbours, we all know as God helps those that help theirselves, and when we look at all them grand ricks of grain, I'm sure we see it's true. And we wish you well, Sarn. And I'm in behopes the young woman'll be industrious too. For I hear tell the next randy we come to at Sarn is to be a wedding. And may it bring more prosperation and not less, though of course we may think our thoughts, knowing where she's from and what's bred in the bone'll come out in the flesh--'

But fortunately there was a stir when he got to that, and a call from the other tables--

'There's two riders at the gate.'

And there was the young squire, and Miss Dorabella with him. They rode across the orchard, and the young man called out, 'Give you good evening, folks, and luck to the corn!'

For he was ever hail-fellow-well-met with all men, I'll say that for un, and it made him well liked.

Miss Dorabella seemed quite to forget she'd quarrelled with Gideon. She drew up by his table and smiled, sparkling her black eyes.

'Well, Sarn,' she said, 'you've worked your will with the farm, I see. You've got a desperate good crop. Are you going to offer us a drink of harvest beer, to drink your health?'

I could see she admired him for a strong man, which he was. I never met but one stronger. And I could see that the Squire had told her to make it up with Gideon, and very likely sent young Mister Camperdine to see she did it, for it was common property that she'd sarved him wi' sauce at the *Mug o' Cider*, and the Squire couldna afford to lose a man that was like to do well. Gideon looked at her straight and sullen, but she kept on smiling for all that, a bit conquering and a bit pleading. Then they gave her up the best pewter measure full of ale, and she says--

'Health and prosperation, Sarn!'

Then she tossed it off, for she could drink ale with any man, and in those days it wunna so long since ale was a lady's only breakfast drink. Then she gave back the measure and leaned down, holding out her hand, stripping off the grand gauntlet, and she says--

'Your hand, Sarn!'

Well, he was done then, for he couldna refuse a lady's hand. So he took it in his great fist, and young Mister Camperdine nodded, as if to say she'd done enough now, and she put on her glove again. All the while I saw Jancis looking at her in a way that meant she was frit of her, and also that she couldna abide her. But looking at Miss Dorabella, with that sort of stony handsomeness she'd got, and then at Jancis, so soft and pinky-sweet, it didna seem to me that Jancis had much to be afraid of. They gave young Mister Camperdine some ale then, and when he'd wished well and drunk it, he said--

'I thought maybe Beguildy was here, but I don't glimpse him.'

Missis Beguildy stood up and curtsied.

'No, sir, he inna here, though a should be. And you'd best not look for 'im at home, sir, for I doubt you wouldna find 'im. But if you come to-day's a week--'

I thought that was right clever of Missis Beguildy. She wanted to give Gideon and Jancis time, and to keep the young gentleman away as long as she durst, while she thought how to manage Beguildy.

'Right!' calls out the young fellow as they rode off. 'To-day week, and mind Venus is there!'

Jancis began to giggle at that. She always did at any mention of the silly affair. And it seemed so funny to her that he should be enquiring so anxious after the very woman his cousin had sarved wi' sauce, and she at table all the while. But I crouched down on the bench, to seem short, and not to let him see my shape, so that Jancis went off into a fit of laughter again, and said I looked for all the world like a broody hen. We had some sport together over the young squire. Then up came Missis Beguildy, very put-about, wondering what to do with Beguildy till the wedding day was safely come. All of a sudden she thought of summat, and laughed and slapped herself till I thought she'd be took ill.

'Dear now,' I've thought of it!' she says. 'I'll ask my cousin from Lullingford, as is here by the mercy of God, to send a message to my maister this very night, to say as hers is took ill (I mun think what he's to have. Summat cruel bad!) and as there's no cure but the old famous cure, to eat seven loaves baked at one baking by the seventh child of a seventh child, and she's to offer good money (you can pay after you be wed, Jancis, for you'll be having butter-money or summat) and off he'll go, dang-swang, to look for a seventh of a seventh, and it'll go hard but we'll be in peace till Michaelmas.'

'Oh, mother,' says Jancis, giving her a kiss, 'you'd ought to have been a great general to ride along with Lord Wellington and lay traps for Frenchmen!'

It was all fixed up before the games and dancing began, and I felt sorry for Beguildy till I remembered what a wicked old man he was, wanting to sell his child unwilling.

By this it was near dark, and the moon rising, big and raddled. They got together a dozen fellows, mostly middle-aged or old, to whistle for the dancing. They danced in the rickyard, among the stacks of golden corn, sweeping up the straw with besoms first. Old Callard had been chosen for a whistler, and very proud he was, for being the oldest he chose the tunes and set the measure, and so he could feel that all the merry life in a manner depended on him, which is pleasing to old folks.

'Barley Bridge!' he says.

The pretty tune sounded out clear on the quiet air.

I was standing under one of the stacks, watching. It was a gay thing to see. Gideon was dancing, holding Jancis close and strong. Missis Sexton was sailing about, and Felena too, jimp as a fairy. Even Mother made shift to dance a few steps.

The twelve were whistling like a nest of throstles, sitting in one of the empty waggons--

'Open the gates as wide as the sky . . .'

when Kester found me.

'So that's where you be,' he said. 'Not dancing?'
'No.'

'For why?'

'I amna like other girls.'

He considered that. Then he said—

'Well, I mun be going. I'm off to prentice myself for ten months to learn the coloured weaving in London Town. Then I can do piecework at home, and care nothing for Grimble and his gang. Coloured weaving brings in a tidy bit, and I'll send it by coach every few months.'

'When'll you be raught back?' I said, as if I was drowning.

'I'll be back for next August fair, and I'll come and talk with you a bit then, Prue Sarn.'

'Maybe you'll forget.'

'I dunna think so.'

'Well, God bless ye,' I says.

'And you.'

He turned to go. Then he turned back.

'But it's foolish in you not to dance,' he says. 'A wench with a figure like an apple-blow fairy!'

He gi'd a little laugh and went.

So he knew about Venus! Oh, I was shamed and dumbfounded! I was angry with Jancis too, for she must have told him, though she never would confess it, but giggled and said he must have noticed my nice shape through my clo'es, so that I was more shamed and vexed than ever.

Mother was tired and wanted me to help her to bed. After, I looked from her window on to the rickyard, that had been void, but for one big haystack, all peopled now with dark shapes. As I stood there, Gideon and Jancis suddenly came round the corner of the house, and as they went by, slow and seeing nought but each other, I plainly heard Gideon say, 'Nay, Jancis, I'll make sure of what's mine. To-morrow night when your father's gone, come down and let me in.'

I didna hear her answer, for they were past the window then, and besides, I drew back, for I canna abide an eavesdropper. So that was in his mind! He couldna trust his dear love even for a sennight, I thought, well, maybe it was no harm, for they would be wed so soon. And indeed, whether it was agen the church or no, I was bound to be glad that Gideon should show any human feeling. Times, he seemed like a frozen man. When all were gone, and the chattels fetched in out of the dew, it was getting on towards dawn. So I went up to the attic and wrote in my book. But first I took a sheet of paper and put down in very neat writing—

'A figure like an apple-blow fairy.'

' 'Twas me he meant,' I said over and over, 'poor Prue Sarn!'

And a glow began in my heart, warm and pleasant as a gledy fire. For what is there in this earth, or in heaven, if it comes to that, like the knowledge that you've found favour in the eyes of him that is your dear acquaintance, and the

Maister? I left off wondering what he thought of my hare-shotten lip, for indeed it seemed he thought of it not at all. I called to mind a thing he'd said while we watched the dragon-flies, about sin. He said if you thought of it rightly it just wunna there. It was gone like the shrouds of the dragon-flies when they'd wrostled free. What did you want to go hunting about after the shroud for, when you could look at the bright fly? Maybe that was how he thought of me. My poor hideous lip was, as it were, my sin, though a kind of innicent wickedness. It was my sin, and all the rest of me was my righteousness, and my glory, and the way I made him glad. I cried a long while for very joy, and such a rushing happiness went through me as seemed to make all the blood in my veins new, and I felt as if it was so pure and strong it might even cure me of my ill. There was some truth in it, too, for my lip did never look quite so bad from that day.

Morning came fresh and sweet, and the rooks went streaming out across the windy sky, to our stubble, with sleepy, contented caws falling scattered here and there. On the way to milk I stopped by the rickyard to give thanks for the corn. Why then in that hour did I think of those words, 'The precious bane'? Why did I think of that which men will garner with their harvest, and treasure, though it is as fire-grass in a haystack? Why did a cold boding horror stir in my heart, where all was gay and warm, as a catch of frost will strike in your garden plot of an autumn evening, when the dahlias are at their proudest--wine-colour and clear gold, every quill in place, blooming high above the wall, with bees about them--so that in the morning all is winter-sad?

Chapter Two
Beguildy Seeks a Seventh Child

That very evening, so Jancis told us next day, Missis Beguildy gave the pretended message, and the day after the love-carriage Beguildy set out, full of importance, with his ash-wood kibba, to find the seventh child and bring back the bread. I said it did seem a shame to deceive the poor man so, but Jancis said, 'No danger! It makes him happy, and we'll give him the money if he finds the seventh child, so what more is to do?'

She was looking as pretty as a pink, was Jancis. She stayed a bit, to help in the washing-up, and then she sat in the kitchen while I worked, sewing a seam in her wedding clo'es. After tea when she was going, Gideon said--

'Mind you dunna forget!'

She coloured up as pink as codlins-and-cream, and ran along the wood-path. After supper Gideon said, careless like, 'If I be late, Prue, and you want to go to bed, put the key over stable door.'

I said I would, and no more. But I saw him shaving hisself very particular, and putting on his Sunday stock, so I knew that whatever date parson met have got fixed for the wedding, the wedding was now, and I fetched a rose for his coat. He looked very bashful over that, but I said that when a fellow went to see his girl so soon afore the wedding he must always wear a flower. That seemed to make it all right, thinking I guessed nought, and off he went, whistling loud and clear, up the wood path where the leaves were turning rusty, and sighs were sounding here and there, and the airs breathing autumn, and the brown cobs falling with little thuds, for lads to play conquer to their own let and hindrance. Sad, and very sad I thought it in the wood path when Gideon's tall figure was passed away, and the mere lapped, and the boat was knocking on the steps, and an owl hooting. Why was it so sad, I wondered, when the wedding was fixed so soon, and the glory roses blooming, corn safe housed, and in my own heart the Maister come? Yet there was that about the evening which you feel when summat has died. I went the rounds to see if all was well. Mother was asleep, brown and small and peaceful in the big bed. Bendigo was in stable, very comfortable, for he was old and nesh, and we fetched him in before October. All was well, and I wondered what the harm was, that I felt in the air. I was to know afore long, though for a little while things kept on as usual. Every night I put the key in the stable, but said nought. Every morning Gideon's bed was all tossed and tumbled, but I knew very well he hadna slept in it. He whistled about the place as merry as any other man, not under breath any more. I was glad for him, and glad to be making ready for Jancis. They were to have the guest chamber, which, not having been used for many years, was in very bad repair. So I'd bought a few rolls of cheap paper out of the butter-money, and I was papering it unbeknown to Gideon. Mother was in the secret, and she'd come and clasp her hands and say, 'Looks a pretty paper! Doing it right well you are, my dear. Roses and all! Roses be lucky, to my mind. Your Aunt Dorcas had roses in her bride-chamber, and not one of her children ever died, nor ailed, nor cried. I mind she made a joke over that. "Neither die nor cry," she says. I hope Sarn's wunna cry much, for I canna bear to hear a child cry. Sarn ud roar ever so, it was awful to hear un. Beat on the cot, a would, summat cruel. Mun always get what a wanted very quick, but if it tarried, he wouldna forget, he'd cry the day long, but he'd get it.'

I'd got the paper on, and I was about putting a bit of glazed calico round the dressing-table when Missis Beguildy came rushing to our place, like a wild woman. It was such pleasant weather too, with little bird in the new ricks and the first apples falling. It was early in the morning when she came. I'd been churning. I hadna seen Gideon, for he'd taken a crust out into the field where he was ploughing. I was in the dairy when Missis Beguildy rushed in.

'Oh, my dear!' she cries out. 'Oh, my dear, the worst as could happen's come to pass.'

'Goodness me, what?'

I was frightened to see her face.

'He comed back!'

'Who? Not Mister Beguildy?'

'Ah! No less. And all going so well. Him away till a fortnit anyway, I thought. And the two of 'em so sweet together. I didna think Sarn could be so fairspoken to anybody as what he was to me, and Jancis like the Queen of the May. "Mother," she says, "I be more gladsome than I thought any could be." Ah, and your brother too. It eased him to see that his doubts and fears about young Camperdine were nought. If I hadna let un come he'd a thought the young man was at our place. 'Twas the only way. The more anybody wants a thing, the more they do think others want it. But seeing all was fair and square, he was fair and square too. "Mother," he says, for indeed it inna long till I shall be afore Him above and all the blessed angels, "Mother, leave me bide the night over from now on, till we be wed. Soon, it is," he says, "or I wouldna ask it. And her's willing." So I gave them our room, and slept on Jancis's box bed in kitchen. I put the best dimity counterpane on their bed, and the best sheets, without a patch, and a tidy bit of drugget on floor, and I killed a fowl and made a nice bit of bread sauce, and left 'em to their supper, pleasant and to theirselves afore the fire, and stayed out till they'd done, though they did say as nice as nice as I mun sup with 'em. But newly wed is newly wed, ring or none. And when they were abed I'd tidy the place and wash up. And I'd just done, and I was setting afore the fire thinking of the time when I wed Beguildy, and what a proper young man he was, though you'd never think it, and deserve my thoughts he didna, the grutching, wicked old man. I was setting there very peaceful, and thinking I must draw the bolt and rake the fire out, when there was a little sound without, and in came Beguildy. I could ha' dropped on floor.

"Well, missus," he says, "where be Jancis?"

"She be asleep," I says.

"And since when did ye give the wench our room and sleep in box bed?"

With that he rushes in, and there they were. 'Twas hell let loose, and no mistake. He put such a curse on Sarn as I never heard nor shall hear.

"And for all you've crept in the like of this, you shanna have the wench in wedlock," he says.

"You canna stop it," says Sarn. "No power in the 'orld can stop it now."

288

"Yet stop it I will," says the mester. "Hanna I cursed ye by fire and by water? Hanna I told ye you were born under the threepenny planet and canna keep money? Hanna I said you'll be poor in life and die in the water? Eh?"

"Well, it's a pity for ye, seeing you be a wise man and all, to be put in the wrong," says Sarn, "but harvest be in and I be a rich man."

"You binna a tenth nor a hundredth part as rich as young squire. His pockets be crammed ooth French money," shouts Beguildy. "You shanna have my girl, Sarn."

"I've got her, seemingly," says Sarn, as calm as calm could be, and that drave Beguildy right out of mind. He puck up the blunderbus as he keeps by the window ready for the fox, and he went for your brother with the butt end.'

'Dear to goodness!'

'You may as well say that, Prue Sarn. I screeched and Jancis screeched, and I ran in from the kitchen, for I'd kept out, thinking Sarn met not like it, him being in his night-shirt, and as fine a man as you could wish, but not wanting to cause any awkwardness more than already. But afore I could get in, Sarn knocked mine flat on floor, and a lay like a log and none deserved it better. For a very curst man is Beguildy, and obstinate, and bearing ill will year after year. I do believe the root of the matter is your dad asking him for that crown when he'd made mind up it was to be a present. Ah! Though mine he is, I canna but say he's a terrible man to bear a grutch. Well, Sarn knocked un flat, and he says, "Take his feet, oot, Mother, and we'll put un in kitchen. For whether he's dead or quick, I'll not be disturbed any more this night." Ah. He said that. And he says, "Swing for it I may, but I wunna be disturbed this night." Cold and quiet as a frozen mere, but a terrible man to rouse, is your brother. So I doused mine with water, and I gid him some spirits, and in a while he come round, but I took the precaution to tie him to the bed afore that. He struggled cruel, but it was a good rope, and I fed spirits to un regular, and in a while he calmed a bit and quietened, and then slept. So in the morning your brother went, and I untied the mester, and when he woke up I says, what fetched him back? So he says, ill news travels fast, and he supposed he'd got ears, and he hadna but just got as far towards the mountains as Mallard's Keep when a man told un Sarn slept at our place now. Interfering meddlers, folks be! So I got him a bit of breakfast and he went out. Quiet as quiet he be, so I've come to warn ye, for when he's quiet-angry he's deadly.'

I said, what harm could an old man the like of that do, and especially as we knew all his spells and what-nots were but foolish games? But it made no difference, and she only kept on saying there was harm brewing, and God send the wedding day quick, and she went off home as wild-seeming as she came, wringing her hands, with wisps of hair blowing in the stormy wind. For there was a real tempest blowing, that had been rising for two or three days, and it blew up the loose straws and the chaff in the rickyard till the air was full of them, dusty and choking. Out in the field I had to go close up to Gideon and shout afore I could make him hear. There was a roar in the treetops like the sound of weirs after the snow melts, and a howling in the chimneys that made you glad of four walls and a roof. I said to Gideon when we were at our tea, did he think it would blow the tops off the stacks? But he said no, they were well weighted. It was only two days now till the dealer came to price the grain, and only three days after that till the wedding. Knowing this, and being easy in mind about Beguildy, since he'd taken no harm from the blow, I listened to the wind very contented, and made some rounds of toast, and thought about Kester. For I do think there's nothing makes you feel so contented as a roaring wind in the chimney when all's well. I said should we go to bed early, and Gideon said we might as well, seeing we'd worked hard and the harvest was in. So we went at eight, and I fell asleep in a minute with the sound of the loud, dry tempest in my ears.

When I woke, sudden, I thought, 'It be the Judgment!' There was a great light and a roaring, very dreadful to hear, and knockings and cries out of the night. I lay there, mazed, saying *'Our Father'* as fast as I could, and wishing I'd been more regular at church. Then I heard Gideon's voice calling from window, and other voices below, and one was the voice of Sexton's Sammy. This comforted me in my foolish fear, for I felt as if Sammy would be able to think of a text, and mouth it too, even on Judgment night. For night it still was, and early too, since we found out after that we'd not been abed much more than two hours. Gideon came rushing past my door, shouting for me, so I got up and put on my clo'es, for I supposed that whether it was the Judgment or not I'd better wear them, though in the pictures the redeemed go in their night rails. But I did feel that I must wait to get to heaven afore I could be at my ease to stand afore Sexton's Sammy in my night-gown.

I ran downstairs and out, and then I saw. I thought even the end of the world would have been better than that, for then we'd have been provided for, with no more harvests to get in nor money to gather with pain and labour. It would be the same for all in that hour, but this was for us only, and crushed us as a waggon wheel crushes an ear of wheat.

For it was the corn burning that made the roaring noise. It was the harvest, all of it, the whole garnering of all those years of work, the very stuff of Gideon's soul, and our future. It was no great comet nor flaming star raging across the sky to herald in the end of all, no trumpet of an archangel pealing and whining along that black night betwixt the trembling worlds. It was only the corn. Only all we had! Only that which was to make a kindly man, a loving man, of our Gideon, since having it he would leave slaving by day and dark, and making us all slave, and would work only like any other man. Only the corn, that meant a bit of comfort for Mother, a bit of hope for me. Only the corn, that would give Jancis dear children, and the place of wife by fireside, and a bit of love, maybe. Oh, my soul, it was the corn! I clung to the rickyard gate, and my hair was lifted in the fierce-hot wind. There were black figures running in the red light, most like a picture of hell, but they were nought, and less than nought. The vasty roaring wind went on, taking the fire with it. I could see that the thing must have started with the barley, that was on the west of the rickyard, whence the wind was coming. There was no barley now. Where it had been were two great round housen made of white fire, very fearful to see, being of the size and shape of the stacks, but made of molten flame. There was no substance in them, and it was marvel how they stood so. Now and again a piece of this molten stuff would fall inward with no sound, and there could be seen within caves of grey ash and red, sullen, smouldering fire. So it will surely be when the world is burned with fervent heat in the end of all. It will go rolling on, maybe, as it ever has, only it will be no more a kindly thing with mists about it, a pleasant painted ball with patterns of blue seas and green mountains upon its roundness. It will be a thing rotten with fire as an apple is rotten when the wasps have been within, light and empty and of no account. So was our barley, falling inwards with no sound, as though one went here and there within, unseen. It was a worse thing to see than if it had fallen down in a heap, for being yet a stack, it seemed like a jest of some demon, saying--'Well, what is to do? There be your stacks of barley! Make barley bread and eat.' I looked at those two abodes of demons, of the roundness and height of our good barley stacks, and I remembered the barley, oh, the sweet barley, rustling in the wind of dawn! I called to mind the ploughing for it, in such good behopes, and the sowing of it, between the sowing of the winter wheat and the sowing of the summer wheat, Gideon and me walking up and down the fields with the bags of seed slung over shoulder, or with a deep round lid to hold enough of seed for one crossing of the field there and back, and swinging out our arms with a great giving movement, as if we were feeding the world, a thing I dearly loved to see. For reaping, though it is good to watch as be all the year's doings on a farm, is a grutching and a grabbing thing compared with sowing. You must lean out to it and sweep it in to you, and hold it to your bosom, jealous, and grasp it and take it. There is ever a greediness in reaping with the sickle, in my sight. There is

291

not in scything, which is a large destroying movement without either love or anger in it, like the judgments of God. Nor is there in flailing, which is a thing full of anger, but without any will or wish to have or keep. But reaping is all greed, just as sowing is all giving. For there you go, up and down the wide fields, bearing that which you have saved with so much care, winnowing it from the chaff, and treasuring it for this hour. And though it is all you have, you care not, but take it in great handfuls and cast it abroad, with no thought of holding back any. On you go, straight forrard, and the bigger your hand the better pleased you are, and you cast it away on this side and on that, till one not learned in country ways would say, here is a mad person. For it would seem as if you were feeding all the birds of the country, since there was always a following of rooks in the furrows, and starlings, and many small birds, which would be very unprofitable chickens.

It is a pretty thing to see the golden seed tossed in the air with sunshine on it and the light spring wind scattering it here and there; or if it is winter wheat, then it will be, very like, a still brown day with the mellowness of old beer in the colours and the scent of the air. I was already ready for the sowing, though Gideon did not care about it, and indeed would often seem to begrutch casting the grain from him, and would sow too thin and so waste land and labour. I thought of all this, and of the fair evenings when we had walked forth, Mother and me, to look at the young barley pushing up, bright and sparse, then thickening, till the brown earth was all greened over, and springing taller and brighter, stiff and pointed, and then softening and lengthening yet more, with the wind running in it like a boat furrowing the water, and finding a voice at last, and a song, and sending up its green, plaited ears to swell and ripen, till at the end they stood perfect as if the Lord had but that moment lifted His hand from them, all made of purest, clearest gold. Gold leaves, gold stalks, gold knops for heads, and these knops bearded thick with gold as well. Yet it was an innicent gold, and not that gold which is called the bane. Oh, how I could mind it, on those still Sunday mornings when I went to the well, and would set down the buckets for a little while and go out into the corn fields that lay beneath the vasty pale blue peace of the sky like creatures satisfied and at rest! There would be a ruffling breeze, and rooks far up the sky, and a second bloom of pale gold flowers on the honeysuckle wrathes against the blue. There would be warmship that lapped you round, and the queenly gift of the scent of corn. What other scent is like it? There is so much in it, beyond other sweets. There is summer in it, and frost. There is water in it, and the heart of the flint which the corn has taken up into its hollow stalks. There is bread in it, and life for man and beast.

All these thoughts, moithered and bewildered, came to me as I clung to the gate with the parching wind upon my face, too stunned to move. There are misfortunes that make you spring up and rush to save yourself, but there are others that are too bad for this, for they leave nought to do. Then a stillness falls on the soul, like the stillness of a rabbit when the stoat looks hotly upon it and it knows that there is no more to be done.

The fire was in the two biggest stacks of wheat now. It had gone upon them and they were not. Soon they would be as the barley was. They were good stacks, those, of a solid squarish oblong, and as high as might be with safety, for we had such a harvest that we could only make room by having the stacks high. It was good wheat too, long in the straw, and no touch of mildew. It had taken the most time of all both to sow and to reap, and in the lugging it had the biggest waggons all day. And now it was gone! It was a great mound of fire with the black shapes of two stacks in it, and soon the fire would be passed on and there would be no more sound, but just two grey-white housen for demons, with baleful red gleams in the crumbling passages within. There were more stacks of wheat by the hedge, but the next to the blazing stacks was the oats. The lovely oats, so pale and fine, like ferns for a lady's table!

They were so sweet, the oats, so very fine and fair, like midsummer grasses come golden. I did ever love the oats best of all. And suddenly I was all mother to the oats. The fire met have the wheat and the barley, but it should not take my oats. I clomb over the gate and ran where the little figures moved. I caught Gideon by the sleeve.

'You mun save the oats!' I screamed. 'Oh, save the oats, as is so fair and fine!'

But he said nought. He was working like a madman, and I saw that it was the oats he was trying to save, the oats and the stacks by the hedge. He and Sammy were digging trenches between the blazing stacks and these, to fill with water.

'Where's Tivvy?' I said, for now I was come to myself I wanted all the help there was.

'Gone for Feyther,' said Sammy, sweating and groaning over his spade, for the fire was gaining on them.

'Shall I take Bendigo and go for help?' I said. 'Or shall I get the buckets and begin fetching water?'

'Ah, that!' says Sammy. 'Do that, for help ud be too late, a power.'

Not a word did Gideon say. He was stricken with a dumb madness, but he worked like ten men. What with the horror of mind and the stress of labour and the great heat of the fire, the sweat ran down his face in a river and his clo'es were as if he had been in the water. And being so wet, and so near the fire, he went in a cloud of steam, which had a very strange look, as if he had been put under some curse or was already in hell.

I loosed Bendigo and the oxen and cows, such as were lying in, and they went pounding away into the woods, half crazy with fear. I woke Mother and told her she must dress and come to the mere and dip while we made a chain for the buckets, to send them from hand to hand. I got together all the pails and buckets, and thought it seemed a pitiful thing that with all that great mere full of water we could only slake our fire with as much as we could get into our little buckets. And I've thought since that when folk grumble about this and that and be not happy, it is not the fault of creation, that is like a vast mere full of good, but it is the fault of their bucket's smallness.

Mother came with me like a child, very mazed and quiet.

'Must I dip now, Prue?' she said.

'You can begin now, and have all the buckets ready,' I answered. 'But the time when you must dip your best will be in a tuthree minutes when we come.'

'Now, Sarn,' says Sammy, 'you mun leave digging and come for water.'

For though it may seem a thing not to be believed, all that awful night, though it was Gideon that did the most of the work, it was Sammy or me that gave the orders. Gideon would go at what he was set at in a frenzy, and go on after it stopped being any use, working like an ox at the threshing floor. He threw down the spade when Sammy spoke, and came with us to the mere. Mother was toiling over the dipping. She looked smaller and smaller as the trouble thickened about her, like a person that had eaten some fairy stuff to make her not able to be seen. She seemed no more than one of those little brown birds that will light down by the water for a while in their journeying and then be gone, nobody knews where.

'Now here comes Feyther, thanks be to the Lord,' said Sammy. He was a good lad that night, was Sammy, and while the fire lasted he never said but one text, and that a very temptuous one, 'Burning and fuel of fire,' though he must have thought of no end of them.

Sure enough there was Sexton bursting through the wood, and Tivvy not far behind, and a angry voice crying on the wind a long way back, that was Missis Sexton, who misliked being by her lonesome.

'Now,' says Sammy, 'Feyther can go in the rickyard and chuck on the water to dout the fire, Tivvy can gather the empty buckets as fast as he throws 'em down, and run back to Missis Sarn with 'em, and you and me and Prue'll run with full ones. I did think we might make a chain and pass from hand to hand, but we be too few, Sarn.'

Gideon spoke for the first time.

'I never,' he said with a wild, pale face, 'never had much strength about me, only me and these two.'

And with that he put his arm across his face as he was used to do when he was a lad and things went badly wrong, and cried.

Ah, I tell you it was a thing few would have cared to see, a great, strong, masterful man like that, crying like a little lad.

'Now, now, Sarn!' says Sexton, shocked as we all were. 'Now, yo munna take on. The Lord gave and the Lord hath taken away.'

At that Gideon came to himself.

'The Lord?' he says. 'No. It wunna the Lord! It was Beguildy. When we've douted the stacks I shall fetch un and roast un.'

No words of mine can tell you the awful way Gideon said that. I wanted to ask how he knew, if he did know, but there was no time for words. We were running to and again with two full buckets each, which, after an hour or so, is enough to try a strong man, leave alone a woman. Water carrying is an easy job if there's no hurry and you can use a yoke. But to run stumbling through a roasting heat, which we did for most of the journey, and to know that if you tarried the oats would go, and maybe if you didna tarry, was enough to take the spirit out of anybody. The oats did go. The fire leapt the ditch and all, and there was a new, tremendous blaze. I lost heart after that, and though I ran, it was with no hope.

'Oh, I be so tired,' said poor Mother. But I couldna let her rest.

'If we canna save it,' I said, 'you'll never get free of tending swine, Mother.'

So she bent her poor old back again, standing half in the water, in spite of the rheumatics. The cry went up to save the barn, for if the barn was lost, the house was lost. At that, Mother left dipping for water, so I was forced to get Tivvy to do it, and we had to bring back our own empty pails. I looked up once, and there was Mother fetching things out of the house. I looked at them after, and there was her sewing and the copper fruit pan, and a sampler she did when she was little, and Father's picture cut out in black paper, done by parson's brother-law, who was part foreign. People thought he must be simple to play with scissors and paper like a child, though they owned that he did it very well, and said that being part foreign he knew no better. Though Mother had been so mortal feared of Father in life, she treasured this picture in the queerest way. So there it was with the other things and six pots of damson cheese, and Pussy in a basket.

It was only at dawn, when the wind dropped and a fine, quiet rain began to fall, that we got the fire under. At least, it had burnt itself out, and we managed to save barn and house. The red light was gone from the sky and the burning from the mere. For all night it had seemed that the water in the mere was turned to fiery spirit, and was burning too. Everything was there, confused and topsy-turvy, the red and yellow flames, the smoke, bellying in the wind, the white-hot stacks, hollow and canting, the farm and the barn and our little black figures like mommets in the tumult.

Not long after it was over came Missis Sexton, who had suffered frittening of Bendigo, that came snorting and trampling through the wood so that she thought it had been the Black Hunstman. There were many hollow trees about the Sarn woods, they being old forest land, so she crept into one, and stayed till the light began to come. And then, once in, she could not get out, for she was more than ornary stout and also had so many clo'es on, and though in the stress of fear she squoze herself in, it was not easy to get out again in cold blood. But when she did come, she soon got us all some breakfast, and indeed we were in need of it, not only for what was past, but to face the day.

'Why, look's Tivvy and Prue white as ghosses!' she said. 'And you, Missis Sarn, should be abed, and to bed you shall go when you've had bite and sup. And as for you, Sarn! Why, man, man, you fritten me worse than Bendigo, indeed to goodness! Now then, where's ours? Draw up now, draw up, take bite and sup, people!'

She said it just as she said, 'Take your places for the game of Costly Colours.'

'But what I'd lief know,' says Mother, 'is how Sexton and Sammy knew our ricks were afire?'

'I knew,' said Sammy, 'because Tivvy and me were coming back latish from the mill, and we saw Beguildy coming along very quiet and sneaking this way. So I says to Tivvy as we'd follow, for I've been keeping an eye on Beguildy a goodish while, he being a wicked old man and the power of the Lord far from him. By their fruits you shall know them. And it seemed a funny time for him to be coming to Sarn, he being one for early bed always. So we followed on slow, keeping a long way back. And just as we came to the end of the wood there was a tremendous blaze from the far corner of the rickyard, and in a minute Beguildy came running up wood path, so we only had just time to hide. As soon as he was past, we did run to the rickyard, and it was the little stack in the corner, and just by it was this.'

Sammy held up the lid of Beguildy's tinder box, which everybody knew well, for he'd put his name on the inside of the lid in red paint, being proud of his writing.

'What a fool, to drop un!' says Missis Sexton.

'Nay, Mother,' says Sexton, 'Beguildy's no fool. 'Twas the hand of the Lord took the tinder box lid off'n un and chucked it there for Sam to see. Ah, so it was.'

'In the hand of the Lord there is a cup, Psalms seventy-five, eight,' said Sammy.

'Only it wunna a cup,' giggled Tivvy, who was always sillier when she was excited, ' 'twas the one-half of an old iron tinder box.'

' 'Tis the curse!' moaned Mother. 'He did curse my son Sarn by fire and by water, and this be the first. Dear Lord knows what the second'll be. 'Tis the sin you did eat, Sarn. There's bin harm on the place ever since you did it. Ah, ever since my poor maister died in his boots the place has been ill to live in, very ill it's been, what with the pigs and the rheumatics and the everlasting ploughing, and now all gone, as if it hadna been.'

'Ah, fire's a greedy feeder,' said Missis Sexton.

'I will consoom them in a moment, Numbers sixteen. This great fire will consoom us, Deuteronomy five. Fire con-soomed the palaces of Benhadad, Jeremiah forty-nine,' said Sammy.

'Three texes at a birth! Good lad, good lad!' cries Sexton.

'Only it's Beguildy did ought to be consoomed,' remarked Missis Sexton.

'And the awful thing about such wickedness,' says Tivvy, 'is that it's in the blood. It goes on from father to child. You'd never know when it ud break out. I wonder at you, Mister Sarn, I do, to be thinking of taking the child of a viper in wedlock. I never did like the Beguildys, Jancis in especial.'

'Indeed to goodness, the girl's right!' cried out her Mother, and Sexton added--

'What's bred in the bone'll come out in the flesh.'

Gideon looked around, with a grey lined face, like an old man's. He was never the same again after that night. You canna knock an ox on the head with the mallet and then expect it to be just as it was. He made to speak, but the words were slow in coming. Just then there was a trampling and traversing without, and Bendigo trotted past the window.

'Ha!' says Gideon, and makes for the door.

I knew what he was going for, and I rushed after him. By good fortune the cows were coming back from the wood, making soft mooing plaints that it was long past milking time. So instead of pleading for Beguildy I said--

'Look's cows coming, they'll be stanked if they inna milked.'

'Ah, you mun mind not to let 'em get like that'n,' Missis Sexton cautioned from the room. 'A brother-law's cousin of mine had the best herd ever you saw. Cheshire, he come from. Grand cows they were, and never ailed, and plenty of everything there was in that house, good milk and butter and cheese, and buckets and buckets of skim for the pigs, and fine fat pigs they were, and a fine fat man by brother-law's cousin was, and a fine fat women he'd got for wife, and twelve fine fat children.'

I may say that Missis Sexton, being so fat herself, always judged folk by it, and if they were thin they might as well never have been born, in her sight.

'Ah,' she went on, 'they were all as fat as butter, filled the pew at church to bursting, until the day he let the cows get stanked. Ah! That was a bad day for 'em. There was no prosperation after. The cows dwined and the pigs dwined, and in a bit the family dwined too, and in a little while, of all that fine fat family there was nought left but fourteen miserable rails.'

Tivvy was in a fit of giggling, for her Mother's stories 'most always made her laugh, though many's the beating she had for it.

'Milk first, lad,' I says to Gideon, 'and go to the Stone House after.'

God forgive me to deceive him so, but I wanted to save him from the sin of murder. No sooner was he in the shippen, milking, then I took Bendigo to the door and cried out to Sexton to mount and ride, and take Sammy too, for Bendigo could carry both as far as Plash, and to take Beguildy and march him off to the parish constable at Lullingford all in a courant, and save him from Gideon. For if he was locked up Gideon couldna get at him, and he'd only suffer what was right according to the law.

'I see,' says Sammy. 'Let me fall into the hand of the Lord, and not into the hand of man. Two Samuel twenty-four. Ah, we'd best go, Feyther.'

'Will Jancis and Missis Beguildy go to prison too?' enquired Tivvy.

'Surely to goodness no! They've done nought. In fact Jancis be a very tidy wench, and if she'd had the right spirit in her, and meekened her soul and gone softly in good sadness, I dunno but I'd have taken her in wedlock myself,' said Sammy.

They only got off just in time, for Gideon came running from the shippen, crying upon them to stop.

'They'll take Beguildy to prison,' I said. 'You munna have murder on your soul, lad, things be bad enough without that.'

'It would have eased me,' he answered with a strange look. 'It's all dammed up within. Choking, choking me. 'Twould have eased me to kill un. I'll never mend of it now.'

'But you couldna kill the father of your wife-to-be,' I said.

'Wife? What wife?'

'Why, Jancis! You'll be wed to Jancis come a week now.'

'What?' he says, with a wild, fierce look. 'Do ye think I'll wed with the devil's daughter? I tell ye, if it was to save my life and all, I'd never wed with her. Nay, I'll never see the wench again, not of choice, not unless she do force herself into my company.'

'Gideon, Gideon! Dunna say it! Oh, Gideon, there be things in life as is better than money and that'n. Leave be, lad! It inna meant for us to be rich. Let you settle down and be content, and marry the poor child as loves you so well, and if so be money comes, all the better. And if so be it dunna, none the worse. But deny the poor girl marriage after what's took place, you canna. Your heart canna be as hard as that.'

'It is. The granite mountain, quartzite, brytes, inna as hard. If you leave that girl come nigh me, I'll tromple out her life like I would a clothes-moth's. And so I warn ye. Rotten. That's what they be. Like father like child. A fause smiling face, but any minute, any minute she met burn the place to the ground. I shouldna wonder but she fetched the flint and the tinder for un last night. Camperdine may take her and welcome. I make him a present of her.'

'But, Gideon, you've bin as good as wed to her this last week. And suppose there was to be a baby, what then?'

'A baby? What? My child and hers? I tell ye, if any such thing came to pass, I'd strangle it. Hark ye, their blood's black. Foul, foxy, vermin. That's what they be. They're not fit to live. Thanks be to God, folks can swing for arson. I'll see he swings for it. And you tell the girl to keep away from me. It'll be the better for her.'

I durst say no more. What could I say, when the human kindness in my poor brother had been scorched up in the fire and was not? Only a fool will dip and dip in a dry well. He looked a deal taller as he stood there, with his back to the dark driving woods, where the rain was lashing now, that would have saved all last night, where the autumn storm was moaning, and the dry leaves churning and boiling in the air as the weeds will in the mere at the troubling of the waters. His clo'es yet clung to him, all scorched and darkened with the fire. His face was grimed, so that the lines that had not showed were very clear to see, and there were more lines, I was sure, since last night. His eyes, that were so cold, like water, blazed with hatred when he thought upon Beguildy or any of hisn, but at other times his face was blank and dim, like the face of one without hope, spent and foredone, a lost face. I said should we dig taters, for I thought maybe it would be a bit of comfort, to think he'd got summat. He came without a word, and worked hard and well, but every now and again he'd stop, and look about him strangely at the chill, silent mere, the overcast heavens and the stormy woods. It seemed to me that the spirit of the man was like a bird with a broken wing. And at noon, when I went to get our meal, he missed to come when I banged the tray, and I found him in the rickyard, where the heaps of ash yet smouldered, lying upon his face, as still and hard of hearing as a dead man, and indeed I do think his heart was dead from that time.

Chapter Three
The Deathly Bane

'Tis hard, and very hard, to write of the wintry time we went through after that night of grief and bitter woe. For when the quill has traced out good words of a kind meaning, it irks to make them sad and evil. But sad and evil that time was, and there is no use in gainsaying it. For many days after the fire, thew ork on the farm stood still, as it often will after a death. Gideon's one thought was to get at Beguildy, or if not that, to make him suffer the utmost of the law. Missis Beguildy was forced to give up the Stone House, for the landlord didna want a man there who burnt ricks, nor his folk, so he made the excuse of the rent being late to turn them out. Everything was sold, and Missis Beguildy and Jancis went off to Silverton, where Beguildy lay in prison waiting for the assizes, with only what they stood in. At least, poor Jancis didna stand, for when she heard the dreadful news of what Gideon had said, which I told her Mother to break to her as best she could, she fell down on the floor and stirred neither hand nor foot, nor spoke a single word. They carried her to the waggon from Plash Farm, which was to take her and her mother away, and they say she lay there like a broken flower. Maybe it was as well, for if her strength hadna gone from her she'd have tried to see Gideon, and I do think he'd have struck her down in his bitter smouldering rage. It seemed to ease him to hear of their misfortune, and when the day came for them to go, he went off to a place in the woods where he could see the waggon pass by, and stood there looking down upon it, with the sullen farm labourer driving, misliking having anything to do with folk in such evil case in men's sight, and poor Missis Beguildy sitting in the waggon all aged and wild, and Jancis lying on some straw at the bottom, like a white waxen image. I know, because Miller's Tom was in the wood at the time, and he came running to me, frit out of his life, pretty near, to tell me all about it.

'Oh, Prue Sarn, I was in the 'ood after a tuthree nuts,' he says, 'and I saw Mister Sarn a-walking by lonesome, very glooming and drodsome, and I was feared, so I did hide in a tree. And Mister Sarn went under the boughs of the big beech, where the road through the woods comes by. And in a while there was a rumbling, and I saw the waggon from Plash, and Missis Beguildy crying and taking on awful, but I couldna see Jancis. So I clomb the tree to see if she was in the bottom of the waggon, and there she was. She did look like a dead maid. Oh, she did look like the picture in the church of the little maid as was dead in the house when they fetched the Lord in, and He says "Rise you up!" He says. Only He hadna said it to Jancis. And I was feared, and I came down quiet from the tree, and I saw Mister Sarn staring down upon the waggon, for you do know there's a bit of a bank just there. And his face did frit me so that I made to run off, only then he stirred, so I kept quiet for fear he might come my way. He gloomed upon the waggon a long while, till the rumbling went ever so quiet, and wunna no more than the noise of a startle-de-buz when it be gone past, and then there was no sound at all, save the noise of a throstle banging a conker on a stone. And Mister Sarn did lift up both his fisses and did shake 'em after the waggon, and oh, Prue! his face was like the face of the Lord Jehovah in Feyther's book, when His anger was not turned away. Then he went away, slow, looking upon the ground, and the throstle went on banging the conker on the stone, and I runned to you.'

And that was how the properest man in our countryside did see the girl of his choice go, a girl like a water-lily bud, as loved him right well.

I said to myself, 'It be the bane. Oh, it be the dreadful bane.'

But after that Gideon seemed more at ease in himself. And I think it was that he had mistrusted his own heart, being afraid if Jancis came to him he'd give in. And his purpose was not to give in, but to begin all over again, and go straight forrard to his fixed end and aim.

The morning after they'd gone, he fetched out the ploughs, and came to the kitchen door and called to me as I was making gruel for mother, who was abed again, and had been ever since the fire, taking nought but gruel or a posset, and he said--

'Come and start of the big field, oot, Prue?'

I thought it was best not to give him a nay-word at all, so I said, Ah, I'd come. I took the gruel to Mother and said should I get Tivvy to come and sit with her a bit now and again, seeing we were starting on the ploughing. And she says--

'Oh, that bitter old ploughing! And maybe all the corn'll be burnt like the last. No wedding, nor house nor china nor nothing, only the pigs to tend again come the spring! But maybe I wunna see the spring. I'm very middling, Prue. You mun get the doctor's mon to me, I doubt.'

And indeed her poor hands were very thin and shrunken, and her small face browner and thinner, and she seemed more like a lost bird or a trapped creature than ever, and more in fear of Gideon.

'Dunna let him come in till I be better,' she'd say. 'Dunna let my son Sarn come and make me feel as I'm a burden. He dunna love me. He'd lief I was dead and sodded.'

301

And she'd lift up her hands, beseeching.

So I got Tivvy to come and mind her, and all that winter of dark weather, dark within as well as without, we ploughed, turning over the stubble of that good harvest we'd lost. We were poorer than ever, and things didna prosper so well as they had, there being no heart in us. There were Tivvy's meals to find as well, for though she came for love, being sweet on Gideon, yet we had her victuals to find, and she was a very hearty feeder. The doctor's man cost a lot, also, and the worse the weather was, the more he charged. About the New Year there was a bitter cold spell, and ice on the roads, so his horse came down and broke its leg, and we had to pay summat towards that. Things seemed to go from bad to worse, for Gideon kept me so hard at it, driving plough, that I was forced to leave the dairy work and the fowls and pigs to Tivvy, and she was ever a bit flighty, and careless, so folks began to complain about the butter, and the fowls laid badly, and the pigs began to look thin and unkind, and Tivvy thought of nothing but to make herself look pretty and temptuous for Gideon. As January went on the weather got worse, and we had a heavy fall of snow, and Mother was so bad one night that I was forced to send for the doctor's man again. At least, send I didna, for nobody would go, the snow being deep. There was nothing for market, the cows being dry all but one, and eggs scarce. So Gideon didna go to Lullingford, and I made up my mind to go on Sunday, when even Gideon didna plough, and once at Lullingford I could send word to the doctor by the Silverton coach. This I did, and a weary day I had of it, and a sad day also, passing the empty house of Kester Woodseaves, and thinking maybe some ill might come to him in the great city, or he might meet a lover there, and so come no more to Lullingford. But I was glad of this weary day after, for there be times when the only comfort a body has is the remembrance of hardship borne for somebody dear.

When the doctor's man came after a good few days, he was forced to bide with us some time, on account of the badness of the roads. This irked Gideon, for the expense of the food and also his nag's keep. He was the more put out because the doctor's man gave a good account of Mother, for he seemed to think she should have been at death's door afore I called the man to come from so far away. I mind we were sitting round the hearth, late on a wild night, with hailstorms taboring on the window, and a good clear fire that we were mighty glad of. The doctor's man was a pleasant-spoken person, round and short and ruddy, with a bright red colour on his cheeks that looked as if it had a good glaze over it. He was always rubbing his hands, as if the last patient had pleased him very well, but you could never tell from this how the person had prospered, for he'd rub his hands as much over a corpse as over a quick person, and indeed, I sometimes thought, more. He was rubbing them while we talked about Mother, though not so much as he did when he told us of Missis Beguildy, who had ailed more and more ever since she got to Silverton, and was now said to be going into a decline. It wasna that he was an unkind man, or wished folk harm, only naturally it was more interesting to him if they were took for death than if they were only a little ailing.

'Missis Sarn'll pull through now. Nicely, she will,' he said.

'Oh!' says Gideon. 'Her'll pull through, will her?'

'Ah. And last a-many years, I shouldna wonder. A wiry old lady! Tough, for all she's thin and nesh-looking.'

'How many years?' says Gideon.

'Oh! It's hard to say. Doctor might be able to, but of course I be only like his 'prentice. But it might be as much as ten, easy. Ah. I should say ten. With care.'

'Ten years!' Gideon said it in a very strange way.

'Ah, but you mun cosset her.'

'Ten years, and always like this?'

'Oh, ah! Her'll be bedridden, winters, and maybe all the year round later on.'

'And she'll be no more use?'

'Use? Why, what use could she be?'

'And you coming over a tuthree times every winter, I suppose?'

'Oh, ah, if you send for me,' says doctor's man, taking a pull at his ale and helping himself to another piece of bread and cheese, which made Gideon scowl.

'Whenever be you going to clear supper, Prue?' he says. 'I've had my bellyful this long while.'

'Oh, but you're such a poor eater, Sarn,' Tivvy cries out. 'It's wonder you're not clemmed. You want a wife to cook for ye and sarve up temptuous dishes. Chitterling puffs, now. They're as different from plain chitterlings as heaven from hell. I made some Sunday was a week, and neither Feyther nor Sammy spoke a word all day after, they were that contented in their innards.'

'Oh, dear me, I do wish I wunna a married man,' says the doctor's chap. 'Ah, in good sadness I wish it!'

'If you wunna, it would be no manner use,' said Tivvy pertly. 'I like a big man.'

Gideon took no notice, any more than he did of the chitterling puffs.

'A very big man,' went on that forrard little piece, 'and dark. Big shoulders, big 'ands, arms with great big lumps of muscle and sinew, big feet, strong legs--'

'Why, missis, you be giving a list like the list in the Song o' Solomon,' says doctor's man.

'And hard,' went on Tivvy, taking no notice, but fixing her eyes on Gideon, 'hard and never tired, lusty and lungeous and ill to thwart, but a good lover, Ah, and fiery, and not to be

303

gainsayed by the girl he's a mind for. That's the man for me! Ah. That's the man Sexton's Tivvyriah would be a right good missus to, with no other thought but to save and scrape and scrat to do his will and make him rich.'

'Well, you should have been a lawyer, Missis, so you should,' says the visitor, 'and if you dunna get what you want, may I be bottled in spirits like a tadpole!'

But Gideon never lifted his eyes to Tivvy at all, only sat and glowered till she'd gone to bed. Then he said again--

'And she'll last for years, always ailing, but lasting on?'

'Ah. Indeed to goodness! Creaking doors, you know. But you mun see you keep her pulse strong. There's the danger. If it wunna kept strong, she'd very likely go off quiet and sudden before you'd time to say sarsaparilla. Keep the pulse strong and she'll be as merry as a robin.' We talked a bit more, and then Gideon said he was going to look the stock afore turning in.

'The brindled longhorn's very middling,' he said. 'Seems to be in a fever all the while. Heart's like to burst sometimes. I suppose a dose of foxglove ud put her right, maybe?'

'Ah. Foxglove'll lower the pulse as quick as anything. But you mun be careful. Be she a young cow?'

'Going four.'

'Dunna give her too much then. When things get old and worn out they canna stand much of it.'

When the visitor was gone to bed, and Gideon back from the shippen, he sat down, hopeless-like, and said--

'Her means dying.'

'What, Brindle?' I says.

'Ah. Seems like the old devil's put a curse on me all right.'

'It's only the weather, and Tivvy being a bit careless, and me so busy at it, ploughing.'

'And there's Mother,' he said, 'as was used to help a bit, no use, and less than no use. A heavy burden! We'll never pick up now she's like that.'

'Dunna let her know you think it.' I said.

But the very next day, when I took her supper, there was Gideon standing in the mid of the room, talking very loud, and Mother like a frittened mouse.

'Well,' he was saying, 'you be very middling, Mother!'

'Ah, I be ailing, Sarn,' she says, with her smile.

'It mun be a sorrow to you that you canna do a hand's turn.'

'Ah. It be, Sarn. But come the warm weather, I'm in behopes to see to the broody hens and the rest of the fowl. Ah! And the ducks and the cade lambs.'

'But not the pigs?'

'Well, if Tim could mind 'em a bit longer I'd be glad. It does make me so rheumaticky, down by the water there.'

'It's a big expense, giving that great lad his tea every day.'

'I know it be, and I'll be as quick as I can getting better, Sarn.'

'I shouldna think life's much of a pleasure to you, ailing so.'

'It be weary time and again, but in between I'm pretty comfortable.'

'What with the rheumatics and the cough and the sinking feeling, I should think you'd as lief be in the Better Land.'

'When it pleases the Lord to take me to the Better Land, I mun go without complaint, but I'd liefer be in life, for life I do know, and the worst of it, but the Better Land I dunna know.'

'You know there's no coughs nor rheumatics there, nor sinking feeling.'

'Nor chimney corners nor cups of tea,' she says, 'and I doubt it'll be too grand for me, Sarn.'

But Gideon, standing in the mid of the room and talking very loud, said--

'You'd as lief be dead as quick.'

He went away then, but every evening he went in again and talked in the same way, which seemed a pity to my mind, for though he might mean to cheer her up, and though folk never seem to think it matters what you say to the sick, yet it seemed to me melancholy talk for a poor old ailing woman. But at last, one evening at the end of March, in a spell of wet, muggy weather, when the rheumatics were very bad, she said, when he came to what he always ended with--'I should think you'd as lief be dead as quick--'

'Well, maybe I would, Sarn.'

And that seemed to content him. He left off coming every evening, which eased Mother, for she was more in dread of him than ever nowadays, so that even Tivvy noticed it. I thought when April came in, things seemed to be going better, Mother being more cheerful, though still very weak. I got on better with my work, being free of worry, and Mother seemed quite happy with Tivvy. We were working harder than ever, and my clo'es hung about me, but I didna mind that. I was sowing the big field with wheat, while Gideon went on ploughing. It was grand out there in the fresh of the morning, with purple shadows on the wet earth, and the sun rolling up beyond the woods, and Sarn Mere like pale blue crackled glass with a light behind it. Times, the sky would be all pale blue too, with larks hanging in it. Times, the big white clouds, like new-washed and carded wool, stood upon the tops of the budding trees. The bright colours made me think of the coloured weaving, which I supposed Kester would have pretty near mastered by now. Though no word had come, since Christmas, of his doings or his well-being, I felt in myself that all was right with him. At Christmas the Silverton coachman had left a little packet for me at the *Mug of Cider*, and when I was raught back to the attic I found within a bit of cloth woven in two colours, and a letter.

LONDON TOWN.

Christmas.

DEAR PRUE SARN,--
This is to wish you well as it leaves me. I can do two colours now, as you see by pattern. The women here are poor things, pale and small, mostly fair, and not a real melting dark eye among them. I was bid to a banquet at the house of an alderman that is a weaver. There was a young wench sat by me that had spared her bodice-stuff but not her blushes. I called to mind a dark stone chamber, and young Camperdine's face in the shadows, and a woman that did what she did for loving-kindness and in bitterness of spirit, but did look like an apple-blossom fairy all the same, and did light a fire in one chap as will be very hard to dout. And so a happy Christmas and a good New year from

KESTER WOODSEAVES.

I may say that letter was in rags by April, as if the mice had been at it.
I had sent him a letter for Christmas also, and this was it.

SARN.

Christmas.

DEAR WEAVER,--
Please find herein a lockram shirt. If you wear it, they say you'll take no harm from the smallpox or other ills. I wove it and made it of hemp, and said a good few old righteous charms over it, but no unrighteous ones. I often call to mind the day we watched the dragon-flies, at the time of the troubling of the waters, when the lilies were in blow. So farewell for now, and God send you happy.

Yours obediently,
PRUDENCE SARN.

The seventh of April being a very clear-coloured morning, I called the weaving to mind, and so, as I went up and down the field sowing the bright seed, I sang *Barley Bridge*.

'Shift your feet in nimble flight,
You'll be home by candlelight.
Open the gates as wide as the sky,
And let the king come riding by.'

Would Kester ever come riding to Sarn from London Town? I wondered. For the fair, he'd said he'd come, at the time of the troubling of the waters, when the lilies were in blow all along the marges of the mere, looking at their angels, and when blue kingfisher-flies and the bright, lustre-coloured damsels were coming out of their shrouds.

I was thinking thus, when I looked up, and there was Tivvy, coming running in a great courant, all distraught. 'Come quick, Prue!' she said. 'Her's took very bad. The tea didna agree. He says, give it her strong, he says, for it'll do more good the like of that'n. So I did. And she said it was a bitter brew. But she drank it. And in a while she went ever so quiet, and I couldna hear her breathe. And then she gave a guggle and whispers--

'Go for Pure.'

I was only just in time to kiss Mother, who was all shrunken down in her pillows. She whispered--

'A bitter brew!' and smiled, and caught her breath, and was gone.

After a while I says to Tivvy--

'Where's that tea?'

But she'd thrown it away.

'Gideon,' I said, 'was there bane in that tea you did tell Tivvy to give Mother?'

'Now what do I know what Tivvy did give to Mother?'

'Oh, Sarn, you did know!' cries Tivvy. 'You said, "Give it her strong," you did.'

'Hold your tongue, you little liar,' shouts Gideon, 'or I'll thank you to tell Prue what you and me were doing in the loft, Sunday's a week.'

With that, Tivvy went as red as fire, and hushed.

I could make nothing of them. I sent for the doctor, to see what Mother died of. And he said, were we in the habit of giving her *digitalis*, a strange word that I didna know, but he spelled it out for me, and I wrote it down. So I said no, I'd never heard tell of it. So he says, 'Foxglove! Foxglove!'

'Foxglove?' I says. 'No. Whatever should I give her that for?'

'What indeed?' he says, looking at me very sharp.

'What do puzzle me, sir,' I says, 'is what Mother died of. She was beginning to pick up so nice.'

'That what I want to know, too,' he says.

'Maybe we'd ought to have a Crowner's 'Quest, sir?' I says.

'Oh, you'd be willing to have an inquest on the body?'

'Why, yes indeed, if it was right and proper.'

'Well, if you're willing to have it, there's no need to have it.'

He was a very peculiar man. I couldna make him out at all.

307

'I was doubtful,' he says, 'but if you're willing . . . It's nothing but old age, I expect. They go like that in the spring sometimes. And it's a great trouble and expense, an inquest . . . all just for the flicker of a doubt . . . and can't do the poor woman any manner of good . . . so, if you're willing, we won't bother with an inquest.'

I could make neither head nor tail of that. But remembering that Doctor was an educated man, I left off trying to understand him. For there's as much of a mystery about an educated man, that's been schooled and colleged proper, as there is about the Trinity. So, being busy over the funeral and all, I thought no more about him, but grieved sorely for Mother, because as she lay in coffin she did look like a frozen bird, foredone with winter.

Chapter Four
All on a May Morning

It was quieter than ever at Sarn without Mother's quiet ways. I missed her a deal more than if I'd depended on her, for it's the folk that depend on us for this and for the other that we most do miss. So the mother is more let and hindered lacking the little creatures clinging to her skirt than she is when they be there, for she has no heart for her work. So in the lengthening April days I'd often sit and cry, calling to mind her poor little hands uplifted, and her way of giving me a right good welcome when I came in tired of an evening. There was only Gideon and me, and Tivvy now and again. The work went on the same as ever, though there was a sadness about it all. Gideon never went into the stackyard but he cursed Beguildy, who was still in prison, with no sentence fixed. We'd heard nought of Jancis nor her mother for a good while, nor had there been another letter from Kester. The market began again. I mean, we began to go again, having plenty to fill the stall. One of us would go, and the other would mind the farm, and I heard that every time Gideon went, Miss Dorabella would come and buy summat. Indeed it was already being said that she was sweet on Gideon, and I could only hope it wouldna come to the Squire's ears. I didna wonder at her being partial to Gideon, for indeed he was a fine, strong man, with a deal of character and power, and very good to look at, and there were few young gentlemen about Lullingford at that time, what with some of them going to bide in London, and some never coming back from the wars. Gideon never said anything to me, but I could see he was flattered at her liking, and I thought once when she came to our door for a drink of milk, that his hand shook a bit when he gave her the cup. But if he was thinking of her, I'm sure it was only the lust of the eye, and youth, and the wish to get on, and not love, such as he felt for Jancis. I didna believe he'd ever love anybody again, since that early love had been poisoned--for indeed the bane seemed to have got into it as it had into everything. But there was no doubt he was very taken up with her, and when it wasna Miss Dorabella it was Tivvy. He didna care a farden for Tivvy, but he was ready to take all she'd give, as many another young man would, especially after such an upsetting of his life, and the losing of his dear acquaintance. He seemed to want to be out along with Tivvy when he wasna working, and if he was restless, and he couldna bear to speak of Mother. This seemed curious to me, for he never appeared to care much about her in life. I mind when May Day came, and we were starting for the market, for the things must be sold, mourning or not, I said I called to mind just where Mother stood to send us last time. And Gideon gave a bit of a start, and looked, nervous like, at the place I pointed to, almost as if he thought she'd come again. And sometimes I noticed that he'd look across at her chair, anxious and brooding. This troubled me, for it was so different from his usual ways. In all else he was the same, and the farm was the same, and the mere, and the spring. May came in warm and splendid, and the buds and blades, the opening petals and the blown petals, the wafts of sweet air and he storms of warm rain drove on over the country as in every other year. The blackbirds kept up their charm the day long, and the cuckoos were at it from four or five in the morning. Out went the coots and their young across the mere, the dippers made their well-roofed house, the wag-tails played beside the water, and the heron stood watching his long shadow in the glassy lake, as if he wondered how soon if would be as long as the steeple. The lily leaves lay green and bright, like empty boats, for the time of lilies were not yet. The young leaves on the forest trees lengthened and broadened, the grass grew long and began to ripple, the corn sprang quick and bright. The Lent lilies in the meadow wilted, and the bluebells came, like smoke bellying up the slopes of the woods. All was made anew, and the brighter the colours were, the more I thought of Kester and his weaving, and the more unkind I felt it to be on my part, to be glad of the spring, with poor Mother in her new-made grave. There came a day in the very mid of all this fine May weather, when the thorn trees along by the mere were so thick-set with blossom that they laid a solid wall of white in the water at their feet. Though it was noon, the charm of bird-song was nearly as loud as it was at dawn, for in May they never seem to weary. We were in the kitchen, having our dinner afore going out to finish earthing up the taters. Tivvy was helping, as she often did now, though she got but little thanks from Gideon, who would brood all the while, and frown, and start up sometimes as if he heard a voice.

309

The kitchen was pleasant after the heat outside, for it was an early year. The sun lay in quiet patches along the quarries, and the lilac outside, just past its prime, and the sweeter for it, sent a strong freshness through the open window.

Something went past the window, and there was a little soft tap on the door. It reminded me of the time when Jancis ran away and came to our door in the snow. I went to open, and there she stood, Jancis, white as a ghost, leaning against the doorpost, with a shawl wrapped about her, and in the shawl, as I could just see, a baby no bigger than a doll.

'Why, Jancis!' I says. 'However in the name of goodness did you come?'

But she only looked past me, as wild and as white as any mermaid in the old tales, peering after her mortal lover.

She gave me neither word nor look. She gave Tivvy no glance even. We wunna there for Jancis in that hour. She just slipped in, like a wreath of mist from off the winter mountain or a drift of blossom from off the summer trees, or a white woman from under the mere. She'd got on the gown she was used to wear for randies, torn and crumpled but still white, and though it didna set her off as well as the blue one, it did, with the white shawl, make her look like a floating spirit out of the air, as she went across the kitchen. There she was, all of a heap at Gideon's feet, and she had set the baby on the floor in front of him, as he sate in the big arm-chair at its head, and Jancis there upon the floor, it did make me think of that story in the Bible when Jesus was at a feast, and some poor peson came and asked summat, and was chid, and did up and say that not even the dogs need lack their crumbs. It was as if all the good of life was outspread there on our oaken table, till it creaked under the weight. There were the fruits of love, there was the homely bread of daily kindness, and the cup to quench all thirst, and salt to make life tasty, and all the lesser pleasures that do make life a good, sweet thing in the living. And Gideon had the helping of them. Sarn of Sarn Mere was the maister of that feast and he might say, if he would, 'Here, let me heap thy plate, and fill up thy mug!' Or he might begrutch it all.

Jancis was kneeling in the patch of bright sunshine, and she seemed as the snowflake when the day turns to a thaw. In the ticking of one moment she might have melted clean away. I called to mind that day in the dairy, when she came in behopes that Gideon might ask her to wed there and then. I called to mind the night I wished her well when Beguildy was gone to look for the seventh child, and the time I saw her coming toërts me between her white oxen, like a lady of old time that has been a long while dead. I remember how she'd sung *Green Gravel* that Christmas when she ran away, and how the light from the window was green upon her face, and how she was used to say--

'O I wanted to play *Green Gravel!*'

All the things she'd ever said or done seemed to be lapped around her as she knelt there with her golden hair all loose about her shoulders. That she was so pale, all white and gold, and that Gideon was so dark, and darkly clad, made it seem yet more as if she came from some other world, and the baby also, for it was white too, and its tiny head, where the wrapper fell aside, was covered with a light yellow down. There was no look of Gideon in it at all. It wunna like a real baby, but like a changeling that came into being in the mid of a summer night on the petal of a lily flower. Oh, it was a strange baby as ever I saw! I leaned against the doorpost with the tears rolling down my face, and so that I shouldna sob out loud I promised myself to give Jancis the best meal ever she had, so soon as this should be over, and she should have a new-laid egg from the slatey game hen, whose eggs were worth a mint of money for setting, she being a prize bird. Though why it should please me so to think of her eating it, when a common egg would have been quite as nice, and bigger, I dunna know. And I promised myself that the baby should have the best wash ever, for indeed it looked as if it had rolled in the ashes. And oh, dear me! how I'd stuff it with milk, and how I'd dress up the old rush cot, and make a little counterpane, and then put the well-stuffed baby to lie in the sun and sleep! And in time it would lose that wisht, awful look, so ancient, as if it knew all there was to know, and didna like it. I wanted to see it with a great big tossy-ball of golden cowslips. And all the while Tivvy sat by Gideon with her mouth fallen open with surprise, and looking almost as frittened as if she'd seen a ghost.

Gideon was like a stone man. There was no feeling in his face at all, neither pity nor anger. All that was over-past, it seemed. It was like an old tale that he'd forgotten, and Jancis was chief lady in that tale, but why she was, and who she was, and what she did was all out of mind, because the tale was lost to his remembrance. Once, at Christmas, maybe, if she'd come, he'd have knocked her down, very likely, in his anger. But then he might have kissed her after. Now he neither struck nor kissed.

All he'd felt for her had died in the fire that night of September, and the sin of the father was visited upon the poor girl. For when Gideon's eye fell on her, he saw his burning ricks, and in her blue glance there were the red reflections of fire, as you will see on some clear morning the last wild smoulderings of the thunderstorm. That was all she meant to him now. And though his hatred of Beguildy was as savage as ever, he had no feeling at all for her, neither hatred nor desire, nor even lust, much less any love. Miss Dorabella

311

had seized upon his mind, and Tivvy had satisfied his body. There was no place for Jancis. There he sat, in our old kitchen, so quiet, yet so full of whispers, so full of the remembrance of all the Sarns that had been here, from Tim, with the lightning in his blood, to Father, passing out from life in a dark snoring after a fit of anger. I thought of Mother spinning here day after day, whirring like a little lych-fowl. I thought of all the other Sarn women, and of myself, striving and slaving for the bane. And it seemed that the bane was like some plant, such as the catch-fly, that does wile living creatures into its banqueting hall, spreading a great feast, and see! when they are in, she catches them and grips them, and binds them, and trammels their feet, so that they cannot go. There was a heavy sweetness from the day-lilies in the border that made me think of death chambers. I wished Jancis would say summat and get it over, whether for good or ill, so that I might the sooner set about the babe. But she didna, and time went on and on. Outside, there was Sarn Mere standing up afore me like a mirror framed in some precious green gem work. There was no sound but the saddish charm of the birds near and far, and the wandering hum of a bee that came in to our kitchen, and misliking it, blundered out again.

Then Jancis lifted up her head and looked at Gideon.

'Sarn!' she said. And again, 'Sarn!'

As she said it, I got the feeling that there were many listeners, leaning down out of the air, crowded together as close as the petals of a white peony, waiting to hear what should come of this meeting.

She clasped her hands and set her blue eyes upon Gideon, seeming to leave the baby aside for a while, as if he should speak up for himself later.

'Do you mind, Sarn,' she said, 'how we used to play *Conquer* with the big pink and white snail-housen down by the water, and you nearly always won, and I lost? Do you mind how I wanted to play *Green Gravel?*'

Her faint voice stopped a while, and a strange thing happened, for as I watched her it seemed to me as if many voices, a long way off, took up the words of that old song and sang it right through, in parts, as is the manner of singers in our country-side. For if anybody sings at all, he or she can sing parts, the people being all very fond of music and having it grained into their souls. So I heard it, with the grace-notes of the trebles and the rolling of the bass voices, and the altos and the tenors taking up the words and playing with them, and all, as it were, making much of the song, and speaking for Jancis through it. Very low and far it seemed, yet rich with many voices.

'Green gravel, green gravel, the grass is so green!
The fairest young lady that ever was seen.
I'll wash you in milk, and I'll clothe you in silk,
And write down your name with a gold pen and ink.'
What it was I heard, I never knew. Parson said it was my busy imagination playing about the past. I canna say. Only, in my imagination or in reality, I did hear it, in very truth, a part song, well sung and tuneful, with every note clear and each part intertwining as it should, but all a very long way off.

'Do you call to mind the even when you saw me under the rosy light, Sarn, when you were coming back from Lullingford ooth the sheep? And the day we found the canbottlins' nest in the spinney, and fourteen young uns in it, and you kissed me once for every canbottlin?'

Still Gideon made no sound, nor stirred.

'And when I ran away, and Prue took me in, you did say to me, standing in the mid of this very kitchen, "Give us a kiss, wench!" And in the dairy once you said I looked as if I was made of may and milk. And at Callard's that evening I held the baby while Mister Callard made 'em all say, "Bull-baiting's bad!' do you mind how Grandfeyther Callard said all of a sudden, "I see two babbies in her arms, ours, and hers as is to come!" And the harvest dance, when they whistled so well, and we danced?'

A quiver went across Gideon's face at the mention of that harvest, and I wondered at Jancis speaking of it, till I saw that she'd forgotten the cause of Gideon's quarrel with her. All she knew now was that he didna love her, and the reason was neither here nor there.

'And when Feyther went to look for the seventh child, and you came, and we were so sweet together? Ah! Even that morning after Feyther came back we were so, and you said, "Come five days, my little dear!" And I said, "God send you happy!' And since that, Sarn, I hanna set eyes on you till this hour.'

Still Gideon made no sign, so she laid her hand on his arm.

'Do you mind it, Sarn?" she says.

'Ah!' he said, indifferent, 'I mind it, but it was long ago. Time out of mind.'

'But the babe wasna. Here be the babe, Sarn! Yours and mine.'

She held the child up as if she'd put it on his knees, but he waved it away.

'A boy!' says Jancis. 'Not a girl, to cumber you with women. A boy, to mind pigs for ye ever so soon, and in a few years he'll be driving plough. Ah. I reckon he'll be a good lad to you, and work well, and gather in twice as much as his grandad scattered abroad.'

The poor babe stirred, as if it felt the heavy burden.

Gideon looked at it, as if when it touched his life's aim it could be seen, though invisible at other times. Then he gave a short, cruel laugh.

'That?' he says. 'You offer me that to help me? Thank ye! Why, if it lives, which I doubt, it'll never be no good but to coddle about in the house and feed on soft food.'

And as if it knew that it hadna passed the test, the poor mite set up a wail. At this Gideon pushed the table aside and got up. He went to the back kitchen door, that being the nearest way to the kitchen garden. At the door he stopped a minute.

'Best go back where you came from,' he said. 'You binna wanted here, neither the one nor the other.'

With that, he shut the door and went out.

Jancis stayed where she was, seeming mazed and dumbfoundered. A pale feather borne along the air, a lily petal wandering on the water, couldna be as lost as she was then. I ran to her, and lifted her and the babe to the settle, for indeed she was so light, it was pity to feel her lightness.

'Now, lookye,' I said, 'never a word shall you speak till you've had bite and sup! Put the kettle on, Tivvy, there's a good girl, while I warm some milk for baby.'

Jancis said nought, but in a little the tears began to steal down her cheeks. She took a sup of tea, and then I asked her how she got here.

'I walked,' she said, 'and poor baby was so heavy. You'd never think, to look at him, what a weight he was to lug.' I knew he scarce weighed more than a good fowl, and so I knew also how weary poor Jancis must have been, to feel so small a burden so heavy.

'Whatever was your mother thinking of, to let you walk?'

'Mother's dead.'

'Dear to goodness! I be sorry for that,' I said. 'She was a right nice woman.'

'There's kind!' says Jancis, but without any heart in it.

She was like one who, in the game of *Costly Colours*, has risked all, playing the card called *Costly*, and lost it. She was out of the game now, with nothing more to gain or lose. I didna like to mention her dad, and she said nothing about him.

'Well, your home's here,' I said. 'You know that, Jancis, my dear.'

'My home canna be here if Sarn dunna love me, Prue.'

'Ah, but it is!' I cried out. 'Though I did swear on the Book to obey Gideon like a 'prentice, a wife, and a dog, yet this day I shall gainsay him. You'll lie in my bed to-night, child, You and the little un will sleep at home from this time on.'

She gave a little sad smile, as if to say, 'I wonder!' and lay holding the babe. But now Tivvy, who'd been looking more and more sulky, burst out—

314

'And will she sleep here indeed, Prue Sarn? I do think not! Maybe you dunna know as I'm going to wed with Sarn myself. Ah! He's got to wed me for my sake and for his own as well.'

Jancis had opened her eyes and was watching her with a look like a Wise Woman's I knew once, who could tell you your own thoughts.

'I know it ud be as well for you, Tivvy, if he did wed with you,' I said, pretty dry and sneering, for I never could abide Tivvy, and that's the truth, 'and I reckon he'd best not be too long about it, neither, and you Sexton's girl and all! But the thing is, will he? And I'm pretty sure he never will. I'm sorry for you, Tivvy, and I'd never have said a word afore Jancis, only you began it.'

Tivvy's face was scarlet, but she didna flinch.

'I said, good for him as well as for me,' she answered.

'I canna see,' I says, and God forgive me for being so sharp with the girl, 'how it ud be good for Gideon, *in any way*, to marry.'

'Oh! Well, I'll soon show you,' she says.

'He did love Jancis once, Tivvy,' I told her. 'And she was his dear acquaintance and his wife, all but the ring.'

She took no notice of that.

'I'll tell you why it ud be good for Sarn to marry me,' she said. 'Foxglove tea! That's why.'

'Foxglove tea? Are you crazy, Tivvy?'

'Everybody knows as I know nought of yarbs. Everybody knows Sarn gave the cow foxglove leaves. You and I know that the doctor said your mother seemed as if she'd had foxglove.'

She spoke slower and slower, leaning forrard with her hands on the table.

'Everybody knows, Prue Sarn, that your brother thought Missis Sarn a burden. Everybody know he does want to get on. And I know, and if he dunna marry me pretty quick everybody else'll know too, what was in the tea he made for his mother and told me to give her strong.'

'What was it?' I said, with a sickness at the heart.

'Foxglove!'

She snapped out the word like a bite. I knew it was true.

'I can prove it,' she said, 'because as it chanced Mother had come to bring Missis Sarn that night-rail she'd been sewing for 'er. And when I came down from giving Missis Sarn her tea, I poured a cup for Mother, there being some left, and Mother said in a minute, "This is foxglove tea." Ah, Mother knows right well what Missis Sarn died of, but she'll never mouth it to a mouse if Sarn weds with me.'

'I'll never believe it!' I cried out. But Tivvy says--

'You will. You believe it now.'

And I did. Jancis did, too. She gave a little moan and whispered--

'It was foreboded, Prue! It was to be. I've no home now, Prue, no home on all this earth. Neither baby nor me's got anywhere to go. What shall us do, baby?'

The baby, being spoken to and being well content with the meal it had just finished, gave a milky smile. Jancis shut her eyes and seemed to care no more what anybody said.

But Tivvy came to the settle, and she says--

'If you stop the night over, we'll publish it all abroad, Jancis Beguildy!'

And then I be sorry to say my temper was out, and I rushed at her and boxed her ears right well.

'Go!' I says. 'Go, you cruel wench, afore I maul you. I never hated afore. But you I hate. How dare you be so curst to that poor child? You may settle with Gideon what you both do. But when you come over the door-sill, out go I. And for this day, out go you!'

And I may say she went pretty quick, very startled to see meek Prue Sarn in such a temper.

'Now lie you still, and rest, my dear,' I said. 'While I go to Gideon.'

'No. Dunna werrit Sarn, Prue,' she says. 'But I'll rest. Ah. Baby and me's both in need of rest. We'll take a good long rest, Prue. And thank you kindly for all.'

Out I went. There was Gideon, working like seven. I do believe those unkind words he said to Jancis were but his way of brazening it out to his own heart. I do believe there was a seed of love there even then, and if it hadna been for Tivvy it might have pushed up and flowered. I was never one to hiver-hover over things, so I walked up to Gideon and said--

'Tivvy says you gave Mother poison. Be it true?'

'By gum, that wench wants a good hiding!' says Gideon. 'And if she forces me to wed with her, that's the bride-gift she'll get.'

'You *did* give her foxglove tea to give Mother, then?'

'Mother told me she'd liefer be dead than quick, and she was a burden.'

He never tried to soften it nor deny it, for that wasna his way.

'Well, you be a murderer, and I've done with you,' I said.

'You swore to do as I said.'

'Murder cancels all vows,' I answered.

'I dunna want Tivvy here. She's no manner use.'

'Seemingly you canna choose,' I said. 'It's Tivvy or hang, as far as I can see. I'd save you if I could, for you be my brother, when all's said, and I like you right well, too. When you've worked along of a person, furrow for furrow and spade for spade, as long as I've worked with you, lad, you do like the person right well, unless you hate him. And you I canna hate, though I've been trying to the last few minutes. Gideon! What for did you do such a wicked thing? Indeed to goodness you mun repent in dust and ashes, and think of nothing else at all, or the devil'll certainly put his mark on you, so you'll come to no good in this life, and go to the lowest hell in the other. Your own Mother, Gideon!'

But all he'd say was—

'She said she'd liefer be dead than quick, and she was a great burden.'

'Well, I'm going, and so I warn you,' I said, in a passion.

'I'm in behopes you'll stay over hay and corn harvest,' he answers, as cool as cool could be, just as if he'd done no wrong at all, which I believe in his own sight he hadna.

'No,' I said. 'Fix up with Tivvy.'

'She's no use in the harvest. She's so bone-idle.'

'I'll stay till she comes, and no longer,' I said. "And I wouldna promise that, only I know she's in a pretty taking to get wed quick. I be right down disappointed with you, Gideon, on every count.'

'You've no right to be. What have I done? Put an old woman to sleep as wanted to sleep. And as for Tivvy, she as good as asked me to.'

Calm? Oh, he was as calm as the mere when it was frozen deep.

'And what about Jancis?' I burst out. 'What about that poor mommet of hers that you've brought into the world? They're neither old nor forrard.'

For answer, he pointed across to the blackened floor of the rickyard, and said—

'You know whose child she is.'

Then, under breath, he said, as if he'd forgotten me—

'But I did love her once.'

So I left him to his thoughts, and ran back to the house, calling out as I opened the back door—

'Here, Jancis, my dear, I've brought the slatey's hen's egg to beat up in milk for you.'

But no one answered, and when I came into the kitchen the settle was empty.

I ran across the fold and out through the gate by the mixen into the road, into that good road the Romans did make, so many a year ago. And yet, to the mere, that long while was but a little, for though it had been troubled two thousand times since then, so Parson said, yet it had been troubled uncounted thousands of times afore, and would be again, till the world and all shrivelled like the cast-off body of a dragon-fly. I ran along the road in the strong heat, and the sandy earth shone in the light, and the shadows were short and very dark. I ran round the first corner, that came soon, and the next, and even the next, in case she'd walked faster than I thought. But there was nobody on the road, no white and gold mother with a white and gold mommet. Only the camomile, in clumps on the banks, was their colour, gold and white, and as I ran the strong scent of it caught my heart. I thought maybe she'd gone up to my room to wash baby. I ran back, calling and searching high and low. But there was nobody in the house save Pussy, who looked at me, sad, and ran into every room a bit in front of me. I looked in the barn and the loft and the shippen. Why I should think she was there I canna say, only I was getting despert eager to find her by this. I ran up the wood path, in case she'd had a fancy to walk there, where Gideon so often went to send her on her way home. I ran on and on, calling till the wood-pigeons flew up with a clattering noise, but nobody answered. Only the forest stood about me. Only the varnished kingcups were yellow round the edges of the mere, each clump of blossoms multiplied by two in the clear water, and the walls of thorn-bloom lay there, white and green. A lost and lonesome feeling crept over me. I went to Gideon in the garden at the back of the house.

'I canna find Jancis,' I said.

'I told her to go back where she came from,' he answered, with the same manner of speaking as he had afore, brazening it out.

'She couldna do that,' I said, 'for she's gotten no money and her mother's dead, and what's come to her father only the assize court knows, seemingly, for she dunna. She walked all the way from Silverton, Gideon. She hadna any money for the coach. All those weary miles she walked to come to you. And how did you make her welcome?'

He said nought to that, but went on with his work.

'You mun come and look for the poor girl,' I said. 'Now. This instant minute, you must come. You must think of somewhere else to look. Oh, think of somewhere else quick, Gideon! For I canna. And if we canna think of anywhere else, there's only--'

With a great shudder I pointed to the mere.

'What?' he said, very angered. 'What, you'd fritten me, would ye?'

He smote the spade into the earth as if there was an enemy hid there, and came with me round the house and the buildings. Then he set off up the road, saying she might have got a lift, which made me afraid for his wits, seeing that there was nobody to give lifts on that road but us and the ghostly chariots that people said you could hear, nights, rolling and grinding along the old road. But in a while Gideon came back, finding no sign of Jancis.

'We must drag the mere,' I said. 'We needna go far, I doubt. She'd soon be out of her depth, being so little and small. And she'd no time to walk far. She must have gone in by the caus'y here.'

318

For, as I said afore, this broad stone caus'y that the Romans made ran from just in front of our house down into the village at the bottom of the mere, where the bells did play, they said, of an evening.

And it turned out that I was right, for there, just where the caus'y went into the water, was one of baby's boots. I'd noticed that the ribbon was out of it, and that it was nearly off, and would have been right off if this un had been like other babes, kicking and laughing to feel its own might. But it was only a poor stilly waxen creature, and so, doubtless, the boot stayed on till it felt the cold water, and struggled to find itself dying as it never did to find itself living.

They lay there in a bed of lily leaves, and we took them up without a word and carried them within. I washed them and dressed them in white, and we laid them on Mother's bed, and I mounded it up with flowers, white lilac, and thorn, golden day-lilies and golden cowslips, that the child should have made into tossy-balls in the time to come.

All the while, Gideon said nothing, nor did he look much at them, but went on with his work about the place.

But the neighbours came, all the three days afore the funeral, from near and far. For the coming back of Jancis, and the child, and the drowning, made such a tale as hadna been in our part of the country, where things go on middling quiet, even in the memory of Grandfeyther Callard.

They came and looked at her, and the women cried, though in her life they'd been hard as flint to Jancis. The younger men stood a while, saying nought, looking down upon her as if they were fain of her.

'The sins of the fathers,' said Sexton, making an oration over those two, 'and not only the sins of the fathers, for it's no use to be mealymouthed, people, and though it be sad to say it, the poor wench was no better than she should be, for the child wunna born in wedlock. No, people, it wunna even a barley child, for there was no ring in the case at all. We dunna know who the man was,' he went on, looking at Gideon in a way that showed he knew right well, and meant to say unless Gideon wed with Tivvy, 'we dunna know that, but what we do know is, *where she came from*. We know who was her feyther, neighbours. We know she was sired by the devil's oddman. We know that the burning or the ricks was as nought, yea, and less than nought, compared with the things he did secret and unbeknown. What's come to pass was only what we had to expect, for what's bred in the bone will come out in the flesh, dear souls.'

'By their fruits ye shall know them, Matthew seven,' added Sammy.

Then, looking down upon the two golden heads a good while, as you might look at some rare bird you'd never see again, he said, to himself and so low that I only heard because I was nighest to him—

'They were lovely and pleasant in their lives, and in their death they were not divided.'

And he catched his breath a bit, forgetting chapter and verse.

Callard's children came two by two, to view the bodies. And as they stood at the foot of the bed after, looking on the babe in the crook of its mother's arm, suddenly they cried out all together, as they were taught to do about the baiting—

'Oh, look's pretty! The little mommet!'

And Miller nodded his head three times, as if to say, here were two kit-cats, where they should be.

Then Grandfeyther Callard stood out, and he said—

'Two funerals in a month! It do make me think of the days when the great sickness was on the land, and we as were quick were weary of the buryings. And strange it is, friends all, that these two should be dead, when their ages added together dunna amount to near thirty years, while I number one-and-ninety years and yet I've so far missed to catch the plague that ravens through this bitter old world—the ancient plague of dying.'

Still Gideon said nothing. But the night afore we took them to the church yard I heard him stirring, and being afraid that in a sudden horror of the spirit he might do himself a mischief, for though a slow, quiet man in daily life, he could be, now and again, hasty of a sudden, I went to see what the matter was.

He was standing beside the bed. As I went in he had just stretched forth his hand and lifted in his great brown fingers the plait of golden hair, so thick and fine, that was ever the pride of poor Jancis. When he turned at my coming, he was like a lad taken in a fault, hanging his head and muttering, as if it should explain his act, which indeed it did—

'I did love her once.'

Chapter Five
The Last Game of Conquer

If it had not been that Parson said I must be careful to write all, and leave out none, since to know all made folks kind, but to know a part made 'em worse than if they knew nothing, if it hadna been for that, I'd never have tried to write of those three months at Sarn betwixt the time of the death of Jancis and the time of the troubling of the waters. For there are some things so hard to write of that even a great scholar might boggle at it, and I, though I can do the tall and short scirpt, am not anything of a scholar, and words be hard to find for some things. I think, times, that in our mortal language there are no words for the things that are of

320

most account. So, when those things come upon us we are
struck silent, and can but feel and feel, till our hearts are like
a bursting dam. Maybe, in the life yonder, that already I
begin to glimpse on the edge of this world, we shall find the
proper words. But not yet. So, if I fail in what I've set out to
do, you must pardon what I canna help, and fill up the glats in
my speech with the brushwood of your own imagining.

The strangest part of that time was the silence of it.
Gideon had always been a silent man, but now he was as bad
as the miller. He'd come and he'd go, but not a word would
pass his lips. And sometimes he'd stop all of a sudden, as he
went about his work, as if he'd been struck of a heap by
summat. His thoughts, I guessed it to be. Then he'd
straighten his shoulders, and mighty shoulders they were, and
go about his work again. I thought it would pass in time, and
as nothing was settled between him and Tivvy yet, I made up
my mind not to leave the poor lad all alone, but to bide still
for a while. Tivvy was in a fix, for she was determined to
have Gideon, and yet she was so mortal afraid of the frittening, for the frittening is said to be very bad in a place
where mother and babe die together, that she durstna set foot
our side of the mere at all. So there we were, in a thick,
cruddled silence, that grew ever more and more solid like
freezing water or souring milk. Save for the birds, that
minded their own affairs and took no thought of us, there
were no voices uplifted at Sarn. Evenings, when they hushed,
it fell so still that I could hear Gideon's boat, moored just by
the beginning of the caus'y, knocking and knocking with small,
reminding taps. And, times, in the kitchen of a night, when
Gideon was out, working late at the hoeing of the young corn
or at the haying, I'd hold up a bit of tasty victuals to Pussy
just to make her mew. And I'd say, 'There, now thee's mewed!
Good Pussy!'

When he was in, Gideon was as dumb as the drowned, save
that once, on a night of bright moonlight when we were
having our supper late after haying, he leaned forrard of a
sudden and said--

'Did ye see that?'

'What?' I says.

'Why, somebody went by the door, in a white gown.'

But it wasna till July, in a spell of very thundery weather,
hot and still and gloomy, that his strangeness came upon him
in good earnest. I was sitting in the doorway, to get what air
there was, for it drew off the mere, evenings. I was carding
wool, and the white of it, heaped up on my black, made me
look like a magpie, I thought. The lilac leaves were limp with
the heat, and the mere like hot lead to look at, with the tall
thick trees around it, carven out of iron. All round the
marges of the mere were the lilies, lying on the heavy water,
their small white buds shining. Not a bird spoke, for all were

in their coverts, since the heat was so great. Even the water-
birds stayed among the reeds, and the boat had given over
knocking on the steps, as if the day was fixed now for the
passenger to come, and there was no more to do till then.
Suddenly Gideon came round the corner all in a sweat of
haste, with the brummock in one hand and his hedging gloves
still on, for he was busy at the hedges between hay and corn
harvest. He stopped when he saw me, and put hand to head,
and then broke out in a passion--

'What for do ye sit there the like of that, making game
you're Mother?'

'I never made game to be Mother,' I said. 'Whatever ails
you?'

'Mother was used to sit there and card wool. I thought you
were Mother.'

'Well, I couldna help that,' I said. 'But what did you come
round the corner in such a courant for?'

'I was pleaching the big thorn hedge, and she came upon
the top of it, all in white.'

'Who came upon the top of it?' I asks, impatient.

'Jancis,' he says, as quiet as could be, not as if he was
saying anything strange, but just as he might speak of seeing
Tivvy or Polly Miller. He said no more, but went back to his
work, though he gave up the hedge. He'd never argue at all
about what he saw, but just say he saw it, and that was all.
The next time was when he was hoeing in the big wheat field.
He came into the house, very hasty, with the hoe and all, and
said he'd seen Jancis ploughing with her two white oxen, in
the barley field, and the child sitting up on the nighest ox.

'Now look you, Gideon,' I said, 'you mun leave thinking of
Jancis, or you'll be possessed. And a man possessed is pretty
far on to madness. You just think of getting on, and scraping
and saving as you used to, and dunna think of Jancis or
Mother till you're more settled in your mind.'

'I dunna think of Jancis. She just comes.'

'Well, set your mind on other things and she wunna.'

'What things?'

'Why, getting rich, and getting the house.'

'What for?'

'For the same reason you began of it. Because you want
it.'

'I dunna want it now.'

'But why? You wanted it so much, you poisoned Mother.
You wanted it so much, you gave the nay-word to Jancis. Let
alone all the things you did afore, you must have been pretty
well clemmed for it to do as you did.'

'Well, I dunna want it now.'

'What for not?'

'Summat went out of it, when I did see 'em in the water.'

'Well, think of Tivvy, then. She'd like to go to the Hunt Ball, I know.'

'I wunna take up with Tivvy. I'd liefer swing.'

'Miss Dorabella, then. She's sweet on you. Take up with her, and she'll spend her money to save you from Tivvy.'

'Dorabella's abron. I like a fair woman. Little. With blue eyes. A woman like may and milk.'

'Well, think of me then. Be a bit of company for me now and again.'

'But you be going.'

'Not till you're more settled in mind, lad. I'll stop on a bit, if you'll keep a cheerful heart, and not call old grief to mind.'

But it was no use. In less than a week he came in all of a hurry and said—

'She's at it again.'

'What, ploughing?'

'Ah. And the barley field's as bald as a coot.'

'It's bad seed,' I says, 'that what it is, Gideon. It's because you had to buy instead of putting in our own.'

But my heart was heavy, and I couldna see what the end of this would be. I even wished Tivvy would come.

It got to be the usual thing for him to say—

'She came again in the wood to-day.' Or he'd say—

'Look ye! There she is, drawing in to the caus'y. There! Now she's coming up the caus'y, dripping wet. There! Now she's gone.'

Once he said she beckoned from the boat. But it was always out of doors he saw her, so the house was a kind of refuge, and when he suffered that strange fear, in he'd come, and be more himself. I was glad he never saw anything in the house. I was glad, too, that he never heard anything. It was like as if, being smitten to the heart with the sight of her in the water, he'd lost the power to choose what he *saw*, but could still choose what he heard. And then, at the beginning of August month, when the corn was just on ripe, he came in and said she'd been singing *Green Gravel* across the water.

'The sound comes in here,' he said, anxious. So I shut the window.

'Best put some wool in your ears,' I said. For indeed it was pitiful to see a man like Gideon trembling at a gleam of white in the hedge or an echo across the water. So he put wool in his ears and we got on pretty well through the first part of August. Then, it was the evening afore the fair at Sarn Mere, and many of the booths were already set up. We sat down early to our supper because there had come a letter from Miss Dorabella, brought by one of their men, with the news in it about Beguildy. So I opened the letter and read it to Gideon, and he took the wool out of his ears to hear; and what it said was that they'd let Beguildy off light, because he'd had great provocation on account of his daughter.

323

'Domm!' says Gideon. The blazing hate in him burnt up afresh at hearing of the light sentence, and I almost thought it might cure him of seeing things. But in a little while he fell into his melancholy again, and said he'd seen Mother in the oak wood, where the pigs were.

'No, dear to goodness,' I said, 'it was nobody in the world but Miller's Polly. She's getting a big girl for her age, and Mother was but little.'

'No,' he said. 'It was Mother. They bother me, Prue.'

'There, there!' I said, patting him on shoulder like a child. For indeed when he spoke of his haunting, he seemed as weak and full of fear as a child in the dark.

'Now see, it'll all come right,' I said. 'You must be well plucked and not mind. You was used to be so fond of *Conquer*. Well, now you must play *Conquer* with your own thoughts.'

But he only looked at me as if he didna understand, and said--

'What she didna like was me speaking unkind of the babe. Very touchy, mothers be, about their babes.'

We sat quiet a bit, and then he said, all of a sudden--

'Hark ye! She's singing *Green Gravel*.'

He listened a long while, though I could hear nothing.

Then he leaned forrard and said she was coming up off the caus'y toërts the house. His face broke out in a sweat, as if he was feared out of his life. But indeed the weather was enough to make anybody sweat without that, it was so hot and dank at once, the worst weather of all at Sarn, which never had much air, being down in a hollow, and which was always damp from the water. On an evening such as this, the walls ran down with water, so that the whitewash shone as if with the tracks of many snails. Over the mere a mist was rising, in trails and wisps, white as wool, thickening and gathering into clotted heaps towards the mid of the mere. Sometimes a wreath of mist would be drawn out like a scarf, and other times it would stand up in the shape of a woman, but wavering upon the air. It seemed to me it might well be one of these ghosts of mist that Gideon had seen. For they rose and sank about the caus'y all the while, as the light airs on the water took them. At Sarn in August there were always heavy mists night and morning, and this was out of the common bad, because we'd had thunder-rain the night before, and a day of brooding heat after it. Bad, I say, because I never could abide mist, and we had such a deal of it, so that sometimes it blotted the farm and the woods and church right out, as if the mere had turned to milk, and risen up and drowned all.

'Hark!' says Gideon. 'Can you hear *Green Gravel?*'

So strong was his mind, and so much it had the mastery over mine, that I almost thought I did hear a wailing song. And then, without any warning, sitting in the big arm-chair with a set, yearning face, like a man enchanted, as I do think he was, Gideon began to sing the song himself. He held up his right hand, solemn, like parson giving the blessing, and he looked out through the doorway toërts the mere and the caus'y and the slow, white, curdling mist. He sang as if some power was on him that made him. You could see he was bound to sing. He had a rolling voice, a fine bass it was; and though he began very softly, it strengthened as he went on, till the music seemed to master the place. And the way he made that childish song mean such a deal!--all the love he'd had for Jancis, and how he'd wanted her to have everything so grand, and go to the ball like a lady, and all the fear and pity of her ending. It seemed as if he was easier in mind after, having, as it were, given in and so made peace. Still watching the door, he says--

'Here's Jancis. Soused with water she is, out of the mere.'

So I said I saw nothing.

'Why, look's the water dripping off her gown!' he said. 'See there, and there, where she goes! Sogging wet she is, by gum!'

He pointed to the floor, and indeed there was water in all the little hollows in the quarries, as if the mere had found a way to soak up through the floor. So I said, yes, I saw the water in the hollows of the quarries.

'Hark at the mud in her boots sooking! Muddy, the mere is. See now, how slow she comes--slow, like she used to walk when she spun with the big wheel. She walks slow because her clo'es are so heavy about her. It's uphill and agen the heart for Jancis, with the mommet to carry all alone.'

Then he said, worried--

'I wish I hadna mocked at the babe.'

A long while went by. The sounds in the room were less than on the evening Father died. It was as if Sarn, all the live part of it, us and our beasts, the trees full of birds, and the wood ways with wild creatures in them, had sunk to the bottom of the mere where the village was. I was beginning to believe all Gideon said, which was not so very different, after all, from many a tale of frittening we'd heard.

'Look ye now!' he muttered. 'She's going toërts the dairy door. There, she's gone! 'Twas in the dairy I gave her the nay-word that time afore she went to Grimbles. There now, she's coming back. Her yellow head does shine so, she makes me call to mind that wandering light at Lullingford New House.'

He was leaning forrard, staring down the dimmery passage that led to the dairy.

'There, look's the wet floor!' he said. 'It's like as if she'd brought the mere in along of her. I never thought she'd come in the house. A castle's easy kept when none comes against it. But now--'

He looked down at the wet quarries a good while.

'Why, she's gone!' he said then. 'Like a golden bee sailing away on the air, and singing as she goes. Look's pretty!'

He stayed brooding a long time. Then he got up and told me he was going to see to the stock, for the evening was well on to night. He said that in his usual way, and I thought the frittening had lifted from his mind. But as he went out, he turned, and looked at me just as he did the night Beguildy went to seek a seventh child, and said—

'If I'm late, put the key over the stable door.'

I thought, no, if he was out so much as a half-hour, I should go after him. Indeed I almost did then. Summat told me to go. But it seemed so queer, when he was only going to see to the stock, to run after him. So I stayed where I was and began looking in Beguildy's book, that I bought at the sale, and in the Bible, to see if I could find any cure for such bewitchments. I hadna been reading more than half an hour, if so much, and I suppose it was about nine o'clock, though it seemed later because of the muffling mist and the silence, when all of a sudden there was a taboring at the door, and in rushed Miller's Tim and Polly too.

'Oh, Prue, Prue! we'd just brought the pigs along, being late because the black un wouldna come out of the rushes, and we'd put 'em in yard, quiet, for fear Mister Sarn ud be angry with us for being late, and we were looking for glow-worms under the orchard hedge, when out comes Mister Sarn. So we hid. And looking from under the hedge we saw him standing by the water, with his head stooped forrard a bit, like a horse with the staggers. And I told Polly what I heard Granfeyther Callard say. "Sarn?" he says, "Oh, Sarn's known frittening of the beautiful bogey out of the mere, and he'll never be his own man again." And while I was whispering that to Polly, Mister Sarn lifted up his head and seemed to look all around at everything, only there was not much but mist. Then he turned toërts the caus'y, going like a chap in his sleep, and went down the caus'y to the boat, and untied the boat, and got in and took up the oars, and rowed with big strokes away from the farm, straight out where the caus'y went, to the mid of the lake. So we ran round to see if we could get a blink of him, but he was in the mist. The noise of the oars went on for a while, and I wished I was in the boat. But in a bit I was glad I was on dry land. The sound of the rowing stopped.'

'Ah. Dead as dead it stopped,' said Polly.

'We held our breath to see if we could hear aught, but no! It was like the text parson learned us last Sunday, "There was silence over all the land till the ninth hour." Oh, it was solemn.'

'You should have come to me then,' I said. 'But quick now! What else?'

'Why nothing else at all,' says Tim, 'saving a great splash. I never heard such a splash, not even when the brindled calf fell into the water.'

'Ah. Dear to goodness, it *was* a splash!' says Polly.

'Then it went quieter and quieter, and we held breath and listened, but there was nought. And I did call on Mister Sarn's name, but none answered. And I was feared and so was Polly, and we ran to you.'

The boat! I must get to the boat. I ran down the caus'y, tearing of my skirt, but there was no need to swim, for the boat was coming back, since the air drew from the other end of the mere, sending the currents toërts us, and these currents were stronger at the time of the troubling of the waters. A dreadful thing it was to see that empty boat come stealing in, slow, slow. I catched it and got in, taking up the oars which Gideon had unshipped, for even in this hour he couldna do anything slipshod or careless. I pulled out, calling to the children to run for Sexton, he being the nighest. They were soon gone, and glad to go. And I rowed out to the mid of the lake, feeling in the water with the oars, looking here and there, and calling his name, though I knew all the while it was too late. I was still rowing and calling when I heard Sexton shout from the shore.

'Me and Sam will go while you rest a bit,' he said. 'But we'll never find Sarn. You canna drag the mere out there. It's too deep. None were ever found that went in there.'

They rowed away, and as they came toward the middle of the mere. I heard them singing, as we'd sung over Father long ago--

'Your good deeds and your bad, dear man,
Afore the Lord shall meet.'

Only they left out about the turf at head and foot, for the water was his grave. Ah! The whole of that great stretch of water wasna too much to make the grave of a man as strong as that one. The mile-long mist that lay upon the place wasna too grand a shroud. For though he was wrong, and did evil, and hurted folks with his strength, yet he never did meanly, nor turned out bad work, nor lied. 'The granite mountain, quartzite, b'yrytes,' he said once to me, speaking of his own hardness. And he was like them all. He could no more give in than the granite can crumble like sandstone. And now he'd played his last game of *Conquer*, and what he played with wasna one of the big pink-and-white ones, but his own life.

And since the other player was one that none can ever hope to conquer, it shivered into brittle fragments in a moment, and so Gideon Sarn lost his last game.

Chapter Six
The Breaking of the Mere

That was a night of grief and fear which nothing in life has ever made me forget. Sexton and Sammy, after a vain search, went home. I was alone under the coverlet of fog, in that place full of ghostly footsteps. I said a prayer for dying men. Then I sat hour by hour beside the fire, in that dim slothfulness of the spirit which a great sorrow or a great amazement will bring. It was the strangest Wake Eve I'd ever known, and the most grievous night of all my life. I thought how Gideon forbade me to go down into the water as folk did of old time, and be cured of my ill. And now, see! he was gone down into the mere himself, to be cured of his own curse. Then I thought of golden Jancis, and the little babe, and Missis Beguildy, and Father and poor Mother, all dead too. It seemed Death had been very busy at it, swiving among us. Ah! It was a bitter watching, for I ever liked those I cared for to be in good case. A year back, there was Jancis chosen for the sport called Heaving the Chair, for which the prettiest girl was always called out. There she was in her blue gown, I minded it well, with a crown of summer flowers on her head and a posy in her hand, lifted high in the chair by two strapping young fellows, while the rest came by, one by one, to see who she'd choose. All the young chaps were in it, but only one girl, so you may guess there was a deal of heart-searching over who'd be chosen.

They gave her a posy, and one fellow held a basin of water, and when she'd chosen her chap, she dipped the posy in the water and smote his face with it, which made everybody laugh.

And Jancis had chosen Gideon, of course, and he'd waited till the very last, because it pleased him to see all the others turned away and to know he wouldna be. And she smacked his face well with the posy, and gave her sweet, tinkling laugh, and then he lifted her down, which was part of the game, and gave her a kiss, which wunna. And I thought now, how untoërt a thing it was that she should have soused his face with water, as if in token that she should baptize him the mere, 'ticing him to his death, and that it was the coming round of the fair day that had been the last straw. So I sighed, thinking--'we be all His momments, and He orders the play.'

I called to mind also how Gideon won the guinea for whistling best and clearest. He could whistle very well, and also he could keep his face straight in spite of all the fooling of the merry-andrew, who tried to make them laugh. For if Gideon was at the making of money he took it in such good sadness that nothing in the world could even make him smile. Beguildy whistled well also, but his best chance of a prize was always the yawning match, in which Granfeyther Callard ran him very close. Beguildy would come to the fair, though it angered Sexton, who persisted in saying it was a festival of the church, and not for wizards, and who made himself very busy about everything, as if he was chief man.

Thinking of all this, I was sick at heart, for what is there more grievous than calling to mind old, merry randies? Then you say, 'Ah, this one or that one was here then.' And you remember how you were so strong in your joy, you could even be merry over jests that played upon great and solemn things. You call to mind how such an one said, 'A goose walks over my grave!' and laughed. And you remember that the one who said it has been under the sod a long while. So the thought of last year's fair set me crying, though the drowning of Gideon didna. Indeed, it was out of the ornary strange, his dying, and not like the common lot, for he neither died in his bed nor by violence, but went into the mist of his own will and wish, and then was not. And that we never found him seemed to me only a rightful ending to a life which so cut itself adrift from all pleasant, feckless human ways and doings. He belonged to none, seemingly, for he gave the go-by to his nearest kin. What he had most truck with was the earth and the water from which he was building himself a life to his mind. Rock, and troubled water, heavy earth, trees groaning yet unyielding in the storm, all these he was kin to, though he didna love them. He took hold of them, browbeat them, made them his'n. And in the doing of it he fell, as it were, among thieves, for they took hold of him and made him their slave. It seemed to me he couldna die like other men, and be sodded, and lie in six feet of soil, and have a name-stone. No. He must have large room and be free of all, roaming at will in the troubled currents of the mere, in the mid of his own farm and his own woodland. How can you cry for such a thing as this? Can you cry about a thunderbolt or a cloud-burst? No. It was only when I remembered those few times when he gave in that I could cry for him, as when I called to mind how he put his arm across his face at the fire, and sobbed.

All that night I thought of him, and the dark was full of cold fear, and a horror gathered about the place, it seemed so lone, as if it didna belong to the world at all. I knew I couldna spend another night there, and I began wondering what to do with the live stock, since nobody else would set foot here after such doings. No, not if it was ever so! Sexton refused out and out, and if he wouldna, nobody would. Not a soul would buy the place, and though I could leave the fields we'd laboured on to go back into wood and heath, yet the live stock must be seen to as long as it was there. Yet I was determined to bide there no longer, but to flee away as they did from the cities of the plain, not for any fault in the place, but for what Gideon had made of it. I'd shift to-morrow. But what to do with the beasts I couldna think, for if I asked anyone even so much as to water them, they'd say, 'No, no, missus, there's summat to be seen there.'

At last came the blessed dawn, and the mist lay like a vasty shining cloud on the place, but as the sun swam up, full of power and warmship, not to be gainsayed, the mist came loose all in a piece, and lifted slow, till there was a space betwixt its under side and the mere, where the coots swam, like bees running about between two boards. Then one half of the tree-trunks came free, so that the forest seemed to be mounded up with snow. It lifted and lifted, and at last went into the sky, and failed amid the clouds of dawn. Then the clouds faded, and there were only the proper heavens, blue as bird's eye. As soon as the mist lifted, I saw that the mere had broken in the night, and the water was thick and troubled, simmering all over, so that the lilies were stirred as they lay anchored. When the blessed sunshine came, a way out came also into my mind. It was fair day. There'd be a sight of people here. Why not take the creatures to the fair, and make a pen, and get somebody to sell them? They could go cheap. Ah. That was it! So when I'd fed the stock, and milked, I fetched all into the fold, to be ready, and tidied the house, drawing the curtains, and set out to Sexton's to ask if I could put up a pen and bring the beasts, and get the crockman to sell them by auction, as he sold his wares. Sexton didna care about it much, but seeing he knew he'd got no authority, and the fair being held in our wood, he could do no else than agree. Tivvy looked very spitefully at me, for she wanted sore to be missus at Sarn, not to speak of her being sweet on Gideon, and she seemed to blame me that all had gone wrong. But I'd no time to waste, for already the first waggons were coming to the fair ground. It was still the custom then to deck out a waggon for each village with flowers and boughs, to bring the people. Or sometimes the young ones would walk, the men and women in separate companies, singing as they came. But they went back two by two, men and maids. They were setting out the booths when I went by, spiced ale and the gingerbread-babies Moll liked, mint cakes and pebble brooches and combs to stand high in the hair. A woman had lit a fire and was getting ready the huge bowl of hasty pudding for the trial, which could eat it hot quickest. The waggons rolled along the wood ways with the same sound as at our harvest home. The folk chattered like a lot of jays, until they came to the fair ground and heard the news about Gideon. I could hear when each waggon heard tell, for a hush fell on all. Then I suppose they thought, well, they were a-nigh the church, that was on holy ground, and the accursed place was at the other end of the mere, so they took heart and began to chatter again. I saw Mister Huglet and Mister

Grimble, thick as thieves, and they scowled at me as I went by.

All along the wood-path there was a great stirring of dragon-flies, and the lustre-coloured damsels looked grand, sailing over the crimson bosses of dragon's blood, that is the wild geranium. I thought, 'The wind lifts in the branches, the lilies be in blow, the dragon-flies be coming out of their shrouds, but Kester Woodseaves has forgot me.' For by this he was to have raught back. And why should he remember a woman with a curse upon her, a hare-shotten woman, in danger of being accused of witchcraft? No, he wouldna call me to mind again. He'd take up with that young woman he spoke of that didna spare her blushes.

When I got home, I gathered together all the sheep and pigs, the cows and oxen, and drove them, riding upon Bendigo, to the fair. By good fortune they were all fain of me and went where I told them. Then I went back and put the fowl and ducks, the geese and turkeys in boxes and hampers, and wheeled them on the barrow. I'd left them shut up, to catch them the sooner. The people stared when they saw me riding through the wood with my flocks and herds afore me, for the creatures made a great stir, baaing and grunting and mooing, misliking the woods. And as we went, there we all were in the troubled water, dimly shadowed, and I thought how we had been reflected there when we buried Father. Then, all the fields and barns, fold and shippen, being void of life, I put Pussy in a basket and locked the door. And I thought, now the ghosts could have the place, yes, all of them, even as far back as Tim, that had the lightning in his blood. My vow that I took to Gideon was cancelled now. I'd no more to do here. What should I stay for, with nobody to ask a hand's turn of me? I was for the road. What road I didna know, but I thought it would be lonely. I'd packed a few things to leave with Miller, for him to take to Lullingford, else, I had what I stood in, and the old Bible, and my book. So I set forth from the farm, where Sarns had been time out of mind. It was hard to leave the fields I'd laboured so long upon, but it would have been harder to stay. I shivered to think how the church spire would point across the water at the haunted house this night, lying over that deepest, darkest place where Gideon was.

They were selling the things by the time I got back to the fair, with a pewter tankard to put the money in. So, not wishing to have part or lot in the merrymaking, I sat down on the churchyard wall to wait till all was done and I might go. The bidding was pretty brisk, for the beasts didna carry any curse, folk supposed, though they did come from an ill place. Sexton bought Bendigo, and Moll's father bought the oxen for his maister. Callard had some of the cows, the other things were bought up in good time, and I gave Pussy to Felena, because I thought she had a good heart, though not much respectability--or maybe it was because of that.

She said--

'Do you get tidings of weaver, Prue?'

'No,' I said. 'We've not heard this long while.'

'He's one in many,' she said. 'Ah! He does seem to me to be of other stuff than we are. As if he came from afar. Do you mind how we played *Costly* for weaver's soul, you and me? But I doubt some fine madam in the city's catched his soul by this.'

All the while, as we talked, and as I sat lonesome on the churchyard wall, I was ware of black looks cast at me, side-glances, a pushing out of the lips, and lifting of shoulders, and some would draw away a bit as I passed. I wondered what this might be, for though the old tales about me had gone on growing in the lonely farms, as I knew, and though a misfortune is enough, times, to turn people against you, as if they thought it was the hand of the Lord meting punishment for sin, yet it didna seem to me enough to explain the looks I got, which did cut me to the heart, for in them I saw hatred. I ever loved my kind, and as I once said, I was like one standing at the lane ends with a nosegay to offer to the world as it rode by. But instead, it rode me down. Ah! On this day of mid August, in the time of the troubling of the waters, it rode me down.

I was considering, and wondering what to do, for I was waiting for some people who were driving to Bramton, and would take me, and so I should be part way to Silverton. If I went now, I'd get no lift, and besides, the money couldna be counted till it was all in, so the crockman could take his pay of so much in the shilling. On both counts I was bound to wait.

Missis Miller came up, quiet, and said she'd been there since the first and she'd heard a deal said about me, and the whispers were started by Grimble and Huglet, here one and there one, saying this and that, with a nod or a wink, maybe, or a shaking of the head, and, 'Pity. A tidy young woman, too!' Or, 'Summat should be done about it. Parson ought to see about it.' So the talk got fixed on me, she said, and no sooner did they tire of speaking of the manner of Gideon's death than they'd start of me. The younger ones had been brought up on tales of how I roamed the country at night in the body of a hare, and had a muse under this very churchyard wall. Miss Dorabella's words at the *Mug o' Cider* had stayed in people's minds, and then the fire had fixed on us the idea of a curse, for though Beguildy did it, yet 'twas though the Lord wouldna have suffered him to do it at a righteous farm. Then the drowning of Jancis made things ten times blacker, and Gideon's death put the last touch to it. There was something here that the folks couldna understand. The only cause for all the misfortune that they could see was the curse of God. There must have been a Jonah in our ship, they thought. And as Mother had always been liked, and Gideon thought pretty well of, as a man bound to get on, it seemed to them that I must be the one that called down the curse. They'd reasoned it out slow, as we do in the country, but once they came to the end of the reasoning they were fixed, and it would take a deal to turn them. This was the reason for the hating looks, the turnings aside, the whispers. I was the witch of Sarn. I was the woman cursed of God with a hare-shotten lip. I was the woman who had friended Beguildy, that wicked old man, the devil's oddman, and like holds to like. And now, almost the worst crime of all, I stood alone. I may say that in our part of the country, whatever happened in other parts, it was thought suspicious to stand alone. This might be because in those lost and forgotten farms in the mountains and the flooded lands about the meres, where in the long winters the winds would howl around the corners of the house like wolves, and there was talk of old terrible things--men done to death in sight of home; the fretting of unhappy ghosts at the bottle-glass windows that once they owned, but now were the wrong side of; the dreadful music of the death pack; the howl of witches such as I was said to be, riding with blown leaves upon the gale; the threat of gentlemen of the road who had long lain at the crossways--nobody could choose to be alone, and nobody without good reason would condemn another to be alone. Therefore, if you were alone you were as good as damned.

I canna tell you what a sinking of the heart all this gave me. For to one that can feel the love and hate of others flowing about her without word spoken, and who can only do well in warmship of the soul, even a little misliking is enough to nip the blossom.

'Now,' says Missis Miller, 'I know what it's like a bit, for mine's said to be under a curse, and cause he gives, indeed, but you dunna, and I say, "Beware of Grimble!" He's fause, is Grimble. Huglet's all of a roar, but you know what he's after. With Grimble you dunna. He'll drop a word here and a word there like thistledown, and you see nought and think nought, but dear to goodness, what a crop of thistles! And I doubt the thistles be all up and just about in blow.'

While she was yet speaking, Tivvy darted up to me, all in black, for she'd given out that she was promised to Gideon, and she says--

'You boxed my ears, Prue Sarn! Now see!'

With that she jumped up on the wall and shouted out--

'People all, I'll speak this once and no more. A wronged woman I am. Sarn was promised to wed with me to-day's five months, and it's five months gone that I should have been Missis Sarn. For Sarn did love me right well. But *she* stopped it. Prue Sarn stopped it. For she put me in such mortal fear, I couldna come near the place. Clouted me, she did. And she being a witch, I was afraid of her. She wanted to be missus there, seesta! Couldna abide anybody else to have a say in things. And see what's come to pass! She's missus there altogether now, and the very next day after my poor Sarn's death she sells all. Oh, she's a heartless piece! There's no wickedness she wouldna do. Five months I'd ought to have been Missis Sarn, but for her. She's so strong, because she's a witch!'

I was astounded at the furious way she said it, till I remembered that she was expecting a love-child, which was ten times worse as she was Sexton's daughter, and what Sexton would do when he knew was awful to think of, and so Tivvy must have somebody to put the blame on. But no sooner was she finished than up gets Grimble. There he stood, with his long nose pointing down as if he was considering, among all he could say, what he'd fix on. 'People,' he began, 'this is a solemn day. In this here water lies a fine farmer. Ah! A man as would have made a mark on Sarn. Look at the ploughing he'd done! Bound to be rich, he was. Promised to a tidy young woman, too, and a righteous, for we know that her brother can come as pat with a text as any man even in the memory of Granfeyther Callard.'

'Ah. That's righteous!' calls out the old man from the cart where he sat. 'But old Camperdine could run him pretty close, the one as Beguildy had in bottle, I mean. Ah! He was a good un with a text when he was in liquor! I've heard him roll 'em out till you wanted a yard-stick to measure 'em. But when he was sober, not a text would he say. Very bawdy he was then. But in liquor, oh, indeed to goodness it was a miracle!'

'As I say,' Mister Grimble, went on in his reasonable voice, 'her brother can mouth a text, her father's Sexton, her mother's Sexton's married wife, so it stands to reason she's a good young woman. And you've heard what she said. I tell you, what she says is true, and more than true. Now listen. Since birth Prudence Sarn's been a woman smitten by the Lord. What she does she canna altogether help, being in the power of Satan. That's why she roams the land, as we know. That's why she was friend to Beguildy, and learned all his wickedness off him, for like finds like. That's why she puts her eye on this one or that one, a child or a beast, or a field of corn, it's no matter. It dwines, whatever it is, dwines and withers away. Or she'll as soon kill outright. What did she do to my dog, as was worth a deal to me? Ah! And darker things yet. Blacker and blacker. What did her mother die of? People, she died of foxglove tea. Poisoned. Sexton's missis is my witness. Who nurses a sick mother? Her daughter. Well, people, what do you say to that?'

334

There was a muttering in the crowd, a pushing and stirring to look at me, where I sat, struck dumb with astonishment. But nobody said anything as yet. Country folk dunna condemn in a hurry. They were ready tinder, but the flint wunna put to it yet.

'And darker,' says Grimble. 'But first let Missis Sexton and Tivvyriah Sexton stand up and say in one word if it be true. Now then. Aye or no?'

'Aye!' said both together.

'Now, why did that feckless young creature, Jancis Beguildy, and her poor child, meet their deaths in the water? Who was alone in the house with them when it took place? Prudence Sarn! Why was Jancis irksome to the witch? Because she knew things. She knew the devil's tricks that were played betwixt her father and the witch. And as she'd no money, she came to threaten to speak unless she was well paid, and that Prudence Sarn wouldna do. So, when nobody was there but the weak, nesh little thing, trammelled with her baby, and Prue Sarn, who's as strong as a man, Jancis Beguildy met her death in the water.'

There were murmurs again, but it would need more than the death of the wizard's daughter, who was in ill odour, to rouse them.

'But there's worse,' said Grimble. 'When Sarn took up with Tivvyriah, her sister didna like it. She wanted to keep on being missus. She wanted no other woman about the place. She'd got rid of her mother on that count. Ah! Liefer would she have no brother, friends, than have a married brother.'

A sigh went through the crowd, which must have numbered three hundred souls, all told, for it was a big fair. 'What did she do?' Grimble went on, and the hate in his eyes when he looked at me was awful to see. 'Why, when dusk drew on and the mist rose, and Sarn was dipping water for the beasts, she did push him in, and then took the boat out to deceive Sexton, having put such dread upon the miller's children that they durstna say the truth.'

He waited a minute for the people to understand. Then he said--

'Hare-shotten! A witch! Three times a murderess!'

And on the instant Huglet roared out--

'Suffer not a witch to live!'

The flint was set to the tinder. A howl went up. There were cries of--

'Tromple on her!'

'Stone her!'

'Let her drown!'

There was nobody to speak for me, except such as would not be heard. Sexton was gone home. He was a fair-minded man, and I think he'd have stood for me. Most of the people were strangers. Some were neither for me nor against me.

Felena pushed her husband forrard, telling him to speak for me, but they shouted--

'Thee's in danger of damnation thyself, shepherd! How do ye pay yer rent?'

They came on me like the rising of a winter flood. They sent some to the church for the ducking-stool. And still the voice of Huglet went roaring on.

'Suffer not a witch to live!'

I do think I fainted for very terror, for I knew no more, till I felt the chill water, and came up gasping, feeling the ropes that tied me to the ducking-stool, and hearing the roaring of Huglet, which seemed like the blaring of some great demon.

Chapter Seven
'Open the Gates as wide as the sky,
And let the King come riding by.'

I came to myself, and opened my eyes, wondering what the great trompling was, and thinking it was Bendigo got loose. Then I remembered that Sexton had taken Bendigo away, so I looked to see what it might be, for all the waggon horses had been taken back to Plash Farm for the day. I looked up, and straightway I thought I must have died, and be now in Paradise.

There, looking down upon me from his nag, with a dwelling gaze so blazing with life that, if I hadna been sure the other way, I should have thought he loved me, was none other than Kester Woodseaves. Older-seeming he was, a little, and his face even cleaner cut than afore, as if the soul had been busy chiseling at it. As for his eyes, all the light of heaven was in them, not to speak of a very pleasant touch of the old Adam. They took me in from head to foot, and I was at rest. Ah! tied to the ducking-stool, in such sad case as no self-respecting woman could choose to be seen in by any man, let alone the man she loved, I was yet at rest. I cared for nothing now. I werrited about nothing. Kester was here. Kester had gotten things in hand. What could ail me? Such was my faith, that though three hundred people, more or less, were set against me, and only Kester for me, yet I knew that I was safe. I could have turned on my side and gone to sleep on that old ducking-stool as if it was a feather bed, so comfortable I was in my mind.

'Well,' says he at last, 'well, Prue, my dear, you be in poor case!'

And he gave a little smile, as much as to say, 'But not for long!'

'I be,' I answered, and my voice was all of a tremble with joy, 'in very poor case, Kester Woodseaves.'

He gave a look round, and then beckoned to Felena. She darted forrard as if she was his slave.

336

'Untie those, 'oot?' he said, pointing to the cords.

As she was doing it, she whispered--

'I dunna care what they do to me. I'll work his will. A man to die for!'

'Is there any fellow here friend to me enough to catch a holt of my nag a minute?' he asks.

Callard called out--

'I will, and welcome.'

Afore he got off, Kester looked all around, and he says--

'Well, you were having a fine randy, I must say! Last time it was a little white ox. Now it's a woman whiter than lily. I know very well who's egging you on.'

Some hung their heads, but most were angered to have their fun stopped.

Kester went up to Grimble.

'You and me's had ado afore, Grimble,' he says. 'You're too mean and twisty to be treated as a man. If you dunna like the treatment you get, you can fight me any time you like. But you're only good enough to laugh at. Your nose is too long, Grimble. It stirs about in everybody's business.'

And with that, he gave Grimble a tremendous blow on the nose with his fist, and Grimble roared so, being a real coward, that the people couldna help but laugh.

Then Kester went to Huglet and he said--

'You're aboveboard all right. You dunna do things secret. Man, I could hear you hollering even to Plash! Oot wrostle?'

Now, for all he was so big, Huglet didna want to wrostle. He hiver-hovered over it a good bit, for he knew Kester was a right proper wrostler. But many of the people knew nothing about Kester, and wouldna have cared if they had, for they only wanted a good day's sport. This was what Kester had reckoned on.

'A wrestling match!' they called out, quite in a pleasant humour again, though what they'd be after, nobody could say.

'Haw-whoop!' cries out old Callard, pretty well beside himself with excitement, and the children, seeing Kester and remembering their lessons folded their hands very primly over their stomachs and sang out--

'Bull-baiting's bad!' which would have made me laugh if I hadna been so uneasy in mind about Kester.

'A ring! Make a ring!'

'Ah, chaps, there's a nice smooth bit of turf there,' says Kester, pointing to a place close by the water. So they made a ring there. Kester stripped off his coat and weskit, and Huglet took his off unwilling. There were some hasty wagers made. Then they set to at it. I thought Huglet would crush every one of Kester's bones, but no! Kester was hard, and a practised wrostler, and when Huglet seemed to have got him safe and sure, he was out of his grip, ready to start all over again. A tuthree times Huglet bore him back till his one shoulder very near touched the ground, but each time he wrostled free, sharp and sudden, so it was only a *foyle*, and didna count. I was in a terror all the while that Huglet, by his great strength, would break Kester's back, and I could see he'd dearly like to, for he'd forgotten everything but hate of the man who'd twice robbed him of his sport. I wondered why Kester didna try, by some feint, to get him down, but Felena whispered--

'He's got summat in mind, Weaver has. He's tarrying for summat.'

All the while Kester kept edging nigher to the water, and I wondered at it, for the mud was very slippery there.

Then, all in a minute, it was done. Though how it was done, I never knew to this day. Kester said it was a new throw he'd learnt in the city. Anyway, in the blink of an eye, Huglet was flung, not only on the ground but clean out into the water. He went in souse, and when he struggled out, which he did with a deal of difficulty, for he'd gone all his length and the mud was very sticky, there was such a roar of laughter that he blenched. And indeed he was comical sight. Miller, who stood by, smiled for the first time in anybody's memory, as if to say, 'Another kit-cat in the water!'

Kester stood a minute, breathed with the tremendous heave, getting his wind. Then he took the rein from Callard, put foot in stirrup, and was in the saddle.

'I'd lief,' says Felena, low, 'I'd lief be on that saddle afore you, Weaver.'

I never saw such worship as was in her green eyes.

But he took no manner notice.

'Prue!' he said.

I rose up.

'Did I say at the harvesting at Sarn that it was to be toërts or frommet?' he asked me.

'Toërts.'

I could only whisper it.

'Come here then, Prue Woodseaves!'

He stooped. He set his arms about me. He lifted me to the saddle. It was just as in the dream I had. And, as in that dream, Felena looked up, imploring, and he took no account of her, and the noise of the people sank away, the laughter, and the curses of Huglet and Grimble, the clapping of the Callard children and the high voice of Granfeyther Callard telling of a wrostling match nearly a century ago. All sank, all faded in the quiet air. There was only the evening wind lifting the boughs, like a lover lifting his maid's long hair.

'Tabor on, owd nag!' says Kester, and we were going at a canter towards the blue and purple mountains.

'But no!' I said. 'It mun be frommet, Kester. You mun marry a girl like a lily. See, I be hare-shotten!'

338

But he wouldna listen. He wouldna argufy. Only after I'd pleaded agen myself a long while he pulled up sharp, and looking down into my eyes, he said--

'No more sad talk! I've chosen my bit of Paradise. 'Tis on your breast, my dear acquaintance!'

And when he'd said those words, he bent his comely head and kissed me full upon the mouth.

Here ends the story of Prudence Sarn.

APPENDIX A

IMPROVING YOUR RESEARCH METHODOLOGY
prepared by Mr. Gene Gregg, Tulsa, Oklahoma

I.   Selecting a topic

    A.   Some will be chosen for you by the instructor.
    B.   Individually selected topics must relate with the objectives of the course syllabus.

*Nothing under the sun is new, but a paper that expresses your observations, your interaction, and your conclusion is, in every sense of the word, original.

*The topic must be of personal interest to you since you will be spending a considerable amount of time with the subject. Do not procrastinate! Start thinking of potential topics early in the semester rather than putting it off until later.

II.   Three factors governing the selection of a topic
    A.   Worthwhileness--Is the topic trivial and routine, or is it timely and important?
    B.   Manageability--Is the topic so broad and nebulous that any attempt to corral the evidence would be futile?
    C.   Availability of information--Does the LRC possess adequate resource materials to facilitate your research?

III.   Eight steps of proper research
    A.   Develop an interest in a general subject (e.g., evidences for the historical resurrection of Jesus)
    B.   Read a general article on the topic--Standard religious dictionaries and encyclopedias would be an excellent place to begin (but a poor place to stop).
    C.   Formulate a tentative thesis statement which will embody the controlling idea of your topic and guide your research. It must be restricted, unified, and concise. Perhaps now you have decided to narrow your research and focus on a particular topic (Shroud of Turin).

D. Prepare a preliminary bibliography--Scour the library to uncover any prospective sources.*

*In order to proceed with this step, the student must be familiar with the library. This is an essential prerequisite!

--Microfiche card catalogue system
--Periodical Indexes--Periodical articles are <u>current</u> and concise.
--Reference room and Periodical room
--Microfiche/film viewers
--Inter-Library Loan

E. Do some preliminary reading--Get a panoramic view of the controversy you are investigating. (Oh yes, good research papers explore issues to which there are generally several possible positions. Your responsibility is to analyze both sides of the subject critically, discerning strengths and weaknesses of each view, and then you must decide which position is more likely.)

F. Evaluate your sources
1. Relevance--Is the source dealing explicitly with your topic or is it only marginally or peripherally related?
2. Type--Primary or Secondary? Why settle for someone else's understanding of a writer's view. Get it straight from the horse's mouth!
3. Perspective--Is the author's presentation impartial and objective or is it biased by negative presuppositions? Did the writer predetermine his conclusions?
4. Author credentials--Is the writer a world-renowned authority on the subject? Does his education or experience qualify him/her to write intelligently on the issue?
5. Readability--Is the source too technical for you to get a clear understanding of the author's position? (This could possibly lead to a misrepresentation of the writer.) Is the source too devotional or sermonic?

G. Formulate a tentative outline--What you intend to do/Where you intend to go, etc.
H. Begin taking careful, accurate notes.

RESEARCH AND WRITING
SKILLS HANDOUT
prepared by Mr. Gene Gregg, Tulsa, Oklahoma

METHOD
1. Is the method I have chosen the most appropriate and reliable means to solve my problem?
2. Is it impersonal and impartial?
3. Do I have sufficient background to use this method?
4. Am I aware of its weaknesses and limitations?
5. Have I stated reasons for my choice, and what steps will be taken to free it from inherent weaknesses?

THE OUTLINE
1. Does it show that I am oriented in the field?
2. Is the logic of the analysis of the problem sound?
   Does each sub-point suggest a logical progression of thought?
   Is each sub-point vitally related to the major heading?
   Are sub-points stated in parallel form?
3. Does the outline furnish a basis for an orderly collection of data?
4. Is it workable, easily adapted to the type or amount of material found?
5. At each stage in the process of research, does it present a complete picture of the problem as I then see it?

COLLECTION OF DATA
1. Am I reading wisely, intelligently, purposefully?
   Have I first scanned materials, using index, table of contents, preface, bibliography, and conclusion?
   Have I then gone to the first paragraphs of chapters, the first sentences of paragraphs?
   Have I spent time only on details of relevance?
2. Do I have a system of note-taking?
   Is it flexible (as with 4x6 cards)?
   Are notes filed for ready accessibility?
      Have I taken notes on one subject on one card?
      Is the subject clearly indicated at the top?
      Is the reference on each card brief and sufficient?
3. Am I taking notes selectively and wisely?
   Are all data pertinent to the study?
   Do I take down enough material to make the notes permanently intelligible?

Am I trying to take the minimum that will attain maximum efficiency?

Does this mean taking more notes than seems necessary, with the understanding that the problem may take an unexpected direction?

Am I taking full reference particulars so that material is easily traced?

Do I quote when:

> The author's words express the thought better than any others could?
>
> The exact position of the author must be made sure?
>
> The authority's exact words lend weight to the argument?
>
> The thought is terse?
>
> Is it a question of laws, regulations, official rulings?

Do I paraphrase when the thought may be summarized effectively?

Is first choice given to primary sources for data?

Am I taking care to collect data?

Am I taking care to collect data from authorities in the field?

Are my sources well distributed? Is one used extensively? Can I justify such use on the basis of:

> Its summary character?
>
> Its representative character?
>
> Its uniqueness?

4. Am I also gathering information about the background and setting of my problem as I read?
5. Have I collected all data significant for the solution of my problem?

ANALYSIS AND INTERPRETATION OF DATA

1. Have I arranged the data so as to permit comparison, contrast, and synthesis of specific findings?
2. Have I analyzed my problem again to see what is necessary for its solution?
3. Am I studying enough factors or elements to yield a satisfactory answer to my problem?
4. Have I noted significant differences in viewpoint between authors where such differences exist?
5. Have I been consistent in analyzing and interpreting facts?
6. Has the evidence been carefully sifted for validity and reliability?
7. Has it been weighed to determine its relative value and relevance?

8. Are all the findings consistent with each other? The cause if not?
9. Have the necessary limitations of the data been recognized and pointed out?
10. Have all data retained the thought of their original context?
11. Have I avoided:
    Yielding to suggestion, without adequate reason?
    Ignoring negative evidence?
    Comparing things not comparable?
    Mistaking a part for the whole?
    Generalizing without adequate support?
    Reasoning from analogy or silence?

SUMMARY/CONCLUSION
1. Could anyone secure the outstanding facts and conclusions without reading my whole thesis?
2. Could anyone reading the whole thesis obtain in the Summary an integrated impression of the whole?
3. By reading it, could anyone decide whether or not he would like to read the whole thesis?

BIBLIOGRAPHY
1. Have I surveyed all possible sources?
    A guide to the professional literature in my field?
    Card catalogs of available libraries?
    Indices of periodical literature?
    Bibliographies of books related to the subject?
    Footnotes in major works?
    Persons familiar with the field and its sources?
2. Have I worked for careful selection rather than absolute completeness?
3. Have I taken down information so legibly that there will be no error later in copying the data for final typing?
4. Have I set up a workable filing system for references?
5. Are all references complete?
6. Have I classified and alphabetized my final bibliography?

SCHOLARSHIP
1. Am I open-minded, unprejudiced, and objective?
2. Do I differentiate between objective fact and unsupported opinion?
3. Am I scrupulously accurate in regard to facts, quotations, the thought of the author when paraphrasing?
4. Do I avoid accepting material as valuable merely because it is in print?
5. Have I fairly examined all sources pertaining to my subject, whether they represent my viewpoint or not?

6. Am I avoiding unwarranted assumptions?
7. Do I faithfully reveal troublesome exceptions?
8. Have all properly relevant data been included?
9. Do I avoid contentious or sarcastic tones in my writing?
10. Am I completely satisfied that I have done my best and arrived at the correct conclusion?

COMPOSITION: THOUGHT
1. Can the reader follow the thought from the clearly defined problem to a critical and scholarly answer?
   Do sentences, paragraphs, and chapters follow each other logically?
   Are there any gaps in thought? Is the thesis "logic tight?"
2. Would another worker using the same problem and data come to the same conclusions?
3. Does each section bear a definite relation to the original problem?
   Does each contribute to the final conclusion?
   Is this relationship clear to the reader?
   Is the conclusion the inescapable result of the research?
4. Have all irrelevant ideas been eliminated?
5. Are all statements worded to avoid ambiguity and confusion?
6. Is there a creative element in the thesis? Is it more than compilation?
7. Are important ideas and facts given proper emphasis?
8. Are there sufficient summaries at the ends of sections and the beginnings of chapters to keep the progress of the proof clear?

COMPOSITION: TITLE
1. Is it descriptive and truly expressive of the contents of the thesis?
2. Is it reasonably short?
3. Is it worded well?

COMPOSITION: FORM
1. Are the following divisions reasonably explicit?
   Definition of the Problem
   Collection of Data
   Treatment of Data
   Discussion of each question to be answered
   Conclusion
2. Does the Table of Contents provide an accurate preliminary synopsis?
3. Have I checked for correct grammar?
4. Have I checked for consistency in punctuation?

5. Have I checked all uncertain spelling?
6. Have I checked in Campbell/Ballou/Slade for correct forms throughout?
7. Have I checked for inconsistencies in form throughout?
8. Has material that would tend to break the trend of thought or that was too long for a footnote been placed in an appendix?
9. Is there unity between paragraphs, chapters, the whole thesis?
10. Is there coherence within paragraphs, chapters, the whole?
11. Is emphasis correctly placed within paragraphs, chapters, the whole?
12. Is the style suitable for a thesis?
    Smooth but not flowery?
    Impersonal?
    Utilizing the intrinsic merits of the investigation to win interest?
    Introducing quotations naturally?
13. Is there variety?
    In sentence structure?
    In introductory and transitional words?
    In the vocabulary in general?
14. Is the vocabulary carefully chosen?
    To find the most appropriate words and phrases?
    To maintain consistent meanings?
    To avoid overworking some words?
    To achieve simple, definite expression of thought?
15. Are footnotes utilized to
    Present and establish validity of the evidence?
    Acknowledge indebtedness?
    Amplify discussions beyond the point permissible in the text?
    Provide cross references to various parts of the thesis?
16. Have I considered the advisability of using charts or graphs?
    To present data that can be tabulated for clarity?
    To buttress the flow of discussion, not interfere with it?
17. Have I edited the final copy for typographical errors?

APPENDIX C
GOOD NOTE-TAKING METHODOLOGY
prepared by Mr. Gene Gregg, Tulsa, Oklahoma

A. You should first have:
1. a solid thesis sentence.
2. a general outline.
3. a working bibliography.
4. done much of your preliminary reading.

B. Note-taking technique
1. Write notes legibly in ink--pencil smears.
2. Use notecards rather than notebooks--This allows you to shuffle and rearrange your notes.
3. Use 3X5 for bibliography cards and 4X6 for notes.
4. Place only one relevant item of information on each card--Once again, you must be free to shuffle your notes.
5. Write only on one side of the card.
6. Record the source and the pagination before you begin taking the note.
7. Key note to outline in pencil.
8. Write out the note using summary, precis, paraphrase, or quotation.
9. Never take notes indiscriminately.
10. Review and edit your notes periodically.

C. Different kinds of notes
1. Rough summary--Rough sketch of material without much concern for style or expression, a pooling together of main points and ideas. (Material of questionable value should be summarized.)
2. Precis--Brief summary in your own words written in a polished style; very condensed (about 1/3 of original) but preserves the tone of the original material (e.g., Satire, Humor). Never sacrifice clarity for brevity.
3. Paraphrase--Restatement of an author's ideas in your own vocabulary using about the same amount of words. (Most notes should be of this variety.) It is better to paraphrase than to quote. If you cannot paraphrase a passage without continually looking at it, you are probably guilty of plagiarism! PLAGIARISM--The failure to give credit to an author for statements or ideas which are not your own. (Merely reversing the order of words or making cosmetic alterations in sentence structure is inadequate.) Plagiarism, whether intentional

or unintentional, is grounds for immediate dismissal from this university.
   a.   Enclose all quoted materials in " " marks.
   b.   Enclose interpolations in brackets.
   c.   Write author's name on notecard before taking note.
4.   Direct Quotations--Nothing more than a bald, unthinking restatement of the author's exact words (Students seriously abuse quotations--Should be no more than 10% of the text of your paper). Many students actually copy entire paragraphs out of books. If you want a perfect duplication, why not xerox? Eventually you must paraphrase anyway. Also, professors might think that you are too unsure of yourself and are only padding your paper. The best way to ruin the effectiveness of the quotation is to overuse it.

When to use direct quotations

A.   When exact wording cannot be improved upon--The author was at the height of literary genius when he made that statement!

B.   A point being made needs substantiation by an authority.

C.   Comparing/Contrasting two views.

D.   A specific statement is being analyzed.

E.   Exactitude is required--stating of a formula, law, or edict.

Why it is better to paraphrase

A.   You have made an effort of thought.

B.   You have practiced the art of writing.

C.   You have taken the first step toward writing your first rough draft.

APPENDIX D

TAKING NOTES

Your reading will include encyclopedia articles, parts of books, and magazine articles. You cannot hope to remember all of the details of information that you collect. Consequently, you will need to take notes.

The most efficient way to take notes is to write them on cards or slips of paper, using a different card for each note. Early in your reading you will find that the subject matter of your report falls into a number of general divisions or topics. Once you have three or four of these, you can use them as headings for your note cards. When you find information that would come under one of these headings, write the heading at the top of the card and underline it. Then write your notes under the heading. Underneath the note write the page number(s) on which you found the information.

Heading	What happened to colonists II.A.	Outline number
Note your own words	Left CROATOAN: carved on postsign that colonists had left for friendly Indian village.	
	2	Source Number
	p. 131	Page Number where the material is found

The number in the upper right-hand corner means that this note was taken from the second bibliography card. Use separate note card for each heading and for each source. For example, the note in the above example is about what happened to the Roanoke colonists. You might also find information on that topic in an encyclopedia and a magazine article. You would than have three note cards with the same heading but different bibliography numbers.

Three ways you can take notes:
1. paraphrase - put the material into your own words
2. summarize - material is giving only the main ideas
3. quote - copy the exact wording and marking it with quotation marks

SELF-EVALUATION CHECK LIST

SUBJECT MATTER
1. Did you limit your subject sufficiently?
2. Have you sought out original, significant, varied source material?

BIBLIOGRAPHY CARDS
1. Did you record all bibliographical information exactly as it appears in the given resource?
2. Did you record all bibliographical information as you used the reference?

NOTE TAKING
1. Did you take notes in your own words, in phrases rather than in sentences, using lists and modified outline form?
2. Did you copy direct quotations exactly, enclose them in quotation marks, and record the specific page on which the quotation was found?
3. As you progressed, did you organize your material according to major divisions and subpoints?
4. Do all of your note cards have specific subject headings, and does the material on the cards refer directly to the subject heading?
5. Does each note card clearly indicate the source of information to be found on the card and the page numbers?

WRITING THE PAPER
1. In writing your paper, were you able to arrange your note cards according to your plan of organization with the help of the headings on the cards?
2. Did you discard those notes that did not directly pertain to the limited subject upon which you had decided?
3. Have you utilized direct quotations sparingly to embellish an idea or strengthen a point?
4. Did you create effective, meaningful, original sentences from the notes you took?
5. Is the style of your paper lively, original, interesting, and at the same time serious, objective, scientific, and accurate?
6. Have you interpreted your notes objectively, avoiding misleading conclusions by taking material out of context?

CREDITING MATERIAL
1. Have you acknowledged all ideas that are not original with you and are not generally or widely known?

APPENDIX E

READING ANALYSIS

STEP I.

1.   What is the theme or subject of the book?

2.   What issues or problems does the author raise?

3.   What resolutions to these issues does the author present?

4.   List and define the important terms.

STEP II.

1.   List in descriptive outline form the sections or parts of the book.

2.   Describe and explain the theme of the book. Assess the validity of the author's position.

STEP III.

1.   Describe the strengths and weaknesses of the author's style, theme, and resolutions to the issues.

2.   How would you change the book? Why?

3.   What part of the book evoked the most meaning or feeling to you personally? Why?

NOTE   For a comprehensive approach to analytical reading, see How To Read a Book by Mortimer Adler and Charles Van Doren, in which some similarities with our analytical ideas can be seen.

LINGUISTIC ANALYSIS

1.   List all new vocabulary with definitions in context.

2.   Enumerate the verbs that affected you most. Why did they?

3.   List the most unique or outstanding adjectives and phrases that made the book interesting or illuminating.

4.   Rewrite one page of the book.

BIBLIOGRAPHY

Some biographical facts were gleaned from the following fine reference works:

Bridgwater, William. (ed.). The Columbia-Viking Desk Encyclopedia. New York: Dell Publishing Company, 1966.

Connolly, Rev. T. L. Poems of Francis Thompson. New York: Appleton-Century-Crofts, Inc., 1960.

Halleck, R. P. History of American Literature. New York: American Book Company, 1911.

Halleck, R. P. History of English Literature. New York: American Book Company, 1900.

Phillips, Robert S. (ed.) Funk and Wagnalls New Encyclopedia, Vol. 8. New York: Funk and Wagnalls, Inc., 1975.

Quarles, Benjamin. Narrative of the Life of Frederick Douglass. Cambridge, Mass.: Harvard University Press, 1960.

Webb, Mary. Precious Bane. New York: Penguin Books, 1989.